AF816381

Contributions to Management Science

The series *Contributions to Management Science* contains research publications in all fields of business and management science. These publications are primarily monographs and multiple author works containing new research results, and also feature selected conference-based publications are also considered. The focus of the series lies in presenting the development of latest theoretical and empirical research across different viewpoints.

This book series is indexed in Scopus.

Bart Derre • Yvette Baggen
Editors

Empowering the Next Generation of Entrepreneurial Change Agents

A Design Science Approach to Transforming Entrepreneurial Education

Springer

Editors
Bart Derre
Center for Entrepreneurship
HOGENT University of Applied Sciences and Arts
Ghent, Belgium

Yvette Baggen
Education and Learning Sciences
Wageningen University and Research
Wageningen, The Netherlands

ISSN 1431-1941 ISSN 2197-716X (electronic)
Contributions to Management Science
ISBN 978-3-031-82250-6 ISBN 978-3-031-82251-3 (eBook)
https://doi.org/10.1007/978-3-031-82251-3

© The Editor(s) (if applicable) and The Author(s), under exclusive license to Springer Nature Switzerland AG 2025

This work is subject to copyright. All rights are solely and exclusively licensed by the Publisher, whether the whole or part of the material is concerned, specifically the rights of translation, reprinting, reuse of illustrations, recitation, broadcasting, reproduction on microfilms or in any other physical way, and transmission or information storage and retrieval, electronic adaptation, computer software, or by similar or dissimilar methodology now known or hereafter developed.
The use of general descriptive names, registered names, trademarks, service marks, etc. in this publication does not imply, even in the absence of a specific statement, that such names are exempt from the relevant protective laws and regulations and therefore free for general use.
The publisher, the authors and the editors are safe to assume that the advice and information in this book are believed to be true and accurate at the date of publication. Neither the publisher nor the authors or the editors give a warranty, expressed or implied, with respect to the material contained herein or for any errors or omissions that may have been made. The publisher remains neutral with regard to jurisdictional claims in published maps and institutional affiliations.

This Springer imprint is published by the registered company Springer Nature Switzerland AG
The registered company address is: Gewerbestrasse 11, 6330 Cham, Switzerland

If disposing of this product, please recycle the paper.

The authors dedicate this book to Jimme's memory, honoring his remarkable legacy, warmth, and commitment. His contributions and expertise, especially in design-science research, will continue to inspire all who had the privilege to know him.

Preface

Dear reader,

In front of you is the result of an iterative, dynamic, and joyful entrepreneurial design process. The idea for the book emerged with the growing desire to support educators and scholars in creating entrepreneurial education that does justice to the iterative, dynamic, and uncertain process of value creation for others—the process that is so typical for those who are willing to address the societal challenges of our time. How can we incorporate the entrepreneurial process of value creation in our education? And what does it take to educate entrepreneurial change agents? We observed that a design-science approach provided promising opportunities. Applying a design-science approach allows us to merge different teaching approaches, methods, and learning theories into entrepreneurial education based on the intentionality and context of education. By starting with our own "bird-in-hand", we used our experience and approached like-minded researchers and teachers from our network to join us in creating the current book.

The journey of creating the book was a design process in itself. What started as a writing exercise turned into a design process over time. In a process of bricolage we connected, adapted, and refined the different artifacts as presented in this book, leading toward the design of the EntreDesign Canvas, which is presented in Chap. 10. We feel eager to elaborate the design-science approach, share concrete, evidence-informed examples of design-science in practice, and provide a future outlook for continuing the design-science journey in entrepreneurial education.

In the book, we mainly speak of *entrepreneurial education.* With entrepreneurial education we refer to both education preparing students to start their own venture and education in which students develop their entrepreneurial skills and mindset in the context of educating change agents who are capable of addressing societal challenges. Especially when referring to literature that specifically targeted entrepreneurship education, we use this term and use it as input for advancing our understanding of entrepreneurial education.

The main aim of Part I (Chapters "Advancing the Field of Entrepreneurial Education: Leveraging a Design Science Approach for Educating the Change Agents of the Future", "Designing Artifacts in Entrepreneurial Education Research", and "The Entrepreneurial Educator as an Architect of Effective Entrepreneurial Education—Design and Redesign of the CBL Course "Innovation Space Project: Innovation and Entrepreneurship Processes"") is to set the stage and define how we perceive the meaning, value, and potential of the design-science approach in entrepreneurial education. In Part II (Chapters "The Entrepreneurial Education Canvas", "The Entrepreneurial Educational Method: A DSR Artifact to Support Educators in Designing Entrepreneurial Education", "A Two Flows Framework Leveraging Challenge-Based Learning for Entrepreneurial Education: A Design Science Approach", "Embracing Failures: Advancing the Entrepreneurial Education Pedagogy through Design Science Approach", "From EntreComp to EntreAct: 16 Validated Design Principles for Making People More Entrepreneurial", and "Design Science Approach to Building a Large University Entrepreneurship Education Ecosystem (EEE)") we share concrete examples of a design-science approach in entrepreneurial education in different contexts. In these chapters, we present different artifacts in the form of tools, frameworks, and design principles that can help educators and scientists. Finally, in Part III (Chapter "Moving Design Science Research and Practice in Entrepreneurial Education Forward") we synthesize the contributions from the authors and present a new (but not final) model, named the EntreDesign Canvas, that could be used by educators and researchers to further advance a design-science approach in entrepreneurial education.

Each chapter has its own perspective and approach toward design-science in entrepreneurship education. What all chapters have in common is the aim to support educators and researchers in educating and investigating entrepreneurial change agents—change agents who are capable of dealing with uncertainty, and who perceive failure as a learning opportunity. They are also able to create sustainable value together with unfamiliar others.

The design process is not an individual effort, but a joint journey of committed stakeholders who together learn and shape an artifact—in this case, the co-authors with whom we designed our book on educating entrepreneurial change agents. On a personal note, we would like to thank the authors of the book—Ákos, Duygu, Gayatri, Gert, Isabelle, Jasmina, Jimme, Judith, Martin, Mathieu, Pedro, Pim, Ralf, Samar, Steven, Thomas, and Tom—for their valuable contributions to the book. We highly appreciate the supportive and constructive atmosphere in which we have been able to write the book together, allowing ourselves and each other to perceive it as a design process—iterating the different chapters and the book as a whole together over time.

We would also like to thank Johan, Reineke and Nele (Vlaio), Julie and Peter (Vlajo), Sylvie (Unizo E&E) for engaging with us in the process of co-creating the EntreDesign Canvas and for introducing our work to the Flemish community.

As each design process, the journey has no final ending. We perceive the design process as an effectual process of bricolage in which we use the resources at hand to take the next step and continue our learning journey. We warmly invite you to join our community in shaping entrepreneurial education and preparing students to become entrepreneurial change agents in their future careers and personal life. These individuals will not only be capable of driving change but will also see change as opportunity to do things differently—and responsibly. They will understand who they are and be empowered to act in creating sustainable impact. Together, we can transform entrepreneurial education and empower the next generation of entrepreneurial change agents.

We hope that you feel inspired and warmly invited to join our community so that together we can further develop, shape, and evaluate entrepreneurial education for educating change agents with entrepreneurial mindsets.

Warm regards, Bart Derre and Yvette Baggen

Ghent, Belgium — Bart Derre
Wageningen, The Netherlands — Yvette Baggen

Contents

About the Editors

Bart Derre is Director at HOGENT University of Applied Sciences and Arts in Ghent, Belgium, and holds the (HOGENT-Xerius) research chair on entrepreneurial learning at the Vrije Universiteit Brussel, Brussels, Belgium. As Director of the Center for Entrepreneurship, he has overseen numerous entrepreneurial education programs. His research, including a Ph.D. from TU Eindhoven (The Netherlands), focuses on the design and implementation of entrepreneurial education that drives meaningful impact.

Yvette Baggen is Assistant Professor at the Education and Learning Sciences group of Wageningen University and Research, specializing in entrepreneurial learning and ecosystems in higher education. Her work empowers students and professionals as change agents, equipping them to tackle real-world challenges. Yvette's research integrates education, entrepreneurship, and societal impact, promoting transformative learning experiences that prepare learners for impactful careers.

Part I
Introduction to the Design Science Approach in Entrepreneurial Education

Advancing the Field of Entrepreneurial Education: Leveraging a Design Science Approach for Educating the Change Agents of the Future

Bart Derre, Yvette Baggen, and Pedro De Bruyckere

Abstract Chapter "Advancing the Field of Entrepreneurial Education: Leveraging a Design Science Approach for Educating the Change Agents of the Future" sets the stage for why a design science research (DSR) methodology could significantly benefit the development of entrepreneurial education for both researchers and practitioners. The chapter argues that DSR can demystify the "black box" of entrepreneurial education and address the current epistemological challenges within the field. By exploring the literature on educational effectiveness, the chapter advocates for a shift towards an ecological approach, aligning well with DSR principles. This approach emphasizes the development of "evidence strategies" over rigid best practices, advocating for adaptable methods that educators can implement across varied contexts. Concluding with a call to action, the book aims to promote DSR among entrepreneurial education researchers and educators, empowering them to become architects of entrepreneurial learning equipping students to become the next generation of change agents prepared to address pressing societal challenges.

B. Derre (✉)
HOGENT University of Applied Sciences and Arts, Center for Entrepreneurship, Ghent, Belgium and Psychology and Educational Sciences, VUB, Brussels, Belgium
e-mail: bart.derre@hogent.be

Y. Baggen
Education and Learning Sciences, Wageningen University & Research, Wageningen, The Netherlands
e-mail: yvette.baggen@wur.nl

P. De Bruyckere
Education, Utrecht University, Utrecht, The Netherlands
e-mail: p.debruyckere@uu.nl

© The Author(s), under exclusive license to Springer Nature Switzerland AG 2025
B. Derre, Y. Baggen (eds.), *Empowering the Next Generation of Entrepreneurial Change Agents*, Contributions to Management Science,
https://doi.org/10.1007/978-3-031-82251-3_1

1 Setting the Stage: The Potential of Entrepreneurship in Educating Change Agents

Europe, like many other regions, faces complex "grand societal challenges" (GSCs) that require multidimensional approaches to resolve (Voegtlin et al., 2022). GSCs are complex, uncertain, and value-laden in nature. Think for instance of the transition towards a circular economy and climate change—these are complex challenges of which the problem and solution side are hard to define, as different systems and stakes are involved, which are changing over time. In its communication "Towards a green, digital and resilient economy: our European growth mode" (EC, 2022), the European Commission explains how the transition to a sustainable, resilient, and inclusive economic model, facilitated by broader dissemination and acceptance of digital and green technologies and skills, will contribute to addressing the main challenges facing Europe today. This concept of a green, digital, and resilient economy reflects the overall efforts of the European Union to promote sustainability and stimulate economic growth by embracing digitization and green technologies.

Given these complex and interwoven challenges, there is a crucial need for higher education institutions to adapt their curricula and approach to educating future professionals as change agents in every discipline (Tassone et al., 2022). We define change agents as individuals who are capable of "initiating, managing or implementing change" (Caldwell, 2003, p. 131). In higher education, change agents have to learn how to create innovative solutions for GSCs and navigate through social, co-creative processes required in circumstances characterized by uncertainties. In this regard, the integration of wide entrepreneurial education into the curriculum addresses and enhances the ability of these future professionals to act as change agents (de Bronstein & Timm, 2023; Cárdenas-Gutiérrez et al., 2023; van Rijnsoever et al., 2023) and can help them develop as entrepreneurial change agents. Entrepreneurial change agents are capable of perceiving change as windows of opportunity (Westley et al., 2013).

Over the past 20 years, we have seen tremendous progress in the field of entrepreneurship education, both in terms of the evolution of the domain and the outcomes achieved. This evolution has transformed entrepreneurship education from a specialized subject primarily found in business schools or management programs to a broad entrepreneurial movement focused on fostering entrepreneurial competencies, mindset, and behaviors that are crucial for empowering students to act as change agents by providing them with the skills needed to innovate, adapt, and lead in various contexts. Walmsley and Wraae (2022), for instance, explore the potential of entrepreneurship beyond its economic orientation and elaborate the potential of the emancipatory function of entrepreneurship. Their conceptual work is part of a wider trend in which entrepreneurship has been introduced beyond the business school, during which both the "what" and the "how" of entrepreneurship education have undergone significant development (Fellnhofer, 2019; Gabrielsson et al., 2020; Hägg & Gabrielsson, 2020). The wide approach to entrepreneurship has a focus on action, co-creation, transformation, empowerment, and identity development (Baggen et al., 2022; Van Rijnsoever et al., 2023; Walmsley & Wraae, 2022).

This transformation aligns closely with the widening of the concept of entrepreneurship from a narrow definition focused on creating new business entities and economic value to a wide definition of entrepreneurship centered on creating value for others, transcending an exclusive focus on economic value. This broader approach was catalyzed by the European Commission's redefinition of entrepreneurship in 2006 as:

> Entrepreneurship refers to an individual's ability to turn ideas into action. It includes creativity, innovation and risk taking, as well as the ability to plan and manage projects in order to achieve objectives. This definition supports everyone in day-to-day life at home and in society, makes employees more aware of the context of their work and better able to seize opportunities, and provides a foundation for entrepreneurs establishing a social or commercial activity. (European Commission, 2006, p. 4)

With a wide definition of entrepreneurship, emphasis is also placed on the importance of an entrepreneurial mindset that results in broad entrepreneurial behavior, with a central tenet being creating value for others in relation to societal issues and the pursuit of nonfinancial motives (Lackéus, 2015) among all citizens. It positions entrepreneurship in the context of change agency in all spheres of life and for catalyzing change in the ongoing, urgent transitions in society (Baggen et al., 2022). Entrepreneurship as a mindset empowers change agents to perceive change as opportunity, deal with uncertainty, and adapt to new circumstances.

More specifically, in wide entrepreneurship education, students are invited to experience the iterative, uncertain process of new value creation in education (Baggen et al., 2022), for instance, by creating an artifact—that has value for others—in heterogenous teams by working together with nonacademic professionals, such as entrepreneurs or governmental organizations. During the process of creating the artifact, students may experience the so-called learning surprises when interacting with different stakeholders, prototyping their product (artifact), and collaborating with their (often unknown) peers. Such learning surprises capture rich learning moments that may help students to develop themselves as change agents.

As early as 2002, Gibb pointed to the societal need for a broader form of entrepreneurial behavior, stating: "A wide range of stakeholders are faced with the need for entrepreneurial behavior, including priests, doctors, teachers, police officers, retirees… entrepreneurship is therefore no longer exclusively reserved for the business sector" (p. 234). Gibb (2002) based his analysis on a thorough political and environmental assessment to determine that both the task environment and the organizational environment of employees are undergoing change. On the one hand, there is increasing uncertainty and complexity, while on the other hand, there is a growing desire among employees for entrepreneurial behavior. Value creation can be social, environmental, cultural, economic, or a combination of multiple forms of value creation. The widening of the definition of entrepreneurship opens the door to introducing well-being as a goal of entrepreneurship, supporting "everyone in day-to-day life at home and in society." Eudaimonic well-being refers to deeper self-realization and the pursuit of deeper values and goals (Deci & Ryan, 2008; Ryff, 2019; Shir & Ryff, 2021).

The publication of the Oslo Agenda "Fostering an Entrepreneurial Mindset through Education and Learning" (European Commission, 2006) and the report "Rethinking Education: Investing in Skills for Better Socio-Economic Outcomes" (European Commission, 2012) have been important drivers for an explosion of attention and funding towards promoting wide entrepreneurial education across European member states and educational institutions (Eurydice, 2016). In educational practice, there is a shift from entrepreneurship education, which traditionally focuses on creating startups and business entities, to entrepreneurial education, which emphasizes entrepreneurial mindsets, competencies, and wide entrepreneurial behaviors among students from all disciplines, not just business-related fields. The focus on the role of universities in educating future-proof professionals (i.e., change agents) who can help address GSCs catalyzes this process. The aforementioned Eurydice report describes the state of entrepreneurship education in European countries, indicating that more than half of the EU countries adopt the wide EU definition of entrepreneurship education (Eurydice, 2016).

In this chapter, we explore how adopting a design science research (DSR) approach can enhance entrepreneurial education research and practice, propelling its evolution to educate a diverse body of students to become effective change agents. Broadly defined, DSR is a method that "establishes and operationalizes research when the desired goal is an artifact or a recommendation" (Dresch et al., 2015, p. 67). This methodology, grounded in the epistemological foundations of "design science" (Dresch et al., 2015), contributes scientifically to transforming existing conditions into desired ones. In his 1996 book *The Sciences of the Artificial*, Herbert Simon identifies education as one of the five domains intimately linked to design science, suggesting that entrepreneurial educational interventions can be viewed as artifacts. Design science offers an alternative to explanatory sciences for entrepreneurial education researchers and practitioners by generating knowledge that creates effective solutions and artifacts, thereby transforming necessary educational change.

2 Why Current Entrepreneurial Education Practice and Research Require a DSR Approach

2.1 Pedagogy as the Key to Enhancing Entrepreneurial Education Effectiveness

Given the significant transition in both the "what" and "how" of entrepreneurial education in recent years (Béchard & Grégoire, 2005a, 2005b; Gabrielsson et al., 2020; Hägg & Gabrielsson, 2020), the question arises whether a design science research (DSR) approach for researchers and practitioners is more of a nice-to-have or a need-to-have. If our guiding principle is to ensure that all students demonstrate increased entrepreneurial behavior and become active change agents in the real world upon graduation, then our focus shifts to educational effectiveness research.

In educational effectiveness research within entrepreneurial education, two fundamental elements carry equal importance: (1) the overall impact of our educational interventions and (2) the variability of that impact. As educators, it is crucial to distinguish between achievement, often indicated by grades, and learning growth, which we seek to measure through impact assessments. Apart from the net effect, variability is crucial to consider. In education, we anticipate a normal range of variability associated with effective teaching, influenced by factors such as personality traits and socioeconomic status (SES). This results in a distribution of both achievement and learning gains. However, it is essential to note that the variability in learning gains should not extend to a problematic situation. We currently observe a high degree of variability, indicating a concerning scenario regarding the effectiveness of education (Hattie, 2015). Many students show no learning gains regardless of their initial achievement. In the context of entrepreneurial education, high variability in learning gains is particularly troubling, especially if our goal is to cultivate entrepreneurial change agents who are capable of addressing GSCs.

Several meta-analyses have yielded contradictory results regarding the effectiveness of entrepreneurial education (Mwasalwiba, 2010; Martin et al., 2013; Nabi et al., 2017; Pittaway & Cope, 2007). However, to gain insight into the extent of variability in the net effect of entrepreneurial education on different learning outcomes, meta-analyses are invaluable (Brandstätter, 2011).

Most of these meta-analyses explicitly report the variability in methodological quality, which spans from selection bias to the utilization of control groups, preexisting discrepancies in personality traits, and the influence of moderators and mediators. Rauch and Hulsink (2015) highlight that only 11 studies included in the meta-analysis by Martin et al. (2013) conducted pre- and post-measurements of the effect variables, and only 7 out of 42 studies examined entrepreneurial behavior as an outcome variable. Notably, these 7 studies reported smaller effect sizes compared to the remaining 35 studies, which primarily focused on entrepreneurial intention (Rauch & Hulsink, 2015).

Nabi et al. (2017) acknowledge the role of methodological or statistical artifacts in explaining the contradictory results and variability, but they also point out other significant factors contributing to the observed variability, such as the nature of the pedagogical intervention or pedagogical heterogeneity. This pedagogical heterogeneity, along with the resulting statistical heterogeneity, may stem from the vague description of pedagogical interventions in scientific work. Entrepreneurship education encompasses a wide range of practices, resulting in significant variation—but it remains unclear how such variety looks like in practice:

> It may be that EET [entrepreneurship education and training] is simply not developed enough at this point. Further studies that examine the impact of course design and teaching methods may help to explain these relatively weak effect sizes and, by identifying important moderators, show that certain types of EET garner larger effect sizes. Such learning, if

incorporated into future EET interventions, may lead to improvements that will make EET more effective generally. (Martin et al., 2013; p. 221)

Statistical heterogeneity stemming from pedagogical diversity may also arise from the application of the same intervention in various contexts. The pivotal aspect of this context is the diverse student populations undergoing the intervention, exhibiting variations in crucial variables that influence the degree to which the intervention leads to specific learning outcomes.

As emphasized by Nabi et al. (2017), researchers should engage in studies that shed light on "which pedagogical models yield specific impacts and under what contextual conditions" (p. 292). Similarly, Lackéus (2015) underscores the necessity for further research to address the question of "when to implement which strategies." This is important especially when educating entrepreneurial change agents who have to learn how to deal with the complexity, uncertainty, and the value-laden character of GSCs (Voegtlin et al., 2022). As stated at the beginning of this chapter, entrepreneurial education should include the iterative, uncertain process of value creation for others—so that students can experience and learn how to address societal education as part of their curricula (Baggen et al., 2022). This requires education that holds learning surprises for students that create value in authentic education, addressing societal issues, which they aim to contribute to solving in co-creation with others.

A review of impact studies in 2017 by Kamovich and Foss corroborated Fayolle's (2013) observations that the alignment between learning objectives, interventions, and evaluation is often lacking in the design of educational interventions. Fellnhofer (2019) conducted a comprehensive systematic mapping study with bibliometric information, analyzing 1773 peer-reviewed documents published between 1975 and 2014. The study concludes that the entrepreneurship education research domain continues to grapple with the challenge of devising "an effective strategy for teaching entrepreneurship theory in a genuinely and deeply engaging manner" (p. 44). Fellnhofer (2019) suggests that future entrepreneurship education research should prioritize inquiries starting with "How to…?"

These findings further endorse Hattie's (2015) stance on the significance of within-school variability and its influence on students' learning outcomes in education. And Hattie (2015) also proposes a way forward:

So, my claim is that the greatest influence on student progression in learning is having highly expert, inspired and passionate teachers and school leaders working together to maximize the effect of their teaching on all students in their care. There is a major role for school leaders: to harness the expertise in their schools and to lead successful transformations. There is also a role for the system: to provide the support, time, and resources for this to happen. (p. 2)

To harness the full potential of entrepreneurial education in educating the change agents of the future, thereby ensuring every student has ample opportunity to cultivate an entrepreneurial mindset, we must scrutinize, support, and improve the pedagogical practices of EE practitioners.

2.2 Shift from Science of Learning to Science of Instruction to Make Entrepreneurial Education Relevant and Rigorous

Since numerous definitions exist, defining and delineating the concept of pedagogy is a necessary first step if we aim to improve the pedagogical practice of entrepreneurial educators. Watkins and Mortimore (1999) provide an interesting approach that encompasses both the learner's and the educator's perspectives by defining pedagogy as: "any conscious activity by one person designed to enhance learning in another' (p. 3).

According to Mayer (2011, 2018), the two distinct perspectives—the learner's perspective and the educator's perspective—are crucial starting points, respectively translated as the Science of Learning and the Science of Instruction, for studying and improving the Science and practice of Education.

In both general education and entrepreneurship education, there is a particular preference to the Science of Learning as a potential source of inspiration for improving educational practice. When discussing the Science of Learning, the three major learning theories—behaviorism, cognitivism, and constructivism—are often referred to, as noted by Mayer (2018), and this is also the case with entrepreneurial education. Learning theories form the basis for developing and shaping pedagogies, for instance, in the form of different learning activities.

Cope (2005) argues that the domain of entrepreneurship should be studied from a learning perspective and refers to Minniti and Bygrave (2001), who argue that "entrepreneurship is a learning process and a theory of entrepreneurship requires a theory of learning" (p. 7). Research within the field of entrepreneurial education has shown a clear emphasis on identifying a learning theory to underpin entrepreneurial education. Hägg and Gabrielsson (2020), in their systematic review of the development of entrepreneurship education pedagogy, conclude that since the 2000s, and especially since the 2010s, educational pedagogical interventions have been based on the constructivist learning theory. A bibliometric analysis conducted by Gabrielsson et al. (2020) shows that the research literature concerning pedagogy in entrepreneurship education has become a homogeneous research area:

> In the third period, 2013–2018, we can identify a significant development where clusters of co-cited works have become largely homogeneous with much stronger interconnections... At the same time, the analysis indicates that a canon of core works has begun to crystallize, many of which can be classified within the field of entrepreneurial education research, for example Pittaway and Cope (2007); Neck and Greene (2011) and Souitaris et al. (2007). (p. 1078)

For Mayer (2018), it is crucial to move away from the pursuit of the right "ism" and instead adopt scientifically supported insights and recommendations on how people learn. He argues against adhering to an untestable doctrine that educational practice must conform to. The persistent struggle within the field of entrepreneurial education to adopt the right "ism" is evident. Mayer (2018) also emphasizes that an exclusive focus on grand learning theories represents a narrow view of Science of

Learning, as middle-range theories such as cognitive load theory and learning strategies have contributed significantly to our understanding of learning over the past 20 years. Mayer (2018) also calls for consideration of emerging theories and insights from research on motivation and emotion, as well as findings from studies on metacognition and neuroscience, in the coming years.

In addition to reducing the Science of Learning to the three major learning theories, there is another issue with using predominantly the Science of Learning to advise educational practice. Mayer (2008) emphasizes this issue of a highly one-sided relationship between the Science of Learning and the Science of Instruction and describes this as a one-way street approach. This one-way street approach establishes a certain path dependency within the Science of Learning and the practice field. Similarly, in the field of entrepreneurial education, this one-way street approach is prevalent. Fayolle and Gailly (2008) argue that when developing an entrepreneurial course, the educator must establish an explicit epistemological position before operationally designing the course. This adopted epistemological stance logically determines the role of both student and instructor, as epistemology is the theory of knowledge. Fayolle and Gaily (2008; pp. 573–574) therefore make an explicit distinction between "to educate" and "to teach," with the former implicitly referring to constructivist learning theories and the latter to more cognitive or behaviorist learning theories. Béchard and Grégoire (2005b) also emphasize that one's worldview should influence how they approach education and teaching, including the design of specific programs, courses, and pedagogical activities.

In this way, the learning theory determines not only the role of the teacher but also that of the student. In constructivist learning theories, the student takes the reins of their own learning process, with the teacher serving as a guide, whereas in cognitive learning theories, the teacher is leading the learning process, and the student is actively involved but does not lead the process.

Mayer (2018) therefore calls for a two-way approach and building a reciprocal relationship between the Science of Learning (SoL) and the Science of Instruction (SoI) with a full-fledged role for the Science of Instruction within the educational field. The Science of Instruction focuses on the ways in which people can be helped to learn. A two-way approach means that the Science of Learning is thereby expanded to explain how learning occurs in an authentic learning context, and the Science of Instruction is enriched with insights into how people learn. There is also a time course in the relationship between the perspective of the educator and the perspective of the learner, where in a one-way street approach as described above, the path runs from the learning theory to determining the instruction. In a two-way approach, the time course runs from instruction combined with the characteristics of the learner to learning, which can be measured, allowing instruction to be subsequently adjusted (see Fig. 1).

Inspired by the work of Stokes (1997), Mayer (2008) associates basic and applied research with the concepts of the Science of Learning and the Science of Instruction, respectively. In this way, Mayer obtains a 2x2 framework with four quadrants (see Fig. 2).

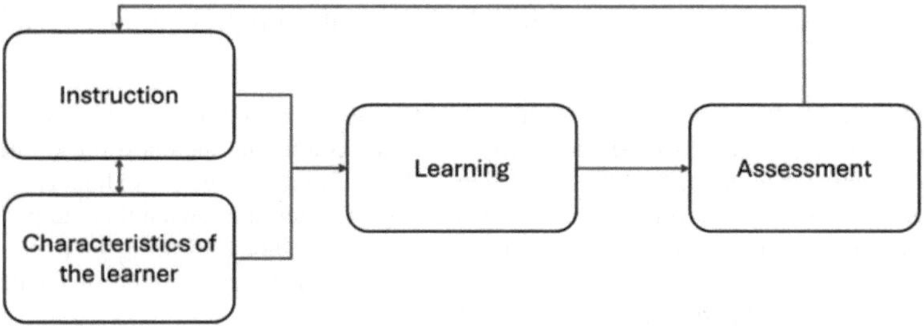

Fig. 1 Two-way approach SoL and SoI. *Note.* Created based on Educational psychology's past and future contributions to the science of learning, science of instruction, and science of assessment, by Mayer, R. E. (2018). Journal of Educational psychology, 110(2), 174–179

	No authentic learning context (SoI)	Authentic learning context (SoI)
No testing of learning theory (SoL)	Nontheoretical studies on contrived learning situations	Nontheoretical studies in authentic learning context
Testing of learning theory (SoL)	Theoretical studies on contrived learning situations	Basic research on applied problems

Fig. 2 2×2 framework SoL and SoI. *Note.* Recreated based on "Applying the science of learning: Evidence-based principles for the design of multimedia instruction." (p. 761), by Mayer, R. E. (2008). *The American Psychologist, 63*(8), 760–769

A certain trend within education, sailing under the flag of evidence-based education, believes that mastering the variability in the quality of pedagogical practice can be achieved by focusing more on "better" research through experimental studies that fit into the bottom-left quadrant. However, according to Daniel and De Bruyckere (2021), such research, with a high emphasis on the internal validity of the research design, is insufficiently capable of providing outcomes that prescribe for qualitative complex authentic learning environments. Just like Mayer (2008; 2017), Daniel and De Bruyckere (2021) point out that there is no "single best way to teach" and advocate for an ecological approach to the combination of the Science of Learning and Science of Instruction, consequently shifting towards the bottom-right quadrant of Mayer (2008). Rather than continuing to focus on best practices, there should be a focus on the development of "evidence strategies, or promising strategies that teachers can deploy across specified contexts, learners, goals, and styles" (Daniel & De Bruyckere, 2021; p. 365). This ecological approach—nicely aligning with DSR—meets the call of several authors (Fayolle, 2013; Fellnhofer,

2019; Nabi et al., 2017) to open the black box of entrepreneurial education and responds to the following call of Lackéus:

> In the future we hope for a greater awareness of the need to develop and establish progression models for entrepreneurial education, rather than continuing the quest for a 'one size fits all' approach to entrepreneurial education … In the future, teachers will hopefully have access to classifications, frameworks and other support material allowing them to pick and choose from a large variety of pedagogical tools and methods allowing them to more quickly identify and hone a teaching style and progression strategy to their own students, contexts and available resources. (Lackéus, 2015, p. 26)

3 How a DSR Approach to Entrepreneurship Education Can Support Both Researchers and Educators

Similar to what Sarasvathy and Venkataraman (2011) suggest for the research domain of entrepreneurship, entrepreneurial education pedagogy can also be studied as a "science of the artificial" (Simon, 1996).

Environmental contingency and human intentionality are two proportions crucial for designing pedagogical artifacts. In his book *The Sciences of the Artificial*, Herbert Simon (1996) defines an artifact in terms of its interface function: an artifact is embedded in two environments simultaneously. The "inner environment" refers to the internal organization or logic of the artifact. The "outer environment" is the broader world where the artifact ultimately aims to have an effect and is influenced.

A key aspect of Simon's theory (1996) is that the designer of an artifact must focus on optimizing the interface between these two environments to realize a specific human intentionality. This means the artifact must effectively connect the internal logic or mechanisms (inner environment) with the external realities and requirements (outer environment). This could mean the artifact adapts certain features of the inner environment or translates them into functionalities usable in the outer environment.

Entrepreneurial pedagogical interventions can be perceived as artifacts. As Simon (1996) suggests, the interventions form the bridge between the internal and external environments. In this case, the internal environment refers to a complex set of pedagogical options—such as learning activities—and components designed by the educator. These need to be aligned with the outer environment, which refers to the environment in which the artifact functions—such as the classroom setting—to achieve a specific learning goal within that context.

A design science research (SDR) approach to entrepreneurial education effectively adopts Mayer's (2008) highly iterative two-way street approach, facilitating collaboration between the Science of Learning and Science of Instruction, to deliver effective education to a diverse group of students, aiming to foster wide entrepreneurial behavior.

Although several methods can be found in the literature that operationalize DSR as a research practice and there is currently no consensus, these methods all share common underlying characteristics (Dresch et al., 2015). DSR can be seen as a highly useful approach that, by forming an intersection between design, which focuses on "how things ought to be," and science, which provides insights into "how things are," ensures relevant solutions are implemented in entrepreneurial education with sufficient rigor due to scientifically substantiated input (Dimov et al., 2023; Romme, 2023). The DSR methodological cycle comprises four major steps (Romme, 2023; Romme & Reymen, 2018): (1) developing design principles or propositions and design requirements; (2) creating new solutions; (3) testing the solutions; and (4) theorizing. Whereas construction or design principles are a coherent set of imperative propositions based on state-of-the-art science, design rules or instructions are rather a coherent set of detailed guidelines embedded in the construction principles. Practitioners can rely on these design rules and instructions to design their specific solutions to problems. Design rules or instructions are described by Romme and Endenburg as "elaborate solution-oriented guidelines for the design process (e.g., 'if condition C is present, to achieve A, do B')" (p. 288). This process is explored in greater detail in Chapter "Designing Artifacts in Entrepreneurial Education Research" of this book.

Central to DSR is the design of new solutions that, although informed by both design principles and propositions and design requirements, do not directly translate into the final design. The "synthesis-evaluation iterations" form the backbone of the design phase (Van Aken & Berends, 2018). The various possible solution concepts are continuously evaluated against the relevant program of design requirements that was the end result of the analysis phase. The main question is to what extent the artifacts or solutions meet the design requirements. Consequently, the design cannot be "derived" from the input data of the build process, but this input is used in the ex-post justification of the evaluation process. The input of the build process consists of both the design requirements and the design propositions. The design propositions and design requirements are formulated on the basis of the cumulative state of the science and include key concepts and theories as well as empirical and pragmatic insights inductively extracted from the real-life context (Romme & Endenburg, 2006). The design requirements are the parameters within which a solution will be designed.

The process of evaluating and testing the designed artifacts is an essential part of DSR (March & Smith, 1995) and refers to the question of to what extent the artifact meets the predefined design requirements (Van Aken & Andriessen, 2011). In DSR, pragmatic validity is therefore paramount (Van Aken & Romme, 2009), which refers to the extent to which the application of the artifact, the design principles, and the design rules included in the instructional design model support the educators' decision-making processes in designing effective entrepreneurial education and contribute to reducing the variability of entrepreneurial educational effectiveness. Van Aken (2004) notes that pragmatic validity testing within DSR also requires special attention and that testing based exclusively on interviews and document analysis leads to lower pragmatic validity than additional observation of behavior and/or the outcomes of that behavior in practice. Usability is also a part of pragmatic validity that needs to be evaluated.

Finally, DSR allows for theorizing about both the problem and the solutions, and it can form the basis for developing design principles as well as for designing and refining constructs and models (Romme, 2023).

This generic approach precisely captures the essence of what differentiates DSR from action research and problem-solving through design thinking (Romme & Reymen, 2018). Moreover, researchers and practitioners can utilize various scientific designs and methods such as case studies, experimental studies, interviews, and both qualitative and quantitative data collection and analysis (Dimov et al., 2023).

A significant advantage of a DSR approach is that it enables the field of entrepreneurial education to transcend discussions among the various epistemological "isms" embedded in grand learning theories. Instead, DSR focuses on designing artifacts that contribute to solving the described class of field problems and ultimately to a better world and is therefore not a neutral descriptive science practice. This means that the researcher and practitioner take a stand and must also try to describe that better world because the artifact derives meaning within that formulation. More specifically, a DSR approach, according to Van Aken (2011), does not refer to a specific philosophical paradigm of science with a closed system of ontological and epistemological views but rather to a nature of research programs or "school of thought" characterized by "a combination of types of research questions, accepted research methods to answer them, accepted means of evidence to justify them, and the nature of research products sought" (Van Aken, 2011; p. 38). According to Goldkuhl (2020), a pragmatic attitude towards design science epistemology should be adopted, and it makes sense to use the concept of "epistemic type": "Different possible knowledge items within design science are epistemologically characterized, i.e., different epistemic types are assigned to the identified DS knowledge items" (p. 44).

In this way, DSR contributes to transcending the epistemological debates among various grand learning theories, focusing on breaking the status quo and homogeneity in the field of entrepreneurial education. DSR opens up the door towards more flexibility in creating entrepreneurial education in which the iterative, uncertain nature of value-creation processes can be captured—not by creating education that is based on one learning theory, but by creating education in which different combinations and variations of learning theories are possible, based on the learning objectives, the target group, and the learning surprises students and teachers experience throughout the learning journey. It provides a more flexible way for designing, implementing, and evaluating entrepreneurial education, with a pragmatic yet systematic and data-driven approach.

In DSR, the design of artifacts to provide often new solutions to old problems (Dimov et al., 2023) remains a central theme, meaning that various types of artifacts can be developed. March and Smith (1995) describe four different types of artifact to solve the described field problem (and by extension class of problems): constructs, models, methods, and instantiations.

- Constructs provide the language in which problems and solutions are defined and communicated. Models use those constructs to represent a real-world situation as a design problem and solution space (Simon, 1996).
- Models support the understanding of both problems and solutions and are the connection between the two that makes it possible to make design choices and implement changes in the real world (Hevner et al., 2004).
- Methods then describe processes that guide the solving of problems in the solution space. These processes can exist in various forms, from algorithms and flow charts to best practices.
- Instantiations are the concrete elaboration and implementation of constructs, models, or methods in a working system. These instantiations underpin applicability and allow researchers to learn in the real world and are also often designed by professionals during design practice. It also indicates the connected link between design science research and evidence-informed design practice.

Romme and Reymen (2018) building on the work of March and Smith's (1995) classification, distinguish between 5 types of design science research output: values, constructs, models, design principles, and practices.

Values, constructs models and design principles can be described as prescriptive artifacts that assist educators in making evidence-informed design decisions. These decisions result in crafting a set of pedagogical interventions aimed at achieving specific learning objectives within a given context. These prescriptive artifacts are a necessary part of the design science research methodology (Dimov et al., 2023). This illustrates how design science can help to close the gap between science and practice (Van Aken, 2004; Dresch et al., 2015; Hevner et al., 2004).

A design science-oriented methodology provides not only a "set of rules" for designing and delivering effective entrepreneurial education but equally a process for adapting the "set of rules" to a changing context and to new scientific insights, both from the explanatory sciences and from individual practice. In contrast to descriptive and hypothesis-testing sciences, DSR aims to effect change in practice by incorporating messy situations, involving multiple dependent variables, flexible design revisions, social interaction, and co-participant design and analysis (Collins et al., 2004). Therefore, it requires a strong and active connection with the field of practice, where several iterative cycles contribute to the quality of the DSR output. McKenney and Reeves (2012) emphasize that the goal of DSR is not merely to enhance practice but also to advance the theoretical understanding of practice.

With this book we aim to contribute to the promotion of DSR among researchers and educators of entrepreneurial education. More specifically, we aim to support educators who want to use an evidence-informed educational design approach in their daily practice. In this manner, the book aims to empower educators to serve as architects of education, capable of realizing entrepreneurial learning outcomes within authentic learning contexts and with different learning outcomes ranging from enhancing entrepreneurial competencies and mindset to explicitly launching ventures. And it is this fostering of an entrepreneurial mindset and behavior that will shape our higher education alumni into the next generation of entrepreneurial change agents, capable of addressing the array of societal challenges that lie ahead.

References

Baggen, Y., Lans, T., & Gulikers, J. (2022). Making entrepreneurship education available to all: Design principles for educational programs stimulating an entrepreneurial mindset. *Entrepreneurship Education and Pedagogy, 5*(3), 347–374.

Béchard, J., & Grégoire, D. B. (2005a). Understanding teaching models in entrepreneurship for higher education. In P. Kÿro & C. Carrier (Eds.), *The dynamics of learning entrepreneurship in a cross-cultural university context (Entrepreneurship education series 2/2005)* (Vol. Issue 2, pp. 104–134). University of Tampere Research Center for Vocational and Professional Center.

Béchard, J.-P., & Grégoire, D. (2005b). Entrepreneurship education research revisited: The case of higher education. *Academy of Management Learning & Education, 4*(1), 22–43. https://doi.org/10.5465/amle.2005.16132536

Brandstätter, H. (2011). Personality aspects of entrepreneurship: A look at five meta-analyses. *Personality and Individual Differences, 51*(3), 222–230. https://doi.org/10.1016/j.paid.2010.07.007

Caldwell, R. (2003). Models of change agency: A fourfold classification. *British Journal of Management, 14*(2), 131–142. https://doi.org/10.1111/1467-8551.00270

Cárdenas-Gutiérrez, A. R., Domínguez-Quintero, A. M., & Bernal-Guerrero, A. (2023). Assessment of entrepreneurial potential in the training of a new generation of change agents in Spain. *Social Sciences, 12*(12), 680.

Collins, A., Joseph, D., & Bielaczyc, K. (2004). Design research: Theoretical and methodological issues. *Journal of the Learning Sciences, 13*(1), 15–42. https://doi.org/10.1207/s15327809jls1301_2

Cope, J. (2005). *Toward a dynamic learning perspective of entrepreneurship* (Vol. 29, pp. 373–397). Entrepreneurship Theory and Practice.

Daniel, D. B., & De Bruyckere, P. (2021). Toward an ecological science of teaching. *Canadian Psychology/Psychologie canadienne, 62*(4), 361.

de Bronstein, A. A., & Timm, J. M. (2023). Transformational sustainability entrepreneurship: Encouraging students to become real change agents. In J. Halberstadt, A. A. de Bronstein, J. Greyling, & S. Bissett (Eds.), *Transforming entrepreneurship education: Interdisciplinary insights on innovative methods and formats* (pp. 67–86). Springer. https://doi.org/10.1007/978-3-031-11578-3

Deci, E. L., & Ryan, R. M. (2008). Self-determination theory: A macrotheory of human motivation, development, and health. *Canadian Psychology, 49*(3), 182–185. https://doi.org/10.1037/a0012801

Dimov, D., Maula, M., Georges, A., & Romme, L. (2023). Entrepreneurship crafting and assessing design science research for entrepreneurship. *Theory and Practice, 47*(5), 1543–1567. https://doi.org/10.1177/10422587221128271

Dresch, A., Lacerda, D., & Antunes, J., Jr. (2015). *Design science research: A method for science and technology advancement*. Springer.

European Commission. (2006). Implementing the community Lisbon Programme: Fostering entrepreneurial mindsets through education and learning. In *Commission of the European Communities*. https://eur-lex.europa.eu/LexUriServ/LexUriServ.do?uri=COM:2006:0033:FIN:en:PDF

European Commission/EACEA/Eurydice. (2016). *Entrepreneurship education at school in Europe*. Publications Office of the European Union.

European Commission. (2012). *Rethinking education: Investing in skills for better socio-economic outcomes* (COM(2012) 669/3). https://eur-lex.europa.eu/legal-content/EN/TXT/?uri=CELEX%3A52012DC0669

European Commission. (2022). *Towards a green & digital future: Key requirements for successful twin transitions in the European Union* (S. Muench, E. Stoermer, K. Jensen, et al., Joint Research Centre). Publications Office of the European Union. https://data.europa.eu/doi/10.2760/977331

Fayolle, A. (2013). Personal views on the future of entrepreneurship education. *Entrepreneurship and Regional Development, 25*(7–8), 692–701. https://doi.org/10.1080/08985626.2013.821318

Fayolle, A., & Gailly, B. (2008). From craft to science: Teaching models and learning processes in entrepreneurship education. *Journal of European Industrial Training, 32*(7), 569–593. https://doi.org/10.1108/03090590810899838

Fellnhofer, K. (2019). Toward a taxonomy of entrepreneurship education research literature: A bibliometric mapping and visualization. *Educational Research Review, 27*, 28–55. https://doi.org/10.1016/j.edurev.2018.10.002

Gabrielsson, J., Hägg, G., Landström, H., & Politis, D. (2020). Connecting the past with the present: The development of research on pedagogy in entrepreneurial education. *Education and Training, 62*(9), 1061–1086. https://doi.org/10.1108/ET-11-2019-0265

Gibb, A. (2002). In pursuit of a new ` enterprise' and paradigm for learning : Creative destruction, new values, new ways of doing things and new combinations of knowledge. *International Journal of Management Reviews, 4*(3), 233–269.

Goldkuhl, G. (2020). Design science epistemology. A pragmatist inquiry. *Scandinavian Journal of Information Systems, 32*(1), 39–80.

Hägg, G., & Gabrielsson, J. (2020). A systematic literature review of the evolution of pedagogy in entrepreneurial education research. *International Journal of Entrepreneurial Behaviour and Research, 26*(5), 829–861. https://doi.org/10.1108/IJEBR-04-2018-0272

Hattie, J. (2015). *What works best in education: The politics of collaborative expertise (issue June)*. Pearson.

Hevner, A. R., March, S. T., Park, J., & Ram, S. (2004). Design science in information research 1. *Design Science in IS Research MIS Quarterly, 28*(1), 75.

Kamovich, U., & Foss, L. (2017). In search of alignment: A review of impact studies in entrepreneurship education. *Education Research International, 2017*(September), 1–15. https://doi.org/10.1155/2017/1450102

Lackéus, M. (2015). Entrepreneurship in education. In *What, why, when, how*. https://www.oecd.org/cfe/leed/BGP_Entrepreneurship-in-Education.pdf

March, S. T., & Smith, G. F. (1995). Design and natural science research on information technology. *Decision Support Systems, 15*(4), 251–266. https://doi.org/10.1016/0167-9236(94)00041-2

Martin, B. C., McNally, J. J., & Kay, M. J. (2013). Examining the formation of human capital in entrepreneurship: A meta-analysis of entrepreneurship education outcomes. *Journal of Business Venturing, 28*(2), 211–224. https://doi.org/10.1016/j.jbusvent.2012.03.002

Mayer, R. E. (2008). Applying the science of learning: Evidence-based principles for the design of multimedia instruction. *The American Psychologist, 63*(8), 760–769. https://doi.org/10.1037/0003-066X.63.8.760

Mayer, R. E. (2011). *Applying the science of learning*. Pearson/Allyn & Bacon.

Mayer, R. E. (2018). Educational psychology's past and future contributions to the science of learning, science of instruction, and science of assessment. *Journal of Educational Psychology, 110*(2), 174–179. https://doi.org/10.1037/edu0000195

McKenney, S., & Reeves, T. C. (2012). *Conducting educational design research*. Routledge.

Minniti, M., & Bygrave, W. (2001). A dynamic model of entrepreneurial learning. *Entrepreneurship Theory and Practice, 25*(3), 5–16. https://doi.org/10.1177/104225870102500301

Mwasalwiba, E. S. (2010). Entrepreneurship education: A review of its objectives, teaching methods, and impact indicators. *Education + Training, 52*(1), 20–47. https://doi.org/10.1108/00400911011017663

Nabi, G., Linan, F., Fayolle, A., Krueger, N., & Walmsley, A. (2017). The impact of entrepreneurship education in higher education: A systematic review and research agenda. *Academy of Management Learning & Education, 16*(2), 277–299. https://doi.org/10.5465/amle.2015.0026

Neck, H. M., & Greene, P. G. (2011). Entrepreneurship education: Known worlds and new frontiers. *Journal of Small Business Management, 49*(1), 55–70.

Pittaway, L., & Cope, J. (2007). Entrepreneurship education: A systematic review of the evidence. *International Small Business Journal, 25*(5), 479–510. https://doi.org/10.1177/0266242607080656

Rauch, A., & Hulsink, W. (2015). Putting entrepreneurship education where the intention to act lies : An investigation into the impact of entrepreneurship education on entrepreneurial behavior. *Academy of Management Learning & Education, 14*(2), 187–204.

Romme, A. G. L., & Endenburg, G. (2006). Construction principles and design rules in the case of circular design. *Organization Science, 17*(2), 287–297. https://doi.org/10.1287/orsc.1050.0169

Romme, A. G. L., & Reymen, I. M. M. J. (2018). Entrepreneurship at the interface of design and science: Toward an inclusive framework. *Journal of Business Venturing Insights, 10*(July), 1–8. https://doi.org/10.1016/j.jbvi.2018.e00094

Romme, G. A. L. (2023). Design science as experimental methodology in innovation and entrepreneurship research: A primer. *CERN IdeaSquare Journal of Experimental Innovation, 7*(2), 4–7. https://doi.org/10.23726/cij.2022.1427

Ryff, C. D. (2019). Entrepreneurship and eudaimonic Well-being: Five venues for new science. *Journal of Business Venturing, 34*(4), 646–663. https://doi.org/10.1016/j.jbusvent.2018.09.003

Sarasvathy, S. D., & Venkataraman, S. (2011). Entrepreneurship as Method: Open Questions for an Entrepreneurial Future. *Entrepreneurship: Theory and Practice, 35*(1), 113–135. https://doi.org/10.1111/j.1540-6520.2010.00425.x

Shir, N., & Ryff, C. D. (2021). Entrepreneurship, self-organization, and Eudaimonic Well-being: A dynamic approach. *Entrepreneurship: Theory and Practice, 46*(6), 1658–1684. https://doi.org/10.1177/10422587211013798

Simon, H. (1996). *The sciences of the artificial* (3rd ed.). MIT Press.

Souitaris, V., Zerbinati, S., & Al-Laham, A. (2007). Do entrepreneurship programmes raise entrepreneurial intention of science and engineering students? The effect of learning, inspiration and resources. *Journal of Business Venturing, 22*(4), 566–591. https://doi.org/10.1016/j.jbusvent.2006.05.002

Stokes, D. E. (1997). *Pasteur's quadrant: Basic science and technological innovation*. Brookings Institution Press.

Tassone, V. C., den Brok, P., Tho, C. W., & Wals, A. E. (2022). Cultivating students' sustainability-oriented learning at the interface of science and society: A configuration of interrelated enablers. *International Journal of Sustainability in Higher Education, 23*(8), 255–271. https://doi.org/10.1108/IJSHE-01-2022-0014

Van Aken, J. E. (2004). Management research based on the paradigm of the design sciences: The quest for field-tested and grounded technological rules. *Journal of Management Studies, 41*(2), 219–246. https://doi.org/10.1111/j.1467-6486.2004.00430.x

Van Aken, J. E. (2011). Domeinafhankelijke ontwerptheorie. In J. E. van Aken & D. Andriessen (Eds.), *Handboek ontwerpgericht wetenschappelijk onderzoek: Wetenschap met effect* (pp. 25–39). Boom Lemma.

Van Aken, J. E., & Andriessen, D. (Eds.) (2011). Handboek ontwerpgericht wetenschappelijk onderzoek: Wetenschap met effect. Boom Lemma uitgevers.

Van Aken, J. E., & Berends, H. (2018). *Problem solving in organizations: A methodological handbook for business and management students* (3rd ed.). Cambridge University Press.

Van Aken, J. E., & Romme, G. (2009). Reinventing the future: Adding design science to the repertoire of organization and management studies. *Organisation Management Journal, 6*(1), 5–12. https://doi.org/10.1057/omj.2009.1

Van Rijnsoever, F. J., Sitzler, S., & Baggen, Y. (2023). The change agent teaching model: Educating entrepreneurial leaders to help solve grand societal challenges. *International. Journal of Management Education, 21*(3), 100893. https://doi.org/10.1016/j.ijme.2023.100893

Voegtlin, C., Scherer, A. G., Stahl, G. K., & Hawn, O. (2022). Grand societal challenges and responsible innovation. *Journal of Management Studies, 59*(1), 1–28. https://doi.org/10.1111/joms.12785

Watkins, C., & Mortimore, P. (1999). Pedagogy: What do we know? In P. Mortimore (Ed.), *Understanding pedagogy and its impact on learning* (pp. 1–19). Sage.

Walmsley, A., & Wraae, B. (2022). Entrepreneurship education but not as we know it: Reflections on the relationship between critical pedagogy and entrepreneurship education. *The International Journal of Management Education, 20*(3), 100726. https://doi.org/10.1016/j.ijme.2022.100726

Westley, F. R., Tjornbo, O., Olsson, P., Folke, C., Crona, B., & Bodin, Ö. (2013). A theory of transformative agency in linked social-ecological systems. *Ecology and Society, 18*(3), 26269375. https://doi.org/10.5751/ES-05673-180327

Bart Derre is Director at HOGENT University of Applied Sciences and Arts in Ghent, Belgium, and holds the (HOGENT-Xerius) research chair on entrepreneurial learning at the Vrije Universiteit Brussel, Brussels, Belgium. As Director of the Center for Entrepreneurship, he has overseen numerous entrepreneurial education programs. His research, including a Ph.D. from TU Eindhoven (The Netherlands), focuses on the design and implementation of entrepreneurial education that drives meaningful impact.

Yvette Baggen is Assistant Professor at the Education and Learning Sciences group of Wageningen University & Research, specializing in entrepreneurial learning and ecosystems in higher education. Her work empowers students and professionals as change agents, equipping them to tackle real-world challenges. Yvette's research integrates education, entrepreneurship, and societal impact, promoting transformative learning experiences that prepare learners for impactful careers.

Pedro De Bruyckere is an educational scientist at Utrecht University and head of Leerpunt, Flanders, a What Works-clearing house in Belgium. He co-authored several popular scientific books such as Urban Myths about Learning and Education and The Psychology of Great Teaching. He is an avid blogger on TheEconomyOfMeaning.com and an often asked public speaker on education. His research interests are currently focused on collective student efficacy.

Designing Artifacts in Entrepreneurial Education Research

Jimme Keizer and Isabelle Reymen

Abstract The methodology known as Design Science Research (DSR) can be broadly defined as a "method that establishes and operationalizes research when the desired goal is an artifact or recommendation" (Dresch, A., Lacerda, D.P., Antunes Jr, J.A.V., *Design science research.* Springer, 2015, p. 67). This approach is deeply rooted in the ontological and epistemological foundations of "design science" (Dresch, A., Lacerda, D.P., Antunes Jr, J.A.V., *Design science research.* Springer, 2015) and contributes scientifically to addressing field problems, as exemplified in the preceding chapter. Researchers such as Berglund et al. (Academy of Management Review, 45:825–846, 2020), Dimov (2016) (Toward a Design Science of Entrepreneurship, Models of Start-up Thinking and Action: Theoretical, Empirical and Pedagogical Approaches, *Advances in Entrepreneurship, Firm Emergence and Growth*, 18). Emerald Group Publishing Limited, Leeds, 2016), Dresch et al. (*Design science research.* Springer, 2015), and Romme & Reymen (2018) build upon the work of Herbert Simon (1996), particularly his distinction between the natural sciences and the "science of the artificial" or design sciences.

Simon's (1996) delineation separates explanatory science, where the phenomenon under study exists independently of the researcher, and the "science of the artificial" or design sciences. In design science, the researcher deliberately creates an artificial phenomenon or artifact with the explicit intention of solving context-related field problems. Illustrating the relevance of the design approach to educational challenges, McKenney and Reeves (*Educational Researcher* 41:16, 2012) define educational design research as "a genre of research in which the iterative development of solutions to practical and complex educational problems also provides the context for empirical investigation, yielding theoretical understanding that can inform the work of others" (p. 7).

J. Keizer · I. Reymen (✉)
Industrial Engineering and Innovation Sciences, Eindhoven University of Technology, Eindhoven, The Netherlands
e-mail: i.m.m.j.reymen@tue.nl

© The Author(s), under exclusive license to Springer Nature Switzerland AG 2025

B. Derre, Y. Baggen (eds.), *Empowering the Next Generation of Entrepreneurial Change Agents*, Contributions to Management Science,
https://doi.org/10.1007/978-3-031-82251-3_2

This chapter proposes the design of artifacts, a key concept in DSR, for entrepreneurial education research. It starts by positioning DSR in the context of scientific methods and describes its main characteristics, including the concept of artifacts. We end with a detailed description of the steps performed in DSR, illustrated with an example of research that includes the design of an artifact for entrepreneurial education.

1 Introduction

Over the past two decades, entrepreneurial education has become a crucial topic in both educational and management literature. A growing stream of publications sheds light on the factors that influence entrepreneurial performance and the need to integrate them into educational curricula and training programs of both profit and nonprofit organizations. Despite these efforts, the question remains to what extent this research actually contributes to the effectiveness of education and training practices, and to what extent it leads to actual entrepreneurial behavior. Impact studies show a mixed picture of successes and disappointments (Brüne & Lutz, 2020; et al. 2015; Kim & Lee, 2019).

On the one hand, positive effects are reported, with entrepreneurial education, based on research, positively influencing entrepreneurial attitudes and intentions. On the other hand, researchers note with disappointment that the outcomes of this academic research often do not reach practitioners. The divide between practitioners and scholars is highlighted, and the slow implementation of insights into practice is an ongoing challenge.

These challenges transcend the domain of entrepreneurial education and are characteristic of practice-based science in general. Collaboration between researchers and professionals is often cited as crucial to connect rigor and relevance.

Besides promoting a culture of dialogical encounter in which collaboration, teamwork, and transdisciplinary work are encouraged (Romme et al., 2015), the question of the appropriateness of the methodology used by researchers should also be addressed. Are the usual descriptive, contemplative, and explanatory studies capable of providing applicable knowledge for diverse practice settings?

Professionals expect active collaboration and dialogue with scientists so that research results are more closely aligned with the real needs and challenges in the field and can be directly applied to real-world problems. They are interested in the latest developments, trends, and best practices and find credibility and reliability of research results important, which gives them the confidence to apply these results in their practice. Furthermore, it is important to professionals that scientific research takes into account diversity in terms of cultural backgrounds, business environments, and individual experiences. They hope that research is relevant to different contexts and not limited to specific situations. Furthermore, professionals expect scientific knowledge to be accessible. This includes understandable language, public access to research findings, and effective communication channels to bridge the gap between academics and professionals.

These are obvious expectations, but scientists often have limited ability to meet them. Characteristics inherent in science such as limited external validity and generalizability; (one-off) measurements under specific, controlled conditions; and accessibility only through academic channels often limit relevance for practice.

Quantitative research, even when focused on specific samples, provides results that are difficult to apply in the culturally and institutionally specific realities of education and business, and qualitative macro and case studies lead to outcomes with limited applicability in the complexity and diversity of other situations.

While researchers are engaged in innovations in both quantitative and qualitative methods and techniques, the gap between research and practice remains. Science is rooted in methodological principles upheld by peer-reviewed journals.

In their analysis of the factors hindering dialogue between practice and science, Romme et al. (2015) conclude that the main problem is the lack of a shared purpose and responsibility within and across scholarly and practitioner communities (p. 547). The expectations and internal ground rules of the communities of professionals and academics are quite different. To bridge these differences, Romme et al. (2015), following Argyris et al. (1985) and others, suggest that the common ground should be the pragmatic question: "Does or will this solution or result work?" This could include—ethically—financial, economic, operational, motivational, satisfaction, and behavioral outcomes.

All these considerations taken together illustrate the relevance of the design research approach to create artifacts that help teaching teams to create effective entrepreneurial education environments.

This chapter highlights the importance of alternative scientific approaches, such as Design Science Research (DSR), which focus on developing practical and acceptable solutions, especially for "wicked problems." This term refers to complex and multifaceted issues that are not easily solved by common methods. A concrete example of a "wicked problem" is creating effective entrepreneurial education and training practices. Other examples of such problems in organizations include changing the organizational culture to enable more innovative performance as a company and developing more effective talent management and staff development due to factors such as competition in the labor market, diversity and inclusion, and the need for continuous professional development.

Solving such issues by creating supportive artifacts often requires collaboration between different disciplines, creativity, and an adaptive approach, as solutions need to be constantly adjusted based on feedback and changing circumstances. Besides striving for workable and acceptable solutions, DSR also aims to generate generalizable knowledge for practice. By generalizable knowledge, we mean identifying possibilities and conditions under which a successful solution can be applied elsewhere, under more or less similar conditions.

2 Basic Scientific Methods

Science often fails badly in helping professionals find solutions to their wicked problems. These are problems that:

- Are complex due to the intertwining of many variables and factors, the boundaries of which are vague and difficult to define
- Are constantly changing so that solutions that seem effective today may not work tomorrow
- Cannot be solved with a single, clearly defined approach
- Are often perpetuated by deep-rooted structural and social factors, making it difficult to make changes because they often have unintended consequences that can further exacerbate the problem or create new ones

To date, there is no single step-by-step plan for solving wicked problems. But there are approaches and methods that can help. A widely used approach is the "soft systems analysis" developed by Rittel and Webber (1973), which focuses on understanding the problem in context and involving stakeholders in finding solutions.

In this chapter, we build on Rittel and Webber's analytical approach and focus on the design methodology needed to achieve effective and sustainable results in solving challenging wicked problems in general and that of designing effective entrepreneurial education in higher education more specifically.

To position the DSR approach in the methodological field, we start with the main methodological distinction between theory-oriented (empirical) research and practice- and solution-oriented (regulatory) research.

The dominant empirical method focuses on generating theoretically relevant statements with which a subject-specific nomological network is built. Such a network consists of relationships of the concept under investigation with other concepts, relationships with operationalizations of those concepts, and relationships between the operationalizations themselves. Testable statements must be derived from it. To the question, "Who do you see as your most important customers?," researchers applying the empirical method would answer, "The reviewers of journals with a high citation impact score." Application of their research findings in practice is not a primary goal.

Especially in practice-oriented sciences such as engineering, health sciences, business administration, environmental sciences, and education science, there is a growing interest in a scientifically sound change and solution-oriented method that connects to the questions and problems of professionals in practice. Figure 1 juxtaposes the two approaches, i.e., the empirical cycle and the regulatory cycle.

The *empirical cycle*, also known as the empirical method or scientific method, is a systematic approach scientists use to acquire and validate knowledge. The usual steps in the empirical cycle are:

Observation. This is the starting point of the cycle, where researchers make objective and systematic observations of phenomena. The aim is to gather facts and patterns without prior interpretation.

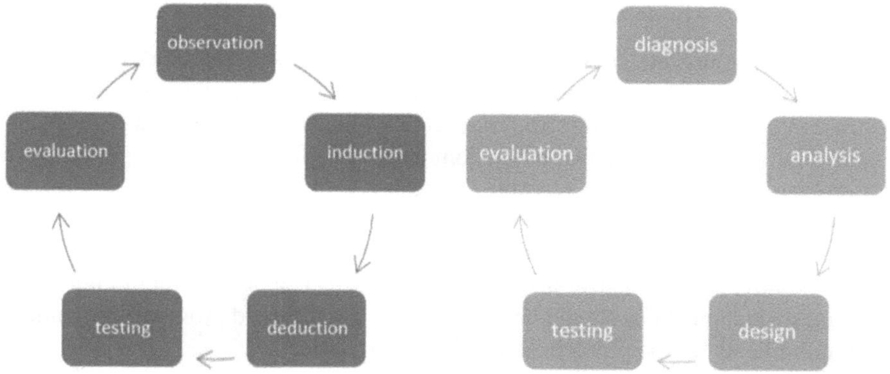

Fig. 1 Steps in empirical cycle (after De Groot, 1961) and regulatory cycle (after Van Strien, 1997)

Induction. Based on the observations, one or more statements are formulated, which include testable generalizations from specific observations to one or more broader hypotheses.

Deduction. Based on the hypotheses, expectations are formulated. These predictions concern specific results that can be observed or measured if the hypotheses prove to be true.

Testing. Researchers design and conduct experiments or collect data to test hypotheses. The aim is to obtain empirical evidence that supports or refutes the hypotheses.

Evaluation. Based on the results of the tests, researchers evaluate whether the hypotheses are supported. If the results are consistent with the predictions, the hypothesis can be strengthened. If the results are inconsistent, the hypothesis can be revised or rejected.

The empirical cycle is an iterative process. If the conclusions indicate that the hypothesis needs to be revised, the process starts again. This method forms the basis of scientific research and helps build reliable knowledge about the world around us. It is a widely used method in the natural and social sciences. The empirical cycle has a positivist background.

For practice-based research, the regulatory cycle was developed (Van Strien, 1997) to provide researchers and professionals—such as psychologists, business administrators, and educationalists—who, in their daily practice, have to give advice, initiate interventions, or develop courses in concrete, often complex, unique situations, with a scientifically sound approach. In many cases, finding a good solution requires interdisciplinary consultation and research. The regulatory cycle has a normative, (inter)subjective background. The variants developed within this approach are basically aimed at finding solutions to specific practical problems. Although developing knowledge is not the primary goal here, developed solutions do consider applications in similar situations.

The *regulatory cycle* usually involves the following steps (Dresch et al., 2015):

Diagnosis. The process starts from a problem tangle. Practice problems are rarely unambiguous. The problem tangle is unraveled in the diagnosis phase. A researcher takes the "detour from science": What does this particular case resemble? Of which family is this one? From unraveling the problem tangle follows a problem formulation with possible causes.

Analysis. Next, the causes of the problem are further investigated. For this, the methodological toolboxes of involved disciplines can be drawn upon. A mix of quantitative and qualitative methods is often used. The problem definition determines which methods should be used. The research should provide a program of requirements for the problem solution to be developed.

Design. The question is asked: which possible solutions (most often in the form of artifacts) can fit the given problem? The program of requirements is leading.

Testing. The identified solutions or artifacts are tested for advantages and disadvantages. The most workable and acceptable solution is worked out in an implementation plan.

Conclusions are drawn regarding implementation.

Evaluation. Finally, it is determined what generalizable knowledge can be distilled from the study. This involves what can be generalized from the $N = 1$ study to the $N = \mathrm{k}$ level.

All these steps involve collaboration with stakeholders.

The pragmatic question stems from the distinction between positivism and pragmatism. The empirical cycle has as its foundation positivism, which states that (Alakwe, 2017) knowledge and truth must be based on empirical facts and scientific observations. Only that which is empirically observable is considered valid knowledge. For positivists, the scientific method is the only reliable means of acquiring knowledge. Hypotheses must be tested and confirmed or rejected on the basis of empirical data. Only factual observations and measurable data are considered valid.

The regulatory cycle stems from pragmatism, which emphasizes (Smaling, 2000) practical experience and utility as criteria for truth and meaning. Pragmatists focus on the usefulness of ideas and argue that the truth of a belief is determined by its positive effects in practice. Theories, models, and research methods are seen as tools that should be practically useful. If a research outcome is effective in solving problems and promoting well-being, it is considered valuable. Pragmatists avoid absolute truths and emphasize that truth is contextual. An idea or solution may be true in certain circumstances, but not necessarily in all situations. In essence, positivism and pragmatism differ in their approach to knowledge and truth.

Positivism emphasizes empirical observations and scientific methods, while pragmatism focuses on the practical utility and effectiveness of research findings in practice. The pragmatic approach has implications for how academics and professionals deal with different methodological orientations, such as quantitative versus qualitative research.

Researchers and professionals have to weigh up which methods and perspectives are most relevant and effective for addressing concrete problems. Choosing between quantitative and qualitative research and distinguishing between descriptive and prescriptive approaches are influenced by the pragmatic lens. The ultimate goal is not only to gather theoretical insights but also to turn them into concrete solutions that contribute to the effectiveness and improvement of everyday practice.

3 Methods According to the Regulatory Cycle

DSR is one of the methods in which the principles of the regulatory cycle are applied. These methods offer different approaches to addressing complex problems and promoting positive change in various contexts. The methods have overlapping characteristics and the choice of one or the other method depends on the specific context of the research and the objectives of the researcher. Some methods that belong to this group include:

Design Science Research (DSR) (e.g., Hevner et al., 2004): DSR focuses on designing, developing, and evaluating innovative artifacts (e.g., systems, processes, products) to address real-world problems. DSR emphasizes on creating solutions that are both effective and efficient.

Participatory Action Research (PAR) (e.g., Reason & Bradbury, 2001): PAR involves active stakeholder collaboration in identifying and solving problems. It combines action and reflection to jointly develop practical solutions and promote improvements in practice.

Soft Systems Methodology (SSM) (e.g., Checkland & Scholes, 1990): SSM focuses on understanding and improving complex human systems. It uses modelling techniques to capture stakeholders' perceptions and interpretations and generate solutions to problems in social and organizational contexts.

Action Research (AR) (e.g., Stringer, 2014): AR integrates cycles of planning, acting, observing, and reflecting to promote change in organizational practices. It actively engages participants in the research process to generate practice-based knowledge.

Adaptive Design Research (ADR) (e.g., Van Aken, 2004): ADR is an approach in which design and evaluation are carried out iteratively, adapting the design based on continuous evaluation. It is particularly suitable for complex and dynamic environments.

Appreciative Inquiry (AI) (e.g., Cooperrider & Whitney, 2005): AI focuses on identifying, leveraging, and strengthening the positive aspects of organizations. It emphasizes understanding and building from strengths and successes to facilitate positive change.

4 Design Science Research

Design Science Research method is thus one of the variants in which the regulatory cycle has been elaborated. The (information) technical, engineering origin of this method is still recognizable from its core concept: design and validation of an artifact.

Herbert Simon is mostly seen as the one who founded the DSR approach. In *The Sciences of the Artificial* (1969), Simon argues for the recognition of a new branch of science, the "sciences of the artificial," in which the focus is on understanding and improving artificial systems. He emphasizes that the design process plays a crucial role in these sciences. The book had a significant impact on several fields, including computer science, systems science, and design theory. It introduced important concepts that were later integrated into disciplines such as information systems and design sciences.

However, the DSR method itself is more of a preliminary outcome of an evolution of ideas that started in the information systems community and was picked up and elaborated upon in practical sciences concerned with how problems can be solved through designing artifacts to achieve goals. No specific individuals can be identified as the sole founders of DSR, as it has rather been an evolution within the academic community. Instead, we can identify different authors that have contributed to the field from different perspectives.

Starting with information sciences, the following authors have contributed to the field of DSR:

- Alan R. Hevner is often cited as one of the main contributors to DSR. He and others have published several articles on DSR in Information Systems (DSRIS), including the influential article Design Science in Information Systems Research published in 2004 (Hevner et al., 2004).
- Shirley Gregor is another prominent researcher in the field of DSR. She has worked with Hevner and others to further develop the principles and methodology of DSR (Gregor & Hevner, 2013).
- Steven T. March contributed to the development of DSR, notably by collaborating with Hevner on early publications on the subject.

Outside information science, DSR has been further developed and applied by researchers such as:

- Christopher Alexander: *A Pattern Language* (1977). Alexander's work emphasizes the importance of patterns in design and architecture. It contains a series of patterns that can be applied in creating buildings and cities.
- Donald Schön: *The Reflective Practitioner: How Professionals Think in Action* (1983). In this book, Schön explores the concept of reflective practice in professional activities, including design.
- Bryan Lawson: *How Designers Think: The Design Process Demystified* (2005). Lawson examines the thinking process of designers and analyzes how designers solve problems and make decisions.

- More recently, Vom Brocke et al. (2020) published a state-of-the-art article on applying DSR. His editorial describes how DSR can be further developed conceptually.
- In management science, DSR principles have been picked up and further developed by Van Aken and Romme (e.g., Van Aken & Romme, 2009 and Van Aken & Romme, 2012). This article explores the integration of design science into organizational and management studies. It argues for adding design-oriented research to the methodological repertoire of these disciplines.
- In educational science, DSR principles have been taken up, for example, by Van den Akker (1999). His article presents principles and methods of developmental research in education. It focuses on developing practical solutions to educational challenges through systematic design research.
- McKenney and Reeves (2012) have published a systematic review of progress in design-based research. It examines the evolution of design-based research and shares insights on the strengths and challenges of this research method in education.

As a methodological note, design science is positioned as a scientific method that can reduce the gap between practice and science. DSR is increasingly applied in fields such as engineering, management, and healthcare to design innovative solutions to complex (i.e., wicked) problems. DSR is still evolving, which is evident from the experience of researchers that it is quite often difficult to get articles published in which the DSR approach has been used (Dimov et al., 2023).

5 The Most Important Characteristics of Design Science Research

The DSR approach has some characteristic features (based a.o. on Simon (1969) and Romme and Dimov (2021)), which we discuss here.

Focus on Artifacts

In the DSR approach, the artifact is a central concept (Hevner et al., 2004; Pfeffers et al., 2007; Gregor & Hevner, 2013; Pfeiffer et al., 2019). An artifact is designed to solve a problem, improve the environment in which it is implemented, and enhance the knowledge base of technology and science. An artifact refers to a concrete, tangible result of research. It is a newly developed or designed object, system, process, model, framework, or any other form of practical knowledge created to solve a specific problem. It is the result of the design process.

An artifact can take very different forms, such as a software application, a process model, a database, a device, a system, a method, a conceptual model, a business model, or a training, course, or curriculum (Romme & Dimov, 2021; Romme et al., 2015). Designing an artifact leads not only to the creation of a new "solution" but also to the development of design theories that provide a better understanding of why the artifact improves the relevant application contexts and can be applicable under different conditions. This involves recognizing the indications and contraindications for application of the artifact.

Examples of artifacts in different settings, in the context of DSR, are as follows:

- Software application designed to improve communication between doctors and patients
- Process model designed to improve the efficiency of production processes in a factory
- Database designed to improve access to medical data
- Framework for developing an entrepreneurship curriculum
- Business model for a new product
- Formula for producing an alternative medicine
- Concept for an innovation center to support SMEs

What these examples have in common is that they bring together different perspectives, ideas, and preferences and are the result of a design process of developing, evaluating, and further shaping the artifact, so that it best serves the need of the target group.

Problem-Oriented
DSR usually starts by identifying a relevant real-world problem that needs to be solved. The aim is to design a solution that addresses the problem and is actually useful.

Collaboration with Stakeholders
DSR requires intensive collaboration between researcher(s) and stakeholders. The problem to be solved is often the problem of an identifiable group. Input from these stakeholders is important in determining the design requirements of the intended solution and in evaluating intermediate and final results.

Cycle of Design and Evaluation
DSR follows an iterative process of design and evaluation. Researchers develop an artifact, evaluate it in a real-world environment, and use the insights gained to improve the artifact. This cycle repeats itself until a satisfactory solution is achieved.

Knowledge Contribution
DSR aims not only to provide practical solutions but also to contribute to scientific knowledge. The research should lead to new insights that are not only relevant to the solved problem but also more widely applicable.

Theoretical Foundations
DSR often integrates existing theories and concepts to inform the design process. The research should be based on sound scientific principles and literature.

Program of Requirements
DSR works toward a solution that meets a program of requirements that combines the scientific knowledge base with stakeholders' requirements and wishes. This promotes support for successful implementation.

Validation and Evaluation

The success of DSR is evaluated based on the effectiveness of the developed artifact in solving the problem. Evaluation often includes field tests and may use standardized methods.

DSR goes through the stages of the regulatory cycle. The research starts in a concrete, complex practice problem. That problem is unraveled, and research questions are formulated that need to be answered to arrive at a clear diagnosis and a program of requirements for the possible solutions. These possible solutions are weighed and tested against each other, and the best-fit one is further detailed and elaborated. To this end, an intervention plan is developed and implemented. Next, the research process is evaluated, and the more generally valid knowledge is formulated. Any new or as yet unresolved problem aspects may trigger follow-up research. Dresch et al. (2015) have described how the basic form of the design cycle has developed in recent years from a technical method to a generally applicable methodology.

6 Applying a DSR Approach to Entrepreneurial Education: Entrepreneurial Education as a Wicked Problem

As indicated before, DSR focuses on developing practical and acceptable solutions, especially for "wicked problems." A wicked problem is characterized by neither a clear problem or clear solution and the involvement of multiple parties with conflicting values or interests (Alford & Head, 2017). There are many unknown unknowns, and the situation is constantly in flux and induces unpredictability. These problems are not easily solved by common methods. They require to first probe and then sense and respond (Snowden & Boone, 2007): it is only in retrospect we can understand why things are happening. By conducting experiments that are safe to fail, instructive patterns can emerge, and the path forward reveals itself (Snowden & Boone, 2007).

DSR helps in solving wicked problems via the creation of supportive artifacts that require collaboration between different disciplines, creativity, and an adaptive approach, as solutions need to be constantly adjusted based on feedback and changing circumstances. Besides striving for workable and acceptable solutions, DSR also aims to generate generalizable knowledge for practice. By generalizable knowledge, we mean identifying possibilities and conditions under which a successful solution can be applied elsewhere, under more or less similar conditions.

Creating effective entrepreneurial education and training practices can be seen as an example of a wicked problem. Higher education institutions are expected and asked to impart entre- and intrapreneurship competencies to their students in addition to study-specific content knowledge and skills. This assignment raises quite a few difficult questions, for instance: What exactly are the envisaged entrepreneurial competencies? How to get students to develop these competencies (like dealing with uncertainty and an action orientation)? How far should students develop them? Is it an independent subject, or should entrepreneurship be integrated into existing subjects? What are the competencies of the responsible teachers? Can educational institutions develop their own approach? Is a common framework being worked toward?

So, DSR seems to fit as an approach to the wicked problem of creating effective entrepreneurial education and training practices, because it focuses on an iterative approach (in contrast to more linear approaches) when creating artifacts and room for experimentation, combined with a data-driven follow-up. But still the question remains to what extent this type of research actually contributes to the effectiveness of education and training practices and to what extent it leads to actual entrepreneurial behavior. Entrepreneurial education is widely promoted on the belief that it strengthens students' entrepreneurial mindset, which in turn is expected to lead to more entrepreneurial action and behavior. Looking at the available evidence regarding the impact of entrepreneurial education on entrepreneurship, there are not many but some hopeful outcomes to note. Positive results are reported with the necessary beats. We mention some impact studies as examples; they show a mixed picture of successes and disappointments.

In their review study, Zampetakis and Moustakis (2011) conclude that it is important to investigate what methods are currently used to design entrepreneurship curricula and how these methods can be improved to better prepare students for the challenges of the labor market.

A survey research (Kautonen et al., 2015) examined the impact of entrepreneurial education on business creation and found that entrepreneurial education has a positive impact on business creation, but that the effects depend on the context in which the education is delivered.

A third (hypothesis testing) study (Maresch et al., 2016) shows that entrepreneurial education increases entrepreneurial intention (EI). However, this does not happen uniformly in all contexts, as specific contexts may require different entrepreneurial education actions. In this study the context-specific questions in two separate categories of students (business students and science and engineering students) are investigated. If context is important, different outcomes are expected from similar EE classes provided to different student groups. The principal results indicate that entrepreneurial education is generally effective for business students and science and engineering students. However, the EI of science and engineering students is actually negatively affected by subjective norms, whereas that effect is not apparent among the business student sample. The authors suggest that future research is needed on effective didactic approaches in entrepreneurial education for science and engineering students.

A systematic review of 21 quantitative and qualitative articles on the effect of entrepreneurial education in schools (Brüne & Lutz, 2020) showed that the effect of entrepreneurial education on children and adolescents depends on their gender and age. For female and older students, entrepreneurial education has a negative effect on entrepreneurship outcomes compared to male and younger students. The positive effect of entrepreneurial education is generally stronger when the program studied is less achievement-oriented.

A subsequent study (Cohen et al., 2020) showed that entrepreneurial education can be effective if designed and implemented properly. A study on the effectiveness of entrepreneurial education programs showed that these programs can have a positive effect on the development of entrepreneurial skills.

Overall, entrepreneurial education seems to have a positive effect on students' entrepreneurial intentions, attitudes, knowledge, and skills toward entrepreneurship. Entrepreneurial education can have a positive impact on entrepreneurial behavior, but the effect depends on several factors. These factors should be considered when designing and implementing entrepreneurial education programs. Here, the researchers point to factors such as:

Target group: It is important to determine the target group for which the program is intended. The program should match the needs and interests of the target group.
Context: The context in which the program is offered affects the program's effect. It is important to consider the cultural, economic, and social context.
Content: The content of the program should match the objectives of the program and the target group. It is important to ensure a good balance between theory and practice.
Teachers: The quality of the teachers affects the impact of the program. It is important to ensure sufficient knowledge and skills among teachers.
Cooperation: Cooperation with business and other relevant parties can contribute to the success of the program. It is important to ensure good cooperation and coordination between different parties.
Evaluation: It is important to evaluate the program to determine whether the objectives have been achieved and to improve the program.

The effectiveness of entrepreneurial education can rightly be called a "wicked problem." It is widely promoted on the belief that it strengthens students' entrepreneurial mindset, which in turn is expected to lead to more entrepreneurial action and behavior.

7 DSR Steps for the Design of Artifacts for Entrepreneurial Education

In this section, we discuss the different steps from the DSR approach. See also Fig. 2, in connection to the development of entrepreneurial education.

Field Problem: Symptoms and Issues

An effective entrepreneurship curriculum should enable students to acquire the skills and knowledge needed to be successful in the current and future labor market. It is important to investigate what methods are currently used to design entrepreneurship curricula and how these methods can be improved to better prepare

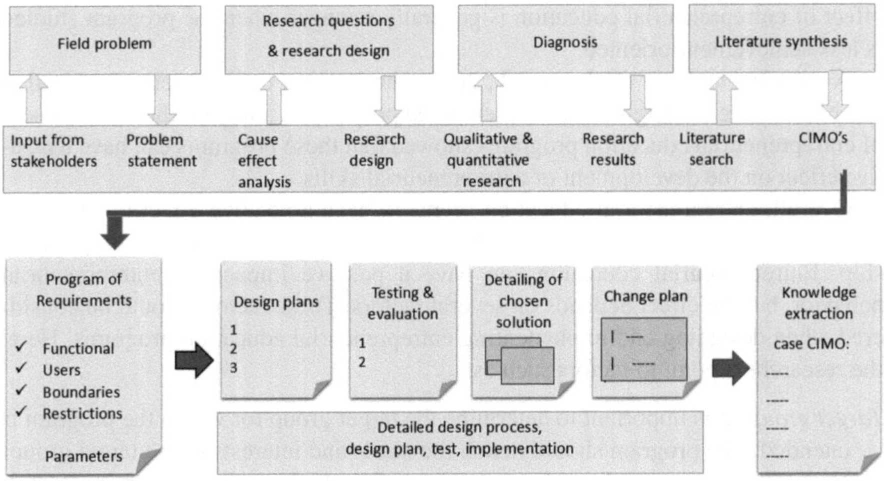

Fig. 2 Steps in DSR

students for the challenges of the labor market. Such research could lead to the development of new and innovative methods for designing entrepreneurship curricula that better meet the needs of students and employers.

The aforementioned research by Zampetakis and Moustakis (2011), Kautonen et al. (2015), Maresch et al. (2016), Brüne and Lutz (2020), and Cohen et al. (2020), among others, has shown that entrepreneurial education program can have a positive effect on the development of entrepreneurial skills if they are well designed and implemented. It is important to investigate what methods are currently used and how these methods can be improved to better prepare students for the challenges of the labor market.

A problem description for a study on improving methods for designing effective entrepreneurship curricula could be: "How can we improve current entrepreneurship curriculum design methods to better prepare students for the challenges of the current and future labor market?"

As a starting point of the DSR research, an "intuitive diagnosis" will be drawn up for the complex situation. The aim is to check the relevance of the assumed problem and get a picture of important aspects. Through interviews with stakeholders, the researcher orients himself on the nature and severity of the assumed problem and checks what others have already published about the symptoms observed and possible underlying causes. Figure 3 outlines in a fishbone diagram the field problem with a number of main and sub-causes that is central to this book: insufficiently effective entrepreneurial education.

Research Questions

After the field problem is formulated, the "intuitive" diagnosis is discussed and further substantiated with those most concerned, the knowledge of the problem field is increased, and the research method to be used is worked out, usually as a form of empirical research.

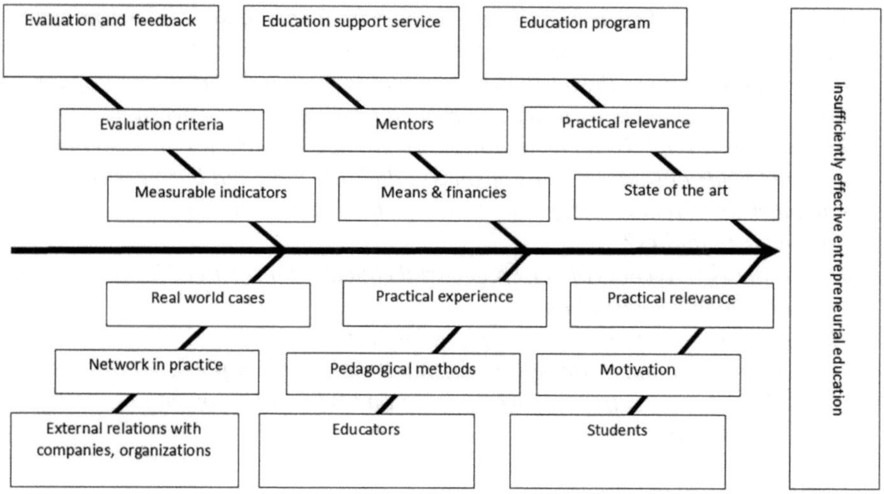

Fig. 3 An intuitive cause-and-effect analysis as an initial ordering of the problem. *Problem formulation: industry engagement, theoretically heavy, leads to insufficiently effective entrepreneurial education*

A distinction is made between diagnostic questions that need to be answered to analyze the existing situation and design questions that anticipate the kind of solution that should eventually be developed.

Diagnostic questions focus on the nature, severity, and improvability of the problem situation, for instance: What facts and circumstances show the seriousness of the problem? What do those involved see as causes and consequences? What have those involved done in their concrete situation to improve it? What worked and what did not work? How satisfied and dissatisfied are those involved with what has been done and tried so far?

Design questions are aimed at forming a picture of the requirements a solution should meet and the conditions under which it should be effective. This type of research question probes what stakeholders see as opportunities for improvement, their expectations, needs, and the requirements they have for an effective solution.

In this phase of the design cycle, methodological choices are also made for how data will be collected and analyzed. Here, a quantitative, qualitative, or hybrid approach can be chosen.

Also fitting into this category of questions is an in-depth literature review that synthesizes what has been published in the academic and professional literature about the problem and the theories, concepts, and models (which are these?) that can be useful building blocks for solutions in the concrete problem situation.

Research questions in a study of effective entrepreneurial education programs:

Diagnostic research questions:

- *What does the literature say about factors affecting the effectiveness of entrepreneurial education?*

- *How do students, teachers, and stakeholders from companies and organizations experience the effectiveness of entrepreneurial education? What (de)motivates them, and what gives them (dis)satisfaction? Is there a difference between more theory-oriented and more practice-oriented education and between primary and higher education? Is there a difference between outcomes in economically oriented fields of study, such as business administration and business economics and marketing, and noneconomic fields of study such as healthcare, social studies, and arts studies?*
- *How is the effectiveness of entrepreneurial education measured? What are symptoms of ineffective education?*
- *How do stakeholders resolve perceived ineffectiveness?*
- *How are teachers and external professional stakeholders prepared for developing and delivering entrepreneurial education? What forms of support and guidance are available, and do they meet needs?*

Design research questions:

- What are the best practices (at home and abroad)?
- What changes and improvements do those involved (students, teachers, and external stakeholders) hope for?
- What requirements must improvements meet?
- How strong will be the resistance to changing the existing practice intertwined with the field problem: does the existing behavior stem from (strong) beliefs, rationales, or go with the flow?

Diagnosis: Empirical Research

In the diagnosis phase, the problem situation in its context is thoroughly investigated through interviews, questionnaires, and analyses of available and/or collected facts and data, culminating in a program of requirements for the solution (the design). Based on the research results, the intuitive diagnosis can be transformed into a more definitive diagnosis. In this phase, qualitative, quantitative, and hybrid methods can be used to identify facts and circumstances as answers to the research questions.

Literature Synthesis: CIMOs

Anyone looking for useful ideas for a particular practice problem in previously conducted research encounters the problem that each study—whether qualitative, quantitative, or hybrid—has its own context, which determines under what circumstances the recommendations described are assumed or proven to be effective. Each study has, so to speak, a leaflet indicating indications and contraindications. Those conditions must be considered in the search process for the best-fit solution to the problem.

In the DSR approach, the results of previously conducted research are used to point the way to possible solutions. Baskerville and Pries-Heje (2019) use the term "projectability" in this context, indicating that it is important in DSR to be as complete and precise as possible in generalizing previous research findings to future situations. They highlight the importance of counterfactuals and contextual contingency. The CIMO method (Denyer et al., 2008) paves the way from theory to the solution of the problem. It helps to answer the following questions: What knowledge and solutions about my research problem are already known? What should I at least consider when looking for an innovative solution?

CIMO stands for Context, Intervention, Mechanism, and Outcome. The chain of reasoning for the CIMO logic reads: "For this specific problem (and similar problems) in this specific Context, it is useful to apply this Intervention, which through these Mechanisms will generate the following Outcomes" (Denyer et al., 2008).

The CIMO logic has the following elements:

Context (C)

Definition: The environment in which the problem occurs and in which the intervention will take place.

Role: It identifies and describes the relevant factors, circumstances, and characteristics of the situation in which the problem occurs.

Intervention (I)

Definition: The solution or intervention designed to address the problem.

Role: It describes the characteristics of the planned intervention and how it is intended to address existing problems in the context.

Mechanism (M)

Definition: The mechanism is the working mechanism or theory behind the intervention. It explains how the intervention is expected to produce the desired results.

Role: It provides a theoretical basis and explanation of how the intervention should work.

Outcome (O)

Definition: The intended results or effects expected from implementing the intervention in the context.

Role: The measurable outcome used to assess whether the intervention has been successful in addressing the problem in the given context.

The CIMO framework is designed to guide researchers in designing, implementing, and evaluating innovative solutions. It helps in structuring the research questions and analyzing the results. Using CIMO also helps communicate findings to both the academic community and practitioners.

See for further explanations and applications of the CIMO-logic: Costat et al., 2018; Holmström et al., 2014; Denyer et al., 2008.

Usually, quite a number of CIMOs are formulated, depending on the extensiveness of the relevant external literature on the subject of study. In Table 1 we provide examples of CIMO formulation from a study that developed a framework for designing effective entrepreneurial education (Derre, 2023).

Table 1 outlines a single intervention, but it is essential to recognize that CIMO-writing typically involves identifying a diverse range of interventions to achieve the desired outcomes. In the study conducted by Derre (2023) on effective entrepreneurial education program design, several distinct interventions were proposed:

Table 1 Example CIMO

CIMO: effective entrepreneurial education programs	
Context	In educational contexts where novice teachers have low prior knowledge or experience in creating entrepreneurial education environments
Intervention	Providing students with the opportunity to gain insight into their entrepreneurial personality traits through a self-administered valid and reliable assessment tool
Outcome	Optimization (stimulation) of personal entrepreneurial characteristics
Mechanism	In the system of the Big Five, personality traits make a difference when entrepreneurs are compared with managers. They are also relevant in predicting entrepreneurial intention and entrepreneurs' performance. (Brandstätter, 2011). Personality aspects of entrepreneurship: A look at five meta-analyses. *Personality and Individual Differences*, 51, 3, 222–230)

1. **Collaborative design perspective**: Consider approaching the design of entrepreneurial education programs from a collaborative standpoint. Engage a community of practice that includes various stakeholders such as entrepreneurial educators, representatives from the work field, educational management, students, and alumni. Additionally, involve experts in educational data management (e.g., Toding & Venesaar, 2018).
2. **Educational vision for self-regulating entrepreneurs**: Another approach is to shape entrepreneurial education programs based on an educational vision. This vision aims to foster the growth of self-regulating entrepreneurial citizens who can confidently navigate uncertainty. Drawing inspiration from Fayolle and Gailly (2008), this perspective emphasizes equipping learners with the skills to handle ambiguity effectively.
3. **Data-driven prototyping process**: Lastly, consider adopting a data-driven prototyping process. Building on the work of Dunn et al. (2019), this approach leverages data insights to inform the design of entrepreneurial education programs. By incorporating real-world data, educators can create more effective and relevant learning experiences.

These interventions offer valuable pathways for enhancing entrepreneurial education and empowering future entrepreneurs.

Research Findings: Program of Requirements

To bridge the gap between answers to the formulated diagnostic and design research questions and the intended problem solution, DSR includes a program of requirements. This brings together the results of the literature review (the CIMOs) and the researcher's own research into answers to the formulated diagnostic and design research questions.

A program of requirements describes the expectations, requirements, and wishes of those involved for a solution to the given research problem (see, e.g., Maedche et al., 2019).

The program of requirements usually contains the following elements:

Functional requirements: These are the requirements that describe what the education program should do. A literature review can provide the input for this. For example, if it is an education program, a functional requirement might be that the program should help students develop certain skills.

User requirements: These are the requirements that describe how the intended users and further stakeholders will use the education program. Interviews, questionnaires, observations, etc. can provide input for this. For example, when it comes to an educational program, a user requirement may be that the program should be easy to use and have an intuitive interface.

Boundaries: These are the nonnegotiable constraints that the educational program must meet. These may include legislation and professional ethical standards. For example, when it comes to an educational program, an institution-wide prescribed educational technology and educational vision may be a constraint.

Design restrictions: These are the constraints imposed by the educational institution concerned. These often include available resources: available teachers and mentors for teaching; time within which the program must be delivered, prepared, and implemented; and budget for designing the teaching program.

Table 2 outlines an example of requirements for designing an educational program.

The functional requirements are usually derived from the problem description and the literature, summarized in the CIMOs, on the problem. The user requirements emerge from qualitative, quantitative, and hybrid research conducted by the researcher(s) on the formulated diagnostic and design research questions. The preconditions are derived from the standards applicable to the situation in which the problem arises. And the design constraints are set by the leadership of the organization concerned.

Designing

For the investigated problem in its complex reality, workable and effective designs are chosen and developed as solutions. A design can consist of a professional reflection or supervision method, a working model, selection method, supervision method, control model, work protocol, step-by-step plan, course, or curriculum design.

Those involved determine how far one wants to go and how radical the solution should be. Then, the question is, for example, whether the innovation should focus on structural measures (organizational structure, (ICT) systems, procedures, protocols, agreements), cognitive interventions (behavioral change through adequate training, coaching, reflection, feedback), or on cultural changes (collective ambition, mission, goals, organizational rules of the game).

Table 3 outlines examples of cultural and structural solutions of bottom-up and top-down types. Solutions in the entrepreneurial education program example could be:

Testing: Internal and External Testing

In the DSR approach, solution options are tested against each other for completeness, soundness, and feasibility.

Table 2 Example of program of requirements for designing an educational program

Design requirements	*Content of requirements*
Functional requirements	Curriculum flexibility: design programs that allow for adaptability and customization based on learners' needs, interests, and changing market dynamics Active learning strategies: incorporate interactive and experiential learning methods, such as case studies, simulations, and real-world projects Assessment mechanisms: develop clear assessment criteria to evaluate students' entrepreneurial competencies and progress Collaboration platforms: create opportunities for collaboration among students, educators, industry experts, and other stakeholders Resource accessibility: ensure easy access to relevant resources, including textbooks, online materials, and industry databases
User requirements	Student-centric approach: understand learners' backgrounds, motivations, and aspirations to tailor the program accordingly Skill development: address specific skills needed for entrepreneurship, such as creativity, problem-solving, communication, and financial literacy Networking opportunities: facilitate connections with mentors, successful entrepreneurs, and industry professionals Holistic learning: integrate business knowledge, ethics, and social responsibility into the curriculum
Boundary conditions	Cultural context: consider cultural differences and adapt content to local contexts Legal and regulatory constraints: ensure compliance with relevant laws and regulations related to entrepreneurship and education Financial limitations: work within budget constraints while maintaining program quality Time constraints: recognize that learners may have other commitments (work, family), and design flexible schedules
Design restrictions	Avoid overload: balance the depth and breadth of content to prevent overwhelming students Avoid repetition: minimize redundancy in course materials and assessments Avoid isolation: encourage collaboration, and discourage siloed learning experiences Avoid bias: design content that is inclusive and unbiased, considering diverse backgrounds and perspectives

Table 3 Example of possible solutions

Cultural solutions		Structural solutions	
Bottom-up	Top-down	Bottom-up	Top-down
Teachers can introduce their own innovative practices and teaching methods, seek collaboration between disciplines, and encourage student participation	The management of the program suggests adjustments to the reward system, feedback and team development sessions, mentorship development, and flexible working	Arrange horizontal collaboration, form self-managing teams, establish innovative incubators, propose flexible work arrangements	Decentralize decision-making, create career perspectives, restructure departments and teams

Within the DSR approach, different possible solutions can be tested for completeness, soundness, and feasibility by developing different solution scenarios. This is an iterative process in which different designs are created and tested to determine which one best meets the set requirements. The possible solution is then evaluated based on the following criteria: completeness, soundness, and feasibility. Completeness refers to the extent to which the solution contains all required features. Soundness refers to the extent to which the design provides the right solution to the problem to be solved. Feasibility refers to the extent to which the solution can be implemented in practice. Testing designs against these criteria can help determine which design is most suitable for the intended application. Testing designs is usually an iterative process. Multiple solution scenarios may be needed to find the design that best fits the established program of requirements.

In an internal test, the researcher or research team critically evaluates the possible solutions on aspects such as fit with the program of requirements, originality, feasibility, impact, efficiency, fit with strategy and culture of the organization, and the extent to which the solution can be demonstrated or visualized to intended users.

In an external test, the solutions are presented to the forum of intended users. Sometimes it is possible to do a pilot test or living lab project (beta test). If that is practically impossible, an alpha test is the obvious choice: the presentation of the selected designs to intended external users, followed by discussion and assessment (Smit, 2018).

DSR claims to be able to provide valid prescriptions for solutions to difficult problems. On the issue of validity, Larsen et al. (2020a, 2020b) proposed a DSR validity framework to integrate validity more fully into DSR research and practice.

Detailing of chosen solution and change plan

DSR is a research approach aimed at developing innovative artifacts to solve complex problems. The implementation of a chosen solution within the DSR approach can vary, depending on the nature of the project and the context. In practice some general steps are often followed:

Designing the chosen solution

The first step after designing a solution is often to elaborate and write out a chosen solution. This can be an artifact: a newly developed or designed object, system, process, model, framework, or any other form of practical knowledge created to solve a specific problem. It is the result of the design process. For designing an effective entrepreneurial education program, the artifact will consist of a comprehensive description of the proposed education program with objectives, teaching methods, roles of teachers and mentors, evaluation and assessment moments, etc.

Pilot testing

Before implementing the solution on a larger scale, it may be useful to conduct a pilot implementation. This involves testing the solution on a smaller scale in a realistic environment to understand how it works and to identify and resolve any problems early on. Thought could be given to starting with one study year in one course.

It is important to formulate in advance some clear measurement points on which the pilot will be assessed.

Iterative improvements
Based on feedback from the pilot testing phase, iterative improvements can be made to the solution. This cycle of testing, evaluation, and improvement can be repeated until the solution meets the set requirements and expectations.

Documentation
An important aspect of DSR is documenting the entire process, including the development and implementation of the solution. This involves looking not only at the end product but also at the learning process and the reasoning behind the decisions taken.

Evaluation of impact
After implementing the solution, it is important to evaluate its impact. This can be done by measuring whether the intended goals were achieved and by looking at the wider effects on the organization or domain to which the solution applies.

Dissemination of the solution
If the solution has proved successful, it can be disseminated to a wider audience or within other contexts. This could include rolling out the new approach in other courses.

Maintenance and continuous improvement
After implementation, it is necessary to maintain and continuously improve the solution based on feedback, changing needs, or new insights. This process of continuous improvement can continue for the lifetime of the solution.

The DSR approach emphasizes the importance of iteration, reflection, and learning throughout the research and development process.

Knowledge Enhancement
The ultimate goal in the DSR approach is not only to develop a solution to a specific problem but also to increase understanding of the design process and contribute to scientific knowledge about the problem under investigation.

Contributing to scientific knowledge within the DSR approach happens in several ways:

Publication of results
Researchers applying DSR often publish their findings in scientific journals and conference proceedings. These present not only the developed artifact but also the design and development process, the rationale behind the choices, and the lessons learned during the implementation of the research.

Literature review and theoretical foundation
DSR requires a thorough literature review in the initial phase of the research to understand and integrate existing knowledge on the topic. The artifact developed should be embedded in existing theories and literature, providing a theoretical foundation for its contribution to scientific knowledge.

Reflection and discussion
DSR research often includes a reflective component in which researchers look back at the design process, the decisions made, and the results. This helps identify implications, limitations, and opportunities for future research and contributes to the scientific discussion of the topic.

Bridging the Gap: Enhancing Research Impact in Applied Sciences
In the realm of academic applied sciences, a growing number of researchers find themselves grappling with a disconcerting reality: their diligent efforts often fail to make a tangible impact on real-world problem-solving. Regrettably, the practical applications of research outcomes frequently become ensnared within the confines of small-scale pilot projects.

Enter the chapter on DSR—a beacon of hope for scholars across diverse disciplines. This chapter extends an invitation: let us collectively reexamine our fundamental methodological assumptions. For practitioners navigating the often chaotic landscape of educational institutions, it encourages a bold step—putting research recommendations to the test in the face of unruly realities.

May this chapter serve as a catalyst, bridging the gap between theory and practice and ushering in a new era of transformative impact.

References

Alakwe, K. O. (2017). Positivism and knowledge inquiry: From scientific method to media and communication research. *Specialty Journal of Humanities and Cultural Science*. Available online at www.sciarena.com, *2*(3), 38–46.

Alexander, C. (1977). *A pattern language: Towns, buildings, construction* (p. 1216). Oxford University Press.

Alford, J., & Head, B. W. (2017). Wicked and less wicked problems: A typology and a contingency framework. *Policy and Society, 36*(3), 397–413. https://doi.org/10.1080/14494035.2017.1361634

Argyris, C., Putnam, R., & McLain Smith, D. (1985). *Action science: Concepts, methods, and skills for research and intervention*. Jossey-Bass.

Baskerville, R., & Pries-Heje, J. (2019). Projectability in design science research. *Jounal of Information Technology Theory and Application, 20*(1), 53–76.

Berglund, H., Bousfiha, M., & Mansoori, Y. (2020). Opportunities as artifacts and entrepreneurship as design. *Academy of Management Review, 45*(4), 825–846. https://doi.org/10.5465/amr.2018.0285

Brandstätter, H. (2011). Personality aspects of entrepreneurship: A look at five meta-analyses. *Personality and Individual Differences, 51*(3), 222–230.

Brüne, N., & Lutz, E. (2020). The effect of entrepreneurship education in schools on entrepreneurial outcomes: A systematic review. *Management Review Quarterly, 70*(3), 275–305.

Checkland, P., & Scholes, J. (1990). *Soft systems methodology in action*. John Wiley & Sons.

Cohen, B., Smith, B., & Mitchell, R. (2020). The effectiveness of entrepreneurship education programs: A meta-analysis. *Journal of Business Venturing, 35*(1), 106088. https://doi.org/10.1016/j.jbusvent.2019.106088

Cooperrider, D. L., & Whitney, D. (2005). *Appreciative inquiry: A positive revolution in change*. Berrett-Koehler Publishers.

Costa, E., Soares, A. L., & Pinho de Sousa, J. (2018). Exploring the CIMO-logic in the design of collaborative networks mediated by digital platforms. In L. Camarinha-Matos, H. Afsarmanesh, & Y. Rezgui (Eds.), *IFIP advances in information and communication technology (pp. 266–277).* Springer Nature. https://doi.org/10.1007/978-3-319-99127-6_23

De Groot, A. D. (1961). *Methodologie. Grondslagen van onderzoek en denken in de gedragswetenschappen.* Mouton.

Denyer, D., Tranfield, D., & Van Aken, J. E. (2008). Developing design propositions through research synthesis. *Organization Studies, 29*(03), 393–413.

Derre, B. F. S. (2023). A design for effective entrepreneurial education in higher education. In *Phd Thesis (Research TU/e / graduation TU/e), industrial engineering and innovation sciences.* Eindhoven University of Technology.

Dimov, D. (2016). Toward a design science of entrepreneurship, models of start-up thinking and action: Theoretical, empirical and pedagogical approaches. In *Advances in entrepreneurship, firm emergence and growth, 18* (pp. 1–31). Emerald Group Publishing Limited. https://doi.org/10.1108/S1074-754020160000018001

Dimov, D., Maula, M., & Romme, A. G. L. (2023). Crafting and assessing design science research for entrepreneurship. *Entrepreneurship Theory and Practice, 47*(5), 1543–1567.

Dresch, A., Lacerda, D. P., & Antunes Jr, J. A. V. (2015). *Design science research.* Springer.

Dunn, R., Hattie, J., & Bowles, T. (2019). Exploring the experiences undertaking educational design research as a form of teacher professional learning. *Professional Development in Education, 45*(1), 151–167. https://doi.org/10.1080/19415257.2018.1500389

Fayolle, A., & Gailly, B. (2008). From craft to science: Teaching models and learning processes in entrepreneurship education. *Journal of European Industrial Training, 32*(7), 569–593. https://doi.org/10.1108/03090590810899838

Gregor, S., & Hevner, A. R. (2013). Positioning and presenting design science research for maximum impact. *MIS Quarterly, 37*(2), 337–355. https://www.jstor.org/stable/24478755

Hevner, A. R., March, S. T., Park, J., & Ram, S. (2004). Design science in information systems research. *MIS Quarterly, 28*(1), 75–105. https://www.jstor.org/stable/25148625

Holmström, J., Tuunanen, T., & Kauremaa, J. (2014). Logic for accumulation of design science research theory. In *Proceedings of the 47th Hawaii international conference on system sciences.*

Kautonen, T., Van Gelderen, M., & Fink, M. (2015). Robustness of the theory of planned behavior in predicting entrepreneurial intentions and actions. *Entrepreneurship Theory and Practice, 39*(3), 655–674.

Kim, Y., & Lee, Y. (2019). The impact of entrepreneurship education on entrepreneurial intention of engineering students in Korea. *Sustainability, 11*(16), 4374.

Larsen, K., et al. (2020a). Validity in design science research. In *International conference on design science research in information systems and technology (DESRIST 2020).* Kristiansand.

Larsen, K. R., et al. (2020b). Validity in design science research. In S. Hofmann, O. Müller, & M. Rossi (Eds.), *Designing for digital transformation. Co-creating services with citizens and industry. DESRIST 2020* (*Lecture notes in computer science*) (Vol. 12388). Springer. https://doi.org/10.1007/978-3-030-64823-7_25

Lawson, B. (2005). *How designers think–the design process demystified* (5th ed.). University Press.

Maedche, A., Gregor, S., Morana, S., & Feine, J. (2019). Conceptualization of the problem space in design science research. In *DESRIST, 11491 of lecture notes in computer science, pp. 18-31.* Springer.

Maresch, D., Harms, R., Kailer, N., & Wimmer-Wurm, B. (2016). The impact of entrepreneurship education on the entrepreneurial intention of students in science and engineering versus business studies university programs. *Technology Forecasting & Social Change, 104*, 172–179.

McKenney, S., & Reeves, T. C. (2012). Systematic review of design-based research progress: Is a little knowledge a dangerous thing? *Educational Researcher, 41*(1), 16–25.

Pfeffers, K., Tuunanen, T., Rothenberger, M. A., & Chatterjee, S. (2007). A design science research methodology for information systems research. *Journal of Management, 24*(3), 45–77.

Pfeiffer, Y., Gschwind, T., & Mettler, T. (2019). Design science in health informatics: A systematic literature review. *Healthcare (Basel), 11*(7), 959.

Reason, P., & Bradbury, H. (Eds.). (2001), Handbook of action research: Participative inquiry and practice, .

Rittel, H. W. J., & Webber, M. M. (1973). Dilemmas in a general theory of planning. *Policy Sciences, 4*, 155–169. https://doi.org/10.1007/BF01405730

Romme, A. G. L., Avenier, M. J., Denyer, D., Hodgkinson, G. P., Pandza, K., Starkey, K., & Worren, N. (2015). Towards common ground and trading zones in management research and practice. *British Journal of Management, 26*(3), 544–559.

Romme, A. G. L., & Dimov, D. (2021). Mixing oil with water: Framing and theorizing in management research informed by design science. *Designs, 5*, 13. https://doi.org/10.3390/designs5010013, Available at SSRN: https://ssrn.com/abstract=3823238

Romme, A. G. L., & Reymen, I. M. M. J. (2018). Entrepreneurship at the interface of design and science: Toward an inclusive framework. *Journal of Business Venturing Insights., 10*(1–8), e00094.

Schön, D. A. (1983). *The reflective practitioner: How professionals think in action*. Basic Books.

Simon, H. A. (1969). *The sciences of the artificial, 1st edition, (3rd edition published in 1996)*. MIT Press.

Smaling, A. (2000). Pragmatics and pragmatism in qualitative inquiry. In N. K. Denzin & Y. S. Lincoln (Eds.), *Handbook of qualitative research* (pp. 849–862). Sage Publications.

Smit, A. J. (2018). Complexe problemen oplossen: design thinking of ontwerpgericht onderzoek? *Onderwijs Innovatie, 20*(2), 17–24.

Snowden, D. J., & Boone, M. E. (2007). A leader's framework for decision making. *Harvard Business Review, 85*(11), 68.

Stringer, E. T. (2014). *Action research*. Sage.

Toding, M., & Venesaar, U. (2018). Discovering and developing conceptual understanding of teaching and learning in entrepreneurship lecturers. *Education + Training, 60*(7/8), 696–718. https://doi.org/10.1108/ET-07-2017-0101

Van Aken, J. E. (2004). Management research based on the paradigm of the design sciences: The quest for field-tested and grounded technological rules. *Journal of Management Studies, 41*(2), 219–246.

Van Aken, J. E., & Romme, A. G. L. (2009). Reinventing the future: Adding design science to the repertoire of organization and management studies. *Organization Management Journal, 6*(1), 5–12.

Van Aken, J. E., & Romme, A. G. L. (2012). A design science approach to evidence-based management. *Organization Management Journal, 6*(1), 5–12.

Van den Akker, J. (1999). Principles and methods of development research. In J. Van den Akker, N. Nieveen, R. M. Branch, K. L. Gustafson, & T. Plomp (Eds.), *Design methodology and developmental research in education and training* (pp. 1–14). Kluwer Academic Publishers.

Van Strien, P. J. (1997). Towards a methodology of psychological practice: The regulative cycle. *Theory & Psychology, 7*(5), 683–700.

Vom Brocke, J., Winter, R., Hevner, A., & Maedche, A. (2020). Special issue editorial–accumulation and evolution of design knowledge in design science research: A journey through time and space. *Journal of the Association for Information Systems, 21*(3), 520–544.

Zampetakis, L. A., & Moustakis, V. (2011). Entrepreneurship education and training: A review of the debate. *International Entrepreneurship and Management Journal, 7*(3), 291–308. https://doi.org/10.1007/s11365-011-0185-0

Jimme Keizer is deceased at the time of publication. His life and career were defined by a deep commitment to education, research, and mentorship, leaving an enduring impact on his colleagues and students. For nearly 27 years, beginning in 1989, he served as an assistant professor at Eindhoven University of Technology (TU/e), where he remained actively involved even after his retirement in 2016. His enthusiasm for teaching, mentoring, and advancing academic development was evident in every role he embraced.

Jimme's professional journey began in 1976 as a researcher in social psychology with the Royal Netherlands Army in The Hague. His interest in workplace dynamics led him to pursue a PhD, completed in 1988 at the University of Groningen, focused on motivation and workjoy among preachers.

Joining TU/e in 1989, Jimme became a member of the department of Innovation, Technology, Entrepreneurship and Marketing (ITEM) within the Department of Industrial Engineering & Innovation Sciences. As a supportive mentor, he guided many bachelor's, master's, and PhD students, leaving a lasting impact on their careers. His influence also extended to curriculum development, where he played a central role, especially as chair of the Innovation Management master's program.

In 2008, Jimme took on a new academic challenge as lector of Innovative Entrepreneurship en Risk Management at Zuyd University of Applied Sciences in Maastricht, a role perfectly aligned with his expertise and interests. In this position, he delved into the themes of innovation and risk management, sharing his knowledge with a new community while maintaining ties with the TU/e ITEM group. Jimme was especially passionate about the design science research (DSR) methodology, a field where he was considered a specialist. His dedication to this approach was exemplified through his collaboration with Piet Kempen on the book *Competent afstuderen en stagelopen* (translated 'competent graduation and doing an internship'), a design science approach aimed at guiding students through higher education projects.

The authors dedicate this book to Jimme's memory, honoring his remarkable legacy, warmth, and commitment. His contributions and expertise, especially in design science research, will continue to inspire all who had the privilege to know him.

Isabelle Reymen obtained a MSc degree in Architecture from KU Leuven, Belgium and completed a PhD degree in Design sciences at the Eindhoven University of Technology (TU/e). Since 2006 she is a member of the Innovation, Technology Entrepreneurship and Marketing Group of the School of Industrial Engineering at TU/e, where she is Full Professor Design of Innovation Ecosystems. She is co-founder, scientific director and general manager of TU/e innovation Space. She combines entrepreneurial thinking with a passion for design processes and aims for system innovation. Her research interests focus on understanding and improving heterogeneous collaboration processes in entrepreneurial innovation ecosystems. She was granted several projects on entrepreneurial topics and on education innovation. TU/e innovation Space received national and international awards for its education innovation. In 2020, she became a Comenius Leadership Fellow and was granted a scholarship to perform research on Challenge-Based Learning.

The Entrepreneurial Educator as an Architect of Effective Entrepreneurial Education—Design and Redesign of the CBL Course "Innovation Space Project: Innovation and Entrepreneurship Processes"

Ákos R. Wetters, Gert Guri, Jasmina Lazendic-Galloway, and Isabelle Reymen

Abstract This chapter systematically explores the design of an innovative entrepreneurship course and its redesign through several iterations over a 7-year period, following a data-driven Design Science Research (DSR) approach. It offers a case study of the "innovation Space Project: Innovation and Entrepreneurship Processes (ISP)" course at the Eindhoven University of Technology. The course uses a Challenge-Based Learning (CBL) approach, engaging students in interdisciplinary teams and tackling open-ended challenges in collaboration with societal stakeholders. We analyse the evolution of the course through the lens of constructive alignment, providing insights into the design decisions that have facilitated its continuous improvement over the years. A longitudinal comparative analysis was conducted to map the changes in learning objectives, activities, and assessment methods. Data-driven DSR prioritises ongoing data collection and analysis as a core component of the educational design process. This involves not just traditional academic performance data but also qualitative feedback from students, reflections from educators, and input from industry and societal stakeholders. This case study contributes to the empirical body of entrepreneurial education knowledge and serves as a model for applying data-driven DSR principles in educational research and practice.

Á. R. Wetters · I. Reymen (✉)
Industrial Engineering and Innovation Sciences, Eindhoven University of Technology, Eindhoven, The Netherlands
e-mail: akos@wetters.me; i.m.m.j.reymen@tue.nl

G. Guri · J. Lazendic-Galloway
TU/e innovation Space, Eindhoven University of Technology, Eindhoven, The Netherlands
e-mail: g.guri@tue.nl; j.lazendic.galloway@tue.nl

© The Author(s), under exclusive license to Springer Nature Switzerland AG 2025
B. Derre, Y. Baggen (eds.), *Empowering the Next Generation of Entrepreneurial Change Agents*, Contributions to Management Science,
https://doi.org/10.1007/978-3-031-82251-3_3

1 Introduction

The realm of entrepreneurial education is dynamic, and it demands high levels of expertise and creativity from educators, who play a pivotal role in shaping the educational landscape tailored to specific contexts and desired learning outcomes. According to Baggen et al. (2022), designing courses and curricula that achieve context-specific outcomes is central to entrepreneurial education. This involves not only the application of scientific insights from the fields of entrepreneurship and education but also the strategic design and implementation of educational artefacts such as courses and curricula. Berglund et al. (2020) underscore that the practice of entrepreneurial education parallels the process of entrepreneurship itself—it is an activity marked by conscious decision-making where educators act as designers, crafting educational experiences that effectively realise entrepreneurial education goals. Entrepreneurial education has increasingly embraced evidence-based teaching approaches (Frese et al., 2014), which aim to enhance learning outcomes by applying pedagogical practices grounded in systematic research (Nabi et al., 2017; Curtis et al., 2020). This integration of teaching strategies with the complex, dynamic nature of entrepreneurial practice, therefore, seeks to boost prospective entrepreneurs' intentionality and effectiveness through targeted educational interventions.

Furthermore, while the literature on entrepreneurial education has extensively explored various frameworks and outcomes, there remains a significant gap concerning the "how" of entrepreneurial education—specifically, the process and mechanisms through which educational practices influence entrepreneurial competencies (Kamovich & Foss, 2017). While studies often discuss what should be taught and why, fewer delve into how educational content should be delivered to enhance entrepreneurial skills and mindset effectively (Baggen et al., 2022). This gap suggests a need for more detailed literature on pedagogical strategies directly linked to fostering essential entrepreneurial behaviours within diverse educational contexts.

A data-driven Design Science Research (DSR) approach can effectively address this gap by systematically investigating and optimising pedagogical strategies through empirical evidence and iterative design (e.g. Hevner et al., 2004). Design science emphasises creating and testing artefacts—in this case, a course design as an example of an educational method. A data-driven DSR approach involves continuously refining educational practices based on feedback and data. The redesign of educational practices enables the optimisation of educational practices to meet learning objectives better. By documenting successful educational methods and the conditions under which they were effective, DSR ensures that these methods can be replicated and scaled across different educational settings. This enhances the broader applicability and utility of research findings in entrepreneurial education. Overall, data-driven DSR enables a scientific and systematic exploration of educational practices in entrepreneurial education, bridging the gap between theoretical knowledge and practical application in nurturing entrepreneurial competencies.

In this chapter, we explore entrepreneurial education through the lens of educators, who are pivotal as both designers (i.e. architects) and implementers of entrepreneurial education. We explore their experiences developing and redesigning an innovative entrepreneurship course, the "Innovation Space Project: Innovation and Entrepreneurship Processes" (ISP) at the Eindhoven University of Technology, initiated in 2017. The course uses Challenge-Based Learning (CBL) to engage students in interdisciplinary teams, tackling open-ended challenges in collaboration with societal stakeholders (Lazendic-Galloway et al., 2021; Reymen et al., 2022). CBL and broader entrepreneurial education share a strong connection through their emphasis on problem-solving, innovation, and experiential learning. CBL encourages students to identify real-world challenges and develop creative solutions, a process that closely mirrors the entrepreneurial journey of spotting opportunities and addressing market needs. Both approaches promote critical thinking, resourcefulness, and resilience. Additionally, CBL's focus on experiential learning—where students actively engage in hands-on projects and learn by doing—aligns with the entrepreneurial mindset of trial and error. This practical, immersive approach prepares students for the dynamic nature of entrepreneurship, where continuous learning, adaptability, and iterative problem-solving are essential.

The ISP course was redesigned through several iterations, following a data-driven DSR approach, providing insights into the design decisions that have facilitated its continuous improvement over the years. We analyse the evolution of the course through the lens of constructive alignment, an educational design framework that ensures that the intended learning outcomes, the learning activities, and the assessment are aligned (Biggs, 1996).

The chapter begins by outlining the context with a brief introduction of the course, its learning environment, and the course's designers. Subsequently, the method of analysing the evolution of course design and outcomes is described. Next, the initial design and continuous redesign are introduced, focusing on the intended learning outcomes, learning activities, and assessment. The chapter ends with discussing the educators' experiences in developing entrepreneurial education, the challenges they perceived, and where they see growth potential. Finally, we reflect on how a data-driven DSR approach can enhance entrepreneurial education, supporting educators in refining their teaching practices and curricula.

2 Context

2.1 *Course Purpose and CBL Learning Environment*

The ISP course is a 10 ECTS elective master course, which runs every semester. It has been developed as an innovative CBL course focused on tackling real-life open-ended challenges, learning in interdisciplinary teams, learning by doing, developing an entrepreneurial mindset, and putting students in the lead of their learning. The motivation for this course was to blend the design and engineering of a product/service/system with the inception of new business ventures, eliminating traditional lectures in favour of studio-style group work, self-directed study, and personal and team development.

The course is a flagship course in TU/e innovation Space (innoSpace in short), meaning that this course is front-running in educational development and continuously improves via new experiments. TU/e innovation Space is the centre of expertise for Challenge-Based Learning and Entrepreneurial Learning at TU/e (Reymen et al., 2022) and the learning hub that facilitates the co-creation of responsible solutions to real-world challenges by interdisciplinary teams of students, with researchers, industry, and societal organisations. In 2021, the team was awarded the first Higher Education Award in the Netherlands for educational innovations. In 2022, the hub received international recognition by winning the European Triple E Award in the "Innovation and Collaboration Space of the Year" category.

The physical space where the course takes place is also of importance. The innoSpace Light Assembly location plays a key role in motivating students and creating the right environment for teamwork and interaction. The space design and its proximity to the prototyping workshops facilitate coaching support and enhance students' activities in a different environment from the classic classroom and closer to a real-life working environment. Students' appreciation for this space structuring is also demonstrated by the students' feedback in the co-creation sessions.

2.2 Main Designers

The course was designed in co-creation with many educators and students. Over time, more coaches, course coordinators, and students got involved in the course design, delivery, and iterative refinement. The first, second, and fourth authors of this chapter are currently involved in the course and are the main contributors to its (re)design. Each brought a unique perspective and expertise (also see the biographical note of the authors) to the course development process, enriching the collaborative, reflective practice and contributing to the multifaceted evaluation of the course's evolution.

Isabelle Reymen initiated the ISP course based on her experience with design projects and entrepreneurial education for industrial engineering students and brought these to the wider university level by also allowing entry to the students from all other master programs. This offered the opportunity for students to work in interdisciplinary teams and tackle more complex and real-world challenges. She is currently the course responsible lecturer.

Ákos Wetters is the primary instructor and coach in the course. He exemplifies the following characteristics: collaboration, innovation, creation, action, advancement, and life-long learning. As an entrepreneur and a "hybrid teacher" at the Eindhoven University of Technology, he brings practical insights from the professional world into the academic setting.

Gert Guri, co-instructor of the course, joined in 2021 and brought in unique expertise in integrating real-life challenges with educational objectives in entrepreneurial courses. His role includes coaching and implementing innovative teaching strategies. Gert's approach is characterised by continuous experimentation, co-creation, and adaptability to evolving educational challenges, focusing on enhancing the effectiveness of team-based student learning.

Jasmina Lazendic-Galloway is a scientist and educationalist with extensive experience in designing and delivering innovative teaching approaches. She joined the course in 2021, initially as an observer, and later took on roles as a coach and researcher. Her research focuses on fostering the development of an entrepreneurial mindset in students. As part of this case study, she conducted reflective interviews with the co-authors and contributed to framing the research process and output.

3 Method

For this study, we use a case study approach based on the principles of DSR, which emphasise creating and evaluating innovative artefacts to solve identified problems and contribute new knowledge to the field (Hevner et al., 2004). In the context of this research, "artefact" is the course itself, undergoing continuous cycles of design, implementation, evaluation, and redesign.

3.1 Data Collection

The primary data for this study consisted of the collaborative reflections of course designers and instructors on the course set-up and delivery, which were documented systematically over 7 years. These reflections included detailed notes on design meetings; alignment sessions (with various staff members and challenge owners); study guides (course descriptions) and iterative revisions to the course materials; quantitative and qualitative feedback from students from the systematic, institutional questionnaires at the end of each course; predominantly qualitative feedback collected via co-creative sessions with students and other course stakeholders; and instructors' observations of student engagement and their attainment of learning outcomes. The reflections were structured around the key elements of constructive alignment (Biggs, 1996), focusing on learning objectives, learning activities, assessment methods, and the alignment between these different building blocks of education.

3.2 Data Analysis

The data analysis was structured around constructive alignment over time, with the analysis focused on how the intended learning outcomes were supported by teaching activities and assessment methods. This alignment was critically assessed to determine its efficacy in fostering desired educational outcomes. A longitudinal approach facilitated mapping and interpreting changes in course design and educational outcomes across different implementation cycles. This mapping helped trace the development of the course over time, highlighting successful adaptations and areas needing further improvement. Ongoing reflective dialogue between the researchers (designers) also contributed to synthesising the longitudinal data, identifying recurring themes and challenges.

4 Initial Design

In 2017, the initial design was created following the DSR approach, which is particularly suitable for designing and analysing innovative interventions, as it involves iterative cycles of design, implementation, analysis, and refinement (Hevner et al., 2004). We began with enquiry phase, where initial ideas were sparked by existing problems, and new insights were derived from educational research and practice of the main designers. Subsequently, we followed the steps of the DSR approach, as also discussed in Chapter "Advancing the Field of Entrepreneurial Education: Leveraging a Design Science Approach for Educating the Change Agents of the Future". We started developing design requirements and, in the next phase, creating a design solution, which, in our case, was the creation of the ISP course, our artefact. We embedded the model of constructive alignment in the DSR approach and as such defined intended learning outcomes, learning activities, and assessments for the course. The next phases of testing solutions and theorising (Romme, 2023; Romme & Reymen, 2018) happened continuously. After the initial course design, continuous redesign took place based on testing the course in practice over 7 years, thereby collecting data and reflecting on these.

4.1 Enquiry Phase

In the enquiry phase of the process, the focus was on identifying the learners' needs and the gaps or opportunities for innovation within the educational context. The foundations of our course lie in the teaching experience of the responsible lecturer in facilitating open-ended projects in collaboration with companies through new project-based design courses in the School of Industrial Engineering. She invited many educators and students with diverse past experiences and competencies to co-create a new course. The course also drew inspiration from other institutions' innovative educational practices and philosophies. We looked to Aalto Design Factory (https://designfactory.aalto.fi) for its pioneering approach to interdisciplinary project-based education, fostering collaboration and creativity among students from various disciplines. Similarly, the hands-on, experimental nature of Parsons Paris' Makelab (https://www.newschool.edu/parsons-paris) provided a blueprint for integrating design thinking into our curriculum. From Stanford University's D. School (https://dschool.stanford.edu), we adopted the ethos of nurturing innovative problem solvers through empathy and a user-centred design process, encouraging students to tackle challenges with a fresh perspective. MIT's Media Lab's reputation for combining technology, multimedia, and design (https://www.media.mit.edu) to push the boundaries of traditional education and research further influenced our approach, encouraging an exploratory and innovative mindset. The amalgamation of these influences was used to create a course that not only equips students with the technical and creative skills necessary for today's challenges but also instils a profound sense of social responsibility and entrepreneurial spirit.

4.2 Design Requirements

Next, we defined clear design requirements for what the course aims to achieve. For this course, we wanted to leverage the potential of a project-based approach towards what we now refer to as CBL (Reymen et al., 2022). The vision was to form interdisciplinary project teams to tackle open-ended assignments, fostering collaboration with high-tech companies, governments, research institutes, and NGOs. The intention was to present business and societal challenges that were sufficiently open and complex to necessitate interdisciplinary teamwork among students. The course was intended to be accessible to all master-level students of all backgrounds interested in developing an entrepreneurial mindset while identifying innovative and creative solutions that are deployable in real-world situations. The aim was to involve a substantial integrative project where students could refine their engineering design skills and actively share their acquired knowledge and expertise with peers from various backgrounds.

The open and complex nature of the business and societal challenges was intended not only to leave ample space for students' creativity but also to require a united interdisciplinary effort to address these challenges thoroughly and innovatively, thereby positioning the course ambitiously within the educational framework. Furthermore, the course aims to nurture a systemic approach to finding solutions by teaching students to observe the complete system rather than a specific component. We steer students' learning journey and acquisition of new knowledge and skills through thematic workshops. The course objectives align with the higher levels of the Bloom Taxonomy (Bloom et al., 1956), such as analysing, evaluating, and creating, as students were expected to devise original solutions—be it a pilot project in collaboration with the challenge owner or a prototype—to tackle real-life challenges effectively.

Running the course over a semester allows sufficient time for students to work on a project and have enough interaction with external stakeholders. Making it an elective course for all TU/e master students enables them to work in interdisciplinary project teams.

4.3 The Initial Course Design

As an artefact of our design process, our ISP course is characterised by several innovative elements, including forming interdisciplinary teams that tackle real-world challenges to create minimal viable products and equipping students with an entrepreneurial mindset. Unlike traditional courses, ISP does not include lectures; instead, it uses extensive coaching from educators, external partners, and fellow students. Participants are encouraged to reflect deeply on their individual and team development. Challenges in the course are offered by external partners in collaboration with innoSpace.

The course consists of a sizeable integrative project in which in-depth engineering design skills are developed and previously acquired knowledge and expertise are shared with students from different backgrounds. The students must creatively devise an original solution—for example, a pilot project implemented in cooperation with the challenge owner or a prototype—to address a real-life challenge. A systemic approach is stimulated by observing the complete system rather than a specific component. Students are in the lead of their learning processes and are encouraged to acquire new knowledge and skills. Several out-of-the-box workshops are offered either online or offline. The course structure developed in the academic year 2017–2018 is given in Fig. 1.

The design of the course structure, as presented in Fig. 1, is based on the constructive alignment approach supported by three fundamental pillars—intended learning outcomes, learning activities, and assessment (Biggs & Tang, 2011)—which we discuss below. Table 1 indicates the alignment between the intended learning outcomes, learning activities, and assessment of the course. For each intended learning outcome, we indicate whether competencies are developed at the individual or team level.

4.3.1 Intended Learning Outcomes (ILOs)

To achieve the course goals, we have designed the ILOs, as presented in Table 1, to enhance students' disciplinary and transversal competencies to analyse, synthesise, and identify the most appropriate solution, building upon interdisciplinarity. The ILOs are specific and measurable with a clearly described set of abilities, which students need to develop at the end of the course to demonstrate that they have

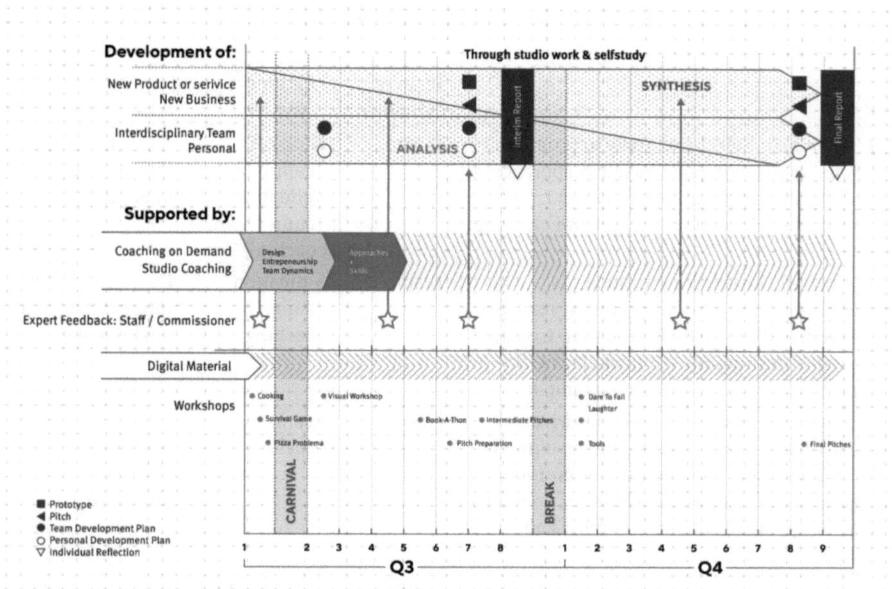

Fig. 1 The course structure from the academic year 2017–2018

mastered the set of ILOs. The course started with six ILOs, which guide the transformation of learners into individuals with entrepreneurial mindsets: Approach, Analysis, Synthesis, Interdisciplinarity, Skills and Behaviour, and Personal and Team Development (see Table 1 for details).

4.3.2 Key Learning Activities

Considering the specific methodology, the involvement of multiple stakeholders, and the focus on entrepreneurial learning and not just the business side, the course starts with the *kick-off workshop* designed to explain to students the course ILOs and philosophy, i.e. students are in the driving seat of their learning and project activities. We have also designed the speed-dating activity, where challenge owners' presence in the kick-off helps enhance cooperation from the beginning. This event also allows students to get to know each other and coaches and student assistants (SAs). Hence, this activity mainly helps to set the stage for the course.

Challenge selection and team forming. Students are instructed to select the challenge based on (1) their disciplinary competencies (where they can contribute the most), (2) what they would like to learn (where their interests lie), and (3) the complementarity of the team members (what they can learn from the others). The freedom to select the challenges adds to the autonomy to form teams alone. Since the course methodology implies teamwork, particular attention is dedicated to team formation to ensure interdisciplinarity and cultural diversity. The team formation

Table 1 Alignment between intended learning outcomes (ILOs), learning activities, and the assessment

ILO	Team or individual	Learning activities	Assessment
1. Approach: Select and apply appropriate design, engineering and business approaches, and tools to create an innovative and science-based solution to a real-life challenge	Team	Kick-off Team-building Validation Team-coaching	Reflection sessions Intermediate and final pitches
2. Analysis: Develop a profound interpretation of a highly complex, real-life problem and the systems around it. Consider customer desirability, technical feasibility, financial feasibility, and societal impact	Team	Validation Team-coaching	Progress pitches Intermediate and final pitches
3. Synthesis: Develop a problem-driven, creative, and integrative design, resulting in an original and validated pilot or prototype that balances customer desirability, technical feasibility, organisational viability, and societal impact	Team	Team-coaching	Intermediate and final pitches Piloting or prototype
4. Interdisciplinarity: Identify, envision, and promote the role and contributions of engineering disciplines in solving problems in business, industrial, and societal environments Integrate diverse contributions—tools, methodologies, approaches—as a validated prototype	Team & individual	Team-building Sharing and coaching sessions Ethics workshop	Intermediate and final pitches Piloting or prototype
5. Skills and behaviour: Develop leadership and agile project management skills to organise and perform an interdisciplinary, hands-on, and team-based engineering design and impact value project Communicate a message at various elaboration levels to all relevant parties, orally and in writing Work independently; be proactive; develop an entrepreneurial mindset	In team & individual	Team-building ESA workshop on culture and team dynamics Weekly pitch progress	Reflection sessions Weekly coaching
6. Personal and team development: Define and regularly reflect on a personal and team development plan, indicating personal & team goals and the needed development	In team & individual	Team dynamics ESA workshop on individual students and teams Pitch training	Self-/team reflection, the investors' pitch, learning festival

(continued)

Table 1 (continued)

ILO	Team or individual	Learning activities	Assessment
*7. Stakeholder management**: Map and reach out to the relevant stakeholders for the project, and ensure that they are informed and/or involved throughout the course	In team & individual	Validation Team-coaching Meetings with challenge owners	Mid-mid-term Mid-term (intermediate pitches) Investors' pitch
*8. Self-regulated learning**: Acquire skills, strategies, and techniques to become a more effective and efficient learner Develop self-awareness and adaptability to optimise their learning process and acquire new knowledge and skills more readily	Individual		Reflection sessions Weekly coaching

(*) These ILOs have been added later (see section A2 of the Appendix)

criteria demand that no more than two students from the same disciplinary background be in the same team. Having people from different cultural backgrounds is another component that aims to foster diverse ideas and build cultural and transversal competencies in students.

Face-to-face workshops on critical concepts, such as problem identification, business model, pitch presentation, etc., are designed offline in a concise way, since various students may be already familiar with some of these concepts. We have also designed online workshops, which are available for those students who would like or need more knowledge on specific aspects, creating a thematically organised wiki. The workshops are designed based on a needs-identified approach, i.e. students recognise their needs during teamwork and apply such concepts in a real-life challenge. If they need to know more, they can visit the online workshop or seek advice from the coaches. The philosophy of this design is to offer customised "just in time" instruction, which students can apply immediately to their projects.

The teamwork is accompanied by weekly *team-coaching support* from the coaches, who visit each team to observe the progress and provide adequate indications. To enhance self-reflection in the learning process, the coaches use questions to enable students to see the challenge or solution from different perspectives and consider different aspects. The coach's feedback is usually conducted at the team's level, since each team has the proper dynamics. Still, there are cases in which this is done plenary, especially when feedback is also relevant for the other teams and enhances peer-to-peer (P2P) learning.

Hence, teamwork, P2P learning, and coaching are fundamental activities that help to identify students' needs and apply the most appropriate teaching technique in each case. The coaching process also includes *technical coaching* provided by challenge owners or technology experts from the TU/e or other institutions. The technical coaching is designed as an integral part of the course. Therefore, we constantly interact and align the activities with the technology experts or challenge owners to assess the teams'/students' needs and address them. Technical coaching is designed in a bi-weekly schedule within the teamwork activities. It may vary from team to team, depending on the coaching availability and the team's needs. Another essential element of the course activities is delivering *pitches* at different core moments of the learning process. In Chapter "From EntreComp to EntreAct: 16 Validated Design Principles for Making People More Entrepreneurial" (Wetters et al.), the full spectrum of learning activities is described.

4.3.3 Assessment

The assessment is composed of two components: the formative and summative assessment. All assessments are formative, except self-/team reflections, the investors' pitch, and the prototype, which are summatively evaluated at the end of the course.

Formative assessment: As explained in the learning activities, the formative assessment includes the weekly feedback provided by the course coaches to students both as a team and individually and is harmonised with the weekly P2P feedback students receive from each other, as well as the regular feedback and coaching received by the challenge owners. Formative assessment is also provided in various official progress presentations, such as mid-term and the "investors' pitch" sessions, by challenge owners and a dedicated jury composed of entrepreneurs or entrepreneurship educators. The objective is to help students reflect on the progress made and undertake necessary improvement steps.

The summative assessment builds upon the formative one and grades the final team and individual reports. The final grade of the ISP course students is broken down into (a) a Team assignment composed of the Team Report + Final Pitch (weight 70%) and (b) an Individual assignment consisting of the Individual Reflection Report (weight 30%). Both reports mirror the students' performance in actively participating in the teamwork to develop a functional prototype of a technically feasible, financially sustainable, and socially/customer-desirable solution while reflecting on team development. Therefore, as a team, students have to go through different steps and processes, including defining and refining a problem and ideas for a solution simultaneously and iteratively through analysis, synthesis, and reflection processes. Students are also expected to be able to communicate the team-developed solution clearly and creatively through an "investors' pitch". Therefore, the assessment focuses on the team assignment, which counts for 70% of the final grade. The main idea is that in real life, you will be working in teams, so you need to know how to develop your capacities within a team and master techniques for achieving results as a team.

The coaches discuss the progress of all teams and informally "grade" the progress; they communicate this progress formally halfway through the quartiles. Although there is a clear set of *assignments*, they may differ from team to team and even from student to student, depending on the project stage for that team. For instance, one team could focus on their mid-term self-reflection assignment, another on validation or interaction with stakeholders depending on their progress, while other teams could focus more on the business component, such as the value network around their project.

Teamwork and weekly team-coaching are harmonised with weekly *P2P feedback*, during which every team presents their weekly progress in a 2-min pitch to address a specific stage of the project and receives feedback from other peers to stimulate P2P learning. We have designed this activity to have benefits at four levels. Firstly, the pitching team receives helpful feedback from their peers. Secondly, it stimulates critical thinking among students. Thirdly, it enhances cooperation within the cohort and stimulates interdisciplinarity at the team and cohort levels. Finally, it makes team-coaching support more effective and efficient because, during these sessions, the coaches focus their feedback on the specific, complex, and less obvious aspects of the project work.

Personal development is also considered. Students need to reflect on the individual abilities they develop during the course and how to replicate such learnings and abilities in real life. The individual component of the assessment is also a tool to assess each student's contribution to the project and to gratify the students who have contributed the most to the project.

At the end of the quartile, formal feedback is given on the interim prototype, pitch, and report. The final team output is an investors' pitch in front of a jury and the external stakeholders involved, the developed prototype, a final report, and a team reflection on ILO achievement.

5 Continuous Redesign

After the initial design, the course was continuously redesigned using a data-driven DSR cycle over 7 years. The feedback from the implemented solution (the first delivery of the course) fuelled further enquiry, making the DSR cycle a dynamic process of continuous improvement. This approach ensures that course design and development are adaptable to new insights, changing cohorts, and educational landscapes. The evaluation phase critically assesses the course's impact and effectiveness against its requirements and beyond, incorporating feedback from various stakeholders. It allows for reflection and learning from the implementation and facilitates the exchange of knowledge and practices, where insights gained can inform broader educational contexts and lead to further innovation into the "how" of entrepreneurial education.

5.1 Data Used for the Redesign Process

Different forms of course evaluation were used as data for the design process, both formal and informal. Since the ISP course adopts the innovative CBL concept, improvements based on the evaluation of the course with different stakeholders can easily be incorporated, thanks to the flexible structure and content of the course. Unlike the more traditional education approaches, the evaluation is based on a method that harmonises the feedback of various stakeholders, such as students, challenge owners (from academia, public institutions, and industry), peers, researchers, and the coaches' self-reflection. The improvements are then re-evaluated at the end of the course to consider their impact and/or to improve them further in a constant and reiterative DSR cycle. The different forms of course evaluation are discussed here in more detail.

Experimentation and self-reflection. Experimentation comes from the intrinsic drive to innovate with learning activities. Self-reflection is based on what worked from the previous improvements and how to integrate these insights in the next course. Thanks to weekly coaching and teamwork with students, evaluation of the implementation results of the course and the learning progress achieved by students took place. Such weekly self-reflection issues can be categorised into (a) suggestions to be fixed during the course, for instance, talking with challenge owners and project teams to see whether a higher meeting frequency would improve the cooperation, and (b) more structural issues, which need a more thorough approach. Structural issues—together with the official students' survey feedback and the co-creation session with students at the end of the course—constitute the raw material for the self-reflection input in the meetings with challenge owners and co-designing sessions with peers and researchers.

Co-creation sessions with students take place at the last lecture of the course. To not influence students' perspectives, the session is organised around three open questions: (a) what they would like to keep in the course and why; (b) what they would like to change and how; and (c) what they would like to remove and why. In this way, the course is redesigned to mirror student's needs. This is also a valuable mechanism to balance the tendency for a low response rate of students in the official end-of-the-course questionnaires.

Feedback sessions with challenge owners in a focus group setting are focused on (a) what we can do in the course to improve the cooperation between students and challenge owners and (b) which students' ability can we further develop in the course to improve the quality of final projects.

Brainstorming sessions with colleagues and peer researchers, in which we discuss the feedback received from students and challenge owners with innoSpace educators, TU/e peers, and CBL researchers to collect different perspectives, practices, and methodologies to redesign the course by integrating students' and challenge owners' suggestions.

Since the redesign is reiterative, each session mentioned above starts by analysing the results achieved by the redesign steps already implemented in the previous cohort course to see whether the improvements have yielded the expected results. If this is not the case, redesign restarts by answering the question: how can we do it differently in the next course?

5.2 *Evolution of the Course*

To map the evolution of the course made over the years, we use the lens of constructive alignment (Biggs & Tang, 2011). Our analysis specifically focused on examining how changes to one course design element influenced the others and how these changes contributed to achieving the desired learning outcomes. Working on societal and business challenges in interdisciplinary teams was vital from the beginning of the course, and it was a distinguishing feature from many other courses. Table 2 lists *examples of redesigned* elements of the course in chronological order. A more detailed overview of the evolution of the ILOs and learning activities (LAs) is given in the Appendix.

5.3 *Students Perceptions of the Course*

To assess the impact of our design (the course), we collected data from student outputs because students produce artefacts (reports or videos) as a part of the course assessment in which they reflect on their learning process. In Table 3 we present quotes that illustrate the impact of the course on students' learning. We contacted students from the last three cohorts (from the 2021 and 2022 academic years) and asked permission to use their final reflection artefacts for our research. The project has been approved by the TU/e Ethics Review Board (no. ERB2021ESOE18). Thirty students gave their permission, and their reflection artefacts were then compiled (videos are converted into text) and anonymised by one of the researchers. Two researchers then performed an inductive analysis of the reflections, identifying emerging themes directly from the data, which were validated through a comparison and linked to the intended learning outcomes of the course. A more in-depth analysis of the impact of the course on the development of the students' entrepreneurial mindset is presented in another paper (Lazendic-Galloway et al., submitted).

6 Discussion and Conclusion

In this section, we reflect on the educators' experiences developing entrepreneurial education, the challenges they perceive, and where they see growth potential. Lastly, we examine the pivotal role of data-driven DSR in enhancing the design and delivery of entrepreneurial education, more specifically how this systematic,

Table 2 Examples of changed course design elements

#	Examples of changed course design elements	How it was before the change	After redesign	Course element
1	Stakeholder management	Stakeholder management was an integral part of the other ILOs	Teams put in more effort earlier to reach out to stakeholders and maintain and grow their stakeholder networks. Some (new) LA nudge and support teams to take appropriate action	ILO
2	Self-regulated learning	With the seven ILOs, great attention was paid to individual and team learning implicitly	Individual students are triggered to become conscious of their personal development, take control of it, and direct their learning path	ILO
3	"Woensel West challenge"	Teams were just encouraged to validate	This workshop "kicked" the teams out of the building to validate with real people outside	LA
4	"Ambassador and Minister of Interior"	Individuals and teams occasionally and spontaneously exchanged thoughts and ideas with each other	Peer-to-peer coaching sessions occur twice a quartile, during which individual students and teams mix, pitch their questions, and give and receive feedback	LA
5	Miro Board	Before the COVID outbreak, we used CANVAS, the LMS at TU/e, and shared folders to save and share materials	During COVID, we started using the Miro Board, a virtual classroom where we share, save, and present content, even today	LA/ ASM
6	"Financial sustainability of the organisation"	"Business viability" was one of the entrepreneurial focus areas (EFA), and it was too often associated with projects that would only lead to commercial startups	Introducing "financial sustainability" better caters to teams focusing more on social entrepreneurship, which is appreciated by many students whose objective is not to become rich but to make a positive societal impact and address a real-life problem	LA

(continued)

Table 2 (continued)

#	Examples of changed course design elements	How it was before the change	After redesign	Course element
7	Workshop on team dynamics	The educators facilitated team forming, gave assignments on boosting teamwork, and coached on team dynamics	Once the students have formed project teams, coaches from ESA** run a workshop on team dynamics and culture in the second week of the course. At the end of the first quartile, a follow-up session takes place	LA
8	Format of the kick-off session	In the first edition of the course, teams were formed, and then they had to choose their challenge based on a paper description and presentation by the challenge owner. This all happened in the first week	After several rounds of speed dating, during which the students use infographics about their skills, hobbies, experiences, and study backgrounds, they form project teams. Then, the teams decide which problem space or technological opportunity to explore	LA
9	Mid-mid-term session	Initially, teams had to pitch their progress twice formally during moments (midterm and final pitch) at the end of each quartile	Teams pitch now twice more, in this case to an external expert, halfway through each quartile. Therefore, they are triggered to accelerate their project development process four times. In this way, they are on time to take corrective measures on aspects highlighted by challenge owners and technology experts	LA/ ASM
10	Learning festival	Each team wrote a final report describing their learning journey and explaining their personal development	On the last day of the course, the teams demonstrate their learning journey in a format they choose (e.g. rap, documentary, board game, and role play). The individual students share their learning portfolios, too. The last part of the festival is a shared lunch with the whole cohort	LA/ ASM
11	One team entirely online	From the beginning, the course was run onsite. During COVID, we ran the course in a hybrid way so that the students could join online, while most of the cohort was onsite	Only once did a team of students from foreign partner universities form a team and participate remotely in the course. It was hard for this team to fully benefit from the dynamics and activities that took place onsite	ILO/ LA/ ASM

(continued)

Table 2 (continued)

#	Examples of changed course design elements	How it was before the change	After redesign	Course element
12	"Feed-forward"	Each team pitched their weekly progress on the project, and the rest of the cohort asked questions or gave advice, followed by the coaches' observations and remarks	After the progress pitches, the students provide tops (what they liked and why) and tips (what and how to improve) on sticky notes on the Miro Board. Individual students improve their co-coaching skills, and the teams can harvest the cohort's input more effectively. That is done thanks to a call to action and a request for help from the cohort, which is the last part of a progress pitch	LA/ASM
13	"Investors' pitch"	During the final pitching session at the end of the course, the teams pitched their project to a jury	This investors' pitch takes place halfway through the second quartile, replacing the second mid-mid-term session. As a result, the teams have time to incorporate the jury feedback and reach out to new stakeholders mentioned or connected by the jury	LA/ASM
14	Demo market	Teams made mock-up models and prototypes that they presented during the mid-term and final pitches	After the investors' pitch session, the teams can work on their mock-up models and prototypes, validate them with stakeholders, and demonstrate them at the "demo market". They can also prepare a pilot for implementing the project in real life	LA/ASM

data-oriented approach can facilitate the creation of more robust and adaptable educational models that effectively meet the needs of students and the evolving market landscape.

6.1 *Educators' Experiences*

Through data-driven DSR, we engage in a dynamic process of entrepreneurial education development that is heavily influenced by direct feedback from students and other key stakeholders. This feedback mechanism ensures that the course remains relevant and highly effective in fostering an entrepreneurial mindset among students. A data-driven DSR approach helps in bridging the gap in understanding the "how" of entrepreneurial education: by systematically investigating and redesigning the course based on empirical evidence and in an iterative process, we find out

Table 3 The impact of our course on students' learning is demonstrated through exemplary quotes linked to the intended learning outcomes

#	Codes	Example quote
1	Approach: co-creation	"The best example of this was at the co-creation session, where [other team member] and I, together with a few people from the Challenge Owner and other people involved, brainstormed about the issue, possible directions and opportunities. These different views really helped us identify the biggest problem to solve and envision our solution better"
2	Approach: embracing failure	"I also learned that to be an entrepreneur is to accept failure and learn from it. I am a very failure-averse person, and I'm prone to not taking risks just because of the possibility of failing. Here I learned however that failing is not the end of the world, and we can learn a lot from it"
3	Personal and team development: team dynamics	"We considered our project as much bigger than just following a course and I am happy that we took the time to get to know each other better and have plenty of fun activities. This created an open, fun and educational environment, in which we knew each other's strengths and weaknesses. What I valued most was everyone's enthusiasm and initiative to work on things"
4	Personal and team development: peer learning	"I developed skills to provide feedback in a clear and constructive manner. At the same time, I learned to implement feedback that same day and improve by the next weekly feedback session. This shows that I am eager to learn and develop a growth mindset"
5	Personal and team development: importance of team dynamics	"I've learned that a team is not only about how skilled and talented we are, but also it's about fun, random talks and food. This team gave me the energy and motivation to not give up and work even harder to achieve our goals"
6	Stakeholder management: engaging external stakeholders	"I became even more conscious of the need to involve the stakeholders in your process to find your best problem-solution fit. Validation with them is very, very, very important. This is something I did mainly with my designs, but less with the feasibility of a business model"

what works in practice and how students best develop entrepreneurial competencies. It also means the course is never "finished". It is a continuous process of changing the course, reflecting on its design based on different perspectives, and aligning it with the needs of students, educators, and external stakeholders. This data-driven DSR also requires teachers to have a mindset of continuous improvement and growth, a certain openness, and an eagerness for renewal and change.

A significant aspect of educators' experiences under DSR is the tailored approach to teaching and learning. This personalisation is evident in the weekly coaching sessions designed to meet specific team or individual needs, which departs from traditional one-size-fits-all educational models. These sessions are an integral part of the course structure, providing timely interventions that address the immediate challenges faced by students. Personalised coaching also facilitates a deeper understanding and application of entrepreneurial concepts, which are often complex and multifaceted.

Interaction with challenge owners and other stakeholders is another dimension of the DSR approach that enriches educators' experiences. These interactions help refine the course content and teaching strategies and bring real-world perspectives into the classroom, making the learning experience more tangible and impactful for students. This external engagement is crucial for maintaining the innovativeness of the education methodologies, as it introduces fresh challenges and ideas into the academic environment, thereby keeping the curriculum vibrant and aligned with current entrepreneurial trends and labour market needs.

Moreover, being actively involved in the design and continuous redesign of the course allows educators to experiment with and implement new teaching methodologies. This experimental freedom is key to discovering what best fosters entrepreneurial skills, such as creativity, problem-solving, and resilience among students. Educators can build a diverse portfolio of teaching techniques, including team-building activities, peer-to-peer feedback sessions, and interactive workshops that enhance individual and collective learning experiences.

Finally, educators' roles extend beyond mere knowledge facilitators to become architects of a learning environment where students are motivated by their discoveries and the potential socio-economic impact of their projects. As Ryan and Deci (2000) highlighted, this intrinsic motivation is significantly nurtured when students are empowered to steer their projects, reflecting a deep engagement with their learning process that transcends traditional educational outcomes.

6.2 Perceived Challenges and Growth Opportunities

One of the educators' core challenges relates to assessment methodologies. Traditional grading systems often fail to capture the essence and progress of students in entrepreneurship courses. These systems typically reward result-oriented performances rather than process and growth, which are more indicative of entrepreneurial learning. For example, in scenarios where students start at different levels of competencies, traditional grades may not reflect their entrepreneurial development or acquired skills. This discrepancy can demotivate students who make significant progress but do not see this reflected in their final grades. The challenge, therefore, lies in integrating more holistic and formative assessment methods that align better with the goals of entrepreneurial education, such as pass/fail systems complemented by detailed feedback mechanisms, which are more reflective of students' actual learning journey rather than a summative grade point.

Additionally, growth opportunities were noted in the co-creation of course content with stakeholders, including the students, which fosters innovation and ensures that the educational offerings remain relevant and responsive to the entrepreneurial ecosystem's actual needs. Another area where significant growth can be achieved is the ability to customise education paths for different teams based on their unique characteristics and ambitions. This customisation allows for a diverse portfolio of teaching techniques and more effective team dynamics.

Another challenge linked to growth, i.e. upscaling this type of courses, is the set of competencies needed for teaching these courses. An "entrepreneurial" lecturer needs to possess a mindset of continuous improvement and growth, embodying the same adaptability, perseverance, and resilience expected of entrepreneurs. They must understand entrepreneurship well from a practical perspective, either from their own practice or professional collaborations, which would allow them to guide students through real-world challenges. Entrepreneurial lecturers also have to deal with uncertainty and be comfortable with their lack of expertise in areas that students may choose for their project development, as well as with the fact that their role shifts from "professing" knowledge to facilitating students' learning process. Additionally, they should be skilled in collaboration, innovation, and creation, promoting an action-oriented approach to learning. Most importantly, their focus should remain on fostering student learning, ensuring their instructional methods are dynamic, responsive, and aligned with students' developmental needs.

6.3 Data-Driven DSR Approach

Applying data-driven DSR to entrepreneurial education provides a strategic framework to enhance course design and delivery, ensuring it is both effective and scalable. This approach leverages data extensively to make informed decisions that continually improve educational outcomes and adapt to the evolving needs of students and the entrepreneurial landscape. We argue that data-driven DSR can be strategically leveraged to address specific challenges and harness opportunities within entrepreneurial education.

We embedded the model of constructive alignment in the DSR approach and used it to define intended learning outcomes, learning activities, and assessments for the course in close alignment. We integrated constructive alignment in the DSR phase of creating a design solution, i.e. the creation of our course. There it can help in making well-aligned design decisions between the different building blocks of education.

Data-driven DSR prioritises ongoing data collection and analysis as a core component of the educational design process. This involves not just traditional academic performance data but also qualitative feedback from students, reflections from educators, and input from industry and societal stakeholders. This data was collected by all people involved in the course and combined and integrated by the course coordinator to discuss systematically. By analysing this data in the team, educators can identify what aspects of the course are most effective and which areas require adjustment. Leveraging data-driven DSR means adopting a cyclical approach to course design, where the course is not seen as a static entity but as a dynamic one that evolves continually. This iterative process is characterised by implementing changes, assessing their impact, and then further refining the course. Such an approach allows educators to experiment with and integrate new pedagogical approaches, such as CBL, ensuring that the course remains at the cutting edge of educational innovation. For scaling purposes, data-driven DSR can help in identifying which components of the course can be standardised and delivered online and which require in-person, bespoke interactions. This is crucial for managing larger cohorts without compromising the quality of education. Data-driven DSR facilitates deeper integration of stakeholders into the educational process. This integration involves regular interaction with industry experts, alumni, and entrepreneurs who can provide real-world insights and challenges to the students. Such engagement not only enriches the learning environment but also ensures that the curriculum remains relevant to current industry standards and needs. Additionally, it provides networking opportunities for students, which is crucial in entrepreneurial education. A critical component of data-driven DSR is the establishment of effective feedback loops. These loops ensure that feedback from all stakeholders is systematically collected and acted upon. This responsiveness to feedback allows for rapid adjustments to the course, which is particularly important in the fast-evolving field of entrepreneurship.

In leveraging data-driven DSR for the design of entrepreneurial education, the focus shifts from merely imparting knowledge to creating a rich, adaptive learning ecosystem that fosters innovation, critical thinking, and practical problem-solving skills. By continuously collecting and analysing data, engaging stakeholders, and iterating on course design, educators can ensure that their programmes not only meet the current educational needs but are also well positioned to adapt to future demands. This strategic use of data-driven DSR not only enhances the quality and relevance of entrepreneurial education but also significantly contributes to the broader goals of developing entrepreneurial competencies in students.

6.4 Conclusion

In conclusion, this chapter examined the dynamic process of course development using a DSR approach, offering insights into the practical and pedagogical complexities of designing innovative educational experiences in entrepreneurship.

We systematically explored the design and evolution of a course over a 7-year period. The primary data encompassed detailed collaborative reflections on the course set-up, including comprehensive notes from design meetings and alignment sessions with staff and challenge owners, iterative revisions to study guides and course descriptions, and feedback from students and instructors' observations on student engagement and attainment of learning outcomes. A longitudinal comparative analysis was conducted to map the changes in learning objectives, activities, and assessment methods. This analysis facilitated an understanding of how each element was adapted over time in response to collected insights and feedback. The iterative cycle of data collection, analysis, and course redesign created a dynamic feedback loop, which continuously enhanced the educational effectiveness and efficiency of the course. This process not only substantiates the application of data-driven DSR in educational settings but also promotes an evidence-based approach to pedagogical decision-making, ensuring that educational interventions are both effective and responsive to student needs. The case study not only contributes to the empirical body of knowledge on entrepreneurial education but also serves as a model for applying data-driven DSR principles in educational research and practice.

Acknowledgement This work was partially supported by the NRO grant 405.20865.714 (JLG).

Appendix

Evolution of the Course: Added Intended Learning Objectives

Redesigns made over the years resulted in two additional ILOs. Firstly, interaction with business and societal organisations is an important element of this course since the course demands outside-class activities in which students create a networking of the key stakeholders, i.e. technical coaches and challenge owners. However, drawing upon our self-reflection and thanks to the feedback received from the key stakeholders, we became aware that their interaction with students was insufficient. Stakeholder management was added as an ILO considering the integrative contribution of the challenge owners in providing technical advice, especially in the evaluation and improvement mechanism of students' technical and impact-making progress in the project. For that reason, we redesigned the course ILOs by adding the seventh one on *stakeholder management*, focusing on more frequent institutionalised meetings related to a particular key milestone of the project, participation of the key stakeholders in the formative assessment, and more cooperation between them.

We introduced the eighth ILO, *self-regulated learning*, as a response to the changing educational environment due to COVID because we felt we had to increase the attention to this. During the team-coaching sessions, we discussed this topic and asked the students to share their self-reflections and related actions. We also noticed different speeds of teams in progressing in their project as well as the different backgrounds and, therefore, different individual learning objectives for each student. Self-regulated learning can also be considered as a key component of customised learning.

Evolution of the Course: New Learning Activities

We have experimented with and piloted tens of learning activities since the start. In the first delivery of the course in 2018, we noticed in team-coaching sessions early on that students were struggling with talking to "strangers" and validating problems and solutions, so we added a learning activity called the *Woensel West challenge*, intended to get them out of the classroom and collect empirical data from the interaction with the people they ran into on the street. This aligned with the ILO "approach" and "analysis".

To boost interaction and peer-to-peer learning, we experimented with the *Ambassador and Minister of Interior* learning activity in the second year of the course. During this activity, the students pitched their progress (the ministers) and asked for feedback from the other teams' students (ambassadors). The pitching and consultation happened in multiple rounds to maximise the cross-pollination. As a result, the ILOs "interdisciplinarity" and "skills and behaviour" were better tackled. As another novelty that same year, we invited external assessors as jury members for the midterm pitch session. Their questions, suggestions, and remarks provided valuable team input and learning points. Ranking the pitches by the jury is an example of formative assessment.

In early 2020, at the beginning of the COVID outbreak, we had to deal with new social conditions that resulted in partly remote working. Consequently, we shifted to a *hybrid delivery model* of the course and made it possible for our students to join from home or to show up on campus. We had to use digital infrastructure like MS Teams for communication and Miro as a virtual classroom or team office when the teams worked independently. Engaging in this hybrid form of collaboration, the students gained new and strengthened existing skills. They also experienced new ways of connecting with (external) experts for their projects.

Thanks to Miro, we further improved the process of weekly progress pitches. After a team finished their pitch, including a call to action, the other students shared their "tips and tops" on digital sticky notes on a template we designed on the *Miro Board*. Tips are points to improve with a short description of how to do that next time and answers or suggestions related to the call to action. Tops are examples of what went well and should be kept in future pitches. This way, the students could improve their pitching and coaching skills.

We added *financial sustainability of the organisation* to our course terminology to replace business viability as one of the entrepreneurial focus areas, based on feedback from students. We invited our colleagues from Education and Student Affairs (ESA) to run a *team dynamics and culture workshop* and coach the teams on these topics, given that several students indicated they were struggling with them. After this learning activity, the coaches shared their observations on the teams with the course educators, which could be seen as another form of formative assessment.

We changed the *format of the kick-off session* to start the course, break the ice, and introduce the challenge owners in 2022. We invited alumni to explain the essence of the course to the new cohort instead of us because these alumni could leverage the peer-to-peer learning effect. Then, we showed short videos about the challenges and interviewed the challenge owners about their motivations for participating in the course. Speed dating with the challenge owners and the students is the last official part of the kick-off, followed by a social networking drink in which they continue the talks informally.

During the three sessions after the kick-off, we facilitated the team-forming process. We learned from the past that investing time and attention at the beginning of the course will eventually result in a better-performing cohort. In multiple rounds of speed dating, the students had ample time to explore the problem space around the challenges and meet everyone in the cohort several times. As a result, all students got to know each other's study backgrounds, experiences, and competencies better.

They also better understood each challenge and had more input for determining their preference for which challenge to work on. Eventually, the students formed the teams themselves and chose a challenge, and they had to meet the criteria of interdisciplinarity and a team size of four to five persons.

Another change we made to boost the teams' performance was introducing, based on self-reflection and talks with the challenge owners, a *mid-mid-term session* with each team and their challenge owners halfway through the first and second quartiles of the course. The challenge owners and the respective teams shared their observations and suggestions to improve the collaboration and progress of the project. In this more informal setting, the challenge owners provide formative assessment. We kept the mid-term and final investors' pitch in front of a jury with the presence of the challenge owners as a formal learning activity.

Still, in 2022, we organised the *learning festival* for the first time. It started as an experiment to complement traditional written reflection reports with a format more congruent with the course's entrepreneurial setting while maintaining the reflections' richness and completeness. The only instruction we gave each team was to "demonstrate" their shared learning journey in front of the others entertainingly and engagingly, and they had the freedom to choose their way. We told the cohort that they had to prepare a "gift" for themselves that would put a smile on their faces when they would think back or be "exposed" in the future. It had to be original as a source of inspiration for others. A rap in a video clip performed by famous artists with the support of AI, a documentary in the style of David Attenborough, on-stage role plays, and interactive board games that the cohorts had to solve were some examples of these "pieces of art". The students captured their journeys in a "portfolio" of learning experiences in the form of a slide deck.

Last year, we ran an experiment by having *one team entirely online* with team members from different foreign universities. Thanks to our and the students' experience during the COVID times, we got the most out of the hybrid set-up of the course. Nonetheless, we felt that having a full in-class or only an online cohort works better because of having a level playing field, so we stopped offering this option. As a follow-up of the bi-weekly team-coaching session on team dynamics and learning, we started to *share a summary of our observations and "feed-forward"* (tips & tops) with the teams in short bulleted messages. This is additional input for the students and teams to keep track of their development.

We made another significant change in the programme by bringing the "final pitch" to the middle of the second quartile and calling it the *investors' pitch* instead. This decision was triggered by the response from the jury in the earlier editions of the course, where they gave suggestions to teams on how to run an experiment and were willing to connect them to potential stakeholders in their networks for further validation. This freed up the last weeks of the course to focus more on creating pre-prototypes and planning and executing a small experiment, the minimum viable project (MVP). In the week before last, we organised a *demo market* where the teams showcased their pre-prototypes, explained the results of their project live, and presented them on a poster. The teams invited their challenge owners and other stakeholders. To optimise the time of the challenge owners, we had an evaluation session with them before the end of the market and the informal snacks and drinks.

References

Baggen, Y., Lans, T., & Gulikers, J. (2022). Making entrepreneurship education available to all: Design principles for educational programs stimulating an entrepreneurial mindset. *Entrepreneurship Education and Pedagogy, 5*(3), 347–374. https://doi.org/10.1177/2515127420988517

Berglund, H., Bousfiha, M., & Mansoori, Y. (2020). Opportunities as artifacts and entrepreneurship as design. *Academy of Management Review., 45*(4), 825–846. https://doi.org/10.5465/amr.2018.0285

Biggs, J. (1996). Enhancing teaching through constructive alignment. *Higher Education, 32*(3), 347–364. https://doi.org/10.1007/BF00138871

Biggs, J., & Tang, C. (2011). *Teaching for quality learning at university: What the student does* (4th ed.). McGraw-Hill Education.

Bloom, B. S., Engelhart, M. D., Furst, E. J., Hill, W. H., & Krathwohl, D. R. (1956). Taxonomy of educational objectives: The classification of educational goals. In *Vol. Handbook I: Cognitive domain*. David McKay Company.

Curtis, V., Moon, R., & Penaluna, A. (2020). Active entrepreneurship education and the impact on approaches to learning: Mixed methods evidence from a six-year study into one entrepreneurship educator's classroom. *Industry and Higher Education, 35*, 443–453. https://doi.org/10.1177/0950422220975319

Frese, M., Rousseau, D., & Wiklund, J. (2014). The emergence of evidence–based entrepreneurship. *Entrepreneurship Theory and Practice, 38*, 209–216. https://doi.org/10.1111/etap.12094

Hevner, A. R., March, S. T., Park, J., & Ram, S. (2004). Design science in information systems research. *MIS Quarterly, 28*(1), 75–105. https://doi.org/10.2307/25148625

Kamovich, U., & Foss, L. (2017). In search of alignment: A review of impact studies in entrepreneurship education. *Education Research International, 2017*(1), 1450102.

Lazendic-Galloway, J., Wetters, Á., Guri, G., & Reymen, I. M. M. J., Development of Entrepreneurial Mindset in STEM Students through Challenge-Based Learning, submitted

Lazendic-Galloway, J., Reymen, I. M. M. J., Bruns, M., Helker, K., & Vermunt, J. D. (2021). *Students' experiences with challenge-based learning at TU/e innovation Space–Overview of five key characteristics across a broad range of courses*. SEFI 49th Annual Conference Engaging Engineering Education: Proceedings.

Nabi, G., Liñán, F., Fayolle, A., Krueger, N., & Walmsley, A. (2017). The impact of entrepreneurship education in higher education: A systematic review and research agenda. *Academy of Management Learning and Education, 16*, 277–299. https://doi.org/10.5465/AMLE.2015.0026

Reymen, I., Bruns, M., Lazendic-Galloway, J., Helker, K., Cardona, A. V., & Vermunt, J. D. (2022). Creating a learning ecosystem for developing, sustaining, and disseminating CBL the case of TU/e innovation space. In E. Vilalta-Perdomo, J. Membrillo-Hernández, R. Michel-Villarreal, G. Lakshmi, & M. Martínez-Acosta (Eds.), *The emerald handbook of challenge based learning* (pp. 13–33). Emerald Publishing Limited. https://doi.org/10.1108/978-1-80117-490-920221002

Romme, A. G. L. (2023). Design science as experimental methodology in innovation and entrepreneurship research: A primer. CERN IdeaSquare journal of experimental. *Innovations, 7*(2). https://doi.org/10.23726/cij.2022.1427

Romme, A. G. L., & Reymen, I. M. (2018). Entrepreneurship at the interface of design and science: Toward an inclusive framework. *Journal of Business Venturing Insights, 10*, e00094. https://doi.org/10.1016/j.jbvi.2018.e00094

Ryan, R. M., & Deci, E. L. (2000). Self-determination theory and the facilitation of intrinsic motivation, social development, and Well-being. *American Psychologist., 55*(1), 68–78. https://doi.org/10.1037/0003-066X.55.1.68

Ákos R. Wetters has co-founded several enterprises, including two consultancy firms focusing on operational and supply chain process improvements and a venture dedicated to intrapreneurship and open innovation. Concurrently, he has significantly contributed to STEM education through teaching, training, and coaching in the academic sector. Before these entrepreneurial ventures, Ákos accumulated over a decade of experience in various corporate roles abroad, particularly in Jakarta and Kuala Lumpur. Today, he is deeply engaged in entrepreneurial education and innovation in education, capitalising on his rich experience to mentor students, professionals, and start-ups. Serving as a "hybrid teacher" at Eindhoven University of Technology, he brings practical insights from the professional world into the academic setting. Ákos' multicultural Dutch-Indonesian-Hungarian heritage enhances his effectiveness in international contexts.

Gert Guri has developed unique expertise in integrating real-life challenges with educational objectives in entrepreneurship courses over a decade at EIT Digital (European Institute of Technology and Innovation). His international background, being an Albanian-born Italian living in France and working in the Netherlands, and his experience in international organisations and with international students have enriched his global perspective and approach to education. Gert coordinates entrepreneurial learning at TU/e, guiding students in hands-on projects that tackle real societal challenges. Through the Challenge-Based Learning (CBL) approach, he fosters an entrepreneurial mindset in curricular and extracurricular settings. As a co-teacher in the Innovation Space Project (ISP) course, Gert empowers students to make tangible societal impacts with their projects. His work is defined by ongoing experimentation, co-creation, and adaptability, enhancing the effectiveness of team-based learning.

Jasmina Lazendic-Galloway is a scientist, educationalist and entrepreneurial academic. She obtained her PhD in Astrophysics in Sydney, Australia, and has worked as a researcher at the Harvard-Smithsonian Center for Astrophysics and Massachusetts Institute of Technology in Boston. She was a senior lecturer and the Astronomy program coordinator at the School of Physics and Astronomy, Monash University, Australia, where she led the implementation of student-centred learning practices at the faculty and university level. In 2021, she was awarded a Senior Fellowship for demonstrated leadership and impact on other colleagues' practices in learning and teaching in higher education. She has experience as an entrepreneur in digital tech and technology transfer. With entrepreneurial experience in digital technology and technology transfer, she has also served as a coach in the Innovation Space Project (ISP) course.

Isabelle Reymen obtained a MSc degree in Architecture from KU Leuven, Belgium and completed a PhD degree in Design sciences at the Eindhoven University of Technology (TU/e). Since 2006 she is a member of the Innovation, Technology Entrepreneurship and Marketing Group of the School of Industrial Engineering at TU/e, where she is Full Professor Design of Innovation Ecosystems. She is co-founder, scientific director and general manager of TU/e innovation Space. She combines entrepreneurial thinking with a passion for design processes and aims for system innovation. Her research interests focus on understanding and improving heterogeneous collaboration processes in entrepreneurial innovation ecosystems. She was granted several projects on entrepreneurial topics and on education innovation. TU/e innovation Space received national and international awards for its education innovation. In 2020, she became a Comenius Leadership Fellow and was granted a scholarship to perform research on Challenge-Based Learning.

Part II
Applying the Design Science Approach in Entrepreneurial Education: Cases, Frameworks and Artifacts

The Entrepreneurial Education Canvas

Yvette Baggen, Judith Gulikers, Tom Hogendoorn, Ralf Mastwijk, and Thomas Lans

Abstract In this chapter, we present the Entrepreneurial Education Canvas (EEC) as a tool towards (re)designing entrepreneurial curricula and evaluate its usefulness for practice. The EEC consists of 11 design principles and can be used by educators to develop, implement and evaluate their entrepreneurial education together with others. The main purpose of the EEC is to steer the discussion among teachers and curriculum developers on how to create entrepreneurial education across educational levels and domains. The EEC should enable the (re)design of entrepreneurial education in such a way that it serves the context (e.g. educational level and domain) and target group (e.g. students from secondary, vocational or higher education with different levels of expertise) of education.

Y. Baggen (✉) · J. Gulikers
Education and Learning Sciences, Wageningen University & Research, Wageningen, The Netherlands
e-mail: Yvette.baggen@wur.nl; judith.gulikers@wur.nl

T. Hogendoorn
Nova College, Hoofddorp, The Netherlands
e-mail: thogendoorn@novacollege.nl

R. Mastwijk
Avans Centre for Entrepreneurship, Avans University of Applied Sciences, Breda, The Netherlands
e-mail: r.mastwijk@avans.nl

T. Lans
School of Business and Communication, HAN University of Applied Sciences, Arnhem, The Netherlands
e-mail: thomas.lans@han.nl

© The Author(s), under exclusive license to Springer Nature Switzerland AG 2025
B. Derre, Y. Baggen (eds.), *Empowering the Next Generation of Entrepreneurial Change Agents*, Contributions to Management Science,
https://doi.org/10.1007/978-3-031-82251-3_4

1 Introduction

The Entrepreneurship Education Canvas was introduced in 2019 as part of a project funded by the Netherlands Initiative for Education Research (file number: 405–17-715; Baggen et al., 2022; Gulikers et al., 2018). As we explain in the current chapter, we resemble the notion of 'entrepreneurial education' as introduced in the preface. Therefore, we call the canvas here the Entrepreneurial Education Canvas (EEC). Since its introduction, the EEC has been used in different educational contexts and across disciplines. How the tool is used differs, making it interesting to evaluate the applicability and relevance of the tool for (re)designing entrepreneurial education. The purpose of this chapter is twofold:

1. Provide insights into how the EEC can be used to (re)design education, in collaboration with teacher teams, and why it is an attractive tool to use in this regard
2. How the use of the EEC leads to actual changes in education (in the design of a new course or in the redesign of an existing course)

For these purposes, this chapter presents the canvas and two cases, one from secondary vocational education and one from a university of applied sciences.

The discussion of the two cases illustrates that the EEC itself is not a static tool, but can be used in different contexts by adopting it in such a way that it suits the design process of a certain educational institution or teacher team. As such, using the EEC is a means to get to an end and not necessarily an end in itself. It also illustrates how the EEC can support teacher teams, curriculum designers and other education staff to (re)design education in joint processes of designing, implementing and evaluating entrepreneurial education. The cases show that the EEC can indeed be used to design entrepreneurial education and change existing programs, making them more entrepreneurial in a stepwise approach.

2 Background: Why Was the EEC Introduced?

In education, we aim to prepare students for their role in society, in which they are expected to contribute to solving the grand societal challenges (GSCs) of our time (Voegtlin et al., 2022), such as the transition towards a circular economy and climate change. What these GSCs have in common is that they are complex, uncertain and value-laden in nature: the problems and solutions are hard to define as they involve multiple (sub)systems, their development is hard (if not impossible) to predict, and different stakeholders are involved—of whom the stakes can change over time.

Increasingly, entrepreneurship is perceived as new value creation for others in relation to GSCs—which can be economic, but also stress social, cultural and environmental value creation (Vedula, 2022). From this perspective, entrepreneurship is about catalysing change in the ongoing, urgent transitions in society. With the introduction of the 'fourth-generation universities' (Garretsen et al., 2023), there is increasing focus on universities as part of larger ecosystems, in which universities have a responsibility in making societal impact and an active role in realizing innovations, together with other stakeholders. An important way of doing so is by facilitating co-creative processes of value creation between universities and (external) organizations. Entrepreneurial education provides promising opportunities for embedding co-creative processes of value creation in education, as it can be perceived as a way of empowering students as change agents (van Rijnsoever et al., 2023)—either by starting their own venture or working as entrepreneurial employee—to perceive change as opportunity, deal with uncertainty and adapt to new circumstances (Westley et al., 2013).

The focus on entrepreneurship as new value creation for others has shifted the focus from learning outcomes (i.e. the 'what') towards pedagogies (i.e. the 'how') of entrepreneurial education (Baggen et al., 2022). Entrepreneurial education should enable students to experience the iterative, uncertain process of new value creation, which can be full of learning surprises. As explained in Chapter "Advancing the Field of Entrepreneurial Education: Leveraging a Design Science Approach for Educating the Change Agents of the Future", in such education—that should allow for flexibility—not a single approach or learning theory should serve as the basis for designing education. Instead, by applying a design science approach, the teacher (in collaboration with others, such as colleagues and the students themselves) should be supported in shaping learning processes that fit the iterative nature of value creation processes in education.

In this regard, Lackéus (2020) presented a typology of (experiential) entrepreneurial education, in which he makes a distinction between idea and artefact creation pedagogy (IACP), value creation pedagogy (VaCP), mini-venture creation pedagogy and full-venture creation pedagogy (both referred to as VeCP). IACP is more inward-focussed compared to VaCP, in which students are stimulated to create value beyond the boundaries of the institution. In other words, in IACP, students create artefacts within the classroom, whereas in VaCP, students create value for external stakeholders. In VeCP, students create their own venture. Lackéus (2020) found that IACP has relatively weak effects on student learning. VeCP showed more promising effects on student learning, but the focus of students was often on themselves—and economic value creation. This was different in VaCP, in which students felt more motivated to create meaningful value for others. In VaCP, students reported high levels of meaningfulness and deep learning of knowledge and skills.

The EEC offers a way to translate different pedagogies—both value creation- and venture creation-driven—to teaching practice in such a way that it fits the learning goals and the target group of education. Specifically, the EEC consists of 3 prerequisites and 11 design principles for designing, implementing and evaluating entrepreneurial education that stimulates the development of an entrepreneurial mindset and entrepreneurial skills. As such, the EEC mainly focusses on the *how* (i.e. learning activities and pedagogies) of entrepreneurial education, instead of the *what* (i.e. learning outcomes). The design principles support teachers to integrate the complex, uncertain and value-laden nature of the societal issues at hand in education in such a way that it fits the education context and target group.

Next, we first present the EEC. Thereafter, we present the two cases in which the use of the EEC in practice is elaborated. The first case is illustrative of value creation-driven entrepreneurial education, while the second case is illustrative of venture creation-driven entrepreneurial education. As such, the cases show how the canvas can be used to create the different forms of (experiential) entrepreneurial education as introduced by Lackéus (2020).

3 The Entrepreneurial Education Canvas

The complete EEC is presented in Fig. 1.

At the bottom of the canvas, the 3 prerequisites are defined as distinctive criteria for entrepreneurial education (Baggen et al., 2022):

1. Authentic, real tasks with multiple solution paths.
2. Undergoing the entrepreneurial process of (1) opportunity identification, (2) opportunity evaluation and (3) opportunity exploration (i.e. getting into action)—either in that order or iteratively.

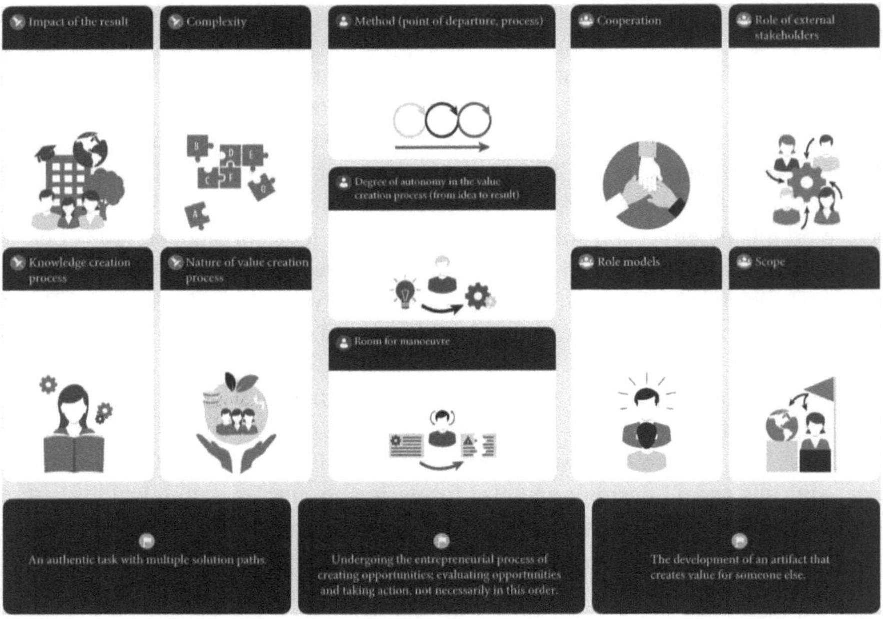

Fig. 1 The Entrepreneurial Education Canvas

3. The development of an artifact to create value for someone else. This can be any kind of value, not only economic value, e.g. sustainable, social, environmental or ethical value.

The 11 design principles are formulated as dimensions and represent ends on a continuum. The principles are organized in three, main categories:

1. The entrepreneurial process (blue)
2. The task (orange)
3. The context and relationships (green)

Table 1 includes the design principles including an explanation per principle and how these can be translated to the 'low' and 'high' ends of the continuum.

The idea of the canvas is that it allows teachers or teacher teams to plot their entrepreneurial course or courses on the principles and dimensions. The canvas can help in discussing the extent to which they are satisfied with the characterization of their course(s) and identify where and what they want to change or how they want courses to build upon one another.

In the next part, we present two cases—in vocational education (*in Dutch: mbo*) and higher education—to illustrate how the EEC has been used in practice so far. The case in vocational education is an example of value creation-driven entrepreneurial education, whereas the case in higher education is an example of venture creation-driven entrepreneurial education.

4 Case 1: Vocational Education, Nova College

Nova College is in the north-west of the Netherlands with a main campus in Haarlem, Beverwijk and Hoofddorp. Nova College offers over 130 vocational education programs across fields varying from automotive engineering, economics and ICT to welfare and healthcare.

Currently, Nova College employs approximately 1200 staff members and has over 12,500 students. About 950 students across the 3 locations are enrolled in one of the programs offered by the ICT Academy at Nova College. These programs include (increasing in level) (1) ICT Support Employee, (2) ICT Support Engineer, (3) Software Developer, (4) Expert IT Systems and Devices and (5) Smart ICT Engineer. In Hoofddorp, around 320 students are enrolled, spread across these IT programs. The Smart ICT Engineer program started in 2019 on this location and has been running for 5 years now, consistently enrolling around 25 students per year. The current case description focusses on Smart ICT Engineer.

This new program was designed from a project-based perspective, with much attention for emergent IT technologies like the internet of things, virtual and augmented reality, 3D design, 3D printing, drones, robotics, blockchain and artificial intelligence. While the starting point was that the program should stimulate the development of students' entrepreneurial skills, the EEC tool was not yet known

Table 1 Overview of the design principles, the related categories, a brief explanation of the principles and how the principles can be used as dimensions (adopted from Baggen et al., 2022, pp. 14–16)

Category	Design principle	Explanation	Low(er) levels of complexity and uncertainty	High(er) levels of complexity and uncertainty
Entrepreneurial process	Method (point of departure, process)	Programs can be based more on methods of *causation* (management, business planning) or more on *effectuation* (starting from: Who am I? What do I want? Who do I know?) or represent a combination of both	Clear goal as starting point (*causation*) and the students apply a more structured approach	The student and their resources as starting point (Who am I? What can I do? Who do I know?). Iterative value creation process (*effectuation*)
Entrepreneurial process	Degree of autonomy in the value creation process	Depending on the level of the student, the student increasingly has autonomy over their own learning and decision-making process in the value creation process	Low levels of autonomy; teacher-centred learning process; learning under supervision of the teacher	High levels of autonomy; student-centred learning process; independent decision-making process
Entrepreneurial process	Room for manoeuvre	In different theories and models (e.g. design thinking), the iterative, experimental character of EE is emphasized. Room for manoeuvre stimulates out-of-the-box thinking, experimenting, prototyping and learning from mistakes but can also be marked off by time or resource constraints	Trial and error in a safe environment without any time pressure	Short cycles of experimenting, prototyping and iterating under time pressure. Risk-taking and learning from mistakes are part of the learning process

(continued)

Table 1 (continued)

Category	Design principle	Explanation	Low(er) levels of complexity and uncertainty	High(er) levels of complexity and uncertainty
Task	Impact of the result	The impact of the value creation process (i.e. the task) can be for peers or teachers, for a more or less hypothetical target group or, more complexly, for external, real (perhaps unknown) stakeholders	The result of the value creation process is targeted to the teacher and/or peers	The result of the value creation process is targeted for 'real' people, outside of the education context. The results can have impact at the level of a domain, sector or society
Task	Complexity	Uncertainty and complexity are key in value creation processes. In progression models, the development levels are characterized by increased complexity and uncertainty in the tasks students are confronted with	Simple but authentic case with multiple options to solve it	Both the problem definition (or challenge) and the solution contain ambiguity (i.e. 'wicked problem'); highly innovative
Task	Knowledge creation process	To innovate or even transform a field, value creation requires new knowledge creation, crossing boundaries between fields or using knowledge and conventions in a different way. Also, domain-specific knowledge and experience play a role in the identification of opportunities	The value creation process is driven by intuition and curiosity; domain-specific knowledge is not necessary or only to a limited extent	Use and creation of new (domain-specific) knowledge; innovative entrepreneurship
Task	Nature of the value creation process	The nature of the value creation process can be of economic, social, environmental or cultural value or a combination (i.e. multiple value creation)	Focus on one form of value creation or a simple combination of multiple types of value creation	Multiple value creation

(continued)

Table 1 (continued)

Category	Design principle	Explanation	Low(er) levels of complexity and uncertainty	High(er) levels of complexity and uncertainty
Context and relationships	Cooperation	The amount and type of cooperation with others may differ, ranging from collaboration with peers and (un)known external parties to collaboration in heterogeneous teams	Mainly individual work or with peer groups	Collaboration in interdisciplinary and/or transdisciplinary teams; across educational, disciplinary and/or institutional levels
Context and relationships	Role of external stakeholders	The role and complexity of involvement of external stakeholders differ, often in relation to the authenticity and complexity of the entrepreneurial challenge at hand	Low levels of alignment with external stakeholders	High levels of alignment with external stakeholders; co-creation
Context and relationships	Role models	Role models with whom students can identify can inspire students to act entrepreneurially or, more strongly, can coach/mentor students in shaping and exploring their ideas. Such role models can support students in developing their own entrepreneurial identity	Heroes and role models serve as inspiration (e.g. in storytelling, a movie or text)	Role models as mentors and coaches that stimulate the development of students; identity formation
Context and relationships	Scope	The value creation process has impact on a certain context, which can differ from local/regional to (inter) national or systemic levels. Students should engage people accordingly	The value creation process has impact on a local or regional level or at the level of a subsystem	The value creation process has impact on a national or even international level or at the level of a system

and used. The initial design principles used were challenging students to (1) work on real-life problems, (2) work together in teams, (3) use design thinking and Scrum to develop and improve new products for real customers and (4) use feedback from customers to improve products. During this process the EEC helped gain a much more detailed insight into what design principles are important for entrepreneurial education and thus to gradually design and improve the education program Smart ICT Engineer.

4.1 Using the EEC to Create a New Program: The Smart ICT Engineer

The Smart ICT Engineer education program can be seen as a successful implementation of value creation-focussed entrepreneurial education. Students of different classes work together in teams of three to five students with different team roles like developer, tester and manager. These roles are often used in professional IT development teams. The students work on projects in sprints of 3 weeks (EEC principle: method). At the beginning of the sprint, the team determines the scope of the sprint in their project plan (EEC principle: scope). At the end of the sprint, they present their work to the other students and/or customer and are formatively assessed using rubrics on the project delivery as a team and on the individual deliveries from the specific team roles (EEC principle: impact of the result). The students have a lot of autonomy to decide on what kind of project they want to work on and what knowledge they want to acquire (EEC principle: degree of autonomy). Examples of projects are building a full stack website, a robot, a drone or a 3D game. The students don't use books but LinkedIn Learning instead. They have to perform a LinkedIn training every 3 weeks. This can be an obligatory training as part of the curriculum or a training of choice based on the student's interests (EEC principle: knowledge creation process). The students are working on real-life problems, occasionally with real customers (EEC principle: role of external stakeholders), and they are challenged to create sustainable and ethical products with value for others. They have access to a large workspace with room for about 60 students.

As each student team works on a different project, the three teachers work as a team and are guiding the student teams and coaching the individual students both on their professional and personal development. In that process, the students are encouraged to find their own resources, such as the right knowledge, hardware, software and expertise (EEC principle: method), to solve complex or 'wicked' problems (EEC principle: complexity). Because the students have relatively a lot of freedom, it is a challenge for the teachers to keep all teams running. The teachers try to achieve this by teaching them to use, for instance, the Scrum method to work on individual tasks on a daily basis and to be responsible for those tasks. The whole setup of the education and curriculum is not static; instead, the teachers and students are in a constant process of reflection to improve parts of the education that are not working well.

4.2 Translating the EEC to the Context of the Smart ICT Engineer: The 'Eight Doors of the Classroom'

Based on the experience with designing the Smart ICT Engineer program, the EEC tool was translated into a simplified version, fitting the educational context of Nova College. More specifically, the 11 EEC principles were translated to the 'eight doors of the classroom' that you can open as a teacher to control how often and to what extent you introduce these elements into your classroom. The idea of the doors was introduced to visualize how these principles could be translated into the classroom. This 'simplification' step was necessary to make the principles tangible, understandable and, thus, workable for the teachers. The lower levels of complexity and uncertainty represent situations in which the doors are closed, whereas the higher levels of complexity and uncertainty represent situations in which the doors are widely open. In Table 2, the eight doors are specified.

Table 2 Overview of 'The eight doors of the classroom', a simplified version of the EEC with levels of complexity and uncertainty

Element of entrepreneurial education	Lower levels of complexity and uncertainty	Higher levels of complexity and uncertainty
Authentic cases	Teacher defines the real-life problem	Students are working on a real-life problem, case or challenge. Outcomes are not predefined
Complexity cases	Simple assignment with a single solution, which requires limited knowledge and resources	Complex casus or problem with different strategies to find solutions that requires different types of knowledge, skills and resources
Real customers	The teacher is the customer	Students work with real customers to clarify the case and get feedback during product development and presentation and demonstration of the final product
Create a product with value	Students work on a product that has no value for others	Students work on a product to create value for others. This can be financial, social, cultural, ecological or ethical value
Prototyping and experimenting	No prototyping or experimenting. Only one possible solution. Other solutions are assessed as faulty	Students experiment and make prototypes to get feedback from customers in order to improve the product. Students learn from the mistakes they make
Cooperation	No cooperation. Students work individually	Students work in different teams, also with students from other educations, customers and with people from companies
Autonomy	The teacher defines knowledge, assignments, assessments and planning	Students define their own planning, tasks, role and learning goals use self- and peer assessments
Finding and using resources	The teacher provides the required knowledge, information and resources	Students find the right knowledge, expertise and resources and use this to solve problems and create products with value for others

4.3 Redesign of the ICT Programs by Using the Eight Doors of the Classroom

In the school year 2023–2024, a project started in Hoofddorp to introduce value creation-focussed entrepreneurial education in the other ICT programs, namely, Software Developer, Expert IT Systems and Devices, ICT Support Employee and Support Engineer. The design of these education programs was more traditional (i.e. representing the 'lower level' end of the eight doors). At that time, students of the Software Developer program mostly worked individually on defined projects and assignments in a fixed curriculum. The other IT programs were mostly subject-based, where the teachers transferred their knowledge to the students on the specific subject and gave them assignments and assessments to incorporate this knowledge. Based on the positive experiences in designing the Smart IT Engineer program, it was explored to what extent a similar approach for redesigning the ICT programs would be feasible.

The purpose of the project was not to completely redesign these programs in one time, but rather to use the eight doors of the classroom (referred to as the 'EEC classroom doors') to introduce more entrepreneurial education in a step-by-step manner. The planning and setup of the project was as follows, spread over the academic year:

1. First, it was investigated which EEC classroom doors were already implemented and which EEC classroom doors could be introduced. Next, it was investigated which parts of the curriculum could be used to implement the identified EEC classroom doors.
2. Next, these parts of the curriculum were redesigned so that the EEC classroom doors could be implemented. Also, the implications for the teacher role were explored, and, if necessary, teacher training was organized to adapt to the new roles.
3. Thereafter, the actual implementation of the curriculum changes was conducted. The EEC classroom doors were used to measure how the students experienced the changes in the curriculum.
4. Finally, a post-test was applied with another questionnaire to find correlations between how often students experienced, for instance, collaboration within the curriculum, and the acquired entrepreneurial skills of the students. Also, an evaluation with the teacher team was organized to discuss how the introduction of the EEC classroom doors was experienced by the students and the teachers.

4.3.1 The Four Steps Further Explained

The project started with an initial assessment of the EEC classroom doors for the complete curriculum, including the five different ICT programs. For this purpose, every door was operationalized into two core questions that the project leaders of each ICT program assessed the curriculum on together with their team. They were questioned whether they already (implicitly) used these doors (and to what extent) in different courses from the curriculum and whether they believed change was necessary for the near future. This first assessment based on the EEC classroom doors resulted in four 'snapshots' of how entrepreneurial education was currently designed and where the project leaders in their particular curricula saw areas for improvement. In Fig. 2, the combined outcome of the whole team is visualized for the complete curriculum in a radar chart. The desired state shows obviously that the teacher team was willing to implement entrepreneurial education.

During the same team session, the separate team sections representing the five different ICT programs worked out a top 3 of the EEC classroom doors, decided which door they wanted to introduce first and determined how often and to what extent they wanted to introduce this classroom door and which parts of the curriculum and activities were suitable for introducing this classroom door. At the end of the session, each section presented their result to the rest of the teacher team. To name a few examples, the section Software Development wanted to start with more

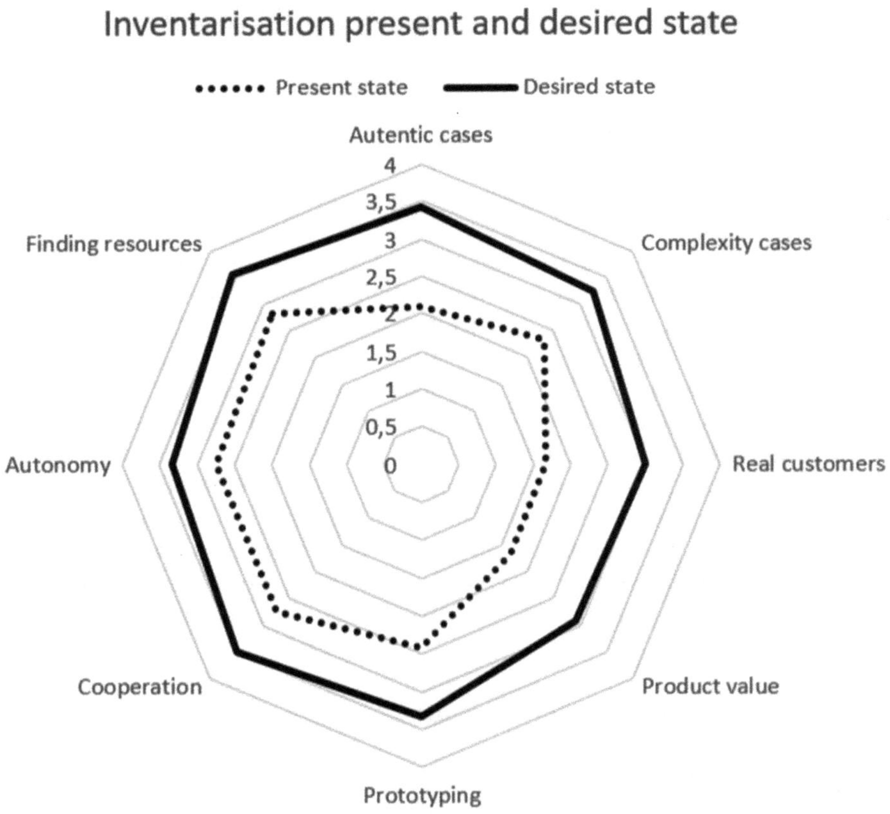

Fig. 2 The EEC classroom doors as currently perceived (dotted line) and desired (bold line) in the ICT curriculum

cooperation between the students and selected a few suitable projects to start with. The other programs wanted to start working with real customers, and these sections brainstormed about possible ways to accomplish this. One promising possibility was to contact retirement homes in the neighbourhood, where students could be placed to help elderly people with ICT-related problems. The section Smart ICT Engineer decided to pay more attention to the autonomy of the students in order to build more gradually on this entrepreneurial skill. To accomplish this, the idea of four different project roles with individual deliveries was introduced to give the students more structure and control over their work during a project (i.e. product owner, manager, developer and tester).

During Q2 these plans were further developed by the sections and made concrete. During another team session at the end of Q2, the sections presented the results of these exertions, and possible problems were discussed. There was no need to train the teachers in order to start implementing the EEC classroom doors into their teaching practice. During Q3 the selected EEC principles were implemented, and the students were asked to fill in a log-tool on a weekly basis. With this log-tool, the students can monitor their own development of entrepreneurial skills. During the implementation phase in Q3 and Q4, students and teachers were supported as much as possible, and the process was monitored to ensure that the implementation was as successful as possible. However, it turned out that only few students were willing to seriously fill in the log-tool during Q3 and Q4 on a regular basis. This shows how challenging it can be to design entrepreneurial education and collect data to change the program based on that data. Currently, alternative strategies are explored to collect data that can further inform the redesign. For instance, by developing a survey for the internship supervisors of the students. The existing internship assessment form will be changed in order to explore the development of entrepreneurial skills of the students in the context of the EEC classroom doors by the internship supervisors of the companies at the end of the internship during the last half year of their program. By collecting data via these assessment forms over multiple years, the relationships between the introduction of the EEC principles in the different ICT programs and the obtained entrepreneurial skills of the students can be explored.

4.4 Preliminary Outcomes of the Project

This is an ongoing project, and it will be prolongated during the coming school years. As usual, the process is more important than the result—we continuously reflect on the entrepreneurial character of our programs and explore ways to collect data, to further improve the (re)design of entrepreneurial education. Already, the result of this project is that the teachers increasingly understand the importance and relevance of using the classroom doors to advance their education and support students in developing entrepreneurial skills.

It is very encouraging to see the outcome of the introduction of entrepreneurial education in the Smart ICT Engineer program. During the 3-year program, the students are immersed in an educational environment where they can fully develop their entrepreneurial skills. In comparison with the students of the other programs, we observe that the students participating in the Smart ICT Engineer program outperform their peers in quickly acquiring knowledge and resources to solve new problems they are confronted with, getting feedback on their work and presenting and demonstrating their results to employees, customers or other stakeholders. Not only is this the observation of their teachers but also of the involved supervisors and employees of the internship companies. The proof of the pudding however will be the outcome of the quantitative research that may show the relationship between the introduced EEC classroom doors and the acquired entrepreneurial skills of the students. Hopefully, this project will inspire other teachers at Nova College to introduce entrepreneurial education in other education programs in the future.

5 Case 2: University of Applied Sciences, Avans

Avans University of Applied Sciences is a renowned higher education institution in the Netherlands, known for offering a wide range of undergraduate and postgraduate programs in fields such as business, engineering, social studies and healthcare. With campuses located in Breda, ‘s-Hertogenbosch and Tilburg, Avans is committed to providing innovative and career-oriented education, combining theoretical knowledge with practical experience to prepare students for the global workforce.

At Avans University of Applied Sciences, the entrepreneurial programs are designed to equip students with the necessary skills, knowledge and mindset to start their own businesses or innovate within existing organizations. These programs often emphasize experiential learning through starting their own business, projects, internships and collaborations with industry professionals, covering topics such as business model testing, value proposition design, human resources, financial management, marketing strategies and innovation management. Avans aims to foster an entrepreneurial spirit among its students, providing them with the tools and opportunities to turn ideas into successful ventures via entrepreneurial programs such as bachelor’s degrees and minors with a focus on entrepreneurship, as well as specialized courses and certifications designed for aspiring entrepreneurs.

5.1 *Using the EEC to Create a New Minor: The Avans Incubator*

The case presented here is about the new minor program, Avans Incubator. It's a venture creation-focussed program of 30 ECTS for the duration of a semester for approximately 20 students in the third or fourth year of their bachelor's program. Students from all universities of applied science in the Netherlands can apply for the minor—as long as they are willing to work 'hands on' on their business (idea), as learning-by-doing is the main pedagogical approach of the minor.

The program was designed and tested between September 2021 and June 2022. Firstly, desk research and interviews were conducted to explore the current issues surrounding entrepreneurial programs at Avans, incubator programs in the startup ecosystem and educational programs, allowing students to determine their own learning goals and paths. From February till June 2022, a pilot was conducted with a group of 12 students, 2 startup professionals and 2 coaches from the Avans Centre for entrepreneurship. With this group of co-creators, meetings were organized every Wednesday afternoon for over a period of 20 weeks. The program was reviewed every 3 weeks, and experimentations with redesigns were conducted. After that, the first edition of the minor was kicked off in September 2022 with the same investigative mindset: to continuously and incrementally redesign the program based on findings in the field with co-creators. That is still the process by which the Avans Incubator program is being improved today.

The EEC was used to provide and maintain an overview during the complete (re) design process. A print on A0 size was placed on the wall. Another way the tool was used was to understand how the building blocks of the minor intertwined. If you change the minor in relation to one of the design principles, you can immediately discuss what effect it might have on the other building blocks of the minor. It creates a holistic view on (the progress of) the educational design and how different design elements connect. Finally it came in very handy as a communication tool for review sessions with co-creators.

How to create a flexible educational environment for student entrepreneurs in which they are motivated to develop themselves, their entrepreneurial mindset and their business? That question was the starting point for the design process of Avans Incubator. The population of the minor consists of students who, during their studies, want to start a business or work on their existing business. By working on their own entrepreneurial idea, they develop an entrepreneurial mindset, which is useful as an entrepreneurial professional in all spheres of life. After interviewing eight students and organizing a panel discussion with six students from the population, five pain points the students experience in reaching their entrepreneurial goals were defined, namely:

1. Little support from teachers and fellow students.
2. No contact with the startup ecosystem.
3. Support from Avans Centre for entrepreneurship is extracurricular.

4. Friction between academic and entrepreneurial ambitions.
5. Misfit between the curriculum and stage of the business or entrepreneur.

Formulating a shared vision and a learning goal with a small group of co-creators was the next step. For this, the Golden Circle was used (Sinek, 2009).

- Why: Enable student entrepreneurs to realize their goals and dreams.
- How: Bringing driven entrepreneurial talent from higher education into contact with each other and the startup ecosystem in an inspiring physical community.
- What: Building open educational, entrepreneurial programs.

From here, the main learning goal of the program was formulated: you are able to shape your own learning process in co-creation and in such a way that you and your business grow.

5.2 Translating the EEC to the Context of Avans Incubator

The design principles of the EEC were used to make design choices that mirrored the vision and learning goal of the minor. The three main categories of the EEC were used as a starting point to structure the design process and understand how the different design principles interact: (1) the entrepreneurial process, (2) the task and (3) the context and relationships. Below is an elaboration of how the EEC categories and design principles were applied in this case.

5.2.1 The Entrepreneurial Process

For each design principle related to the entrepreneurial process, a high level of complexity was implemented in the design of Avans Incubator. The EEC design principle 'method' inspired the minor to kick off with a focus on the birds in the hand (Who am I? Who do I know? What can I do? What do I have?; Sarasvathy, 2001) of the students and how to learn and develop themselves and their business from here on. Furthermore, during the minor students were monitored on the principles of effectuation theory and coached towards an entrepreneurial mindset.

A high level of autonomy is experienced by students because they can work on their own business (idea), formulate their own long-term and short-term goals and choose their own learning activities and content just in time (EEC principle: degree of autonomy). In the program, autonomy is embedded in a structure where the students have to formulate a 20-week goal and six sprint goals and commit to behavioural principles and attendance rules. This tight structure provides a safe playfield in which the students determine the play.

Focusing on the practical part of entrepreneurship and having students actually engage with their potential customers and partners to (learn how to) create value for them, create a high level of complexity. In the minor, students have to get out of the building in order to validate their (idea for a) business model (EEC principle: room to manoeuvre). They have to discover who their target audience is, what challenges they experience towards reaching their goals and test the solution for the business they want to start or develop with their target audience. During this process, they learn how to deal with rejections, be open to new insights and to network. One initiative of the students themselves that exemplifies this is 'Nee Monday', which means 'No Monday' and refers to hearing 'no' so many times before you get a 'yes'. Students team up, motivate each other and actively approach potential customers and partners to learn more about their goals, challenges and needs, or to pitch their solution. This is how they train their so called GOB—'get out of the building'—mindset. Formative assessments and reflection are critical for personal and venture growth in the minor. It encourages regular evaluation of progress, learning from experiences and making informed adjustments to strategies and goals.

5.2.2 The Task

Two agile principles were implemented to create an iterative structure and to lean more towards high levels of uncertainty and complexity: sprints and reviews (EEC principle: complexity). A sprint is designed to achieve a specific (learning) result and make a decision on an important topic within a time frame of 2 weeks. The topic of a sprint is determined by the student in agreement with stakeholders (e.g. co-students, entrepreneurs, coaches, supply chain partners) and is based on what is most important to explore or exploit at this moment. For example: which market segment should I focus on? A sprint goal also provides focus on the learning activities and learning content: what activities, content and partners do I need to reach my goal(s)?

A review week takes place after a 2-week sprint and consists of interventions concerning three topics: retrospective, (peer) review and goal-setting. Retrospective sessions are centred around interventions that make it visible how students worked towards their goal(s) and how they contributed to the community (EEC principle: impact of the result). During review sessions, students send the progress they made during a sprint to a fellow student, entrepreneurs or experts, for instance, from B'wise (an incubator in Breda with strong ties to Avans University of Applied Sciences) and their progress coach for feedback. The feedback focusses on the execution and the progress made within that particular sprint. Seeing examples from other students and receiving feedback from actual entrepreneurs also help students feel more competent and get a sense of quality. The feedback is analysed together with teams of four to six students and a coach in so-called 'low stake conversations' and is intended as feedforward to guide the entrepreneurial learning process (EEC principle: cooperation). More specifically, it provides input to formulate the next sprint goal, which is the third topic of the review week: goal-setting.

In order to focus on the practical part of starting and growing a venture and the mindset you need to work on this venture, a low level of complexity was implemented concerning the EEC design principle 'knowledge creation'. Students were facilitated to share insights, help each other and get help from coaches, experts and entrepreneurs at B'wise. As mentioned earlier, the sprint cycles create the opportunity to develop both their knowledge and skills at the one hand and their mindset and processes at the other.

Avans Incubator also works with its own Wikipedia. In each sprint, students determine which specific knowledge, skills, methods and tools are relevant to delve into. They are co-owner of creating and maintaining content about entrepreneurial skills, mindset and knowledge (EEC principle: knowledge creation). For example, students organize 'just in time' theme sessions in which they invite entrepreneurs from B'wise to discuss current topics. Together with the coaches, they invite relevant guests to facilitate workshops or keynotes. The minutes of the theme sessions and learnings from the workshops are added to the wiki. In this way, knowledge is created and documented for the incubator.

The EEC design principle 'nature of the value creation' made us think about the importance of incorporating the creation of value for others in the program, whether it be financial, social, cultural or ecological. Students are introduced to the concept of multiple value creation via workshops from the Centre of Expertise Wellbeing Economy and New Entrepreneurship at Avans. However, the students are not assessed on the level of multiple value creation. For most students, it is a tremendous accomplishment to actually create some customer value and make money with their business idea. They are concerned with viability and being able to make rent. Making impact is for most student entrepreneurs a bridge too far in this stage of their life. Therefore, a low level of complexity was chosen concerning this principle.

At the end of each minor, an event is organized where the students can pitch their startup in front of approximately 100 people from the startup ecosystem and network afterwards. Together, these interventions provide a real-life setting that intwines with the environment (EEC principle: impact of the result).

5.2.3 The Context and Relationships

Community building with strong local ties and local impact and working with mainly peer groups was placed at the centre of the design after evaluating the EEC design principles 'cooperation' and 'scope'. Avans Incubator should be a place where students and stakeholders actually want to work—a space where they are visible to each other and want to help each other to reach their goals. This puts the design principles 'scope' and 'cooperation' at a low level of complexity. The implementation of the design principles 'external stakeholders' and 'role models' is crucial for providing real-world relevance and opportunities for validation. Therefore, a high level of complexity was chosen for these principles.

More specifically, to create a strong community, the following interventions were used:

- Five rules were jointly (re)formulated: (1) Everyone blocks Tuesday, Wednesday and Thursday from 09:00 h to 13:00 h in their calendar. On Monday and Friday, students are also welcome to work at the incubator. (2) Everyone is installed by 09:15 h at the latest. (3) Everyone attends the standup from 09:15 h to 09:30 h. (4) Optional: joint lunch between 12:30 h and 13:00 h. (5) Everyone works full-time on their business. READ: 'Get Out of The Building' activities start at 13:00 h.

- Peer-to-peer feedback: The goal is to support a culture of collaborative learning in which both the individual student entrepreneur and the community as a whole learn how to learn. Members of the community are not only responsible for their own learning process, but are also co-responsible for the (learning) process of other participants (EEC principle: cooperation). Peer-to-peer feedback is applied to the standups, weekly progress meetings, review weeks and panel assessments in which students are part of each other's panels.

  - Progress meetings: Weekly team meetings are held with a group of five to six students and a coach. In these gatherings, they discuss their progress in depth to really get to the core of why the progress is what it is, using methods such as 'five times why'.
  - Every Tuesday, Wednesday and Thursday, there is a standup at 09:15 h, where three questions are answered very briefly: (1) What was the progress since yesterday afternoon? (2) What progress do you want to make this morning? (3) How can the community help you this morning? After the standup, everyone works on their planned progress, with the help of other students, experts from the startup ecosystem, entrepreneurs from B'wise and/or the coaching of Avans teachers (EEC design principles: cooperation, role of external stakeholders and role models).
  - Panel assessments: All relevant materials, products, feedback and reflections about progress are collected by the students in a so-called roadmap (i.e. portfolio). This roadmap is shared with the assessment panel members: the progress coach, a fellow student and a relevant expert/entrepreneur (EEC design principles: role of external stakeholders and role models) from our network. The panel members are asked to describe their own take on the development of the young entrepreneur based on their experience in the incubator and the roadmap.

Furthermore, a group of six or seven students of the bachelor's Entrepreneurship and Retail Management form the student board of Avans Incubator. They transfer their knowledge, experience and mindset to student entrepreneurs in the incubator that don't have any prior education in the domain of business or entrepreneurship. The mission of the student board is to create a valuable community for their minor cohort. They organize alumni events and team-building activities, invite guest speakers and help with the promotion and recruitment for the next edition of the minor. They are also the representatives of the community towards B'wise and the coaches at Avans.

To conclude, the location of the minor is at an actual incubator, B'wise, in Breda. Here, students are surrounded with professional facilities, startup/scale-up entrepreneurs and relevant domain experts. Interaction is facilitated through speed dating sessions, events, customized connections and knowledge-sharing sessions. Also, the student board maintains, expands and documents an open customer relationship management system. Each edition, our network grows with both alumni and up-to-date partners who are willing to help student entrepreneurs.

6 Discussion: The EEC in Practice

In this chapter, the Entrepreneurial Education Canvas (EEC) is presented together with two cases from practice, illustrating the use of the canvas in (re)designing education. The main purpose of the chapter was to provide insights into (1) how the EEC can be used to (re)design education, in collaboration with teacher teams, and why it is a useful tool to use in this regard and (2) how the use of the EEC leads to actual changes in education. The cases at Nova College and Avans University of Applied Sciences illustrate how the EEC can be used across contexts and for different target groups.

At both institutions, the EEC was adapted and changed in such a way that it fitted the context of the institution. At Nova College, the 11 design principles were translated into 'Eight doors of the classroom', which were practical, comprehensible and workable for the teacher team. Speaking of 'doors' instead of 'design principles' helped to support teachers in visualizing and explicating changes in the classroom. The design principles were presented as doors, which can be closed or opened, similar to the original dimensions of the EEC. In the new model, the 'low' levels not necessarily represent entrepreneurial education. For instance, education programs that are teacher-centred, without collaboration between students and standalone (external) stakeholders, are not in line with the initial prerequisites of entrepreneurial education as presented in the introduction of the current chapter. However, formulating the doors in such way helped the teachers to start designing entrepreneurial education from a low entry level, making them aware what to think of when designing entrepreneurial education—especially from a value creation perspective. The levels were formulated in such a way that they closely matched the reality of the teachers working in vocational education. This helped the teachers recognize the 'eight doors of the classroom', allowing them to propose, develop and implement changes in the curricula that matched their learning goals and target groups—increasing the level of entrepreneurialism in education.

At Avans University of Applied Sciences, the curriculum was designed and evaluated by using the three main categories of the EEC as a starting point, namely, (1) the entrepreneurial process, (2) the task and (3) the context and relationships. The main purpose of using the EEC was to keep the overview throughout the process of designing and shaping the minor. The tools were used to make connections between the different categories of the EEC (i.e. the entrepreneurial process, the task and the context) and its more specific design principles, resulting in a coherent minor on venture creation. The minor was developed in such a way that it supported students in learning not only how to create their own venture but also how to develop entrepreneurial skills and an entrepreneurial mindset that can be useful in all spheres of life.

The Smart ICT Engineer program fits more strongly in the notion of entrepreneurship as value creation, whereas Avans Incubator is more venture creation-driven. In the Smart ICT Engineer program, both elements of artefact creation pedagogy (IACP) and value creation pedagogy (VaCP) can be recognized, whereas Avans Incubator includes elements of VaCP and venture creation pedagogies (VeCP). As such, the design principles do not limit educators to using just one pedagogy in their design, but allow them to choose and combine elements from different pedagogies in the design of their educational program, in line with their learning goals and target audience.

The cases illustrate how the EEC can be a useful tool in (re)designing education and how it can facilitate collaboration within and beyond teacher teams. It provides a shared language, supports the process of developing a shared understanding of the meaning of entrepreneurial education and helps in keeping the overview of what changes are desirable—or not—in the process of developing entrepreneurial education. Adjusting the canvas to the context of the knowledge institution was key, emphasizing the importance of not perceiving the canvas as a 'one-size-fits-all' solution. Instead, it can be used as a starting point—a tool that helps to steer the discussion on entrepreneurial education and find relationships to their current (often more traditional, subject and knowledge oriented) curriculum and that can be practically used by aligning it with the needs of the teacher team (and other stakeholders involved). As such, it nicely fits into the design science approach, as it allows teachers and teacher teams to develop, implement, evaluate and—on the go—change entrepreneurial education, based on the learning needs of the students and the preference of the teacher. Having a concrete tool (or artifact) seems to support the development of entrepreneurial education, making it comprehensible what it could actually mean for teaching practice and guiding a more structured approach for curriculum (re)design, as well as discussing and aligning courses within the curriculum.

Guidelines for Using the EEC for Steering Entrepreneurial Education (re)Design

Based on the results, different guidelines for using the EEC in practice can be formulated:

- Translate the canvas to your own context.
  - In relation to other theories or tools that are relevant in the context of the (re)design
  - In relation to the target group you work with (e.g. bachelor or master students; novices or experts in entrepreneurship)
- Use the EEC as a discussion tool, steering the conversation on the meaning of entrepreneurship and what is important in the entrepreneurial courses.
- Plot current courses and curricula in relation to the principles, as well as the desired curriculum. This allows mapping differences between the current and

desired curricula and discussing how different courses build on one another in terms of entrepreneurship.

- Print the EEC and show it on the wall, to make the (re)design explicit. By using sticky notes, new ideas could be added and old ones removed. A golden rule when using the canvas is not to allow writing on the canvas itself. By using sticky notes, new insights can be added, and sticky notes can be removed or adopted.
- Pay specific attention to the relationships between the different design principles. Change in relation to one of the design principles may lead to changes in relation to other design principles too.
- The EEC can be used in teacher teams, but also, for instance, to show the management the relevance of education (re)design and to make this (re)design tangible. It can also help to use the EEC to communicate and align with non-academic stakeholders, such as entrepreneurs or professionals from businesses who participate in entrepreneurial education.

References

Baggen, Y., Lans, T., & Gulikers, J. (2022). Making entrepreneurship education available to all: Design principles for educational programs stimulating an entrepreneurial mindset. *Entrepreneurship Education and Pedagogy, 5*(3), 347–374. https://doi.org/10.1177/2515127420988517

Garretsen, H., Van De Goor, I., & van de Mheen, D. (2023). Dutch experiences in new partnerships between science and practice in health promotion: Toward a fourth-generation university. *Health Promotion International, 38*(4). https://doi.org/10.1093/heapro/daab194

Gulikers, Baggen, Lans, & Christoffel (2018). *Leren voor breed ondernemerschap. Analyse van leeruitkomsten en leeractiviteiten.* End report NWO-PPO overview study with file number 405-17-71. Retreived via: http://bit.ly/breedondernemerschap

Lackéus, M. (2020). Comparing the impact of three different experiential approaches to entrepreneurship education. *International Journal of Entrepreneurial Behavior & Research, 26*, 937–971. https://doi.org/10.1108/IJEBR-04-2018-0236

Sarasvathy, S. D. (2001). Causation and effectuation: Toward a theoretical shift from economic inevitability to entrepreneurial contingency. *Academy of Management Review, 26*(2), 243–263. https://doi.org/10.2307/259121

Sinek, S. (2009). Start with why: How great leaders inspire everyone to take action. *Portfolio.*

van Rijnsoever, F. J., Sitzler, S., & Baggen, Y. (2023). The change agent teaching model: Educating entrepreneurial leaders to help solve grand societal challenges. *The International Journal of Management Education, 21*(3). https://doi.org/10.1016/j.ijme.2023.100893

Vedula, S. (2022). Entrepreneurship for the public good: A review, critique, and path forward for social and environmental entrepreneurship research. *Academy of Management Annals, 16*(1). https://doi.org/10.5465/annals.2019.0143

Voegtlin, C., Scherer, A. G., Stahl, G. K., & Hawn, O. (2022). Grand societal challenges and responsible innovation. *Journal of Management Studies, 59*(1), 1–28. https://doi.org/10.1111/joms.12785

Westley, F. R., Tjornbo, O., Olsson, P., Folke, C., Crona, B., & Bodin, Ö. (2013). A theory of transformative agency in linked social-ecological systems. *Ecology and Society, 18*(3) https://www.jstor.org/stable/26269375

Yvette Baggen is Assistant Professor at the Education and Learning Sciences group of Wageningen University & Research, specializing in entrepreneurial learning and ecosystems in higher education. Her work empowers students and professionals as change agents, equipping them to tackle real-world challenges. Yvette's research integrates education, entrepreneurship, and societal impact, promoting transformative learning experiences that prepare learners for impactful careers.

Judith Gulikers is associate professor and teacher educator at the Education and Learning Sciences group of Wageningen University & Research. Her research focusses on assessment: formative assessment, programmatic assessment and assessment in and of innovative learning, such as entrepreneurial learning. Her mostly participatory types of research combine the design of innovative educational (assessment) practices with teacher professional development.

Tom Hogendoorn is an experienced ICT educator at Nova College in Hoofddorp, where he has been teaching since 2001. With over two decades of experience, Tom has a deep passion for fostering innovation in education. From 2010 to 2012, he completed a Master's degree in Education, which significantly shaped his approach to teaching and learning. Since then, he has been actively involved in educational reform, particularly focusing on enhancing the skills acquisition process for students. Tom believes that equipping students with relevant skills is key to preparing them for the rapidly changing technological landscape. His work emphasizes the integration of practical, hands-on learning methods, helping students apply ICT concepts in real-world scenarios. Dedicated to the ongoing development of his students and the education sector, Tom continues to explore innovative teaching strategies to better engage learners and improve educational outcomes.

Ralf Mastwijk experiments with personalized learning in entrepreneurship education through his role as Innovation Director at the Avans Center for Entrepreneurship, part of Avans University of Applied Sciences. His approach focuses on making educational choices concerning autonomy and relatedness, aiming to closely meet the learning needs of young entrepreneurs while maintaining a sense of belonging. Ralf has been involved in various entrepreneurship program initiatives. For example a new open learning curriculum for the entrepreneurship program in Breda, the minor 'Avans Incubator' and events connecting entrepreneurial talent, researchers and the startup ecosystem in Breda through the theme 'impact-driven entrepreneurship'. In this chapter, Ralf shares insights gained from developing, implementing, and refining the minor Avans Incubator in which his vision for personalized entrepreneurship education aligns with putting it into practice.

Thomas Lans is a professor of Entrepreneurship at HAN University of Applied Sciences. His interest in entrepreneurship research began during his master's at Wageningen University in 2001, where he studied entrepreneurial competencies in the energy transition within horticulture. He completed his PhD in 2009, focusing on entrepreneurship and competency development in small businesses. From 2009 to 2019, as an assistant professor at Wageningen University & Research and a visiting professor in Italy, he concentrated on (sustainable) entrepreneurship education and published extensively. In 2010, he founded Quente, a company assessing entrepreneurial behavior in schools and businesses. In early 2020, he became a senior research manager at CINOP-ECBO, focusing on practice-based research in vocational education. Since September 2021, he has been at HAN, integrating his experiences as a researcher, lecturer, and entrepreneur.

The Entrepreneurial Educational Method: A DSR Artifact to Support Educators in Designing Entrepreneurial Education

Bart Derre, Pedro De Bruyckere, and Mathieu Weggeman

Abstract This chapter introduces the entrepreneurial educational method (EEM), an artifact developed using a design science research (DSR) methodology to enhance the instructional decision-making processes of higher education educators. With a focus on ensuring entrepreneurial learning gains for all students, the chapter emphasizes instructional quality as a crucial factor, particularly as entrepreneurial education expands from elective groups to the full student population. Drawing on Mansoori's (2017) concept of entrepreneurial methods, the EEM is defined as a set of entrepreneurial education principles and structured guidelines that help guide educators in their instructional design (ID) decisions. The EEM features a three-layered structure: the first layer encompasses ten design propositions, the second contains the ELED protocol as a sub-artifact, and the third layer includes multiple CIMOs and tools, all organized in a nested, Russian doll-like configuration. Together, these layers offer a flexible framework to assist educators in implementing effective and context-sensitive entrepreneurial education.

B. Derre (✉)
HOGENT University of Applied Sciences and Arts, Center for Entrepreneurship, Ghent, Belgium and Psychology and Educational Sciences, VUB, Brussels, Belgium
e-mail: bart.derre@hogent.be

P. De Bruyckere
Education, Utrecht University, Utrecht, The Netherlands
e-mail: p.debruyckere@uu.nl

M. Weggeman
Industrial Engineering and Innovation Sciences, Eindhoven University of Technology, Eindhoven, The Netherlands
e-mail: m.c.d.p.weggeman@tue.nl

© The Author(s), under exclusive license to Springer Nature Switzerland AG 2025
B. Derre, Y. Baggen (eds.), *Empowering the Next Generation of Entrepreneurial Change Agents*, Contributions to Management Science,
https://doi.org/10.1007/978-3-031-82251-3_5

1 Introduction

In a complex and rapidly changing society, every student requires and deserves entrepreneurial education that provides the competencies to become a change agent, contributing to major societal challenges and the student's well-being. Becoming an entrepreneurial citizen is closely tied to the student's ability to take on the role of a change agent. To achieve these positive outcomes, it is crucial that the entrepreneurial education received leads to entrepreneurial learning gains for every student participating in entrepreneurial courses. It is, therefore, appropriate for entrepreneurial education practice to link with the educational effectiveness research (EER) domain that attempts to study both the net effect of teaching on learning outcomes or the percentage share of teaching in the observed learning gain differences and the variability of that net school effect for different learning outcomes (Creemers & Kyriakides, 2006; Kyriakides and Creemers, 2009; Nilsen et al., 2016; Reynolds et al., 2014; Scheerens, 2013). Educational effectiveness is a multilevel construct, with various factors directly or indirectly influencing student outcomes (Nilsen et al., 2016). Educational activities during a course directly and significantly impact student learning outcomes, involving both teacher and instructional quality. Nilsen et al. (2016) define instructional quality as "those features of teachers' instructional practices known to positively influence student outcomes, both cognitive and affective" (p. 14). Teacher quality encompasses "both qualifications and characteristics (inputs) that shape instruction (process) and affect student outcomes," including education level, teaching experience, professional development, and traits like self-efficacy (Nilsen et al., 2016). To ensure that all students achieve entrepreneurial learning gains, optimizing instructional quality is a key lever, especially as participation shifts from elective groups to the entire student population (Fayolle, 2013; Fayolle & Gailly, 2008; Fellnhofer, 2019; Lackéus, 2015; Nabi et al., 2017; Kamovich & Foss, 2017).

This article introduces an artifact developed through a design science research methodology to improve instructional quality by supporting educators in designing courses that foster entrepreneurial learning within a specific context. Designing entrepreneurial courses and curricula to achieve context-specific learning outcomes is considered the core process of entrepreneurship education (Gulikers et al., 2019). It represents the final product of a systematic didactic process in which educators align multiple interacting variables (Kamovich & Foss, 2017). In this way, the artifact can contribute to the further professionalization of educators, improve instructional quality, and, ultimately, optimize the education of a future generation of change-makers.

2 Background: Why Was EEM Introduced

Instructional design (ID) refers to the systematic process of developing educational and training curricula and courses (Branch, 2009). It can range from making minor course revisions to creating entirely new curricula (Brown & Green, 2018). Instructional design models, described as "conceptual tools to visualize, direct, and manage processes for creating high-quality teaching and learning materials" (Branch & Kopcha, 2014, p. 85), rest on three assumptions endorsed in this study: (1) instruction includes both teaching and learning, (2) education involves macro-learning activities, and (3) instruction focuses on micro-learning activities (p. 78). Teaching, here, is viewed as the organization of intentional learning, which is goal-oriented but also allows for unplanned cognitive, social, and emotional learning.

Since the 1960s, the proliferation of ID methods has led to the question of which method yields the best outcomes in specific contexts (Branch & Kopcha, 2014; Edmonds et al., 1994). Although instructional design methods and learning theories are distinct, they are interrelated, with learning theories influencing the structure of instructional design models, including the role of the student, teaching methods, and assessments (Khalil & Elkhider, 2016; Costa et al., 2022). The three main learning theories—behaviorism, cognitivism, and constructivism—are commonly linked to these models (Costa et al., 2022; Khalil & Elkhider, 2016). Despite the numerous ID models, most are based on the ADDIE framework, which includes the five core phases: analyze, design, develop, implement, and evaluate (Branch, 2009; Branch & Kopcha, 2014; Stefaniak & Xu, 2020). According to Branch (2009), ADDIE is a product development paradigm for creating complex, intentional learning environments rather than a model.

For the specific design of entrepreneurial education, several authors (Alberti et al., 2004; Béchard et al., 2005; Fayolle & Gailly, 2008; Maritz & Brown, 2013; Maritz, 2017; Toding & Venesaar, 2018) have developed instructional design (ID) models, often presented as teaching or learning models. A key difference among these models is the distinction between prescriptive and descriptive. Béchard et al. (2005) explore how educators' pedagogical decision-making is influenced and employ the educational concept of the "teaching model" to design an analytical framework. This framework captures educators' epistemological and ontological motivations and their manifestations in courses and programs through their pedagogical decisions. Béchard et al. (2005) approach the teaching model from a descriptive perspective, aiming to describe a learning environment and speculate on how key variables might be affected (Edmonds et al., 1994, p. 60).

According to Béchard et al. (2005), this theoretical foundation should not be narrowly defined and includes not only codified academic knowledge but also the educators' "deeply personal experiences" (p. 2). They argue that teaching models' relevance lies in the connection between educators' conceptions of teaching and their actual instructional behaviors. A teaching model, therefore, encompasses multiple constructs, which are divided into ontological and operational levels. Specific expressions of these constructs generate various teaching model "archetypes" in entrepreneurship education.

Béchard et al.'s (2005) framework consists of three ontological dimensions: (1) the philosophical paradigm, (2) the theoretical foundation or human agency grounded in different disciplines, and (3) educators' conceptions of education. These ontological dimensions shape a teaching model's operational dimensions, including goals, knowledge, pedagogical models, methods, and evaluation. As Béchard et al. (2005) argue, "how one views the world influences how that person approaches education and teaching, including the design of specific programs, courses, and pedagogical activities" (p. 3).

Fayolle and Gailly (2008) emphasize the significant influence of an educator's ontological and epistemological perspectives on the various stages of the ADDIE model. They also apply their teaching model to create learning environments that effectively stimulate three key student learning processes: (1) learning to become an enterprising individual, (2) learning to become an entrepreneur, and (3) learning to become an academic. According to Fayolle and Gailly (2008), these three learning processes, shaped by differing ontological views of entrepreneurship education, define the specifics at the educational level. Their design propositions, particularly at the educational level, integrate elements from the ADDIE model: analyze (P4, for whom), design (P3, why), develop (P6, what; P7, how), and evaluate (P5, for which results).

Toding and Venesaar (2018) take a different approach from Fayolle and Gailly's (2008) three types of learning processes. They focus on fostering an entrepreneurial mindset and developing entrepreneurial skills, supplemented by domain-specific knowledge for those pursuing entrepreneurship and academic knowledge for students pursuing scholarly careers. They explicitly incorporate student factors—specifically, prior knowledge, metacognitive ability, and self-regulation—into the presage phase of the ADDIE model's analysis activity, alongside teacher and learning environment factors. In doing so, they reference the constructivist paradigm that underpins Biggs' 3P model (Biggs, 1996), emphasizing the formulation of pedagogical objectives and expected outcomes based on a shared understanding of entrepreneurship and the entrepreneurial mindset. The transition from novice to expert learner involves a shift from passive learning (e.g., traditional lectures) to active methods (e.g., problem-based learning). This progression occurs gradually across the entire curriculum, with objectives at its core. In constructive alignment, curriculum objectives guide decisions about learning activities and assessment, with the ultimate goal of students reaching the highest level of proficiency, reflected in their behavior (Biggs, 1996).

Toding and Venesaar (2018) also recommend that educational leadership adopt a systematic approach that integrates entrepreneurial curriculum design with EE educators' professional development. They highlight that a teaching model can support the effective design of entrepreneurial education and emphasize that EE educators "need to understand and apply these models" (p. 712). Novice educators, in particular, require a more structured, activity-based professional development approach.

Toding and Venesaar's (2018) recommendations align with the "design for learning" movement in educational sciences, which advocates for the widespread adoption of instructional design models within educational processes, focusing on professional development and educator expertise (Brown & Green, 2018; Dunn et al., 2019; Goodyear, 2015). Consequently, improving educational effectiveness centers on the educator's ability to enhance student learning through effective instructional practices. However, just as in entrepreneurial education for students, professional learning and behavioral change for educators require more than knowledge transfer, making an activity-based approach essential. Thus, educators are the key agents of change in a collaborative design approach that fosters individual and team learning.

Goodyear and Dimitriadis (2013) argue for a "design for learning" approach, which is not only multi-stakeholder but also a complex, systemic process consisting of several key sub-processes: (1) design for learning (focused on what students and other agents do); (2) design for orchestration (supporting educators during learning time); (3) design for reflection (gathering actionable data to inform evaluation); and (4) design for redesign (making conscious design choices that facilitate modifications in future iterations). This approach highlights that design for learning is a multi-stakeholder, iterative process involving collaboration between researchers, educators, and students.

While design for learning retains the basic features of the ADDIE model, it expands beyond its linear structure, emphasizing the intimate relationship between design and redesign, which occur at various levels of time, knowledge, and actions (Goodyear & Dimitriadis, 2013). The shift in management's focus ensures that design for learning becomes part of daily educational practice, rather than project-based work, with educators being viewed as "knowledgeable, helpful actors with bounded capabilities" (Goodyear & Dimitriadis, 2013, p. 4).

Goodyear (2015) also stresses the importance of pedagogical content knowledge in the design for learning process. He notes that designing complex learning environments requires "epistemic fluency," which is often rare and sometimes undervalued in educational practice (p. 40). A critical task for educators, as part of co-creative design processes, is to minimize "accidental variation"—which can disrupt student learning—by carefully structuring the design, even when it may not be well received by students (Goodyear, 2015, p. 42). Goodyear acknowledges the value of experimentation and reformulation, but emphasizes that scientifically supported design requirements should take precedence. Educators thus move beyond being mere developers and implementers of research-informed entrepreneurial courses; they become architects in a continuous, data-driven cycle of improvement and redesign of courses and curricula. However, the assessment of learning gains across various dimensions and levels of classroom interventions—a key component for evaluation, reflection and redesign—remains underdeveloped, both in entrepreneurial education research (Duval-Couetil, 2013; Longva & Foss, 2018) and in practice (Krueger, 2021).

To manage this complexity and ensure that universities become "more congenial homes for design" (Goodyear, 2015, p. 37), managers and educators must clarify the foundations of design knowledge. Educators often make decisions based on uncertain and fragmented information, which creates a need for "actionable knowledge" (Goodyear, 2015, p. 38). This actionable knowledge supports educational innovation while remaining grounded in research-based pedagogical practices.

However, for universities to truly become such "homes for design," the existing instructional design models are no longer adequate to support entrepreneurial learning. There is a need to assist educators based on their proficiency in executing four aligned sub-processes: (1) designing entrepreneurial learning courses, (2) orchestrating learning environments, (3) reflecting on learning through data-driven evaluation, and (4) redesigning courses by systematically incorporating iterative improvements. Effective entrepreneurial learning design must be embedded in an educational vision that fosters students' entrepreneurial growth, cultivates self-regulated entrepreneurial mindsets, and promotes a wide range of entrepreneurial behaviors.

Like entrepreneurship (Berglund et al., 2020), entrepreneurial education is an activity of deliberate design that focuses on creating artifacts that enable effective entrepreneurial education. Prescriptive artifacts can support educators in making evidence-informed design decisions, especially when descriptive or explanatory sciences do not yet provide all the answers, and where the social complexity of the context requires adapting explanatory, hypothesis-testing knowledge.

Drawing on Mansoori's (2017) definition of entrepreneurial methods, the artifact developed, referred to as an entrepreneurial educational method (EEM), is defined as a set of entrepreneurial education principles and instructions designed to guide the behavior of EE educators by providing strategies to support their instructional design (ID) judgment. The EEM consists of three layers (see Fig. 1):

- The "logic" level of the framework encompasses the design principles for creating effective entrepreneurial education. In this study, "a set of design principles" is used in place of "logic." These general guidelines support educators in design-

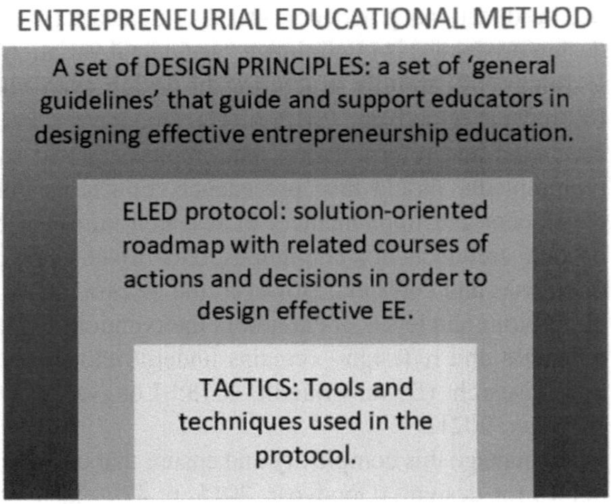

Fig. 1 Visual representation of EEM. Note. Adapted from Entrepreneurial Methods as Vehicles of Entrepreneurial Action (Doctoral dissertation), by Mansoori, 2017, Chalmers University of Technology (https://doi.org/10.13140/RG.2.2.30625.51040). Copyright 2017 by Y. Mansoori

ing impactful entrepreneurial education. They will also inform the development of a protocol that educators can use as a solution-oriented roadmap throughout the design process.
- The "model" level within an EE method specifies the courses of action required to carry out the essential activities in the design process to implement the underlying principles. In this design science research study, the term "entrepreneurial learning (EL) educational design protocol" (ELED) describes the minimum set of actions and decisions educators must take to create effective entrepreneurial education. A protocol, as defined by Van Aken and Andriessen (2011), refers to an "arrangement of interventions" with a time dimension or causal dependency between the interventions. Thus, the complete solution for supporting entrepreneurship educators in designing effective courses includes various design propositions or interventions that collectively lead to creating a curriculum, curriculum line, or course unit. Unlike a model, which is a simplified representation of reality, a protocol offers action implications for different stages of a social process. It dynamically stimulates the creation of a desired reality.
- The "tactics" level refers to collecting techniques and tools that facilitate and enhance the different components of the described "EL educational design protocol."

3 Methodology

The research methodology is grounded in "design science" as both its ontological and epistemological foundation (Dresch et al., 2015). Like other researchers (Berglund et al., 2018; Dimov, 2016; Gilsing et al., 2010; Romme & Reymen, 2018; van Burg & Romme, 2014), it builds, as described in Part 1 of this book, on the work of Herbert Simon (1996) in *The Sciences of the Artificial.* Simon distinguishes between the natural sciences and the "science of the artificial" or design sciences. Holmström et al. (2009) note a fundamental ontological distinction between design science and explanatory (natural) science. In explanatory science, phenomena exist independently of the researcher, who observes, describes, and makes predictions through data collection and analysis. In contrast, design science, which Holmström et al. (2009) refer to as "exploratory research," involves the creation of artificial phenomena (or artifacts) by researchers to solve context-specific field problems.

The developed artifact does not refer to the creation of an entrepreneurship education course or curriculum, which falls within the educator's domain. Instead, it addresses a higher level of abstraction, focusing on scientific design knowledge that can be applied to solve a "class of problems" (Dresch et al., 2015; Van Aken & Romme, 2009). While effective EE courses and curricula are ultimately designed by individual educators within specific contexts, these programs share common features. Educators introduce variations to these features to prevent or address the same class of problems discussed in this study: ineffective entrepreneurial learning (EL) instructional design.

Hevner et al. (2004) developed a framework that is useful for combining design science research (DSR) with behavioral research in the information systems (IS) field, proposing seven guidelines to help researchers effectively operationalize and conduct DSR. Behavioral sciences, grounded in hypothesis-testing and explanatory science, aim to develop theories that explain and predict phenomena, ultimately seeking "truth." In contrast, DSR focuses on solving real-world problems by designing innovative artifacts, pursuing "utility." As Hevner et al. (2004) note, it is valuable to combine DSR with behavioral research, despite their differing ontological and epistemological foundations, to ensure that artifacts developed in IS research are both "relevant" and "rigorous" or, as Hevner et al. (2004) describe it, where truth and utility inform one another.

In addressing the class of problems for which the artifact is being developed—namely, ensuring the educational effectiveness of entrepreneurial education—this complementarity is essential. For DSR to be effective, it must be relevant to educational professionals, enabling them to solve practical problems. At the same time, rigor is essential to ensure the research is valid and reliable and contributes meaningfully to the broader knowledge base.

For an artifact to fulfill its predefined purpose, three mutually aligned components are required: (1) the purpose, (2) the nature of the artifact (DSR), and (3) the environment in which the artifact operates (Simon, 1996). An artifact acts as a boundary object, connecting its inner environment with the external environment it must interact with to achieve a change aligned with its intended purpose. The set purpose is linked to the needs of the external world, which in this study are described as field problems. These three elements are also present in the model of Hevner et al. (2004), where they are connected to a "knowledge base" that provides input to the inner environment.

The operationalized DSR research methodology encompasses three key processes, each of which is detailed further in this chapter:

Ex ante empirical research: This phase leads to the development of design requirements and propositions. The design propositions and requirements are formulated based on the cumulative state of the art, incorporating key concepts, theories, and empirical and pragmatic insights inductively derived from real-world contexts (Romme & Endenburg, 2006). The design requirements are the parameters within which the solution will be developed. The methodology Van Burg (2010) describes is used to formulate the design proposition. This approach (van Burg & Romme, 2014; Sagath et al., 2019) employs a combination of "emergent" and "deliberate" design, which is operationalized through three steps

1. Practice-based design propositions: These are developed by making the implicit experiential knowledge of entrepreneurship education professionals explicit. To extract the tacit knowledge of educational professionals regarding the instructional design of entrepreneurial education and transform it into actionable knowledge in the form of CIMOs, the methodology proposed by Plsek et al. (2007) is adapted and applied. Plsek et al.'s (2007) method aligns with Yin's (2009) case study methodology.

2. Research-based design propositions: These are extracted from existing scientific literature. They not only help to understand and improve current practices but also provide new insights for potential solutions. According to Khalil and Elkhider (2016), design models translate general learning principles and instructional strategies into a procedural framework that educators can use to create interventions and learning environments that effectively lead to desired learning outcomes. In designing the EEM, the entrepreneurial learning principles that enhance the capacity to perform entrepreneurial behavior must be incorporated into the artifact. Therefore, two literature reviews—one extracting entrepreneurial learning propositions and the other extracting instructional design propositions—are conducted using the narrative literature review methodology described by Denyer et al. (2008).
3. Synthesis of design propositions: In the final step, the practice-based and research-based design propositions are synthesized into a cohesive set of design propositions.

Designing the artifact: This process results in the creation of the artifact, which includes design principles, a set of design rules presented as an extended instructional design model, along with the associated tools and methodologies.

Testing the artifact: This phase involves formative assessment, which informs modifications to the artifact, ultimately leading to its finalized version. To test the artifact, an alpha test was conducted, which is a field test aimed at gathering formative feedback from entrepreneurial education educators in higher education on the soundness, usability, feasibility, and potential (perceived) effectiveness of the developed entrepreneurial educational method (EEM) (McKenney & Reeves, 2012). In this testing phase, prospective users were asked to independently—without any interference or influence from the researcher—conduct a thorough review and study of the entire EEM and provide their evaluation.

4 The Artifact

4.1 The Full EEM Artifact

The entrepreneurial education method (EEM) is defined as a nested set of entrepreneurial educational design principles and instructions aimed at supporting higher education educators in the decision-making processes for designing, implementing, monitoring, and improving entrepreneurial courses, whether embedded in curricula or not. These courses are intended to foster participating students' entrepreneurial mindset and behavior. The EEM consists of three nested layers, with the second and third layers containing multiple sub-artifacts, represented as Russian dolls (see Fig. 2):

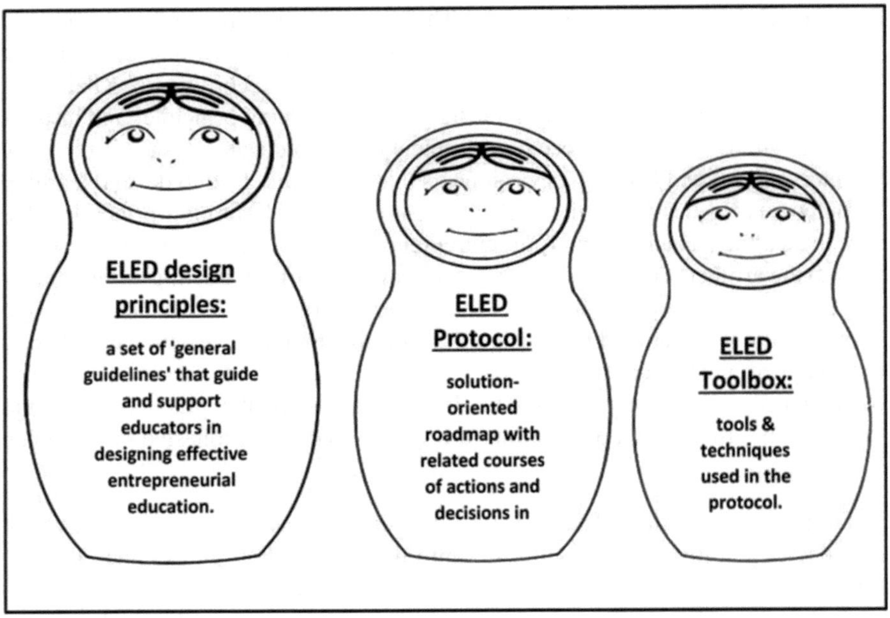

Fig. 2 EEM visualization

- *Design principles:* The first layer of the EEM includes the logic or set of "general guidelines" that guide and support educators in designing effective entrepreneurial education. These design principles are derived from and synthesize the extracted EL-CIMOs and ED-CIMOs. They are specifically designed for expert practitioners in entrepreneurial education but also inform the creation of a protocol for less experienced, novice educators, providing them with a solution-oriented roadmap for the design process of effective entrepreneurial education.
- *Design protocol:* The second layer of the EEM represents the minimum set of actions and decisions educators must take to design effective entrepreneurial education. A protocol in this context is understood as an "arrangement of interventions" with a dependency between the interventions. This complete solution supports entrepreneurial educators—particularly novice educators—in designing effective entrepreneurial education. It includes various design propositions or interventions that lead to developing a curriculum, curriculum line, or course unit.
- *Tactics:* The third, innermost layer of the EEM refers to the collection of techniques and tools that facilitate and catalyze the various parts of the quick and full EEM protocols.

The three layers of the EEM are further discussed in detail below.

4.2 Layer 1 EEM: The Design Principles

The design principles serve as "general guidelines" that guide developing a protocol to help educators design entrepreneurship education that effectively stimulates entrepreneurial behavior and actions in students. These principles are not "ready-made recipes"; rather, they offer guidance for the design process.

The set consists of ten design principles that address both the "what" and "how" of entrepreneurial education, as well as the connection between them, ensuring the design leads to effective, context-specific entrepreneurship education:

1. *Three design principles* focus on the "what" of entrepreneurial education: What is entrepreneurship education about?
2. *Three design principles* address the "how" of entrepreneurial education: How can the desired outcomes be achieved?
3. *Four design principles* shape the link between the "what" and "how": How can designing entrepreneurial education be structured?

Table 1 lists the ten design principles, with a description provided for each one.

Education professionals with sufficient expertise, who can be regarded as experts, may find the design principles adequate to begin designing, implementing, and monitoring entrepreneurial education in alignment with their context and intentions. They recognize that the design process is not a straightforward mathematical exercise where outcomes logically follow from inputs. Instead, it is characterized by "synthesis-evaluation iterations" that involve a "creative leap" through an abduction process. These iterations are not purely cognitive but are "situated" within the social work context of the educator.

However, the EEM is not designed solely for expert educators; it is also intended to support the decision-making processes of novice educators with limited expertise. Therefore, these design principles serve as the input for developing the second layer of the EEM—the ELED protocol.

4.3 Layer 2 EEM: The ELED Protocol

Based on both entrepreneurial learning and instructional design propositions, as well as design requirements extracted from the literature and practice, an ELED (entrepreneurial learning educational design) protocol is designed as a structured arrangement of interventions. These interventions are interdependent, meaning they follow a sequence and exhibit iterative characteristics when applied in the design of artifacts that foster entrepreneurial learning in a specific context by educators. It is important to note that the protocol does not arise as a logical consequence of the extracted design propositions but is instead the outcome of a design process characterized by "synthesis-evaluation iterations" that involve a "creative leap," as described by abduction (Van Aken, 2004). These iterations are not solely cognitive

Table 1 The design principles of the EEM

Design principle	Description
WHAT	
1. Stimulate situated "social-emotional and cognitive" entrepreneurial learning	Entrepreneurial education refers to the stimulation of entrepreneurial learning (gains) as a social-emotional and cognitive process of acquiring new or modifying existing knowledge and decision-making processes, resulting in a transition from novice to expert entrepreneurial mindset and entrepreneurial behavior. Personality traits partly determine entrepreneurial behavior but are learnable, and every student can achieve entrepreneurial learning gains through effective entrepreneurial education that contributes to the evolution of an entrepreneurial individual
2. Design EE as an entrepreneurial journey from novice to expert entrepreneurial behavior and entrepreneurial citizenship	Entrepreneurial education refers to an entrepreneurial journey from novice to expert entrepreneurial mindset and entrepreneurial behavior, resulting in entrepreneurial citizens. An entrepreneurial mindset is the capacity to perform entrepreneurial behavior in uncertain conditions. Entrepreneurial behavior is defined as a broad, value-driven (giving meaning), opportunity-detecting or opportunity-creating, resource-allocating (going into action) process under uncertainty that changes over time due to the interaction of the person with the opportunity and/or context. Broad entrepreneurial behavior refers to both venture- and non-venture-creating value
3.Focus on entrepreneurial behavioral learning outcomes	Entrepreneurial education is about designing, implementing, monitoring, and improving interventions and learning environments that promote entrepreneurial learning outcomes as visible entrepreneurial behavior
HOW	
4. Design "activity-based" learning tasks embedded in an authentic entrepreneurial learning practice and environment	Entrepreneurial education is activity-based and features a backbone of authentic entrepreneurial learning tasks. Completing authentic entrepreneurial tasks serves as a means of stimulating cognitive and noncognitive entrepreneurial competences, entrepreneurial mindset, and behavior. These entrepreneurial learning tasks are embedded and carried out in an authentic entrepreneurial learning environment
5. Focus on situated self-regulated entrepreneurial learning and deep reflection	Entrepreneurial education leads to expert professionals who can sustain the entrepreneurial learning process in a self-regulated way. Entrepreneurial learning includes stimulating deep reflection and activating metacognition and cognitive adaptability
6. Use the guiding principle, "It's all in the timing," when choosing the didactical and supporting learning strategies	Entrepreneurial education has a "student-centered" approach where the degree of personalization and self-regulation within a spiral curriculum is designed at the right time. The pedagogical/didactic methods are designed to function the predetermined learning objectives and the present "prior cognitive and noncognitive knowledge and skills." Gradually phasing out, at the right time, just enough scaffolding is used in the learning process

(continued)

Table 1 (continued)

Design principle	Description
Linking the HOW and the WHAT	
7. Embed entrepreneurial education in domain-specific knowledge learning paths and/or curricula	Entrepreneurial education embraces domain-specific knowledge as an important lubricant to stimulate higher entrepreneurial competences such as critical thinking and creativity. Novices have a greater need for explicitly teaching domain-specific knowledge than experts, and effective entrepreneurship education takes this into account. That domain-specific knowledge may be focused on entrepreneurship as well as non-entrepreneurship
8. Use an impact data-driven design science approach	For the educators, designing entrepreneurial education is a process of educational design. Measuring and monitoring impact data on educational effectiveness supports this process and, more specifically, the educators' learning process
9. Design and use of multidimensional student entrepreneurial learning gains assessment tools	Multidimensional student assessment tools give educators a reliable and valid insight into the impact of their designed entrepreneurship education on the students' achieved learning gains
10. Design EE within a community of practice and stimulate educational professional development from novice to expert educator	Designing entrepreneurial education is a situated socio-emotional and cognitive process, together with different stakeholders such as colleagues, educational managers, entrepreneurs, students, educational experts, and data analysts, that fosters professional development from novice to expert EE educator

but are "situated" within the social work context of the researcher. Furthermore, there has been regular consultation with experts in entrepreneurial education. These continuous "situated" interactions between the researcher and the object of study during the design process align with the definition of an artifact as "a meeting point—an interface between an 'inner' environment, the substance and organization of the artifact, and an 'outer environment,' the surroundings in which it operates" (Simon, 1996, p. 28).

4.3.1 Basic Architecture for Designing Complex Entrepreneurial Learning Artifacts

The ultimate goal of designing a learning intervention that stimulates entrepreneurial learning is to foster an entrepreneurial mindset, ultimately leading to entrepreneurial behavior. Entrepreneurial behavior is defined as a value-driven, opportunity-detecting or opportunity-creating, resource-allocating process under uncertainty, which evolves through the interaction of the individual with the opportunity and/or context. Hence, entrepreneurial learning is broadly defined as a socio-emotional and cognitive process of acquiring new or modifying existing decision-making processes, leading to a transition from novice to expert entrepreneurial behavior. The ultimate goal, however, is not only to foster an entrepreneurial mindset within an educational setting but also to stimulate entrepreneurial behavior in the real world beyond the educational context. That said, “real-life” entrepreneurial behavior is a multilevel concept. The broad entrepreneurial behavior that higher education alumni are expected to demonstrate in their everyday lives depends on both the environment in which they operate and their capacity to exhibit “effective” entrepreneurial behavior when they find themselves in highly conducive environments for entrepreneurship.

A complex learning artifact aimed at stimulating entrepreneurial learning consists of four essential building blocks that make up the entire artifact: entrepreneurial learning objectives, entrepreneurial learning tasks, entrepreneurial method, and assessment (see Table 2).

The educator designing these building blocks now has the opportunity to develop these four individual components, informed by (the extracted) entrepreneurial learning design propositions. A design proposition provides a generic intervention for a certain class of field problem that leads to a certain outcome through a generic mechanism. These design propositions are presented in a CIMO logic as discussed in chapter “Designing Artifacts in Entrepreneurial Education Research” (see Table 3).

The extracted CIMOs that can provide support are divided into three groups or lenses. The design of the four essential building blocks can thus be approached from

Table 2 The essential building blocks of an entrepreneurial learning artifact

Essential building block	Description
Entrepreneurial learning goals	The learning goals are a concrete description of the desired behavior and/or concrete knowledge, skills, and attitudes at a certain proficiency level that should be achieved at the end of the course unit. In contrast to learning outcomes, these learning goals are more concrete and linked to a course unit and refer to the desired outcome of the course unit
Entrepreneurial learning tasks	The “backbone of entrepreneurial learning tasks” describes the (sequential) activity-based tasks students must perform to activate entrepreneurial learning, as designed. A distinction can be made between content-based entrepreneurial learning tasks, which stimulate the acquisition of entrepreneurial knowledge and skills, and more process-based entrepreneurial learning tasks, which stimulate deep reflection, self-regulated learning, and metacognition
Entrepreneurial method	The method (or work format) describes the interaction pattern with the students and how the entrepreneurial learning tasks are presented and supported. The entrepreneurship education method offers the possibility to educate students about the epistemology of expert entrepreneurs or, in other words, to inform the pedagogy of expert entrepreneurs. Note that the entrepreneurial method is not synonymous with using epistemology as pedagogy. The education team can use various entrepreneurial methods to educate the epistemology of expert entrepreneurs. Also, problem- or challenge-based methods involving “wicked” challenges embedded in an uncertain and volatile context can be used. It is clear that there is a close link with the “entrepreneurial learning tasks” building block
Entrepreneurial assessment	The EE assessment describes how assessment is performed in alignment with the entrepreneurial learning goals and learning activities

Table 3 Overview of the CIMO logic

Component	Description
Context (C)	The surrounding factors and the nature of the human actors influence the intervention (I). They include age, educational experience, competence, entrepreneurial experience, etc. of the educator. Interventions are embedded in the social school context and are affected by the individual, the interpersonal relationship, the institutional setting, and the wider infrastructural system
Intervention (I)	The broad interventions educators have at their disposal to influence the student entrepreneurial behavior
Mechanism (M)	The mechanisms that in a certain context are triggered by the intervention
Outcome (O)	The outcome of intervention in its various aspects and levels, such as learning and behavioral outcomes at student, class, or school level

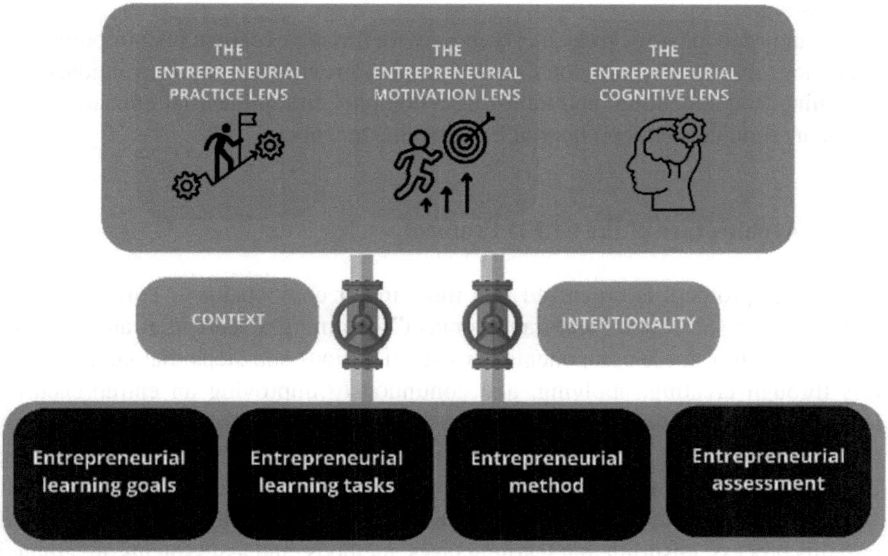

Fig. 3 Designing the essential entrepreneurial learning artifact building blocks

a multifocal perspective, in which the following interconnected lenses are combined and aligned as a function of both the context and the intentionality of the designed entrepreneurial education:

- The entrepreneurial cognitive lens
- The complex entrepreneurial motivational lens
- The entrepreneurial practice lens

Specifically, this means that the emphasis on a particular lens can vary depending on the intentionality and context and the specific interventions determined by that same context and intentionality from a given lens (see Fig. 3).

This underscores the design-oriented CIMO approach, where interventions are linked to a specific context and aligned with a desired outcome. In entrepreneurial education, the context includes factors such as the student's proficiency level. The intentionality highlights the broad range of potential outcomes of entrepreneurial education, including the possibility that change agents may or may not be associated with creating new ventures.

For this study, 16 entrepreneurial learning CIMOs (EL-CIMOs) were extracted, as presented in the Appendix. However, this is not *the* definitive set of CIMO's. On the contrary, using the EEM artifact and designing entrepreneurial education for various contexts and intentionalities can only expand this set by adding practice-based EL-CIMOs. Moreover, new insights from the scientific community can also contribute by adding research-based CIMOs. It becomes a living system where practitioners and researchers share knowledge in a way that educators can utilize in their daily practice.

To support educators, particularly those with limited expertise in entrepreneurial education, the ELED protocol was designed to provide step-by-step guidance in designing, implementing, and adjusting a complex entrepreneurial education artifact that stimulates entrepreneurial behavior in students.

4.3.2 Architecture of the ELED Protocol

The ELED protocol is organized into three major components—"build," "implement and measure," and "learn and connect"—forming a sequential and iterative process. Each of these components consists of various sub-steps that guide educators through creating, applying, and continuously improving an entrepreneurial learning artifact. In the *build component*, the basic architecture for designing complex entrepreneurial learning artifacts is included, where the essential building blocks of an intervention are designed from three key lenses, depending on context and intentionality. Additionally, the concept of constructive alignment is integrated into this process, ensuring that learning tasks, methods, and assessments are aligned to support entrepreneurial learning goals and outcomes. Figure 4 provides a schematic overview of the three components of the ELED protocol presented as a canvas.

These three major components do not occur in isolation but follow a sequential and iterative flow. The iterative nature ensures that the entrepreneurial learning artifact is continuously refined and optimized for the specific learning context. This structured approach provides educators with a clear data-driven process for designing, testing, and refining complex learning artifacts aimed at fostering entrepreneurial skills in learners.

The ELED protocol can be utilized by educators with sufficient expertise, who can independently navigate the canvas and protocol. Still, it can also be employed by novice educators working within a *community of practice*. The underlying data-driven design science methodology and the design-implement-learn clusters enable and encourage expert educators to design new, innovative teaching strategies that can be tested and evaluated inductively. This process ultimately contributes to

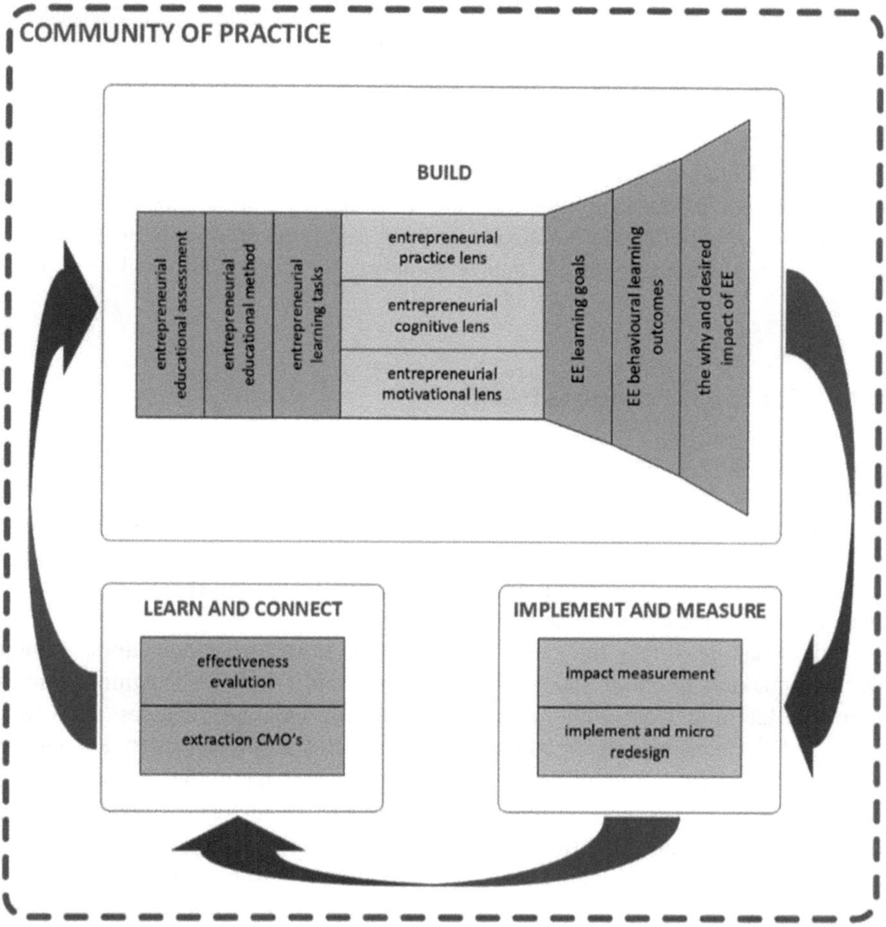

Fig. 4 The ELED protocol presented as a canvas

improving the ELED protocol and toolbox, which in turn enhances professional development and the effectiveness of entrepreneurial education. Furthermore, the data-driven approach enables evaluating and comparing entrepreneurial education practices across different educational institutions and over time.

The community of practice adds further value by involving various stakeholders in designing, implementing, and improving entrepreneurial education, including fellow higher education teachers, entrepreneurs, experts in pedagogy and impact measurement, and students.

The ELED protocol fosters communication between educators, practitioners, entrepreneurs, and the scientific community. Including research-based CIMOs in the ELED protocol enhances the context-specific effectiveness of the designed entrepreneurial education. Conversely, the ELED protocol offers the opportunity to introduce inductively extracted CIMOs to the research community, initiating follow-up research.

Finally, the ELED protocol supports a broad scope in designing various entrepreneurial learning (EL) artifacts. In other words, it is applicable whether a single course is being designed or redesigned or whether the focus is on designing a curriculum or a learning pathway that integrates multiple interlinked courses. If the educator or education team aims not only to design entrepreneurial education for the purpose of qualification but also to develop entrepreneurial individuals, then at a minimum, a learning pathway, and preferably a full curriculum, will need to be designed.

4.3.3 The ELED Protocol in Detail

The ELED protocol supports entrepreneurial education (EE) educators or teams in designing entrepreneurial courses through a process flow consisting of 12 activities (steps) and decision-making processes, divided into 4 clusters: curriculum and course design, implementation, and the learning phase (see Fig. 5). The three main components—build, implement, and learn—remain intact, but the build phase has been divided into curriculum and course design.

This structure offers the designing educator, or team of educators, greater decision-making freedom, along with heuristics and tools for designing, implementing, learning from, and redesigning both curricula and courses. However, increased decision-making freedom requires a higher level of expertise from the designing educators, beyond novice level. On the other hand, the protocol allows novice educators to progress from novice to expert EE designers by working within a heterogeneous team supported by educational experts.

In the further discussion, the term "team" refers to a group of educators, preferably supplemented by other stakeholders such as entrepreneurs, educational specialists, and data experts. The protocol also enables educators to think outside the box, using design-oriented methodology to inductively create new educational interventions, implement them, and monitor their effectiveness through a data-driven approach.

For each activity, a description is provided, along with the decisions that educators need to make and the heuristics available to help them make those decisions. Heuristics as problem-solving strategies or approaches that provide a practical, experience-based method for making decisions or solving problems are typically used as shortcuts to simplify complex decision-making processes, allowing educators to arrive at satisfactory solutions efficiently.

In instructional design, heuristics do not guarantee a perfect solution but are useful for making reasonable decisions quickly, especially in situations of uncertainty or complexity.

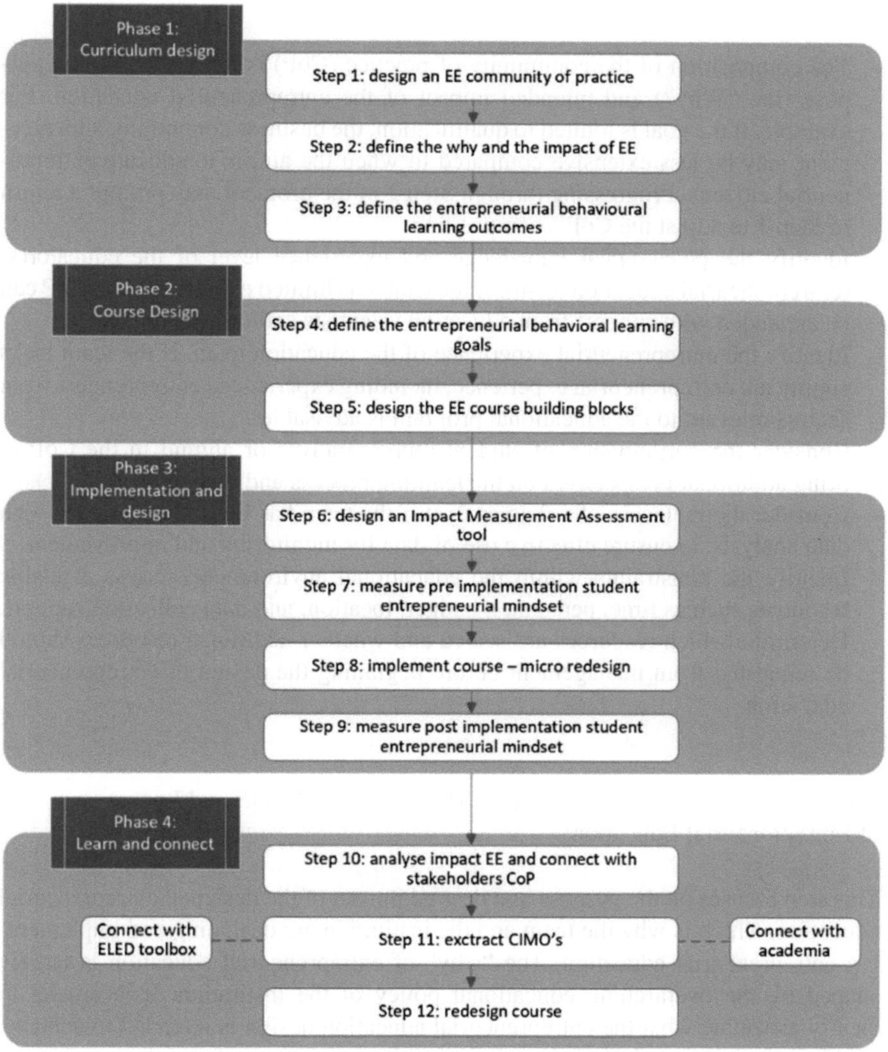

Fig. 5 Flowchart of the ELED protocol

PHASE 1/Step 1: Design an EE Community of Practice

The first step in designing entrepreneurial education is to establish a *community of practice (CoP)*, where various relevant stakeholders collaborate to design, monitor, and improve entrepreneurship education that is scientifically grounded and data-driven. This collaboration facilitates the integration of authentic entrepreneurial learning environments, ensuring educational practices are closely aligned with real-world entrepreneurial contexts.

Heuristics

- The composition of the community of practice (CoP) is influenced by the purpose (the "Why") and intended impact of the entrepreneurial education. For example, if the goal is limited to qualification, the business community's involvement may be less extensive compared to when the aim is to educate entrepreneurial citizens. Progressing through Step 2 of the protocol may prompt a return to Step 1 to adjust the CoP's composition.
- Identify the pedagogical knowledge and experience level of the educator(s) (entrepreneurial education team). If the team has limited experience, the CoP can be expanded with support from education scientists and/or researchers.
- Identify the entrepreneurial experience of the education team. If the team lacks significant entrepreneurial experience, including experienced entrepreneurs from sectors relevant to the educational program is advisable.
- Consider the participation of student representatives or alumni in the CoP to bring additional perspectives on the learning process and outcomes.
- Consider the inclusion of a data analyst if the team has limited experience with data analysis, to ensure effective use of data for monitoring and improvement.
- Identify the constraints within the educational environment. Assess available resources such as time, personnel, budget, location, and data collection support. Determine which resources are scarce and whether additional resources should be requested from management before beginning the design of entrepreneurial education.

PHASE 1/Step 2: Define the Purpose (The Why) and the Desired Impact of Entrepreneurial Education

This step focuses on the purpose and desired impact of the designed entrepreneurial education, which is why the team and the institution are designing and implementing entrepreneurial education. The "why" of entrepreneurial education is largely shaped by the overarching educational policy of the institution. It is crucial to clearly articulate what the entrepreneurial education design is intended to achieve, as this will significantly influence the specific decisions made by the team in the subsequent steps.

Heuristics:

- The team should first examine the overall goals and mission of the educational organization to align entrepreneurial education (EE) accordingly. However, entrepreneurial education can also contribute in a bottom-up manner, influencing and steering the purpose of the educational organization in a certain direction. In this way, the team designing entrepreneurial education can act as a change agent for the organization, serving as a catalyst for broader institutional transformation. This dual approach ensures that EE fits within the existing framework and has the potential to shape and enhance the organization's educational objectives.

Entrepreneurial education serves several overlapping and complementary purposes. The following purposes are possible, but not exhaustive options:

- *Qualification and acquisition of entrepreneurial knowledge and skills.* The entrepreneurial education focuses on stimulating entrepreneurial knowledge, skills, and behavior through entrepreneurial learning, emphasizing acquiring formal qualifications.
- *Becoming an entrepreneurial person.* The entrepreneurial education aims to foster complex entrepreneurial behavior, specifically emphasizing belonging to an entrepreneurial community.
- *Becoming an entrepreneurial citizen.* Here, the focus is on encouraging broad entrepreneurial behavior, referring to the development of an individual as an entrepreneurial citizen—an entrepreneurial individual who acts as a change agent within society, contributing to the resolution of complex societal issues.

- The team should translate the often abstract purpose of entrepreneurial education into measurable outcomes, as this ensures that the impact—the measurable, concrete realization of its purpose—can be evaluated and adjusted as needed. However, in a design-oriented approach, making outcomes measurable does not equate to a hypothesis-testing method, where effectiveness is solely based on measurable results. Instead, space is left for unintended consequences and unplanned learning gains, with this reflective exercise contributing to the design process by anticipating both expected and unforeseen outcomes. The impact can be evaluated at different levels and for various stakeholders. Impact evaluation is a broad concept that refers not only to quantitative but also to qualitative evaluations. In this context, impact measurement refers to the evaluation of the designed entrepreneurial learning (EL) artifact, which was implemented in a specific context for a group of students. While assessment of individual students may form part of this impact evaluation, the concept of evaluation is broader and aligns with the design science approach. Evaluation often combines several of the possible levels outlined below. The impact can be assessed at different levels and for various stakeholders:

  - *Impact on student learning gains.* This level of impact focuses on entrepreneurial learning gains achieved during and after entrepreneurial education.
  - *Impact on complex entrepreneurial behavior in the educational context.* This approach takes a more holistic view by evaluating visible complex entrepreneurial behavior that manifests within authentic environments during the student's educational career. A typical example is the inclusion of student entrepreneurship and startups during the educational career, but other non-venture activities can also indicate entrepreneurial behavior.
  - *Impact on sustainable "in real life" entrepreneurship, change agent behavior, sustainable employment, intrapreneurship, and alumni well-being.* This impact extends the socialization and subjectification objectives, focusing on the outcomes of individual entrepreneurial behavior after graduation. These outcomes can be operationalized as (growth of) entrepreneurship, intrapreneurship, sustainable employment, and alumni well-being. Specific forms of

entrepreneurship, such as social entrepreneurship, or sectoral focuses, such as healthcare, can also be highlighted.

- *Societal level.* This impact refers to realizing sustainable social value or developing entrepreneurial citizens through the "in real life" entrepreneurial behavior of alumni. It can be measured by evaluating the economic and non-economic impact of entrepreneurship, intrapreneurship, sustainable employment, and alumni well-being at different times. For entrepreneurship, operational measures could include survival rates after 5, 10, or more years.

PHASE 1/Step 3: Design the Entrepreneurial Behavioral Learning Outcomes

The entrepreneurial behavioral learning outcomes refer to the observable entrepreneurial behaviors students demonstrate at the end of the designed learning pathway or curriculum. Consequently, these learning outcomes are typically not tied to a single course but span a learning trajectory or curriculum. This approach allows the design of multiple aligned courses that collectively form a learning pathway, where complex entrepreneurial behavior becomes evident at the end of the pathway or curriculum. This enables the development and operationalization of a trajectory from novice to expert across different courses, all working toward a final outcome. If the team is designing a course that is not part of an integrated learning pathway or curriculum, then only the behavioral learning outcomes specific to that course will be formulated. In this case, these outcomes refer to the course's learning objectives, which ideally also focus on observable entrepreneurial behavior. These objectives should encompass the acquisition of both cognitive and noncognitive competencies.

Heuristics:

- Designing entrepreneurial education that leads to entrepreneurial behavior is complex and extends beyond the scope of a single course. Entrepreneurial education is more akin to a marathon than a sprint, as effective entrepreneurial education rarely consists of a single course. This complexity requires the education team to embrace the *concept of a spiral curriculum.* This approach involves breaking down the learning outcomes for the entire curriculum or learning pathway into separate courses, each with its own corresponding learning objectives. As students progress through these courses and achieve the respective objectives, they ultimately work toward a set of learning outcomes that support complex entrepreneurial behavior and transfer learning. The education team translates the entrepreneurial learning outcomes into learning paths and courses. Ultimately, it is within these courses that students acquire the necessary competencies to achieve the entrepreneurial behavioral learning goals. The students' attainment of these learning goals follows a trajectory from novice to expert.
- When designing learning outcomes, it is essential for the team to first reflect on the *primary and secondary knowledge domains* of the entrepreneurial education. The primary knowledge domain refers to the goal of the curricular program or

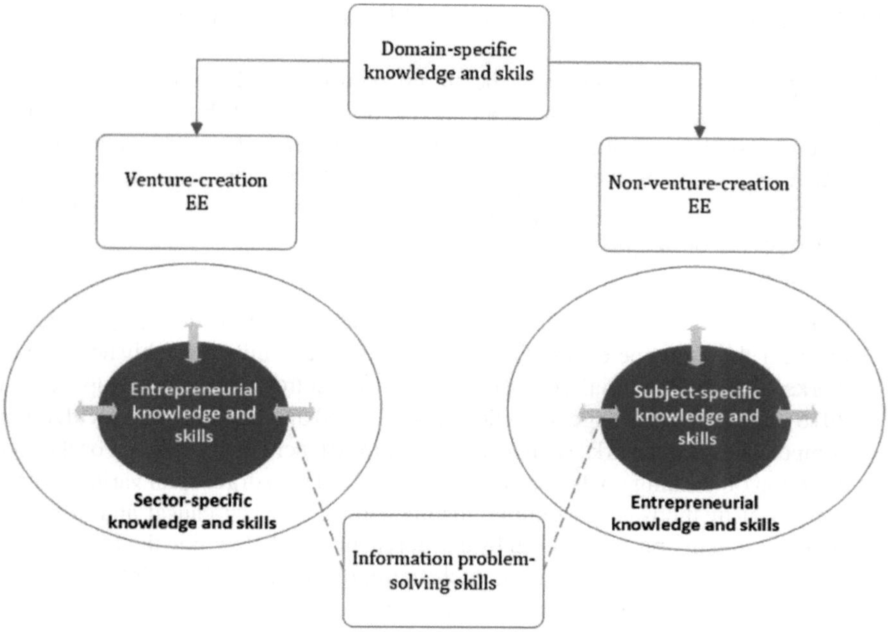

Fig. 6 Primary and secondary knowledge domains within venture and non-venture creation EE

learning pathway and can be divided into two major clusters: *venture creation and non-venture creation* entrepreneurial education. In the first case, the primary objective is to start a venture, meaning that the learning outcomes must be designed to lead toward that goal. This primary knowledge domain can also be further refined, for example, to focus on sustainable and circular entrepreneurship, where students will need to acquire specific learning outcomes tailored to these areas by the end of the program. For non-venture creation entrepreneurial education, the primary knowledge domain is sector-specific. For instance, if the goal is to train nurses who can act as entrepreneurial change agents, the learning outcomes should ensure that graduates are equipped with the necessary skills and knowledge to succeed in that profession. The secondary knowledge domain refers to the entrepreneurial methods, in the sense of "through entrepreneurship." The specified purpose of the entrepreneurial education guides the fine-tuning of the secondary knowledge domain. For venture creation education, the secondary knowledge domain may relate to the specific sector in which the venture is to be established. The link between the primary and secondary knowledge domains is facilitated by *information problem-solving skills*, which must also be integrated into the final learning outcomes (see Fig. 6).

PHASE 2/Step 4: Design the Entrepreneurial Behavioral Learning Goals

This step focuses on the design of the entrepreneurial learning goals at the course level. These learning goals provide a concrete description of the desired behavior, knowledge, skills, and attitudes at a specific proficiency level that students are expected to achieve by the end of the course. Unlike broader learning outcomes, these learning goals are more specific, directly tied to the course, and reflect the intended results of that particular course.

Heuristics:

- Learning goals refer to entrepreneurial competences and the desired proficiency level for these competences. The education team can utilize established frameworks of entrepreneurial competences such as EntreComp (Bacigalupo et al., 2016) and ENTRE-Spiegel (Kyndt & Baert, 2015) and combine them with other competences frameworks such as GreenComp (Bianchi et al., 2022). For the formulation of learning goals, the education team can also draw upon various entrepreneurial methods. For example, distinguishing between causal and effectual decision-making processes used by entrepreneurs can help guide the formulation of learning goals. Incorporating such entrepreneurial methods into the goal-setting process further supports students' progression from novice to expert.
- When formulating learning goals, the team needs to consider the three described lenses, adjusting the emphasis on each lens depending on the context and the purpose of the entrepreneurial education. For example, when working with students at a lower proficiency level, there needs to be a greater focus on learning goals related to the cognitive entrepreneurial lens. This adjustment ensures that the learning goals are aligned with the students' current abilities and the intended outcomes, allowing for a tailored approach that supports their development.
- When formulating the proficiency levels of the entrepreneurial learning goals, the team must create an optimal learning tension. This is achieved by considering the existing proficiency level of the selected competences (the "as is" situation) in relation to the desired learning goals (the "to be" situation). Establishing this balance between the "as is" and "to be" states prevents excessive cognitive load while enabling meaningful learning and progression along the novice-to-expert trajectory. To assess the proficiency level of students' entrepreneurial competences, educators can make a theoretical estimation based on the curriculum when designing the course. Additionally, educators can have students complete an assessment prior to the start of the course to gain deeper insights into their existing proficiency levels.

PHASE 2/Step 5: Design the EE Course Essential Entrepreneurial Building Blocks

This step deals with the design of the essential entrepreneurial building blocks of the course. The team needs to design three crucial building blocks for the course, namely, entrepreneurial learning tasks, entrepreneurial method, and entrepreneurial assessment.

Heuristics:

- These three building blocks are designed in alignment with the learning goals, taking into account the context and, in particular, the proficiency level of the participating students. Ideally, the proficiency level is also reflected in the learning goals. This context and intentionality determine to what extent the team emphasizes certain lenses—the entrepreneurial practice lens, the entrepreneurial cognitive lens, and the complex entrepreneurial motivational lens—and which specific CIMOs are considered during the design process. The CIMOs, by definition, specify which intervention can be used for which context (proficiency level) and desired outcome and are therefore the ideal DNA building blocks that the team can utilize in the concrete construction of the intervention. Working with such CIMOs, as DNA building blocks, also contributes to a meaningful evaluation of the complex designed learning artifact. Instead of relying on broad terms such as challenge-based learning or experiential learning or broad entrepreneurial methods, the DNA components are clearly defined and tailored to the specific context to achieve the intended goal. This approach effectively opens the black box of entrepreneurial education, making the design and implementation processes more transparent and purpose-driven.

PHASE 3/Step 6: Design an EE Impact Evaluation

This step focuses on designing a measurement evaluation instrument to monitor the impact of the entrepreneurial course formulated in Step 2. As discussed, impact can be measured at different levels, and the choice of the measurement level also determines the necessary duration of the longitudinal follow-up of the participating students. The aim of this step is not to assess individual students (which is a separate component of the EE course) but rather to evaluate the impact of entrepreneurial education at the group level. Although evaluation is not synonymous with assessment, evaluation often incorporates assessment data, providing insights into students' learning gains. Therefore, the design of the evaluation is introduced as a step following the design of the assessment. This sequence ensures that the evaluation process not only measures the broader impact of the course but also draws on assessment data to offer a comprehensive understanding of both individual and group-level learning outcomes. This provides the education team with insights into the effectiveness of the EE course and potential areas for improvement.

Monitoring the impact of education can be conducted through various methodological approaches—qualitative, quantitative, or mixed methods. Additionally, the content being monitored, such as entrepreneurial competences or the impact on learning gains, can be assessed in different ways. The choice of methodology will naturally affect the reliability and validity of the impact measurement. Ensuring reliability and validity is essential for drawing meaningful conclusions about the impact and effectiveness of entrepreneurial education.

Heuristics:

- Educators should recognize that the evaluation of entrepreneurial education should not be approached as a "cookbook" method, where only the specific learning goals identified in Step 4 are measured in the impact evaluation instrument. Instead, entrepreneurial education often leads to broader, unanticipated learning gains beyond the predefined learning goals. In the design-oriented approach underlying the developed artifact, it is essential that educators monitor a wide range of potential learning outcomes. As such, it is appropriate to use competence frameworks and adopt a broad perspective on the antecedents of entrepreneurial mindset and behavior.
- Educators must also ensure that the selected competences are operationalized in a reliable and valid manner and then choose an appropriate methodology for data collection. Quantitative, qualitative, and mixed-method approaches can all be considered.
- Additionally, factors such as personality traits and variables like parental entrepreneurship, which may influence entrepreneurial mindset and behavior, should be accounted for. To validly assess the learning gains attributable to education (educational effectiveness), these variables must also be measured.
- Designing such an integrated evaluation methodology requires time, effort, and methodological expertise. For this reason, this approach is best suited for educators working within a community of practice, where data experts are available to support the process.

PHASE 3/Step 7: Verify Whether the Theoretically Anticipated Proficiency Level of the Participating Students Aligns with the Actual Proficiency Levels of the Students in the Course

When designing entrepreneurial education, particularly the essential building blocks, the context—especially the proficiency level of the students—is a critical variable that determines which lenses and CIMOs take precedence in achieving specific outcomes. In education, the design is completed before implementation and the first contact with students. Therefore, it is crucial during the initial interaction with students to assess whether the anticipated proficiency level accurately reflects reality.

Evaluating the proficiency level is important not only at the group level—since education is generally designed for a cohort of students—but also at the individual student level. This assessment allows each participating student to gain insight into their own proficiency level, enabling them to make individualized adjustments within tolerance limits to the essential building blocks or undertake additional actions. For example, students with a lower-than-expected proficiency level may need to review supplementary learning materials before engaging in the planned activities and methods. Conversely, students with a higher proficiency level can set additional, more complex learning goals and take on extra activities. This approach introduces personalized learning within standard educational frameworks.

When the proficiency level significantly deviates from expectations, beyond acceptable tolerance limits, the student, in consultation with the educator, may decide that a different course would be more suitable.

Heuristics:

- The team has several options for estimating the proficiency level. They can use the designed assessment methodology, but a broader approach can also be employed, such as measuring the entrepreneurial mindset, which extends beyond the exclusive assessment of entrepreneurial competencies. It is essential that the team uses validated instruments as much as possible, and when using self-designed instruments, the validity and reliability must be rigorously tested.
- Clearly communicate the rationale for impact measurement and how the results will contribute to both more effective current and future entrepreneurial education and help students understand their entrepreneurial strengths and weaknesses so they can identify personal learning goals.

PHASE 3/Step 8: Implement Course and Micro-redesign

This step addresses the implementation of the designed course, ensuring that students actively engage with the entrepreneurial education learning tasks, methods, and assessments. Due to the nature of entrepreneurial education, as embedded in the proposed design principles, students participate in a highly interactive manner as part of a social system involving fellow students, teachers, and entrepreneurs. As a result, the implemented course becomes a dynamic, living system. Consequently, educators must anticipate the need for micro-redesign during the course to achieve the predefined entrepreneurial learning goals and realize impact.

Heuristics:

- The design of formative assessment is an ideal methodology to quickly track during implementation whether the planned learning artifact is achieving its intended outcomes. Formative feedback, as designed in Step 5, is crucial for facilitating micro-redesign at both the individual student level and the group level. It is essential that the education team not only plans for this iterative process but also ensures its qualitative execution throughout the course.
- This formative feedback is a two-way process, in which the educational team may need to (re)design additional learning tasks to achieve the desired learning activities and learning goals. The process of formative feedback and deep reflec-

tion can be supported by digital learning platforms and/or web-based tools or apps. LoopMe, as discussed in Chapter "From EntreComp to EntreAct: 16 Validated Design Principles for Making People More Entrepreneurial" of this book, is one such platform, developed for scientific purposes by the company MeAnalytics. Users can access the platform via an app on their smartphone or tablet or through the web. The LoopMe app not only supports the design of learning tasks but can also be used as a tool for data collection, analysis, and formative feedback.
- The implementation phase concludes with the assessment of the course unit, as designed in Step 5.

PHASE 3/Step 9: Execute the Planned Entrepreneurial Education (EE) Impact Evaluation

This step ensures that the planned evaluation measurement from Step 6 is effectively executed and that data is collected and analyzed. The impact of entrepreneurial education can only be meaningfully analyzed in Step 10 if data is collected in a reliable and valid manner. When conducting an evaluation, having pre-measurements—data collected before the course begins—is particularly valuable for analysis. Therefore, assessing the proficiency level of the participating students at the start of the course can be especially useful for collecting this data.

Heuristics:

- When collecting the quantitative data by means of self-assessment questionnaires, it is important to clearly communicate the rationale for the second measurement and how the results will contribute to both more effective current and future entrepreneurial education.
- It is valuable not only to collect quantitative data but also to incorporate qualitative data, as this allows for the identification of unintended consequences of the learning artifact. As mentioned, a design-oriented approach is not focused on hypothesis testing; rather, the goal is to evaluate the designed artifact. In this process, unplanned learning effects also play a crucial role.
- The qualitative data can be extracted from the digital learning platforms or web-based tools and apps, or, if educators do not use these tools, they can hold post-implementation impact interviews with students.
- Evaluation not only encompasses short-term impact effects but also, by definition, takes into account elements that become visible over time. This means that the team must consider establishing monitoring systems capable of collecting longitudinal data over several years. Such systems enable tracking the long-term impact of entrepreneurial education on alumni, allowing for a comprehensive evaluation of its effects over an extended period.
- The team can assess both the learning gains and the value added (VA). VA indicates how much more or less learning gain was achieved than could be expected, based on the individual background characteristics of the students. Learning

gains can be evaluated for constructs such as the entrepreneurial mindset and can also be broken down into the various dimensions of this construct. Additionally, the progression of intentions to engage in entrepreneurial behavior, as well as constructs such as entrepreneurial flow, can be analyzed.
- The education team may also analyze longitudinal data to track startup and survival rates of ventures, though this data spans several months to years, compared to the more immediate data reflecting learning gains.

PHASE 4/Step 10: Connect with Stakeholders' CoP and Discuss the Evaluation Results

Within the community of practice, different participating educators (or teams of educators) can design various courses, allowing for the comparison of results with those of colleagues. In this comparison, the specific contexts and intentionalities of the different courses are taken into account. This approach provides an opportunity to discuss and compare their own results, fostering social learning and generating additional insights.

In the design-oriented approach of the ELED protocol, the use of data and statistical analysis is not intended to test or reject hypotheses, but rather to facilitate learning from each other and to pose further questions to the scientific community or various stakeholders in the community.

Instead, the use of data helps prevent biases from educators and their epistemological beliefs from dominating the analysis of the impact of entrepreneurial education (EE). The objective is to make a valid evaluation of the impact of the artifact within a specific context and intentionality.

PHASE 4/Step 11: Extract Practice-Based CIMOs (Design Principles)

Consistent with the design-oriented underpinning of the ELED protocol, the education team inductively extracts design principles based on their analyses and decisions from Step 10. These design principles are articulated in CIMO format: In Context X, Intervention Y will lead to Outcome Z. The Mechanism (M) in CIMO explains why the educational intervention in the specific context (C) leads to the desired outcome (Z).

Heuristics:

- The CIMOs extracted by different education teams are gathered into a "toolbox" that fellow educators can consult when designing entrepreneurial education. By doing so, the effectiveness of entrepreneurial education is enhanced in a data-driven, design-oriented way. Following these steps also contributes to the professional development of novice entrepreneurial education educators.
- During this step, it is also possible to engage with the academic community if the education team has questions or comments requiring further academic input or

study. This connection offers an opportunity for the academic community to apply significant research findings in practice through the formulation of CIMOs, making them available to the educational team.

PHASE 4/Step 12: Redesign the course

Based on the analysis and discussion of the results of the impact measurement in Step 10 and the extraction of CIMOs in Step 11, the education team, together with the stakeholders of the community of practice (CoP), can decide whether to redesign the course or, if necessary, the learning path or curriculum.

Heuristics:

- If the team decides to maintain the goals, impacts, and learning outcomes, then only the course is redesigned. This redesign process begins in Step 5.
- If the team decides to also change the goals, behavioral learning outcomes, and impacts, the redesign process starts in Step 2. In this case, the related curriculum is also implicitly modified (unless the course is not embedded within a curriculum).
- The team may also opt to critically re-evaluate and adapt the ELED protocol before redesigning the course or curriculum.

4.4 Layer 3 EEM: The Toolbox

The toolbox contains all operational concepts, frameworks such as specific entrepreneurial competency models, entrepreneurial methods, and CIMOs that can be utilized by the team during the various steps of the process. As previously mentioned, the contents of the toolbox are primarily determined by the team designing the entrepreneurial education. Unlike other instructional design models for entrepreneurial education, no specific epistemological stance is adopted. This toolbox should therefore be regarded as an evolving system that receives input from both practice and science. As new insights, methods, and frameworks emerge from both practical applications and academic research, the toolbox is continuously updated and refined, ensuring it remains relevant and effective for designing entrepreneurial education. The Appendix includes research-based entrepreneurial learning CIMOs that can be used as resources.

5 Discussion and the Way Forward

Embedded in the design research methodology, an artifact, *the entrepreneurial education method (EEM)*, was designed to support educators in making instructional design decisions that lead to the design of contextualized courses and curricula that stimulate students' entrepreneurial learning and enhance their capacity to engage in entrepreneurial behavior.

Building on Mansoori's definition of entrepreneurial methods (2017), the entrepreneurial education method (EEM) is defined as a set of entrepreneurial education principles and guidelines that aim to guide the behavior of the EE educator by providing strategies to support instructional design (ID) judgment. This three-layered, nested Matryoshka doll design of the EEM method, with layers two and three containing multiple sub-designs, ensures that both expert and novice educators can use the artifact to design entrepreneurial education for different purposes.

The EEM can be regarded as a generic artifact, enabling the integration of existing entrepreneurial competency frameworks, such as EntreComp (Bacigalupo et al., 2016), and/or entrepreneurial methods. The focus of the EEM is not to develop or prioritize a single set of entrepreneurial competencies that are then activated one by one. Rather, it focuses on the design of artifacts that ultimately stimulate entrepreneurial behavioral change, a complex phenomenon requiring the simultaneous stimulation of various competencies in a way tailored to the specific context (Van Merriënboer & Sweller, 2005). Furthermore, entrepreneurial behavior aimed at shaping change agents involves competencies that may not be explicitly included in existing entrepreneurial frameworks, such as green or digital competencies. In a rapidly changing environment, key competencies—such as those related to artificial intelligence—may also play a significant role. As a result, the EEM takes a broad, eclectic approach, focusing on entrepreneurial behavior while allowing for flexibility in the competencies it engages, adapting to emerging needs and contexts.

The EEM neither adopts a specific epistemological stance, thereby facilitating a shift in the well-known debate in the entrepreneurial education field between "innovative" and "traditional" approaches. Instead, it moves toward a data-driven, design-oriented approach, employing the appropriate entrepreneurial educational method at the right time.

The data-driven monitoring of the evaluation of the designed entrepreneurial education artifacts by the teams is an important and explicit component of the EEM. It is particularly operationalized at various steps in the ELED protocol. This addresses a widespread call in the entrepreneurship education literature and practice for more data-driven approaches to tracking the impact of entrepreneurial education. In an "Entrepreneurship Education Manifesto," Krueger (2021) emphasizes, based on the EPIC project and scientific literature, the importance for educators to "triangulate" various metrics they use (p. 25), with a particular focus on measuring learning progress. The significance of data-driven support for practice is also mirrored in the growing research attention in the field. However, two critical concerns can be raised regarding the potential risks associated with improperly using this data-driven approach.

The first concern relates to the design-oriented paradigm within which this data-driven approach is embedded. There is a risk that it could shift toward a hypothesis-testing paradigm, which would undermine the core principles of the EEM. The fundamental objective of this data-driven approach is to support educators in both the design and evaluation of entrepreneurial education while also providing students with tools to develop a data-driven understanding of their entrepreneurial learning. This enables students to take ownership of their learning, contributing to "assessment as learning" (Dann, 2014), benefiting both students and educators. Moreover, the data-driven approach of the EEM artifact ensures that innovative entrepreneurial education methodologies can be designed, implemented, and evaluated inductively in the complexities of practice, further promoting design-oriented educational research.

A second concern relates to reducing a data-driven approach to merely conducting quantitative pre- and post-course questionnaires aimed at measuring entrepreneurial competencies or mindset. As mentioned, such a reductionist approach is not what the data-driven approach in the ELED protocol advocates. On the contrary, it emphasizes a balanced approach where qualitative data collected throughout the learning process, as part of "assessment for learning" (Dann, 2014), is equally important. In this regard, the ELED protocol explicitly highlights tools like the LoopMe app. As presented in chapter "From EntreComp to EntreAct: 16 Validated Design Principles for Making People More Entrepreneurial" of this book, Martin Lackéus' (2020) work on developing LoopMe as an innovative form of experience sampling methodology in entrepreneurial education is a particularly valuable research direction for introducing and further evaluating the data-driven EEM.

The data-driven monitoring of the impact of the designed entrepreneurial education emerged as a key issue during the ex ante and alpha test interviews conducted while designing the EEM artifact. However, it is perceived as a particularly challenging task. Specifically, educators noted two main difficulties: first, the lack of useful measurement instruments, and second, the labor-intensive nature of data collection and processing.

In addition to the data-driven approach, the nested structure of the EEM that supports the design of entrepreneurial education, as revealed by the alpha test results, contributes to the perceived complexity of the artifact among educators who are expected to use it. The educators who participated in the alpha test highlighted the challenge of balancing the complexity of the artifact, which arises from the need to strike a balance between scientifically informed soundness, supporting a holistic approach, and the usability of the artifact.

Both elements of this equilibrium influence educators' ability to design effective entrepreneurial education. An increase in scientific underpinnings and holistic approaches within the artifact may lead to a perceived decrease in usability for educators. Educators who perceive usability as low, or anticipate that using the artifact will require significant effort, are less likely to implement it in the practical, everyday context. On the other hand, enhancing usability by reducing the artifact's holistic nature and scientific rigor may encourage greater adoption by educators. Still, it could also increase the risk that, despite its use, the artifact will not effectively contribute to supporting educators. This is a particular concern because a scientifically grounded and holistic artifact that is not, or cannot be, effectively used by educators due to its complexity will not address the challenges in the field.

Although a community of practice was initially incorporated into the artifact, based on the alpha test results, it was defined as *an inclusion criterion* for using the EEM. This practice community helps manage the tension between a holistic approach and high usability. Furthermore, the alpha test introduced an additional inclusion criterion, emphasizing the need for contextual structural support from higher management and leadership for professionals. Further research into the organizational (pre)conditions necessary for implementing a community of practice and the leadership requirements of educational management could provide valuable insights for the broader implementation of the EEM.

The designed EEM artifact also implicitly offers a way to reconcile different approaches to using design science methodology within the entrepreneurial education research field, allowing for comparing and enriching accumulated design science knowledge. The EEM artifact consists of the content component and the EEM skeleton, within which the content component is incorporated.

As described in this article, the EEM builds on the work of Mansoori (2017) who introduced the overarching model of "entrepreneurial methods" (EM) to cross-reference prescriptive entrepreneurial theories that aim to change the behavior of entrepreneurs (see Fig. 7).

The *logical level* within this EM artifact includes the overarching theoretical and epistemological rationale guiding the entrepreneurial process, and entrepreneurial actions are embedded at this level, revealing the path dependency within entrepreneurial models. The *model level* includes the specific entrepreneurial actions,

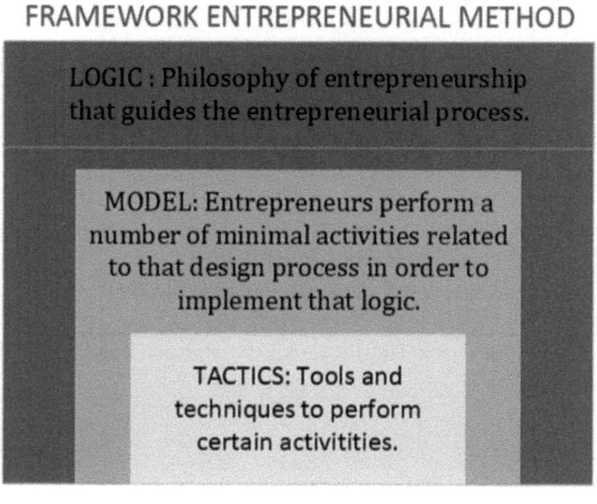

Fig. 7 Framework entrepreneurial method. Note. From Entrepreneurial methods as vehicles of entrepreneurial action [Doctoral dissertation], by Mansoori, 2017, Chalmers University of Technology (https://doi.org/10.13140/RG.2.2.30625.51040). Copyright 2017 by Y. Mansoori

arranged in a logical order, that are necessary to operationalize and implement the logic of the entrepreneurial method. The model serves a crucial bridging function between the logic and *tactics levels*, which refers to the collection of techniques and tools designed to facilitate and catalyze the various stages of the entrepreneurial process.

Adapting the EM artifact from the domain of entrepreneurship to the EEM in entrepreneurial education can be highly relevant for researchers using the DSR methodology, as the three-layered skeleton provides a structured approach for comparing designed entrepreneurial educational artifacts focusing on changing the behavior of educators by researchers. The adaptation is particularly valuable, as epistemological embeddedness in entrepreneurial education directly influences the practical implementation of concrete actions by the educators or those recommended by prescriptive theories. As described in chapter "The Entrepreneurial Education Canvas", Baggen and colleagues have also developed design principles similar to those in this article, subsequently creating a canvas with references to tools. This suggests that Baggen and colleagues' work could also be embedded within the EEM skeleton structure.

By using the EEM skeleton in the same way Mansoori (2017) applied it to entrepreneurial methods aimed at influencing the behavior of entrepreneurs, artifacts designed to influence the behavior of educators can be compared. This approach creates opportunities for the design of new artifacts through *bricolage*. This exercise emerged spontaneously during the writing of this book, leading to the proposal of a new integrated entrepreneurial learning canvas presented in the final chapter "Moving Design Science Research and Practice in Entrepreneurial Education Forward" (Tables 4, 5, 6, 7, 8, 9, 10, 11, 12, 13, 14, 15, 16, 17, 18, and 19).

Appendix

Table 4 EL-CIMO 1

In educational contexts (C) characterized by venture- or non-venture-creating EE in higher education **in order to** effectively stimulate entrepreneurial learning and the resulting growth toward expert entrepreneurial behavior **(O)**:
I1: Approach entrepreneurial learning from a complex cognitive learning lens involving complex cognitive entrepreneurial skills **(I)**
That invoke particular **generative mechanism (M):**
M1: See Gielnik et al. (2015, 2017); Karlsson and Moberg (2013); Shepherd and DeTienne (2005); Rauch and Hulsink (2015); Atmojo and Ragil (2020); Sánchez (2011, 2013); Souitaris et al. (2007)

Table 5 EL-CIMO 2

In educational contexts (C) characterized by novice learners with low entrepreneurial prior knowledge, skills, and venture EE **in order to** optimize (stimulate) complex cognitive learning **(O)**:
I1: Determine the set of entrepreneurial constituent skills and subskills (including (prior) knowledge) as a partial or whole venture creation process relevant to achieving the learning objectives of the particular entrepreneurial course by using entrepreneurial methods
I2: Measure the determined set of entrepreneurial skills (and prior knowledge) before the start of the course, and communicate to the participating students
I3: Stimulate participating student's regulation ability through the formulation of personal learning objectives based on their pre-measurement results and the predetermined overall learning goals
I4: Translate the set of entrepreneurial skills and subskills into a sequence of authentic entrepreneurial learning tasks that form the backbone of the activity-based venture creation EE course
I5: Stimulate shared control of selecting the authentic learning tasks, and ensure a balance between what is imposed on the program in terms of learning tasks (and therefore also learning objectives) and the possibilities of the student to have partial control. For novices the partial control is limited
I6: Integrate learning tasks that stimulate information problem-solving skills into the backbone of entrepreneurial learning tasks
I7: Ensure a high degree of scaffolding of entrepreneurial supportive and procedural information
I8: Ensure a high degree of scaffolding of sector-specific entrepreneurial information
That invoke particular **generative mechanism (M):**
M1: See Van Merriënboer and Sweller (2005); Brand-Gruwel and Wopereis (2006)
M2: See Sweller et al. (2019)
M3: See Paas et al. (2005)
M4: See Van Merriënboer and Sweller (2005); Brand-Gruwel and Wopereis (2006)
M5: See Corbalan et al. (2008)
M6: See Brand-Gruwel and Wopereis (2006)
M7: See Van Merriënboer and Sweller (2005)
M8: See Shepherd and Patzelt (2018)

Table 6 EL-CIMO 3

In educational contexts (C) characterized by expert learners with high knowledge, skills, and venture EE **in order to** optimize (stimulate) complex cognitive learning **(O)**:
I1: Determine the set of entrepreneurial constituent skills and subskills as a whole venture creation process relevant to achieving the venture creation learning goals of the particular entrepreneurial course by using entrepreneurial competence frameworks or entrepreneurial methods
I2: Measure the determined set of entrepreneurial skills (and prior knowledge) before the start of the course, and communicate to the participating students
I3: Stimulate participating student's regulation ability through the formulation of personal learning objectives based on their pre-measurement results and the predetermined overall learning goals
I4: Translate the set of entrepreneurial skills and subskills into a sequence of authentic entrepreneurial learning tasks that form the backbone of the activity-based venture creation EE course
I5: Stimulate shared control of selecting the authentic entrepreneurial learning tasks, and ensure a balance between what is imposed on the program in terms of learning tasks (and therefore also learning objectives) and the possibilities of the student to have partial control. For experts the partial control is high
I6: No scaffolding of sector-specific entrepreneurial information
I7: No scaffolding of entrepreneurial supportive and procedural information
That invoke particular **generative mechanism (M):**
M1: See Van Merriënboer and Sweller (2005); Brand-Gruwel and Wopereis (2006)
M2: See Sweller et al. (2019)
M3: See Paas et al. (2005)
M4: See Van Merriënboer and Sweller (2005); Brand-Gruwel and Wopereis (2006)
M5: See Corbalan et al. (2008)
M6: See Shepherd & Patzelt, 2018
M7: See Van Merriënboer and Sweller (2005); Kalyuga et al. (2003)

Table 7 EL-CIMO 4

In educational contexts (C) characterized by novice learners with low prior knowledge or skills and non-venture EE **in order to** optimize (stimulate) complex cognitive learning **(O)**:
I1: Take a subject-specificity position, and determine the backbone of entrepreneurial constituent skills and authentic learning tasks relevant to achieving the learning goals of the particular subject-specific course by using entrepreneurial competence models or entrepreneurial methods
I2: Integrate or translate the authentic entrepreneurial learning tasks into the backbone of the subject-specific learning tasks
I3: Measure the determined set of entrepreneurial skills (and prior knowledge) before the start of the course, and communicate to the participating students
I4: Stimulate participating student's regulation ability through the formulation of entrepreneurial personal learning objectives based on the pre-measurement results and the predetermined overall learning goals
I5: Stimulate shared control of selecting the authentic entrepreneurial learning tasks, and ensure a balance between what is imposed on the program in terms of learning tasks (and therefore also learning objectives) and the possibilities of the student to have partial control. For novices the partial control is limited
I6: Integrate authentic learning tasks that stimulate information problem-solving skills into the backbone of subject-specific learning tasks
I7: Ensure a high degree of scaffolding of entrepreneurial supportive and procedural knowledge
I8: Ensure a high degree of scaffolding of subject specific knowledge
That invoke particular **generative mechanism (M):**
M1: See Brand-Gruwel and Wopereis (2006)
M2: See Brand-Gruwel and Wopereis (2006)
M3: See Corbalan et al. (2008)
M4: See Van Merriënboer and Sweller (2005); Brand-Gruwel and Wopereis (2006)
M5: See Corbalan et al. (2008)
M6: See Brand-Gruwel and Wopereis (2006)
M7: See Van Merriënboer and Sweller (2005)
M8: See Van Merriënboer and Sweller (2005)

Table 8 EL-CIMO 5

In educational contexts (C) characterized by expert learners with high prior knowledge or skills and non-venture EE **in order to** optimize (stimulate) complex cognitive learning **(O)**:
I1: Take a subject-specificity position, and determine the backbone of entrepreneurial constituent skills and authentic learning tasks relevant to achieving the learning objectives of the particular subject-specific course by using entrepreneurial competence models or entrepreneurial methods
I2: Integrate or translate the authentic entrepreneurial learning tasks into the backbone of the subject-specific learning tasks
I3: Measure the determined set of entrepreneurial skills (and prior knowledge) before the start of the course and communicate to the participating students
I4: Stimulate participating student's regulation ability through the formulation of entrepreneurial personal learning objectives based on the pre-measurement results and the predetermined overall learning goals
I5: Stimulate shared control of selecting the authentic entrepreneurial learning tasks, and ensure a balance between what is imposed on the program in terms of learning tasks (and therefore also learning objectives) and the possibilities of the student to have partial control. For experts the partial control is high
I6: No scaffolding of entrepreneurial supportive and procedural information
I7: No scaffolding of subject specific information
That invoke particular **generative mechanism (M):**
M1: See Brand-Gruwel and Wopereis (2006)
M2: See Brand-Gruwel and Wopereis (2006)
M3: See Corbalan et al. (2008)
M4: See van Merriënboer and Kirschner (2007); Brand-Gruwel and Wopereis (2006)
M5: See Corbalan et al. (2008)
M6: See Van Merriënboer and Sweller (2005)
M7: See Van Merriënboer and Sweller (2005)

Table 9 EL-CIMO 6

In educational contexts (C) characterized by venture- or non-venture-creating EE in higher education **in order to** effectively stimulate entrepreneurial learning and the resulting growth toward expert entrepreneurial behavior **(O)**:
I1: Approach entrepreneurial learning from a complex motivational lens **(I)** through stimulating: – I11: Cognitive entrepreneurial learning – I12: Entrepreneurial goal choice and goal striving – I13: Entrepreneurial passion and flow – I14: Entrepreneurial self-efficacy – I15: Self-regulated entrepreneurial learning – I16: Socio-emotional regulation – I17: Cognitive adaptability
That invoke particular **generative mechanism (M):**
M1: – I11: See Panadero (2017) – I12: See Collewaert et al. (2016) – I13: See Cardon and Kirk (2015); D'Intino et al. (2007); Yen and Lin (2020) – I14: See Gielnik et al. (2015); Gielnik et al. (2017) – I15: See Mets et al. (2021); Payne and Jesiek (2018); Zimmerman (2002, 2013); Winkler et al. (2021) – I16: See Lobczowski et al. (2021) – I17: See Haynie et al. (2012); Haynie et al. (2010) – I18: See Panadero (2017)

Table 10 EL-CIMO 7

In educational contexts (C) characterized by venture- or non-venture-creating EE in higher education **in order to** effectively stimulate entrepreneurial goal choice and goal striving **(O)**:
I1: Stimulate entrepreneurial goal choice by supporting students in understanding their preferred "object of entrepreneurial passion" or entrepreneurial domain and their preferred entrepreneurial role
I2: Stimulate entrepreneurial goal choice by explicitly explaining the concept of "entrepreneurial identity" to novice students
I3: Encourage goal striving by developing learning strategies that: – I31: Stimulate entrepreneurial passion and flow – I32: Stimulate entrepreneurial self-efficacy – I33: Stimulate entrepreneurial self-regulated learning and deliberate practice – I34: Stimulate cognitive adaptability – I35: Use authentic entrepreneurial learning environments
That invoke particular **generative mechanism (M):**
M1: See Cardon et al. (2017); Murnieks et al. (2020)
M2: See Murnieks et al. (2020)
M3: – I31: See Cardon and Kirk (2015); D'Intino et al. (2007); Yen and Lin (2020) – I32: See Gielnik et al. (2015); Gielnik et al. (2017) – I33: See Mets et al. (2021); Payne and Jesiek (2018); Zimmerman (2002, 2013); Winkler et al. (2021) – I34: See Haynie et al. (2012); Haynie et al. (2010) – I35: See Panadero (2017)

Table 11 EL-CIMO 8

In educational contexts (C) characterized by venture- or non-venture-creating EE in higher education **in order to** effectively stimulate entrepreneurial passion and flow **(O)**:
I1: Support students in understanding their preferred "object of entrepreneurial passion" or entrepreneurial domain and their preferred entrepreneurial role
I2: Explicitly explain the concept of "entrepreneurial identity" to novice students
I3: When designing educational interventions, take into account the within-person variability of benefits and passion, and ensure entrepreneurial flow by: – I31: Stretching existing skills but not insurmountable – I32: Ensure the formulation of proximal objectives and clear feedback – I33: Stimulate deep reflection by the student with regard to critical experiences – I34: Stimulate self-regulated learning within student teams – I35: Stimulate deliberate practice
That invoke particular **generative mechanism (M):**
M1: See Cardon et al. (2017); Murnieks et al. (2020)
M2: See Murnieks et al. (2020); Donnellon et al. (2014)
M3: See Collewaert et al. (2016); D'Intino et al. (2007) – I31: See Nakamura and Csikszentmihalyi (2003) – I32: See Nakamura and Csikszentmihalyi (2003) – I33: See Cope (2005) – I34: See van den Hout (2016) – I35: See Panadero (2017)

Table 12 EL-CIMO 9

In educational contexts (C) characterized by venture- or non-venture-creating EE in higher education **in order to** effectively stimulate entrepreneurial self-efficacy **(O)**:
I1: Support students in active mastery by designing part-task entrepreneurial practice or deliberate practice for novice students. Provide sufficient feedback from educators on these entrepreneurial practices (see EL-CIMOs 19 and 20)
I2: Design gender-sensitive peer mentoring with perceived similarities with the mentor. Target mentorship programs primarily to students who score low on "learning goal orientation"
I3: When designing activity-based entrepreneurial practice (both in real life and by using simulation-based learning interventions), it is important to pay attention to the challenge skill balance that creates an entrepreneurial flow
I4: Make sure expert students do not experience a reversal effect by giving too much feedback. For expert students, a self-regulated experiential practice can be designed
I5: When designing educational interventions for novices, apply a combination of the following four self-efficacy building strategies: – I51: Implement anxiety coping mechanism before or at the start of the course – I52: Implement expert modelling examples – I53: Implement mastery experience strategy (see I1) – I54: Implement effort feedback at the end of each practice session
That invoke particular **generative mechanism (M):**
M1: See Wood and Bandura (1989)
M2: See Elliott et al. (2020); St-Jean et al. (2018)
M3: See Yen and Lin (2020)
M4: See St-Jean et al. (2018)
M5: See Huang et al. (2020)

Table 13 EL-CIMO 10

In educational contexts (C) characterized by venture- or non-venture-creating EE in higher education **in order to** effectively stimulate self-regulated entrepreneurial learning **(O)**:
I1: Design SRL strategies as a growth trajectory from novice to expert self-regulated learning, depending on students' current level of self-regulation. For novices this means observation and emulation as a level of regulation and for experts, self-control and self-regulation
I2: Design SRL strategies aligned with the strategies used in designing entrepreneurial learning through a complex cognitive lens. – I21: For novices, process-related learning tasks stimulating observation or emulation can be introduced into the backbone of content-related learning tasks (stimulating cognitive learning) – I22: For experts, process-related authentic learning tasks that stimulate self-control or self-regulation can be introduced into the backbone of content-related learning tasks (that stimulate cognitive learning) – I23: For experts, it is also possible to use more abstract content-related authentic learning tasks and switch to a problem-solving pedagogy

(continued)

Table 13 (continued)

<u>I3</u>: Support the growth path from novice to expert self-regulated learner by designing an entrepreneurial deliberate practice learning environment (see EL-CIMO 19). During deliberate practice, provide sufficient scaffolding of the following SRL strategies: – I31: Support students in setting personal learning goals – I32: Inform students of possible learning strategies they can employ: • Imagery: refers to the creation of distal future images that can support motivation and performance • Task strategies: refers to such things as breaking down complex tasks into smaller, more manageable components. It also refers to using a variety of decision-making support tools. Risk management strategies that visualize possible pitfalls and risks and develop scenarios can also be considered as a touch strategy • Volitional strategies: set of strategies that support motivation and perseverance • Attention focus strategies: a set of strategies that help students to stay focused on the tasks at hand • Self-instruction strategies: a set of strategies that help students to find information autonomously (see also "information problem-solving skills") • Find help strategies: a set of strategies that help students to seek help and support from educators, peers, coaches, and stakeholders – I33: Support students' self-efficacy – I34: Link a forethought phase to deliberate practice in which students take action in an authentic entrepreneurial learning environment – I35: Encourage students to reflect on their performance while performing their task – I36: Encourage students to reflect on the need to employ new strategies when circumstances change – I37: Inform students of possible learning strategies they can employ to support self-control: • Imagery: refers to the creation of distal future images that can support motivation and performance • Volitional strategies: set of strategies that support motivation and perseverance – I38: Encourage students to engage in self-evaluation at the end of the task where performance is measured against the stated objectives. Learning protocols in order to facilitate this reflection and monitoring. Those learning protocols or diaries encourage students to report their progress and applications of SRL strategies – I39: Encourage students to reflect on the need to employ new strategies when circumstances change – I310: Encourage students to assign correct, objective attributions and causal links to the outcomes after the self-assessment – I311: Encourage students' learning effect by facilitating learning from failure or success and reflecting on changing their predetermined goals, strategies, mental models, and heuristics that were used – I312: Encourage students to celebrate successes – I313: Encourage students to "unlearn" strategies, heuristics, and mental models by proposing new strategies, heuristics, and mental models to test in a new SRL cycle
That invoke particular **generative mechanism (M):**
<u>M1:</u> See Zimmerman (2013)
<u>M2</u>: See Zimmerman (2013); Holcomb et al. (2009)
<u>M3</u>: See Zimmerman (2002, 2013); Winkler et al. (2021); Theobald (2021)

Table 14 EL-CIMO 11

In educational contexts (C) characterized by venture- or non-venture-creating EE in higher education **in order to** effectively stimulate socio-emotional regulation **(O)**:
I1: Support students in their socio-emotional regulation by explicitly informing them of the importance of using the following possible regulatory strategies: – Behavioral regulation strategies (e.g., being by yourself, going for a walk) – Interpersonal regulation strategies (e.g., encouraging others, offering to help, providing relief) – Cognitive regulation strategies (e.g., correcting misunderstanding, finding information) – Motivational regulation strategies (e.g., breaking down the problem, prioritizing) – Motivational/cognition strategies (e.g., delegating to future self, focusing on the future)
I2: In particular, as an educator, support groups of students who score low on emotional experiences, and monitor the use of regulation strategies
That invoke particular **generative mechanism (M):**
M1: See Lobczowski et al. (2021)
M2: See Lobczowski et al. (2021)

Table 15 EL-CIMO 12

In educational contexts (C) characterized by venture- or non-venture-creating EE in higher education **in order to** effectively stimulate cognitive adaptability **(O)**:
I1: Explicitly explain the concept and the importance of "cognitive adaptability" to novice students
I2: When designing activity-based entrepreneurial practice (both in real life and by using simulation-based learning interventions), it is important to pay attention to incorporating tasks or challenges that require students to make decisions outside their comfort zone
I3: When designing educational interventions, provide ample opportunity for feedback when students are faced with tasks or challenges that elicit strong emotional responses I31: Provide plenty of cognitive-based feedback, especially for expert students I33: For novices also provide outcome-based feedback
I4: Explicitly teach novice students entrepreneurial metacognitive learning strategies, including how to plan, monitor, and evaluate their entrepreneurial learning (see EL-CIMO 12)
I5: Promote and develop metacognitive talk in the authentic learning environment
I6: Model your own entrepreneurial thinking (or ask an entrepreneur if no expertise) to help students develop their entrepreneurial metacognitive skills
That invoke particular **generative mechanism (M):**
M1: See Quigley et al. (2018); Haynie et al. (2010)
M2: See Haynie et al. (2012)
M3: See Haynie et al. (2012)
M4: See Quigley et al. (2018)
M5: See Quigley et al. (2018)
M6: See Quigley et al. (2018)

Table 16 EL-CIMO 13

In educational contexts (C) characterized by venture- or non-venture-creating EE in higher education **in order to** effectively stimulate entrepreneurial learning and the resulting growth toward expert entrepreneurial behavior **(O)**:
I1: Approach entrepreneurial learning from an entrepreneurial practice lens **(I)** through designing: – I11: Part-task entrepreneurial practice for novice students – I12: Deliberate practice for novice and intermediate students – I13: Self-regulated experiential practice for expert students
That invoke particular **generative mechanism (M):**
M1: See Kozlinska et al. (2020); Ranabahu and Barrett (2020) – I11: Van Merriënboer and Sweller (2005) – I12: See Baron and Henry (2010); Anders Ericsson and Harwell (2019); Ucbasaran et al. (2009); Unger et al. (2009) – I13: See Park et al. (2019)

Table 17 EL-CIMO 14

In educational contexts (C) characterized by venture- or non-venture-creating EE in higher education for novice students with no prior knowledge **in order to** effectively design part-task entrepreneurial practice **(O)**:
I1: Connect the design of part-task practice to the EL-CIMOs of the cognitive lens, and design a backbone of authentic recurring entrepreneurial learning tasks aimed at acquiring domain-specific knowledge and automating primarily procedural entrepreneurial knowledge
I2: Take a more "educator-centered approach," meaning both the learning goals and the learning tasks are mainly designed by the educator, as is adequate scaffolding
I3: Connect the design of part-task practice to the EL-CIMOs of self-regulated learning with the regulation level at observation or emulation. Design an authentic learning environment that stimulates social learning, in which students also acquire, as collateral profit, important skills such as personal initiative, perseverance, and adaptation
I4: Non-venture creation entrepreneurship education can also make use of "value creation" problem-solving or challenge-based strategies to design part-task practice. When designing challenge-based strategies, the incorporation of worked examples and the scaffolding of entrepreneurial procedural and domain-specific declarative knowledge is highly appropriate
I5: When designing part-task practice, make sure that sufficient opportunities for feedback are available. Take a proactive stance as an educator with regard to giving feedback
I6: Non-venture creation entrepreneurship education can also make use of "transdisciplinary project-based learning interventions" to design part-task practice. However, for novices, first dwell on problem-scoping exercises before jumping immediately into problem-solving
I7: Design authentic learning tasks in order to elicit emotional learning events, and scaffold students by giving them instruction on how to use socio-emotional regulation strategies (see EL-CIMO 15). However, ensure novice students' self-efficacy is supported when implementing learning tasks that trigger emotional events (see EL-CIMO 11)
That invoke particular **generative mechanism (M):**
M1: See van Merriënboer and Krischner (2007)
M2: See Ismail et al. (2018); Sweller et al. (2019); Kirschner et al. (2008)
M3: See Zimmerman (2013); Rauch and Hulsink (2015)
M4: See Sweller et al. (2019)
M5: See van Merriënboer and Krischner (2007)
M6: See Payne and Jesiek (2018)
M7: See Gielnik et al. (2017) Lackéus (2020)

Table 18 EL-CIMO 15

In educational contexts (C) characterized by venture- or non-venture-creating EE in higher education for novice students with no or little prior knowledge **in order to** effectively design entrepreneurial deliberate practice **(O)**:
I1: Design a backbone of authentic entrepreneurial learning tasks. These entrepreneurial learning tasks can: – Be aligned with the "learning strategies" in self-regulated learning – Be aligned with activities included in the "entrepreneurial methods" – Be a combination of entrepreneurial methods and self-regulated learning activities
I2: Design a "two-component" deliberate practice that includes a period in which the student engages individually in deliberate practice and the continuous repetitive practice of the entrepreneurial learning tasks to achieve the imposed learning goals and a learning moment together with the educator, who then has the opportunity to monitor progress, give feedback, and set new learning goals
I2: Both the learning goals and the learning tasks are mainly designed by the educator, as is adequate scaffolding that is gradually phased out
I3: Connect the design of part-task practice to the EL-CIMOs of self-regulated learning with the regulation level at self-control or self-regulation
I4: Non-venture creation entrepreneurship education can also make use of "value creation" problem-solving or challenge-based strategies to design deliberate practice
I5: When designing deliberate practice, make sure that sufficient opportunities for feedback from educators and other stakeholders are available
I6: Non-venture creation entrepreneurship education can also make use of "transdisciplinary project-based learning interventions" to design deliberate practice
I7: Design authentic learning tasks in order to elicit emotional learning events and the use of their socio-emotional regulation strategies (see EL-CIMO 15)
That invoke particular **generative mechanism (M):**
M1: See Sonnentag and Kleine (2000); Unger et al. (2009); Dew et al. (2015); Ranabahu and Barrett (2020)
M2: See Anders Ericsson and Harwell (2019)
M3: See Anders Ericsson and Harwell (2019)
M4: See Anders Ericsson and Harwell (2019)
M5: See Stambaugh and Mitchell (2018)
M6: See Payne and Jesiek (2018)
M7: See Gielnik et al. (2017); Lackéus (2020)

Table 19 EL-CIMO 16

In educational contexts (C) characterized by venture- or non-venture-creating EE in higher education for intermediate or expert students **in order to** effectively design self-regulated experiential entrepreneurial practice **(O)**:
I1: Design educational interventions with minimal scaffolding of declarative and procedural knowledge, and prescribe only process-related entrepreneurial learning tasks
I2: Take a student-centric approach, meaning both the learning goals and the learning tasks are mainly chosen and designed by the student. Emphasize the importance of the entrepreneurial activity of "value creation for others" in uncertain circumstances as a determining activity and learning task of entrepreneurial learning
I3: When designing self-regulated experiential entrepreneurial practice, make sure that opportunities for feedback are available, but take a reactive stance as an educator with regard to giving feedback
I4: For venture-creating entrepreneurship education, implement "full" venture-creating programs and/or the implementation of "real-life" minimum viable products within the programs
I5: For non-venture-creating education, implement transdisciplinary challenge-based and problem-solving education
I6: Connect the design of part-task practice to EL-CIMO 12 of self-regulated learning with the regulation level at self-regulation. Design an authentic learning environment that stimulates interaction with external stakeholders and social learning
I7: Design educational interventions that foster metacognitive mindfulness
I8: Emphasize the importance of effectuation as entrepreneurial method and decision-making strategy for expert students in dealing with uncertain and volatile contexts
I9: Track whether students experience emotional learning events during the learning experience and how they deploy their socio-emotional regulation strategies to deal with these events
That invoke particular **generative mechanism (M):**
M1: See Kalyuga et al. (2003); Sweller et al. (2019)
M2: See Bruyat and Julien (2001); Lackéus (2020); Sweller et al. (2019)
M3: See Stambaugh and Mitchell (2018)
M4: See Huber et al. (2014); Karlsson and Moberg (2013)
M5: See Payne and Jesiek (2018); Pepin and St-Jean (2019)
M6: See Zimmerman (2013)
M7: See Yeganeh and Kolb (2009)
M8: See Sarasvathy (2001)
M9: See Lackéus (2020)

References

Alberti, F., Sciascia, S., & Poli, A. (2004). Entrepreneurship education: Notes on an ongoing debate. In U. of N. F. II (Ed.), *14th annual IntEnt conference. University of Napoli Federico II (Italy), 4-7 July 2004* (Issue July).

Anders Ericsson, K., & Harwell, K. W. (2019). Deliberate practice and proposed limits on the effects of practice on the acquisition of expert performance: Why the original definition matters and recommendations for future research. *Frontiers in Psychology, 10*(OCT), 1–19. https://doi.org/10.3389/fpsyg.2019.02396

Atmojo, W., & Ragil, I. (2020). Effectiveness of CEL-Badis learning model on students ' creative- thinking skills: Case on the topic of simple food biotechnology. *International Journal of Instruction, 13*(3), 329–342.

Bacigalupo, M., Kampylis, P., Punie, Y., den Brande, G. V., & European Commission. Joint Research Centre. (2016). *EntreComp: The entrepreneurship competence framework*. Publications Office.

Baron, R., & Henry, R. (2010). How entrepreneurs acquire the capacity to excel: Insights form research on expert performance. *Strategic Entrepreneurship Journal, 4*, 49–65. https://doi.org/10.1002/sej

Béchard, J., Grégoire, D., & b. (2005). Understanding teaching models in entrepreneurship for higher education. In P. Kÿro & C. Carrier (Eds.), *The dynamics of learning entrepreneurship in a cross-cultural university context, entrepreneurship education series 2/2005* (Vol. Issue 2, pp. 104–134). University of Tampere Research Center for Vocational and Professional Center.

Berglund, H., Bousfiha, M., & Mansoori, Y. (2020). Opportunities as artifacts and entrepreneurship as design. *Academy of Management Review, 45*(4), 825–846. https://doi.org/10.5465/AMR.2018.0285

Berglund, H., Dimov, D., & Wennberg, K. (2018). Beyond bridging rigor and relevance: The three-body problem in entrepreneurship. *Journal of Business Venturing Insights, 9*(February), 87–91. https://doi.org/10.1016/j.jbvi.2018.02.001

Bianchi, G., Pisiotis, U., & Cabrera Giraldez, M. (2022). *GreenComp—Cadre européen des compétences en matière de durabilité* (M. Bacigalupo & Y. Punie, Eds.). Office des publications de l'Union européenne. https://doi.org/10.2760/17791.

Biggs, J. (1996). Enhancing teaching through constructive alignment. *Higher Education, 32*(3), 347–364. https://doi.org/10.1007/BF00138871

Branch, R. (2009). *Instructional design: The ADDIE approach*. Springer Science + Business Media. https://doi.org/10.1007/978-0-387-09506-6

Branch, R., & Kopcha, T. (2014). Instructional design models. In J. M. Spector, M. D. Merrill, J. Elen, & M. J. Bishop (Eds.), *Handbook of research on educational communications and technology* (4th ed., pp. 77–87). Springer Science + Business Media. https://doi.org/10.1007/978-1-4614-3185-5

Brand-Gruwel, S., & Wopereis, I. (2006). Integration of the information problem-solving skill in an educational programme: The effects of learning with authentic tasks. *Technology, Instruction, Cognition and Learning, 4*(January), 243–263. http://hdl.handle.net/1820/1682

Brown, A. H., & Green, T. D. (2018). Beyond teaching instructional design models: Exploring and expertise. *Journal of Computing in Higher Education, 30*(1), 176–186. https://doi.org/10.1007/s12528-017-9164-y

Bruyat, C., & Julien, P. A. (2001). Defining the field of research in entrepreneurship. *Journal of business venturing, 16*(2), 165–180.

Cardon, M. S., & Kirk, C. P. (2015). Entrepreneurial passion as mediator of the self-efficacy to persistence relationship. *Entrepreneurship: Theory and Practice, 39*(5), 1027–1050. https://doi.org/10.1111/etap.12089

Cardon, M. S., Glauser, M., & Murnieks, C. Y. (2017). Passion for what? Expanding the domains of entrepreneurial passion. *Journal of Business Venturing Insights, 8*, 24–32.

Collewaert, V., Anseel, F., Crommelinck, M., De Beuckelaer, A., & Vermeire, J. (2016). When passion fades: Disentangling the temporal dynamics of entrepreneurial passion for founding. *Journal of Management Studies, 53*(6), 966–995. https://doi.org/10.1111/joms.12193

Cope, J. (2005). Toward a Dynamic Learning Perspective of Entrepreneurship. *Entrepreneurship Theory and Practice, July*, 373–397.

Corbalan, G., Kester, L., & van Merriënboer, J. J. G. (2008). Selecting learning tasks: Effects of adaptation and shared control on learning efficiency and task involvement. *Contemporary Educational Psychology, 33*(4), 733–756. https://doi.org/10.1016/j.cedpsych.2008.02.003

Costa, J. M., Miranda, G. L., & Melo, M. (2022). Four-component instructional design (4C/ID) model: A meta-analysis on use and effect. *Learning Environments Research, 25*(2), 445–463. https://doi.org/10.1007/s10984-021-09373-y

Creemers, B. P. M., & Kyriakides, L. (2006). Critical analysis of the current approaches to modelling educational effectiveness: The importance of establishing a dynamic model. *School Effectiveness and School Improvement, 17*(3), 347–366. https://doi.org/10.1080/09243450600697242

Dann, R. (2014). Assessment as learning: Blurring the boundaries of assessment and learning for theory, policy and practice. *Assessment in Education: Principles, Policy & Practice, 21*(2), 149–166. https://doi.org/10.1080/0969594X.2014.898128

Denyer, D., Tranfield, D., & Van Aken, J. E. (2008). Developing design propositions through research synthesis. *Organization Studies, 29*(3), 393–413. https://doi.org/10.1177/0170840607088020

Dew, N., Read, S., Sarasvathy, S. D., & Wiltbank, R. (2015). Entrepreneurial expertise and the use of control. *Journal of Business Venturing Insights, 4*, 30–37.

D'Intino, R. S. D., Goldsby, M., Houghton, J., & Neck, C. (2007). Self-leadership: A process for entrepreneurial success. *Journal of Leadership and Organizational Studies, 13*(4), 105–120.

Dimov, D. (2016). Toward a design science of entrepreneurship. In C. Corbett & J. A. Katz (Eds.), *Advances in entrepreneurship, firm emergence and growth, volume 18, models of start-up thinking and action (Vol. 18, pp. 1–31)*. https://doi.org/10.1108/S1074-754020160000018001

Donnellon, A., Ollila, S., & Williams, K. (2014). *Constructing entrepreneurial identity in entrepreneurship education*. 12, 490–499. https://doi.org/10.1016/j.ijme.2014.05.004.

Dresch, A., Lacerda, D., & Antunes, J., Jr. (2015). *Design science research: A method for science and technology advancement*. Springer.

Dunn, R., Hattie, J., & Bowles, T. (2019). Exploring the experiences of teachers undertaking educational design research (EDR) as a form of teacher professional learning. *Professional Development in Education, 45*(1), 151–167. https://doi.org/10.1080/19415257.2018.1500389

Duval-Couetil, N. (2013). Assessing the impact of entrepreneurship education programs: Challenges and approaches. *Journal of Small Business Management, 51*(3), 394–409. https://doi.org/10.1111/jsbm.12024

Edmonds, G. S., Branch, R. C., & Mukherjee, P. (1994). A conceptual framework for comparing instructional design models. *Educational Technology Research and Development, 42*(4), 55–72. https://doi.org/10.1007/BF02298055

Elliott, C., Mavriplis, C., & Anis, H. (2020). An entrepreneurship education and peer mentoring program for women in STEM: Mentors' experiences and perceptions of entrepreneurial self-efficacy and intent. *International Entrepreneurship and Management Journal, 16*(1), 43–67.

Fayolle, A. (2013). Personal views on the future of entrepreneurship education. *Entrepreneurship and Regional Development, 25*(7–8), 692–701. https://doi.org/10.1080/08985626.2013.821318

Fayolle, A., & Gailly, B. (2008). From craft to science: Teaching models and learning processes in entrepreneurship education. *Journal of European Industrial Training, 32*(7), 569–593. https://doi.org/10.1108/03090590810899838

Fellnhofer, K. (2019). Toward a taxonomy of entrepreneurship education research literature: A bibliometric mapping and visualization. *Educational Research Review, 27*, 28–55. https://doi.org/10.1016/j.edurev.2018.10.002

Gielnik, M. M., Frese, M., Kahara-Kawuki, A., Katono, I. W., Kyejjusa, S., Ngoma, M., Munene, J., Namatovu-Dawa, R., Nansubuga, F., Orobia, L., Oyugi, J., Sejjaaka, S., Sserwanga, A., Walter, T., Bischoff, K. M., & Dlugosch, T. J. (2015). Action and action-regulation in entrepreneurship: Evaluating a student training for promoting entrepreneurship. *Academy of Management Learning and Education, 14*(1), 69–94. https://doi.org/10.5465/amle.2012.0107

Gielnik, M. M., Uy, M. A., Funken, R., & Bischoff, K. M. (2017). Boosting and sustaining passion: A long-term perspective on the effects of entrepreneurship training. *Journal of Business Venturing, 32*(3), 334–353. https://doi.org/10.1016/j.jbusvent.2017.02.003

Gilsing, V. A., van Burg, E., & Romme, A. G. L. (2010). Policy principles for the creation and success of corporate and academic spin-offs. *Technovation, 30*(1), 12–23. https://doi.org/10.1016/j.technovation.2009.07.004

Goodyear, P. (2015). Teaching as design. *HERDSA Review of Higher Education, 2*(2), 27–50. http://www.herdsa.org.au/wp-content/uploads/HERDSARHE2015v02p27.pdf

Goodyear, P., & Dimitriadis, Y. (2013). In medias res: Reframing design for learning. *Research in Learning Technology, 21*(SUPPL.1), 1–13. https://doi.org/10.3402/rlt.v21i0.19909

Gulikers, J., Baggen, Y., Lans, T., & Christoffels, I. (2019). *Leren voor breed ondernemerschap: Analyse van leeruitkomsten en leeractiviteiten.*

Haynie, J. M., Shepherd, D. A., & Patzelt, H. (2012). Cognitive adaptability and an entrepreneurial task: The role of metacognitive ability and feedback. *Entrepreneurship Theory and Practice, 36*(2), 237–265. https://doi.org/10.1111/j.1540-6520.2010.00410.x

Haynie, J. M., Shepherd, D., Mosakowski, E., & Earley, P. C. (2010). Journal of business venturing a situated metacognitive model of the entrepreneurial mindset. *Journal of Business Venturing, 25*(2), 217–229. https://doi.org/10.1016/j.jbusvent.2008.10.001

Hevner, A. R., March, S. T., Park, J., & Ram, S. (2004). Design science in information research 1. *Design Science in IS Research MIS Quarterly, 28*(1), 75.

Holcomb, T., Ireland, R., & Holmes, R., Jr. (2009). Architecture of entrepreneurial learning: Exploring the link among heuristics, knowledge, and action. *Entrepreneurship Theory and Practise, 33*, 167–192.

Holmström, J., Ketokivi, M., & Hameri, A. P. (2009). Bridging practice and theory: A design science approach. *Decision Sciences, 40*(1), 65–87. https://doi.org/10.1111/j.1540-5915.2008.00221.x

Huang, X., Mayer, R. E., & Usher, E. L. (2020). Better together: Effects of four self-efficacy-building strategies on online statistical learning. *Contemporary Educational Psychology, 63*(101924), 1–15.

Huber, L. R., Sloof, R., & Van Praag, M. (2014). The effect of early entrepreneurship education: Evidence from a field experiment. *European Economic Review, 72*, 76–97. https://doi.org/10.1016/j.euroecorev.2014.09.002

Ismail, A. B. T., Sawang, S., & Zolin, R. (2018). Entrepreneurship education pedagogy: Teacher-student-centred paradox. *Education and Training, 60*(2), 168–184. https://doi.org/10.1108/ET-07-2017-0106

Kalyuga, S., Ayres, P., Chandler, P., & Sweller, J. (2003). The expertise reversal effect. *Educational Psychologist, 38*(1), 23–31. https://doi.org/10.1207/S15326985EP3801_4

Kamovich, U., & Foss, L. (2017). In search of alignment: A review of impact studies in entrepreneurship education. *Education Research International, 2017*(September), 1–15. https://doi.org/10.1155/2017/1450102

Karlsson, T., & Moberg, K. (2013). Improving perceived entrepreneurial abilities through education: Exploratory testing of an entrepreneurial self efficacy scale in a pre-post setting. *International Journal of Management Education, 11*(1), 1–11. https://doi.org/10.1016/j.ijme.2012.10.001

Khalil, M. K., & Elkhider, I. A. (2016). Applying learning theories and instructional design models for effective instruction. *Advances in Physiology Education, 40*, 147–156. https://doi.org/10.1152/advan.00138.2015

Kirschner, P. A., Beers, P. J., Boshuizen, H. P., & Gijselaers, W. H. (2008). Coercing shared knowledge in collaborative learning environments. *Computers in Human Behavior, 24*(2), 403–420.

Kozlinska, I., Rebmann, A., & Mets, T. (2020). Entrepreneurial competencies and employment status of business graduates: the role of experiential entrepreneurship pedagogy Entrepreneurial competencies and employment status of business graduates: the role of experiential entrepreneurship pedagogy. *Journal of Small Business & Entrepreneurship, 0*(0), 1–38.

Krueger, N. (2021). From instructors to educators, from pupils to learners: What do we in entrepreneurship education owe students? *ICSB Global Education Report*, 19–28.

Kyndt, E., & Baert, H. (2015). Entrepreneurial competencies: Assessment and predictive value for entrepreneurship. *Journal of Vocational Behavior, 90*, 13–25. https://doi.org/10.1016/j.jvb.2015.07.002

Kyriakides, L., & Creemers, B. P. (2009). The effects of teacher factors on different outcomes: Two studies testing the validity of the dynamic model. *Effective Education, 1*(1), 61–85.

Lackéus, M. (2015). *Entrepreneurship in education.* What, why, when, how. https://www.oecd.org/cfe/leed/BGP_Entrepreneurship-in-Education.pdf

Lackéus, M. (2020). Comparing the impact of three different experiential approaches to entrepreneurship in education. *International Journal of Entrepreneurial Behavior & Research, 26*(5), 937–971. https://doi.org/10.1108/IJEBR-04-2018-0236

Lobczowski, N. G., Lyons, K., Greene, J. A., & McLaughlin, J. E. (2021). Socioemotional regulation strategies in a project-based learning environment. *Contemporary Educational Psychology, 65*(March), 101968. https://doi.org/10.1016/j.cedpsych.2021.101968

Longva, K. K., & Foss, L. (2018). *Measuring impact through experimental design in entrepreneurship education: A literature review and research agenda.* 6025. https://doi.org/10.1177/0950422218804912.

Mansoori, Y. (2017). *Entrepreneurial methods as vehicles of entrepreneurial action.* (Doctoral dissertation). Chalmers University of Technology.

Maritz, A. (2017). Illuminating the black box of entrepreneurship education programmes: Part 2. *Education + Training, 59*(5), 471–482. https://doi.org/10.1108/ET-02-2017-0018

Maritz, A., & Brown, C. (2013). Enhancing entrepreneurial self-efficacy through vocational entrepreneurship education programs. *Journal of Vocational Education and Training, 65*(4), 543–559.

McKenney, S., & Reeves, T. C. (2012). *Conducting educational design research.* Routledge.

Merriënboer, van., J., & Kirschner, P. (2007). *Ten Steps To Complex Learning. A systematic approach to the four component instructional design.* Taylor & Francis, Inc.

Mets, T., Holbrook, J., & Läänelaid, S. (2021). Entrepreneurship education challenges for green transformation. *Administrative Sciences, 11*(1). https://doi.org/10.3390/admsci11010015

Murnieks, C. Y., Cardon, M. S., & Haynie, J. M. (2020). Fueling the fire: Examining identity centrality, affective interpersonal commitment and gender as drivers of entrepreneurial passion. *Journal of Business Venturing, 35*(1), 105909. https://doi.org/10.1016/j.jbusvent.2018.10.007

Nabi, G., Linan, F., Fayolle, A., Krueger, N., & Walmsley, A. (2017). The impact of entrepreneurship education in higher education: A systematic review and research agenda. *Academy of Management Learning & Education, 16*(2), 277–299. https://doi.org/10.5465/amle.2015.0026

Nakamura, J., & Csikszentmihalyi, M. (2003). Creativity in later life. In R. Sawyer (Ed.), *Creativity and development* (p. 243). Oxford University Press.

Nilsen, T., Gustafsson, J., & Blömeke, S. (2016). Conceptual framework and methodology of this report. In T. Nilsen & J. Gustafsson (Eds.), *Teacher quality, instructional quality, and student outcomes* (pp. 1–20). Springer Nature.

Paas, F., Tuovinen, J. E., Van Merriënboer, J. J. G., & Darabi, A. A. (2005). A motivational perspective on the relation between mental effort and performance: Optimizing learner involvement in instruction. *Educational Technology Research and Development, 53*(3), 25–34. https://doi.org/10.1007/BF02504795

Panadero, E. (2017). A review of self-regulated learning: Six models and four directions for research. *Frontiers in Psychology, 8*(APR), 1–28. https://doi.org/10.3389/fpsyg.2017.00422

Park, S., Martina, R. A., & Smolka, K. M. (2019). Working passionately does not always pay off: The negative moderating role of passion on the relationship between deliberate practice and venture performance. In *He anatomy of entrepreneurial decisions (pp. 173-195).* Springer. https://doi.org/10.1007/978-3-030-19685-1_8

Payne, L., & Jesiek, B. (2018). Enhancing transdisciplinary learning through community-based design projects: Results from a mixed methods study. *International Journal for Service Learning in Engineering, Humanitarian Engineering and Social Entrepreneurship, 13*(1), 1–52. https://doi.org/10.24908/ijsle.v13i1.11147

Pepin, M., & St-jean, E. (2019). Assessing the impacts of school entrepreneurial initiatives school level. *Journal of Small Business and Enterprise Development, 26*(2), 273–288. https://doi.org/10.1108/JSBED-07-2018-0224

Plsek, P., Bibby, J., & Whitby, E. (2007). Practical methods for extracting explicit design rules grounded in the experience of organizational managers. *Journal of Applied Behavioral Science, 43*(1), 153–170. https://doi.org/10.1177/0021886306297013

Quigley, A., Muijs, D., & Stringer, E. (2018). *Metacognition and self-regulated learning: Guidance report*. Education Endowment Foundation. Retrieved from https://d2tic4wvo1iusb.cloudfront.net/production/eef-guidance-reports/metacognition/EEF_Metacognition_and_self-regulated_learning.pdf?v=1730639151

Ranabahu, N., & Barrett, M. (2020). Does practice make micro-entrepreneurs perfect? An investigation of expertise acquisition using effectuation and causation. *Small Business Economics, 54*(3), 883–905.

Rauch, A., & Hulsink, W. (2015). Putting entrepreneurship education where the intention to act lies: An investigation into the impact of entrepreneurship education on entrepreneurial behavior. *Academy of Management Learning & Education, 14*(2), 187–204.

Reynolds, D., Sammons, P., De Fraine, B., Van Damme, J., Townsend, T., Teddlie, C., & Stringfield, S. (2014). Educational effectiveness research (EER): A state-of-the-art review. *School Effectiveness and School Improvement, 25*(2), 197–230. https://doi.org/10.1080/09243453.2014.885450

Romme, A. G. L., & Endenburg, G. (2006). Construction principles and design rules in the case of circular design. *Organization Science, 17*(2), 287–297. https://doi.org/10.1287/orsc.1050.0169

Romme, A. G. L., & Reymen, I. M. M. J. (2018). Entrepreneurship at the interface of design and science: Toward an inclusive framework. *Journal of Business Venturing Insights, 10*(July), 1–8. https://doi.org/10.1016/j.jbvi.2018.e00094

Sagath, D., Van Burg, E., Cornelissen, J. P., & Giannopapa, C. (2019). Journal of business venturing insights identifying design principles for business incubation in the European space sector. *Journal of Business Venturing Insights, 11*(February), e00115. https://doi.org/10.1016/j.jbvi.2019.e00115

Sánchez, J. C. (2011). University training for entrepreneurial competencies: Its impact on intention of venture creation. *International Entrepreneurship and Management Journal, 7*(2), 239–254. https://doi.org/10.1007/s11365-010-0156-x

Sánchez, J. C. (2013). The impact of an entrepreneurship education program on entrepreneurial competencies and intention. *Journal of Small Business Management, 51*(3), 447–465. https://doi.org/10.1111/jsbm.12025

Sarasvathy, S. D. (2001). Causation and effectuation: Toward a theoretical shift from economic inevitability to entrepreneurial contingency. *Academy of Management Review, 26*(2), 243–263. https://doi.org/10.5465/AMR.2001.4378020

Scheerens, J. (2013). The use of theory in school effectiveness research revisited. *School Effectiveness and School Improvement, 24*(1), 1–38. https://doi.org/10.1080/09243453.2012.691100

Shepherd, D. A., & Detienne, D. R. (2005). Prior knowledge, potential financial reward, and opportunity Identificatio. *Entrepreneurship Theory and Practice, 29*(1), 91–112.

Shepherd, D. A., & Patzelt, H. (2018). *Entrepreneurial cognition. Exploring the mindset of entrepreneurs*. Palgrave Macmillan.

Sonnentag, S., & Kleine, B. M. (2000). Deliberate practice at work: A study with insurance agents. *Journal of Occupational and Organizational Psychology, 73*(1), 87–102. https://doi.org/10.1348/096317900166895

Souitaris, V., Zerbinati, S., & Al-Laham, A. (2007). Do entrepreneurship programmes raise entrepreneurial intention of science and engineering students? The effect of learning, inspiration and resources. *Journal of Business Venturing, 22*(4), 566–591. https://doi.org/10.1016/j.jbusvent.2006.05.002

Stambaugh, J., & Mitchell, R. (2018). The fight is the coach: Creating expertise during the fight to avoid entrepreneurial failure. *International Journal of Entrepreneurial Behaviour and Research, 24*(5), 994–1015. https://doi.org/10.1108/IJEBR-09-2016-0287

Stefaniak, J., & Xu, M. (2020). An examination of the systemic reach of instructional design models: A systematic review. *TechTrends, 64*(5), 710–719. https://doi.org/10.1007/s11528-020-00539-8

St-Jean, E., Radu-Lefebvre, M., & Mathieu, C. (2018). Can less be more? Mentoring functions, learning goal orientation, and novice entrepreneurs' self-efficacy. *International Journal of Entrepreneurial Behavior & Research, 24*(1), 2–21.

Simon, H. (1996). *The sciences of the artificial* (3rd ed.). MIT Press.

Sweller, J., van Merriënboer, J. J. G., & Paas, F. (2019). Cognitive architecture and instructional design: 20 years later. *Educational Psychology Review, 31*(2), 261–292. https://doi.org/10.1007/s10648-019-09465-5

Theobald, M. (2021). Self-regulated learning training programs enhance university students' academic performance, self-regulated learning strategies, and motivation: A meta-analysis. *Contemporary Educational Psychology, 66*(May), 101976. https://doi.org/10.1016/j.cedpsych.2021.101976

Toding, M., & Venesaar, U. (2018). Discovering and developing conceptual understanding of teaching and learning in entrepreneurship lecturers. *Education + Training, 60*(7/8), 696–718. https://doi.org/10.1108/ET-07-2017-0101

Ucbasaran, D., Westhead, P., & Wright, M. (2009). The extent and nature of opportunity identification by experienced entrepreneurs. *Journal of Business Venturing, 24*(2), 99–115. https://doi.org/10.1016/j.jbusvent.2008.01.008

Unger, J. M., Keith, N., Hilling, C., Gielnik, M. M., & Frese, M. (2009). Deliberate practice among south African small business owners: Relationships with education, cognitive ability, knowledge, and success. *Journal of Occupational and Organizational Psychology, 82*(1), 21–44. https://doi.org/10.1348/096317908X304361

Van Aken, J. E. (2004). Management research based on the paradigm of the design sciences: The quest for field-tested and grounded technological rules. *Journal of Management Studies, 41*(2), 219–246. https://doi.org/10.1111/j.1467-6486.2004.00430.x

Van Aken, J. E., & Andriessen, D. (Eds.). (2011). *Handboek ontwerpgericht wetenschappelijk onderzoek: wetenschap met effect*. Boom Lemma uitgevers.

Van Aken, J. E., & Romme, G. (2009). Reinventing the future: Adding design science to the repertoire of organization and management studies. *Organisation Management Journal, 6*(1), 5–12. https://doi.org/10.1057/omj.2009.1

van Burg, E. (2010). *Creating spin-off designing entrepreneurship conducive universities Elco van Burg*. Eindhoven University Press.

van Burg, J., & Romme, A. (2014). Creating the future together: Toward a framework for research synthesis in entrepreneurship. *Entrepreneurship Theory and Practice, 38*(2), 369–397.

van den Hout, J. J. J. (2016). *Team flow: From concept to application [Doctoral dissertation, Technische Universiteit Eindhoven]*. Technische Universiteit Eindhoven.

Van Merriënboer, J. J. G., & Sweller, J. (2005). Cognitive load theory and complex learning: Recent developments and future directions. *Educational Psychology Review, 17*(2), 147–177. https://doi.org/10.1007/s10648-005-3951-0

Winkler, C., Fust, A., & Jenert, T. (2021). From entrepreneurial experience to expertise: A self-regulated learning perspective. *Journal of Small Business Management, 00*(00), 1–26. https://doi.org/10.1080/00472778.2021.1883041

Wood, R., & Bandura, A. (1989). Social cognitive theory of organizational management. *Academy of Management Review, 14*(3), 361–384.

Yeganeh, B., & Kolb, D. (2009). Mindfulness and experiential learning. Handbook for strategic HR: Best practices in organizational development from the OD Network, 152–161.

Yen, W. C., & Lin, H. H. (2020). Investigating the effect of flow experience on learning performance and entrepreneurial self-efficacy in a business simulation systems context. *Interactive Learning Environments, 30*(9), 1593–1608. https://doi.org/10.1080/10494820.2020.1734624

Yin, R. K. (2009). *Case study research: Design and methods* (4th ed.).

Zimmerman, B. J. (2002). Zimmerman–2002–becoming a self-regulated learner an overview. *Theory Into, 41*(2), 64–70.

Zimmerman, B. J. (2013). From cognitive modeling to self-regulation: A social cognitive career path. *Educational Psychologist, 48*(3), 135–147. https://doi.org/10.1080/00461520.2013.794676

Bart Derre is Director at HOGENT University of Applied Sciences and Arts in Ghent, Belgium, and holds the (HOGENT-Xerius) research chair on entrepreneurial learning at the Vrije Universiteit Brussel, Brussels, Belgium. As Director of the Center for Entrepreneurship, he has overseen numerous entrepreneurial education programs. His research, including a Ph.D. from TU Eindhoven (The Netherlands), focuses on the design and implementation of entrepreneurial education that drives meaningful impact.

Pedro De Bruyckere is an educational scientist at Utrecht University and head of Leerpunt, Flanders, a What Works-clearing house in Belgium. He co-authored several popular scientific books such as Urban Myths about Learning and Education and The Psychology of Great Teaching. He is an avid blogger on TheEconomyOfMeaning.com and an often asked public speaker on education. His research interests are currently focused on collective student efficacy.

Mathieu Weggeman is emeritus-professor of Organizational Science and Innovation Management at Eindhoven University of Technology (Netherlands). He obtained a MSc in Industrial Engineering from TU/e and a PhD degree from Tilburg University. Prior to joining Eindhoven University of Technology, he worked as a management consultant for Philips. Mathieu's primary expertise lies in the field of organizational design, innovation management and work processes in knowledge-intensive organizations.

A Two Flows Framework Leveraging Challenge-Based Learning for Entrepreneurial Education: A Design Science Approach

Ákos R. Wetters, Jasmina Galloway-Lazendic, Duygu Keskin, Gert Guri, Pim Widdershoven, and Isabelle Reymen

Abstract This chapter presents a new framework for entrepreneurial education (EE) that builds on the concept of challenge-based learning (CBL). Using a Design Science Research (DSR) approach, an innovative "Two Flows" educational framework was created that fosters students' learning-to-learn and business competencies, combining launching a business and developing entrepreneurial competencies. Student testimonials substantiate the efficacy of our framework in enhancing core entrepreneurial traits, particularly team dynamics and adaptability. The study addresses the "how EE is delivered" gap in the literature, making it very useful for educators and policymakers and serving the academic discourse.

1 Introduction

Entrepreneurial education (EE) encompasses diverse approaches with distinct learning objectives. Lackéus (2015) classifies EE into two broad categories: "narrow" EE focuses on business development, while "wide" EE emphasizes personal development. The chosen focus significantly influences the expected learning outcomes. Traditionally, pedagogies in entrepreneurial education have been grounded

Á. R. Wetters (✉) · D. Keskin · I. Reymen
Industrial Engineering and Innovation Sciences, Eindhoven University of Technology, Eindhoven, The Netherlands
e-mail: akos@wetters.me; d.keskin@tue.nl; i.m.m.j.reymen@tue.nl

J. Galloway-Lazendic · G. Guri
TU/e innovation Space, Eindhoven University of Technology, Eindhoven, The Netherlands
e-mail: j.lazendic.galloway@tue.nl; g.guri@tue.nl

P. Widdershoven
Faculty of Behavioural and Movement Sciences, Vrije Universiteit Amsterdam, Amsterdam, The Netherlands
e-mail: p.widdershoven@vu.nl

© The Author(s), under exclusive license to Springer Nature Switzerland AG 2025

B. Derre, Y. Baggen (eds.), *Empowering the Next Generation of Entrepreneurial Change Agents*, Contributions to Management Science,
https://doi.org/10.1007/978-3-031-82251-3_6

in business and management (Fayolle & Gailly, 2015). Often, the focus lies on individualistic notions of entrepreneurship (Welsh et al., 2016). However, creating new added value and learning lies at the core of entrepreneurship (Lackéus, 2015). Narrow entrepreneurship is associated with opportunity identification, self-employment, venture creation, and growth, whereas wide entrepreneurship relates to personal development, creativity, self-reliance, and initiative-taking (e.g., Fayolle & Gailly, 2008). The choice of which approach to use for EE by instructors has a crucial impact on educational objectives, course content design, teaching methods, and student assessment procedures, leading to a wide diversity of approaches and different target audiences (Mwasalwiba, 2010).

This dichotomy between the "narrow" and "wide" approaches to EE creates a schism wherein there is an evident lack of integration and synergy between entrepreneurial education's business and personal dimensions. Existing curricula seldom provide a balanced blend of both perspectives, thus failing to cultivate well-rounded entrepreneurial individuals (Lackéus, 2014).

In recent years, there has been a growing interest in the wide EE due to the recognition of the competencies that EE brings. However, as noted by Baggen et al. (2021), the existing literature focuses mainly on the "what" of the wide EE, describing desired competencies and outcomes without elaborating on what learning activities to implement for such outcomes to be fulfilled (i.e., the "how" of the wide EE—Naia et al., 2014; Nabi et al., 2017; Kamovich & Foss, 2017; Turner & Gianiodis, 2018). Therefore, there is a need for studies that describe what happens in the classroom and which learning activities significantly impact students' learning when implementing wide EE approaches.

Furthermore, to address the limitations of conventional frontal education, there has been a growing interest in Challenge-Based Learning (CBL) for delivering EE (Reymen et al., 2022). CBL allows learners to apply entrepreneurial competencies in real-world contexts, emphasizing learning through action rather than "static" knowledge acquisition and replication. The central idea behind CBL is to achieve learning objectives by analyzing and designing solutions to address societal challenges (Gallagher & Savage, 2020).

Moreover, CBL aims to cultivate students' entrepreneurial mindset and behavior, enabling them to think critically, identify opportunities, and act upon them (İyigün, 2015), which resonates with the objectives of both narrow and wide EE. CBL can be applied to and is valuable for both approaches to EE. Personal and team development, professional growth, and self-regulated learning are also crucial components of CBL, as they foster the acquisition of essential competencies. Acquiring these competencies aligns well with the objectives of wide EE. CBL also creates opportunities to validate innovative solutions in the real world, allowing students to go beyond the theoretical conceptualization of entrepreneurship and experience many aspects of an entrepreneurial journey while guided and coached by their instructors. Validation in the real world is fundamental for both narrow and wide EE.

In the swiftly evolving educational landscape, aligning pedagogical strategies with the dynamic nature of entrepreneurship has become necessary. The narrow and wide approaches to EE are valuable and have different purposes. However, there is also a need for combining these approaches. Moreover, most research thus far has focused on the "what" instead of the "how" of EE, whereas the "how" is crucial in experiential learning approaches such as CBL. Therefore, this study aims to answer the following research question: *how to deliver EE by combining narrow and wide approaches and combining them with the CBL concept?* The current chapter presents a Design Science Research (DSR) study for designing an integrated EE framework, which we call the "Two Flows" framework. The framework can be used to design courses for EE that wish to combine the wide approaches to EE (personal and team learning journey) with the narrow approaches to EE (financial sustainability). Furthermore, our study presents the "how" of EE (Kamovich & Foss, 2017), and it aims to help practitioners interested in adopting innovative practices for EE, such as CBL, by making course structure and activities tangible.

2 Method

Design Science Research (DSR) has emerged as a robust method in the field of information systems and has progressively found its footing in other domains, including education. The inception of this approach can be traced back to the seminal works of Simon (1996) and Hevner et al. (2004), which conceptualized DSR as a means to bridge the gap between empirical research and the creation of actionable knowledge. The primary essence of the DSR approach is its dual focus on theory and solutions to problems in practice. The approach consists of a series of methodological steps: problem identification, objectives for a solution, design and development, demonstration, evaluation, and communication. In educational research, DSR can facilitate a thorough examination and refinement of course designs based on feedback and outcomes through iterative cycles striving for continuous improvement (Hevner et al., 2004).

In developing our nuanced approach to EE, we engaged in continuous discourse, actively discussing, refining, and aligning insights and experiences from the course deliveries. This process covered over 7 years and resulted in the design of an innovative entrepreneurship course, "Innovation Space Project: Innovation and Entrepreneurship Processes", as presented in Chap. 2 (Wetters et al.). This process enabled the emergence of our "Two Flows" framework, enriched with diverse perspectives and expertise and characterized by a deep commitment to nurturing lifelong learners with a strong entrepreneurial mindset and a "get stuff done" attitude.

Therefore, our DSR method was as follows:

1. Problem identification: In Sect. 3.1, we outline the literature gap and the need for innovative EE courses that combine the narrow and wide aspects.
2. Objectives for a solution: Section 3.2 outlines the objectives that guided the design solution. Additionally, in Sect. 3.3, we present the context of our design.
3. Design solution: in Sect. 4, we describe our design solution—the educational framework.
4. Demonstration and evaluation: In Sect. 5, we demonstrate and assess the impact of our design solution.
5. Communication: In Sect. 6, we discuss the main contribution of our work.

3 Design Process

This section describes the first two steps in the DSR process: problem identification and objectives for a solution (including the context). These steps led to the integrative educational framework combining narrow and wide EE perspectives with CBL presented in sect. 4.

3.1 Problem Identification

In the evolving educational landscape, fostering entrepreneurial competencies through practical pedagogical approaches has garnered significant attention from educational researchers and practitioners alike. The burgeoning interest in this area emanates from the realization that traditional lecture-based methods of teaching entrepreneurship have numerous shortcomings (Blenker et al., 2011; Lackéus, 2015). Furthermore, the existing literature points to a discernible gap between narrow and wide approaches to EE (e.g., Jones & Iredale, 2010). Integrating novel pedagogical concepts like CBL, characterized by its collaborative and problem-solving nature, can bridge these gaps by fostering an integrated approach to EE that balances business development with personal development (Kolb, 2014).

Furthermore, current literature predominantly addresses the "what" of EE, delineating the desirable competencies and outcomes without adequately addressing the "how" of EE, that is, what are the teaching methodologies and learning activities that can facilitate the attainment of these outcomes (Fayolle, 2013). More discourse must be devoted to the methods to foster these competencies, covering a critical gap in the literature and practice of entrepreneurial education.

Therefore, this research seeks to augment the existing body of knowledge by providing a comprehensive teaching methodology through the "Two Flows" framework. This framework addresses the identified gaps and promotes a holistic and hands-on approach to EE using CBL.

3.2 Defining the Objectives of the Design Solution

To define the objectives for our design solution, we began by reflecting on our teaching practices. Teaching is shaped by individual beliefs and philosophies, which in turn influence instructional methods and interactions with students (e.g., Laundon et al., 2020). Therefore, the teaching philosophy of the primary instructor (the first author), who is an entrepreneur himself, and of the course-responsible lecturer (the last author) shaped the following primary course objectives:

1. Maximize individual and team learning while boosting student self-confidence.
2. Create a transformative, meaningful learning experience for students and stakeholders (e.g., coaches, teaching assistants, challenge owners).

3. Encourage students to develop a "Minimum Viable Project" and set up sustainable organizations (social or commercial).

The course, the foundation for developing the Two Flow framework, is called the Innovation Space Project: Innovation and Entrepreneurship Processes (ISP). The course design is built on the following teaching pillars, reflected in the formula: ISP = (AQ + EQ + IQ) + FF.

1. *AQ (Adaptability Quotient)*: Focusing on enhancing individual and team learning, fostering agility, and developing a "Get Stuff Done" mindset (Higgins & Elliott, 2011) crucial for entrepreneurship.
2. *EQ (Emotional Quotient)*: Encouraging self-awareness, resilience, and empathy, preparing students for leadership in sustainable ventures.
3. *IQ (Intelligence Quotient)*: Providing the discipline knowledge required to tackle course challenges.
4. *FF (Fun Factor)*: Ensuring the course remains engaging and enjoyable, promoting a vibrant learning environment.

CBL supports these objectives by transforming theoretical concepts into practical problem-solving experiences, helping students adapt and collaborate effectively in entrepreneurial settings.

3.3 Design Context: The ISP Course

Reflections on the initial design and subsequent iterations of the ISP course over the years have led to the development of the Two Flow framework, which encapsulates key insights and best practices from ongoing evaluation and refinement. In this section, we outline the foundational elements of the course to provide the context in which the framework emerged. Chap. 2 in this book presents the course elements and evolution in more detail (Wetters et al.).

The ISP course is a flagship offering at TU/e Innovation Space, a hub for Challenge-Based Learning (CBL) and student entrepreneurship (Reymen et al., 2022). It is a 10 ECTS master-level course open to students from all faculties, running twice yearly since the 2017 academic year. It engages interdisciplinary teams of students in tackling real-world challenges provided by industry and societal organizations, focusing on designing innovative solutions and business development.

The course consists of three phases, which make up the *Entrepreneurial Phases* (EPs): (1) value creation, (2) value capturing, and (3) value delivery (Lepak et al., 2007), which aligns with narrow EE. In the value creation phase, we focus on problem exploration and ideation around the solution. In the second phase, value capturing, the emphasis lies on designing the value network and business development. During the last phase, value delivery, the teams spend most of their attention on setting up an experiment or pilot, the so-called "minimum viable project." They also work on a go-to-market strategy and an operational and financial plan. The course integrates four *Entrepreneurial Focus Areas* (EFAs): (1) Customer Desirability, (2) Technological Feasibility, (3) Financial Sustainability, and (4) Societal Impact,

Table 1 Intended Learning Outcomes (ILOs) for the ISP course

#	Title	Description
ILO1	Approach	Select and apply appropriate design, engineering, and business approaches and tools to create innovative and science-based solutions to a real-life challenge.
ILO2	Analysis	Develop a profound interpretation of highly complex, real-life design problems and the systems around them. Consider the perspectives of desirability, feasibility, viability, and societal impact (the entrepreneurial focus areas).
ILO3	Synthesis	Develop a problem-driven, creative, and integrative design, resulting in an original and validated prototype that balances the entrepreneurial focus areas.
ILO4	Interdisciplinarity	Identify, envision, and promote the role and contributions of engineering disciplines in solving problems in business, industrial, and societal environments. Integrate those diverse contributions in the form of a validated prototype.
ILO5	Skills and behavior	Develop leadership and project management skills to organize and perform an interdisciplinary, hands-on, and team-based engineering design and business development project. Communicate a message orally and in writing at different elaboration levels to all relevant parties. Work independently; develop an entrepreneurial mindset.
ILO6	Personal and team development	Define and regularly reflect on a personal and team development plan, indicating personal and team challenges and needed development.
ILO7	Stakeholder management	Effectively manage stakeholders, demonstrate communication proficiency, and search for a win-win situation.
ILO8	Self-regulated learning	Acquire skills, strategies, and techniques to become a more effective and efficient learner. Develop self-awareness and adaptability to optimize their learning process and acquire new knowledge and skills more readily.

influenced by the works of Osterwalder et al. (2014), Chesbrough (2003), Schaltegger and Wagner (2011), and Mair and Marti (2006). Throughout all entrepreneurial phases, the teams must navigate the different focus areas to stay innovative and meet stakeholders' expectations when exploring the problems and opportunities and designing and implementing the solutions.

Learning activities include studio-style group work, coaching, peer feedback, and interactive workshops, emphasizing CBL and wide entrepreneurial education. Throughout the course, students engage in progress pitches, team coaching sessions, and mid-term and final evaluations, receiving feedback from peers, challenge owners, and experts. The course promotes self-directed learning, teamwork, and the practical application of theoretical knowledge to real-world problems.

The course has eight *Intended Learning Outcomes* (ILOs), listed in Table 1, based on the key principles of the early TU/e CBL framework (Lazendic-Galloway et al., 2021): working in interdisciplinary teams, tackling sufficiently open and complex real-world challenges, and close collaboration with high-tech companies and societal organizations.

The *Learning Activities* (LAs), which form the building blocks of the course, are listed and briefly described in Table 3 in the Appendix. In the first part of the course, the emphasis lies on infusing a positive attitude in the cohort and strengthening the students' interpersonal relationships, the process of team formation, adopting an entrepreneurial mindset, and exploring the problem space. The second half of the course focuses on value capturing and value delivery phases.

The assessment setup aligns with the entrepreneurial spirit of the course, focusing on transparency and allowing teams to prioritize their projects and skill development. Following constructive alignment principles, the assessment connects learning outcomes, activities, and evaluation to encourage deep learning (Biggs, 1996). Modern higher education trends emphasize innovative methods like portfolios and self- and peer assessments (Struyven et al., 2005).

The involvement of peers, challenge owners, ESA (Education and Student Affairs) staff, and independent juries enhances learning and ensures objective assessment. Students are evaluated on project progress pitches, team reflections, and mid-term/final pitches with prototypes. The weekly formative assessments by coaches contribute to cumulative impressions, which are included in the final summative assessment. Team performance accounts for 70% of the grade, with 30% based on individual contributions.

Table 2 lists the expected outputs from the teams (who are also involved in assessing these outputs), the type of assessment it relates to, and which ILOs that assessment addresses.

Table 2 Assessment for the ISP course

What student does (Output)	What assessors do	Assessors	Type of assessment	Intended learning outcomes
Weekly progress pitch on the development of the project	Give tips and tops	Coaches and peers	Formative	ILO1, ILO2, ILO3, ILO5, ILO7
Weekly reflection on the teams' learning, team dynamics, and individual development	Coach and mentor the teams	Coaches (and challenge owners during mid-mid-term)	Formative	ILO1, ILO4, ILO5, ILO6, ILO7, L08
Reflection on the teams' learning, team dynamics, and individual development, plus relevant questions	Listen and give feedback	ESA (education and student affairs) coaches	Formative	ILO4, ILO5, ILO6, ILO8
Mid-term and final pitch with prototype	Share feedback, including tips and tops	Jury and challenge owners	Formative	ILO3, ILO5, ILO7
Deliverables: Learner reflections based on the learning objectives of the course	Assess and provide feedback	Coaches	Summative	ILO1, ILO5, ILO6, ILO8

4 Design Solution: The Two Flows Framework

Reflecting on our approach to delivering EE, as described in the previous section, the DSR method allowed us to identify the key components of our teaching methodology and systematically organize them into a coherent educational framework. The primary purpose of developing this framework was to share our lessons learned with the wider community while addressing gaps in the literature and practice.

At its core, the framework groups various Learning Activities (described in Table 3 in the Appendix) as the basic blocks of our practice into broader categories, which we call "Learning Activations" or simply "Activations"(described in Table 4 in the Appendix). These Activations are designed to help students acquire and apply knowledge while demonstrating entrepreneurial behavior. The Activations are aligned with the three main course objectives (listed in Sect. 3.2), covering both the wide and narrow aspects of EE. The wide aspect, focused on personal and team development, is called the "Learning to Learn" flow, while the narrow aspect, focused on business development, is called the "Cracking the Challenge" flow. While the framework emerged from our practice, it also has a basis in established educational theories.

Cracking the Challenge Flow develops students' abilities to tackle real-world challenges by creating innovative entrepreneurial solutions. Students start with an open challenge and aim to develop a "minimum viable project" by the end of the course. They work on the four key Entrepreneurial Focus Areas (EFAs): Customer Desirability, Technological Feasibility, Financial Sustainability, and Societal Impact. This flow draws from Sarasvathy's theory of Effectuation (Sarasvathy, 2001), where students are encouraged to use their existing skills and networks to create opportunities, and Ajzen's Theory of Planned Behavior (Ajzen, 1991), which emphasizes fostering a positive attitude toward entrepreneurship. Additionally, ethical and sustainable considerations are integrated into this flow, aligning with Mezirow's Transformative Learning Theory (Mezirow, 1998), which promotes a shift in students' thinking about societal and ethical responsibilities.

Learning to Learn Flow emphasizes personal and team development, encouraging students to step out of their comfort zones and adapt to changing environments. "Personal and team effort together with a positive attitude" is the input for this process, and the output is a more resilient and adaptable "Learner 2.0." Peer-to-peer (P2P) learning strategies, such as team progress pitches and inter-team feedback ("tips and tops"), create a collaborative learning environment where students can actively support and learn from each other. This aligns with Vygotsky's Social Constructivism (Newman & Latifi, 2020), which emphasizes the role of social interactions in learning. Additionally, the flow promotes metacognitive awareness (Fleur et al., 2021), where students learn to reflect on and adjust their learning strategies, fostering lifelong learning. This flow also reflects Kolb's Experiential Learning Theory (Kolb, 2014), as students engage in cycles of experiencing, reflecting, thinking, and acting through P2P exchanges and hands-on activities.

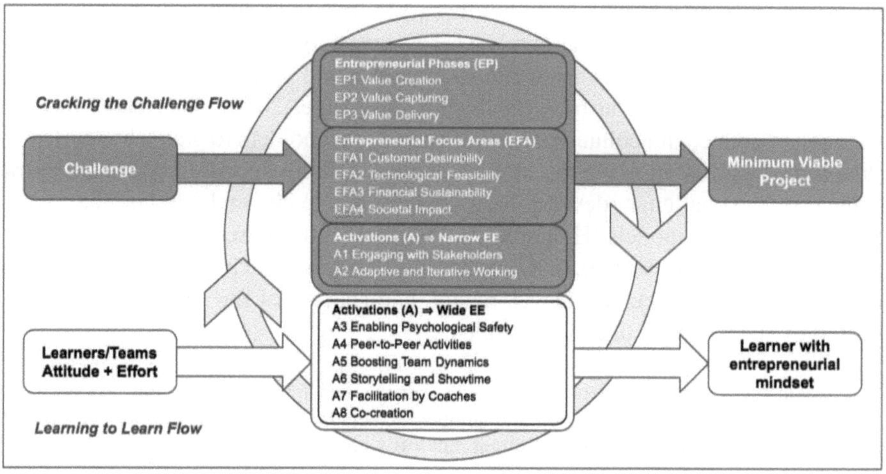

Fig. 1 A graphical representation of the "Two Flows" framework

These two parallel flows combine business development and personal/team growth into a unified approach to EE, forming the basis of our "Two Flows" framework, which is graphically shown in Fig. 1.

5 Demonstration and Evaluation

In this section, we describe each activation in more detail, link them to the existing body of knowledge, and demonstrate their impact on our learners. We also aim to inspire other educators by sharing the specifics of our innovative teaching practices and encouraging them to share their own approaches. More details can be found in the Appendix, where Table 3 offers examples of learning activities and Table 4 illustrates how these learning activities are mapped to learning activations.

To demonstrate and evaluate the impact of our design solution that transforms our students into lifelong learners and entrepreneurial individuals, we collected quantitative data. As mentioned previously, our students produce deliverables like reports or videos as a part of the course assessment in which they reflect on their learning process. These deliverables can be used to demonstrate if our learning intentions for the course have been met. We contacted students from three cohorts from academic years 2021–2022 and 2022–2023 and asked permission to use their final reflections for our research. The project has been approved by the TU/e Ethics Review Board (no. ERB2021ESOE18). Thirty students gave their permission, and their reflections were compiled (videos are converted into text) and anonymized by one of the researchers. Two researchers then performed a contextualized analysis of the reflections based on the eight activations.

Engage and co-create with stakeholders (A1) In a CBL setting, involving external stakeholders, such as mentors, experts, investors, customers, and suppliers, offers opportunities to learn from and about real-world problems and establish professional working relationships (Gallagher & Savage, 2020). The teams have to engage, co-create, and collaborate with external stakeholders to gain a better understanding of the real needs in the market, acquire domain-specific knowledge in the context of the challenge, develop their professional skills, and validate their solutions and business models (Heinonen & Poikkijoki, 2006). According to Burg et al. (2008), it is crucial to interact with the stakeholders to achieve higher levels of innovation, entrepreneurship development, and success of the startups, as demonstrated by the words of one of the students:

> I became even more conscious of the need to involve the stakeholders in your process to find your best problem-solution fit. Validation with them is very, very, very important. This is something I did mainly with my designs, but less with the feasibility of a business model.

Adaptive and iterative way of working (A2) The CBL approach to education follows a cycle of activities in three stages: engage, investigate, and act (Nichols & Cator, 2008). Design thinking has a similar approach with five steps: empathize, define, ideate, prototype, and test (e.g., Dym et al., 2005). The Lean Startup method consists of three steps: build, measure, and learn (Ries, 2011). This activation leverages the aforementioned approaches. Teams must apply adaptive, iterative, and agile working methods to respond to change, learn from experiences, and improve outcomes through feedback loops in a dynamic world. When working with an iterative approach, they can test hypotheses and assumptions early on, reducing the risk of failure and increasing the chances of success. By repeating this cycle of testing and evaluating, teams can achieve incremental progress toward their goals (Ries, 2011). One of our students summarized in the following manner:

> I also learned that to be an entrepreneur is to accept failure and learn from it. I am a very failure-averse person, and I'm prone to not taking risks just because of the possibility of failing. Here I learned however that failing is not the end of the world, and we can learn a lot from it.

Establishment and maintenance of psychological safety (A3) This type of activation is the basis for all learning. Edmondson (1999) demonstrated that psychological safety is essential for enabling individuals to reach their full potential in personal growth. Such team members are also likely to be better team players, resulting in stronger and better-performing teams (Kahn, 1990). These teams have a greater chance of progressing toward cracking the challenge with their project. By fostering a sense of safety and openness (Ryan & Deci, 2000), educators can help learners feel more engaged, motivated, and confident in their abilities, leading to more successful learning outcomes. One team highlights their thought in the following words:

> We considered our project as much bigger than just following a course and I am happy that we took the time to get to know each other better and have plenty of fun activities. This

> created an open, fun and educational environment in which we knew each other's strengths and weaknesses. What I valued most was everyone's enthusiasm and initiative to work on things.

Peer-to-peer activities (A4) This activation intends to unite all the participants and teams within the cohort and intensify collective learning. Peer-to-peer learning is essential in higher education because it encourages active participation, engagement, and collaboration among learners (Stigmar, 2016). This improves transversal skills like critical thinking, problem-solving, and communication (Liu & Carless, 2006), enhancing self-confidence and empathy. To achieve this, peer-to-peer learning requires a supportive and inclusive learning environment and a sense of community feeling. Such an environment allows students to take ownership and lead their learning (Topping, 1996). The following quote shows the impact of peer learning:

> I developed skills to provide feedback in a clear and constructive manner. At the same time, I learned to implement feedback that same day and improve by the next weekly feedback session. This shows that I am eager to learn and develop a growth mindset.

Boosting team dynamics (A5) This activation aims to trigger teams to become more energized, connected, proactive, and motivated to get the most out of themselves and the project. Boosting team dynamics and teamwork is essential in educational and entrepreneurial settings (Slavin, 1980). Strong team dynamics in an educational environment can lead to cooperative learning, where team members develop new insights into solving complex problems. Teamwork depends on efficient and effective team members, essential to achieving increased productivity and profitability in a high-performance organization (Katzenbach & Smith, 2015). This student highlights how the teams provide energy:

> I've learned that a team is not only about how skilled and talented we are, but also it's about fun, random talks and food. This team gave me the energy and motivation to not give up and work even harder to achieve our goals.

Storytelling and showtime (A6) This activation is used to communicate to the cohort the importance of storytelling and showtime. The world needs to know about good teams and the added value they provide. Entrepreneurial teams can convey their messages attractively and compellingly orally and in written form. The message could vary from a simple challenge description to a full flash investor pitch. Through storytelling, individuals can connect with the experiences and emotions of others and can evoke empathy and understanding (e.g., Polkinghorne, 1988). Storytelling can facilitate knowledge transfer and promote critical thinking in a learning environment. It helps the audience recall and understand information more quickly because it activates brain parts linked to learning and memory (Zacks & Tversky, 2001). Storytelling offers entrepreneurs and learners in an entrepreneurial setting a powerful way to effectively communicate what added value the (potential) startup brings to their investors and customers (Martens & Jennings, 2007). The following two student quotes show the impact of this activation:

> Although my study background is in physics which is very scientific and often asks for some explanation, I noticed that as I progressed in the Innovation Space Project my graduation project slides got more and more concise, to the point and my meeting got shorter and more efficient.

> For me personal during a pitch, don't explain the content on the slides. Tell a story with additional value that guides listeners through the slides.

Facilitation by coaches (A7) Facilitation by the coaches (in this case, the ISP and the ESA coaches) makes it possible to tailor the interaction with the learners, resulting in customized learning journeys at individual and team levels. The role of facilitators in CBL is essential because they provide guidance, feedback, and support to learners throughout the learning process. When experiencing effective facilitation, learners can produce improved learning outcomes, show more engagement, and feel more satisfied with their learning (Thomas, 2013). Another activity of facilitators is to create and protect a safe and stimulating learning environment. In this environment, learners feel more confident about taking risks, experimenting, and learning from their failures. Facilitators also encourage learners to collaborate, share ideas, and engage in peer-to-peer learning, resulting in deeper learning and critical thinking (Lave & Wenger, 1991). One student sums it up in the following way:

> I also learned to ask for help from ESA and the main coaches in situations that are eventually not in the best interest of the team, or individuals.

Co-creation on the course itself (A8) This type of activation strongly emphasizes constructive co-creation and enjoyability to obtain a win–win–win situation within the course for the cohort, challenge owners, and coaches. In general, co-creating the courses with the cohort can improve student engagement, participation, and learning outcomes because it promotes a more learner-centered and engaging learning environment, and it gives learners a sense of ownership and control of their learning Windle et al. (2011). Furthermore, co-creating an entrepreneurial course with learners enhances their learning experience, fosters a sense of ownership, and increases motivation (Fayolle & Gailly, 2015).

6 Discussion and Conclusion

Our "Two Flows" framework, which focuses on the "Cracking the Challenge" and "Learning to Learn" flows, integrates both narrow and wide perspectives of EE while drawing from insights in the existing literature. The innovation of the framework lies in its seamless integration of these elements into a cohesive learning experience aligned with the CBL concept. Our design addresses the gaps identified by Kamovich and Foss (2017) by providing a structured yet flexible approach to entrepreneurial learning. This is particularly relevant in today's educational landscape, where the demand for creative problem-solving and entrepreneurial competencies is at its peak.

The framework's objectives were rooted in the course instructors' teaching philosophies and daily practices. These objectives aimed to cultivate an entrepreneurial mindset by maximizing individual and team learning, encouraging the creation of financially sustainable organizations by developing a minimum viable project, and crafting a meaningful learning experience. Student feedback on various aspects of their learning further supports the framework's effectiveness.

Flexibility and Adaptability

The "Two Flows" framework is highly flexible and adaptable, making it a versatile tool for addressing the complex and dynamic needs of modern EE. It is particularly beneficial for courses that aim to seamlessly blend "narrow" and "wide" EE approaches in an agile and effective way.

- *Modular Design*: The framework's "Activations" can be tailored to fit the specific needs of different courses. For example, a course focused on fostering life skills might emphasize the "Learning to Learn" flow, while a product development course might lean more into the "Cracking the Challenge" flow.
- *Customizable Learning Outcomes*: The "Two Flows" are adaptable to different learning objectives. Instructors can adjust focus areas (e.g., customer journey, financial sustainability) or entrepreneurial phases (e.g., value creation, delivery, and capturing) without losing the essence of the framework.
- *Flexible Delivery Mode*: The framework's adaptability extends to various educational formats, whether on-site, hybrid, or online. It is resource-efficient and primarily relies on interaction, making it suitable for diverse educational settings.

Limitations and Further Research

Despite the promising results from our iterative design process, there are limitations to consider. The "Two Flows" framework has been tested in a specific course at a single university, which may not represent the broader population of entrepreneurial learners. Further research is needed to explore how this framework can be customized for different educational settings and entrepreneurial domains. Additionally, while the framework has shown immediate impact, a longitudinal study would help assess the long-term effects of this pedagogical approach on entrepreneurial success.

Conclusion

This chapter outlines our approach to designing entrepreneurial education using DSR, integrating the CBL concept, and combining narrow and wide EE perspectives. Our findings show that the "Two Flows" framework, underpinned by a strong teaching philosophy, effectively fosters an entrepreneurial mindset, enhances learning competencies ("Learning to Learn"), and helps students deliver a minimum viable project ("Cracking the Challenge"). This framework also provides a suitable way to address the "how" gap in EE literature.

Furthermore, the model can serve as a valuable tool for educators and researchers looking to apply a DSR approach in their own teaching and research. By adopting this framework, they can systematically reflect on and improve their teaching methods while contributing to the broader discourse on innovative pedagogical practices.

Acknowledgment This work was partially supported by the NRO grant 405.20865.714 (JLG).

Appendix 1: Table 3

Table 3 The list and short description of Learning Activities (LAs) used as building blocks of our teaching framework. The wide and narrow approach to EE is also indicated, as well as to what Entrepreneurial Phase (EP) the activity corresponds

#	Name	Short description	EE	EP
LA1	Kick-off	Setting the scene and initiating cohort building with an "effectual dinner"	Wide	
LA2	Hello moments	Social start of each session throughout the whole course, with a free flow of coffee (checking in)	Wide	
LA3	Spinning around	Speed dating sessions with challenge owners and "team formers" in the first 2 weeks	Wide	
LA4	Mindset and culture	Workshops on "YES AND...!", team dynamics, culture, learning and performance ambitions	Wide	
LA5	Unleash creativity	Ideation speedily and effectively as a first step in problem/opportunity exploration	Narrow	Value creation
LA6	Check and imagine all	Moonshot thinking, systems thinking, vision (problem/opportunity exploration)	Narrow	Value creation
LA7	Campus validation experience	Basic prototyping, external validation, and fun experience for problem exploration	Narrow	Value creation
LA8	Giant potato	Problem/opportunity exploration, from concept to context	Narrow	Value creation
LA9	Twisted perspectives	Reframing and creativity around problem/ opportunity exploration	Narrow	Value creation
LA10	Competition is your best friend	Exploration and ideation around problem/ opportunity	Narrow	Value creation
LA11	Prototyping workshops I and II	Ideation and validation (I: Problem/ opportunity and II: Solution)	Narrow	Value delivery
LA12	Value added transformation	Value stream mapping in networks (i.e., early stage/small-scale ecosystems)	Narrow	Value capturing
LA13	Oops, ops exercise	Analyze and transpose a day-to-day operation of an ongoing business in the same domain to own project (preferably pilot)	Narrow	Value delivery
LA14	Hit the road, Jack, and please come back	Plan and pave the road ahead in the form of an action plan (road map)	Narrow	Value delivery
LA15	Money talks and walk the talk	Get startup finance on the "table"	Narrow	Value capturing
LA16	The team theme	The greatest asset of all! Teams assess and reflect on their strengths and capabilities again	Wide	Value delivery
LA17	Weekly Progress pitches	Weekly progress pitch with a call for action by a random presenter, followed by tips and tops by the cohort	Narrow	Value capturing
LA18	Call for a peer coach	The rotating consultant game and peer-to-peer reflection and advice within the cohort	Narrow	All phases
LA19	Individual and team coaching	Providing different perspectives while giving freedom	Narrow and wide	All phases

(continued)

Table 3 (continued)

#	Name	Short description	EE	EP
LA20	Mid-final and final pitch moments	Stakeholder management and external perspective by jury	Narrow	All phases
LA21	Stakeholder alignment sessions	Stakeholder management and coaching on professional behavior	Narrow	All phases
LA22	Newsflash	Highlights, learnings, word of the day, worries, a parody of the coaches (memes)	Wide	
LA23	Co-creation sessions with the cohort	Halfway and at the end of the course, the cohort and staff evaluate and design improvement	Wide	

Appendix 2: Table 4

Table 4 Learning activations and their link with the learning activities from Table 3

#	Activations	Related learning activities (LA#) from Table 3
Narrow EE aspect		
A1	Engaging stakeholders	Spinning around (LA3) Mid-final and final pitch moments (LA20) Stakeholder alignment sessions (LA21)
A2	Adaptive and iterative way of working	Unleash creativity (LA5) Check & imagine all (LA8) Campus validation experience (LA7) Giant potato (LA8) Twisted perspectives (LA9) Competition is your best friend (LA10) Prototyping workshops I and II (LA11) Value added transformation (LA12) Oops, ops exercise (LA13) Hit the road, Jack, and please come back (LA14) Money talks and walk the talk (LA15)
Wide EE aspect		
A3	Establishing psychological safety	Kick-off (LA1) Hello moments (LA2) Mindset and culture (LA4) Newsflash (LA22)
A4	Peer-to-peer activities	Weekly progress pitches (LA17) Call for a peer coach (LA18) Stakeholder alignment sessions (AL21) Newsflash (LA22)
A5	Boosting team dynamics	Mindset and culture (LA4) The team theme (LA16) Individual and team coaching (LA19)
A6	Storytelling and showtime	Weekly progress pitches (LA17) Mid-final and final pitch moments (LA20) Stakeholder alignment session (LA21) Newsflash (LA22)
A7	Facilitation by coaches	Weekly progress pitches (LA17) Call for a peer coach (LA18) Individual and team coaching (LA19)
A8	Co-creation	Co-creation sessions with the cohort (LA23)

References

Ajzen, I. (1991). The theory of planned behavior. *Organizational Behavior and Human Decision Processes, 50*(2), 179–211. https://doi.org/10.1016/0749-5978(91)90020-t

Baggen, Y., Lans, T., & Gulikers, J. (2021). Making entrepreneurship education available to all: Design principles for educational programs stimulating an entrepreneurial mindset. *Entrepreneurship Education and Pedagogy, 5*(3), 347–374. https://doi.org/10.1177/2515127420988517

Biggs, J. B. (1996). Enhancing teaching through constructive alignment. *Higher Education, 32*(3), 347–364. https://doi.org/10.1007/bf00138871

Blenker, P., Elmholdt, S. T., Frederiksen, S. H., Korsgaard, S., & Wagner, K. (2011). Entrepreneurship as everyday practice: Towards a personalised pedagogy of enterprise education. *Industry and Higher Education, 25*(6), 413–423.

Burg, V. J., Romme, G., Gilsing, V. A., & Reymen, I. M. (2008). *Creating university spin-offs: A science-based design perspective*. https://doi.org/10.1111/j.1540-5885.2008.00291.x

Chesbrough, H. (2003). *Open innovation: The new imperative for creating and profiting from technology*. Harvard Business Press.

Dym, C. L., Agogino, A. M., Eris, O., Frey, D. D., & Leifer, L. J. (2005). Engineering design thinking, teaching, and learning. *IEEE Engineering Management Review, 34*, 65–65.

Edmondson, A. C. (1999). Psychological safety and learning behavior in work teams. *Administrative Science Quarterly, 44*, 350–383. https://doi.org/10.2307/2666999

Fayolle, A., & Gailly, B. (2008). From craft to science: Teaching models and learning processes in entrepreneurship education. *Journal of European Industrial Training, 32*, 569–593. https://doi.org/10.1108/03090590810899838

Fayolle, A. (2013). Personal views on the future of entrepreneurship education. *Entrepreneurship & Regional Development, 25*(7–8), 692–701. https://doi.org/10.1080/08985626.2013.821318

Fayolle, A., & Gailly, B. (2015). The impact of entrepreneurship education on entrepreneurial attitudes and intention: Hysteresis and persistence. *Journal of Small Business Management, 53*, 75–93. https://doi.org/10.1111/jsbm.12065

Fleur, D. S., Bredeweg, B., Bos, W., & v. d. (2021). Metacognition: Ideas and insights from neuro- and educational sciences. NPJ science of. *Learning, 6*(1), 13. https://doi.org/10.1038/s41539-021-00089-5

Gallagher, S. E., & Savage, T. (2020). Challenge-based learning in higher education: An exploratory literature review. *Teaching in Higher Education, 28*, 1135–1157. https://doi.org/10.1080/13562517.2020.1863354

Heinonen, J., & Poikkijoki, S. (2006). An entrepreneurial-directed approach to entrepreneurship education: Mission impossible? *Journal of Management Development, 25*, 80–94. https://doi.org/10.1108/02621710610637981

Hevner, A. R., March, S. T., Park, J., & Ram, S. (2004). Design science in information systems research. *MIS Quarterly, 28*(1), 75–105. https://doi.org/10.2307/25148625

Higgins, D., & Elliott, C. T. (2011). Learning to make sense: What works in entrepreneurial education? *Journal of European Industrial Training, 35*(4), 345–367. https://doi.org/10.1108/03090591111128324

İyigün, N. Ö. (2015). What could entrepreneurship do for sustainable development? A corporate social responsibility-based approach. *Procedia - Social and Behavioral Sciences, 195*, 1226–1231. https://doi.org/10.1016/j.sbspro.2015.06.253

Jones, C., & Iredale, N. (2010). Enterprise education as pedagogy. *Education + Training, 52*(1), 7–19. https://doi.org/10.1108/00400911011017654

Kahn, W. A. (1990). Psychological conditions of personal engagement and disengagement at work. *Academy of Management Journal, 33*, 692–724. https://doi.org/10.2307/256287

Kamovich, U., & Foss, L. (2017). In search of alignment: A review of impact studies in entrepreneurship education. *Education Research International, 2*, 1–15. https://doi.org/10.1155/2017/1450102

Katzenbach, J. R., & Smith, D. K. (2015). *The wisdom of teams: Creating the high-performance organization*.

Kolb, D. A. (2014). *Experiential learning: Experience as the source of learning and development*. FT Press.

Lackéus, M. (2014). An emotion based approach to assessing entrepreneurial education. *International Journal of Management Education, 12*(3), 374–396. https://doi.org/10.1016/j.ijme.2014.06.005

Lackéus, M. (2015). *Entrepreneurship in education: What, why, when, how*. Entrepreneurship360 Background Paper, OECD. Retrieved from https://www.oecd.org/cfe/leed/BGP_Entrepreneurship-in-Education.pdf

Laundon, M., Cathcart, A., & Greer, D. (2020). Teaching philosophy statements. *Organizational Behavior Teaching Review, 44*(5), 577–587. https://doi.org/10.1177/1052562920942289

Lave, J., & Wenger, E. (1991). *Situated learning: Legitimate peripheral participation*. Cambridge University Press.

Lazendic-Galloway, J., Reymen, I. M. M. J., Bruns, M., Helker, K., & Vermunt, J. D. (2021). Students' experiences with challenge-based learning at TU/e innovation Space–Overview of five key characteristics across a broad range of courses. In *SEFI 49th Annual Conference Engaging Engineering Education: Proceedings*.

Lepak, D. P., Smith, K. G., & Taylor, M. S. (2007). Value creation and value capture: A multi-level perspective. *Academy of Management Review, 32*(1), 180–194. https://doi.org/10.5465/amr.2007.23464011

Liu, N., & Carless, D. (2006). Peer feedback: The learning element of peer assessment. *Teaching in Higher Education, 11*, 279–290. https://doi.org/10.1080/13562510600680582

Mair, J., & Marti, I. (2006). Social entrepreneurship research: A source of explanation, prediction, and delight. *Journal of World Business, 41*(1), 36–44. https://doi.org/10.1016/j.jwb.2005.09.002

Martens, M. L., & Jennings, P. D. (2007). Do the stories they tell get them the money they need? The role of entrepreneurial narratives in resource acquisition. *Academy of Management Journal, 50*(5), 1107–1132. https://doi.org/10.5465/amj.2007.27169488

Mezirow, J. (1998). On critical reflection. *Adult Education Quarterly, 48*(3), 185–198. https://doi.org/10.1177/074171369804800305

Mwasalwiba, E. S. (2010). Entrepreneurship education: A review of its objectives, teaching methods, and impact indicators. *Education + Training, 52*(1), 20–47. https://doi.org/10.1108/00400911011017663

Nabi, G., Liñán, F., Fayolle, A., Krueger, N., & Walmsley, A. (2017). The impact of entrepreneurship education in higher education: A systematic review and research agenda. *Academy of Management Learning and Education, 16*, 277–299. https://doi.org/10.5465/amle.2015.0026

Naia, A., Baptista, R., Januário, C., & Trigo, V. (2014). A systematization of the literature on entrepreneurship education: Challenges and emerging solutions in the entrepreneurial classroom. *Industry and Higher Education, 28*, 79–96. https://doi.org/10.5367/ihe.2014.0196

Newman, S., & Latifi, A. (2020). Vygotsky, education, and teacher education. *Journal of Education for Teaching International Research and Pedagogy, 47*(1), 4–17. https://doi.org/10.1080/02607476.2020.1831375

Nichols, M. H., & Cator, K. (2008). *Challenge based learning white paper*. Apple, Inc.

Osterwalder, A., Pigneur, Y., Bernarda, G., & Smith, A. (2014). *Value proposition design: How to create products and services customers want*. John Wiley & Sons.

Polkinghorne, D. E. (1988). *Narrative knowing and the human sciences*. Suny Press.

Reymen, I., Bruns, M., Lazendic-Galloway, J., Helker, K., Cardona, A. V., & Vermunt, J. D. (2022). Creating a learning ecosystem for developing, sustaining, and disseminating CBL the case of TU/e innovation space. In E. Vilalta-Perdomo, J. Membrillo-Hernández, R. Michel-Villarreal, G. Lakshmi, & M. Martínez-Acosta (Eds.), *The emerald handbook of challenge based learning* (pp. 13–33). Emerald Publishing Limited. https://doi.org/10.1108/978-1-80117-490-920221002

Ries, E. (2011). *The lean startup: How today's entrepreneurs use continuous innovation to create radically successful businesses*. Crown Currency.

Ryan, R. M., & Deci, E. L. (2000). Self-determination theory and the facilitation of intrinsic motivation, social development, and Well-being. *The American Psychologist, 55*(1), 68–78. https://doi.org/10.1037/0003-066x.55.1.68
Sarasvathy, S. D. (2001). Causation and effectuation: Toward a theoretical shift from economic inevitability to entrepreneurial contingency. *The Academy of Management Review, 26*(2), 243. https://doi.org/10.2307/259121
Schaltegger, S., & Wagner, M. (2011). Sustainable entrepreneurship and sustainability innovation: Categories and interactions. *Business Strategy and the Environment, 20*(4), 222–237. https://doi.org/10.1002/bse.682
Simon, H. A. (1996). *The sciences of the artificial* (3rd ed.). MIT Press.
Slavin, R. E. (1980). Cooperative learning. *Review of Educational Research, 50*(2), 315–342. https://doi.org/10.3102/00346543050002315
Stigmar, M. (2016). Peer-to-peer teaching in higher education: A critical literature review. *Mentoring & Tutoring: Partnership in Learning, 24*, 124–136. https://doi.org/10.1080/13611267.2016.1178963
Struyven, K., Dochy, F., & Janssens, S. (2005). Students' perceptions about evaluation and assessment in higher education: A review1. *Assessment & Evaluation in Higher Education, 30*, 325–341. https://doi.org/10.1080/02602930500099102
Thomas, L. (2013). What works? Facilitating an effective transition into higher education. *Widening Participation and Lifelong Learning, 14*, 4–24. https://doi.org/10.5456/WPLL.14.S.4
Topping, K. J. (1996). The effectiveness of peer tutoring in further and higher education: A typology and review of the literature. *Higher Education, 32*, 321–345. https://doi.org/10.1007/BF00138870
Turner, T., & Gianiodis, P. (2018). Entrepreneurship unleashed: Understanding entrepreneurial education outside of the business school. *Journal of Small Business Management, 56*(1), 131–149. https://doi.org/10.1111/jsbm.12365
Welsh, D. H., Tullar, W. L., & Nemati, H. R. (2016). Entrepreneurship education: Process, method, or both? *Journal of Innovation & Knowledge, 1*, 125–132. https://doi.org/10.1016/j.jik.2016.01.005
Windle, R., McCormick, D., Dandrea, J., & Wharrad, H. (2011). The characteristics of reusable learning objects that enhance learning: A case-study in health-science education. *British Journal of Educational Technology, 42*(5), 811–823. https://doi.org/10.1111/j.1467-8535.2010.01108.x
Zacks, J. M., & Tversky, B. (2001). Event structure in perception and conception. *Psychological Bulletin, 127*(1), 3. https://doi.org/10.1037/0033-2909.127.1.3

Ákos R. Wetters has co-founded several enterprises, including two consultancy firms focusing on operational and supply chain process improvements and a venture dedicated to intrapreneurship and open innovation. Concurrently, he has significantly contributed to STEM education through teaching, training, and coaching in the academic sector. Before these entrepreneurial ventures, Ákos accumulated over a decade of experience in various corporate roles abroad, particularly in Jakarta and Kuala Lumpur. Today, he is deeply engaged in entrepreneurial education and innovation in education, capitalising on his rich experience to mentor students, professionals, and start-ups. Serving as a "hybrid teacher" at Eindhoven University of Technology, he brings practical insights from the professional world into the academic setting. Ákos' multicultural Dutch-Indonesian-Hungarian heritage enhances his effectiveness in international contexts.

Jasmina Galloway-Lazendic is a scientist, educationalist and entrepreneurial academic. She obtained her PhD in Astrophysics in Sydney, Australia, and has worked as a researcher at the Harvard-Smithsonian Center for Astrophysics and Massachusetts Institute of Technology in Boston. She was a senior lecturer and the Astronomy program coordinator at the School of Physics and Astronomy, Monash University, Australia, where she led the implementation of student-centred learning practices at the faculty and university level. In 2021, she was awarded a Senior

Fellowship for demonstrated leadership and impact on other colleagues' practices in learning and teaching in higher education. She has experience as an entrepreneur in digital tech and technology transfer. With entrepreneurial experience in digital technology and technology transfer, she has also served as a coach in the Innovation Space Project (ISP) course.

Duygu Keskin obtained a MSc degree in Industrial Design from the Middle East Technical University, Turkey and a PhD degree in Industrial Design Engineering from the Delft University of Technology, the Netherlands. Her PhD focused on product innovation processes within sustainability-oriented new ventures. From 2007 to 2015, she worked a researcher, project manager and lecturer at Delft University of Technology. Since 2016, she works as an Assistant Professor at the Innovation, Technology Entrepreneurship and Marketing Group of Industrial Engineering at TU/e and teaches several design and entrepreneurship-related courses. Her research interests include the design and creation of new firms and innovation ecosystems, sustainable entrepreneurship and entrepreneurship education.

Gert Guri has developed unique expertise in integrating real-life challenges with educational objectives in entrepreneurship courses over a decade at EIT Digital (European Institute of Technology and Innovation). His international background, being an Albanian-born Italian living in France and working in the Netherlands, and his experience in international organisations and with international students have enriched his global perspective and approach to education. Gert coordinates entrepreneurial learning at TU/e, guiding students in hands-on projects that tackle real societal challenges. Through the Challenge-Based Learning (CBL) approach, he fosters an entrepreneurial mindset in curricular and extracurricular settings. As a co-teacher in the Innovation Space Project (ISP) course, Gert empowers students to make tangible societal impacts with their projects. His work is defined by ongoing experimentation, co-creation, and adaptability, enhancing the effectiveness of team-based learning.

Pim Widdershoven was a student and coach in the Innovation Space Project (ISP) course on technology entrepreneurship at the Eindhoven University of Technology. He guided students using Challenge-Based Learning (CBL) methods, helping them address real-world challenges and develop technology-driven solutions that meet societal needs. In addition to coaching, he contributed to the thematic analysis for this chapter, deriving insights from student experiences and project outcomes.

Today, Pim is pursuing a PhD at the Vrije Universiteit of Amsterdam, where he focuses on the Problematic Use of the Internet. His research interests lie in the complex interplay between people and technology, examining how digital interactions impact well-being and behaviour. This work informs his approach to research and teaching, where he aims to foster a deeper understanding of technology's role in modern society.

Isabelle Reymen obtained a MSc degree in Architecture from KU Leuven, Belgium and completed a PhD degree in Design sciences at the Eindhoven University of Technology (TU/e). Since 2006 she is a member of the Innovation, Technology Entrepreneurship and Marketing Group of the School of Industrial Engineering at TU/e, where she is Full Professor Design of Innovation Ecosystems. She is co-founder, scientific director and general manager of TU/e innovation Space. She combines entrepreneurial thinking with a passion for design processes and aims for system innovation. Her research interests focus on understanding and improving heterogeneous collaboration processes in entrepreneurial innovation ecosystems. She was granted several projects on entrepreneurial topics and on education innovation. TU/e innovation Space received national and international awards for its education innovation. In 2020, she became a Comenius Leadership Fellow and was granted a scholarship to perform research on Challenge-Based Learning.

Embracing Failures: Advancing the Entrepreneurial Education Pedagogy through Design Science Approach

Samar Billi Noaman and Gayatri Nair

Abstract Entrepreneurial education (EE) research has identified several trends in fostering students' entrepreneurial mindsets with a growing focus on sustaining entrepreneurial activities, covering topics such as ideation, business planning, market analysis, strategic management, and innovation. Nevertheless, the heightened rate of startup failures urges entrepreneurship educators to reconsider failure in entrepreneurship and how it is addressed within entrepreneurship curricula. This research aims to examine the status quo of the topic of entrepreneurial failure management in current curricula across universities. It further proposes an applicable method for incorporating productive failure into EE. The study's findings reveal a notable gap in the inclusion of business failure as a formal topic of study. Instead, current curricula emphasize the positive and successful aspects, potentially leaving students underprepared to confront challenges and setbacks in their entrepreneurial ventures. Furthermore, the frameworks that guide students in navigating failures in entrepreneurial pedagogies are still undetermined with a focus on preventing failure rather than navigating it. At one level, this research aims to examine the status quo of the topic of entrepreneurial failure management in current curricula across universities. It further develops the applicable method to incorporate productive failure into the learning pedagogy. The design science research approach (DSR) was considered, offering theoretical framework that identifies field challenges while aiming to develop futuristic, applicable solutions. This chapter outlines a step-by-step process aligned with the DSR method, guiding educators through identifying problem areas, analyzing the type and root cause of the failure, creating productive responses, and evaluating and sharing outcomes. The study provides educators with reliable practical applications to implement in class at each step of the process.

S. B. Noaman · G. Nair (✉)
Management, Canadian University Dubai, Dubai, UAE
e-mail: samar.noaman@cud.ac.ae; gayatri.nair@cud.ac.ae

© The Author(s), under exclusive license to Springer Nature Switzerland AG 2025

B. Derre, Y. Baggen (eds.), *Empowering the Next Generation of Entrepreneurial Change Agents*, Contributions to Management Science,
https://doi.org/10.1007/978-3-031-82251-3_7

1 Introduction

With the 50% decline in entrepreneurial ventures since 1978, entrepreneurial education (EE) adopted an overarching trajectory of promoting the development of entrepreneurial willingness and intention, particularly that the support of new entrepreneurs will contribute to economic growth (Dobson et al., 2017; Gonul & Litzky, 2018). Governments worldwide endorsed and promoted youth entrepreneurship and innovation by issuing policies that aim to encourage entrepreneurial activities and ventures (Aftab et al., 2022).

In their analysis of the literature on EE, Winarno et al. (2019) classified the distribution of articles across various entrepreneurial domains. They noted that 32% of the examined articles on EE were focused on educational processes or training designed to influence individual attitudes, behaviors, values, or intentions toward entrepreneurship, either as a potential career or to foster a greater appreciation for its societal role. A parallel emphasis (32%) was on EE linked to the development of personal skills in entrepreneurship. Additionally, some articles were associated with the establishment of new businesses (18%), recognition of opportunities (9%), and the management of existing small enterprises (9%). Research on the preparedness to face the challenges in their entrepreneurial endeavors is still limited.

It is recognized that one of the main deterrents to establishing a new business is the fear of failure (GEM, 2023). By knowing the negative consequences of failure, potential entrepreneurs may feel the fear of being failed and adopt an instinctive emotional aversion. The lack of preparedness to handle failure adds to the ambiguity and complexity that would be faced and increases the impact of failure (Edmondson, 2023). Such failure aspects contradict the rationale of the current EE which pivots on delivering and promoting business success for current and potential students and focuses on competencies associated with startup desirability and feasibility (Oser & Volery, 2012).

Nevertheless, compared to success, startup failure has acquired a higher rate over the years (Bryant, 2024). Current EE has been blamed for the unintentional contribution to this failure by not raising enough awareness on the dark sides of entrepreneurship (Bandera et al., 2021), a fact that extends a moral obligation to bring responsible education on the precautionary and active handling of failure in entrepreneurship (Shepherd, 2003; Shepherd, 2004; Oser & Volery, 2012). This proposition does not intend to stifle the initiative of launching new ventures. Yet, since experiencing failure is intrinsic to achieving success (Timmons, 1999), this scheme intends to bring to light the set of competencies that one needs to be equipped with to manage the complex phenomenon of failure.

EE brings a pivotal opportunity for students to get the knowledge and training that would prepare them to come to terms with failure-related economic ramifications and personal sorrow. The benefits of bringing failure as a concept and an aspect of management education into the classroom are multifaceted. Youth can realize self-regulation and control of their cognition and behavior which can improve their dynamic adaptability to entrepreneurial dilemmas. It also prepares students for real-world scenarios while facilitating the transfer of experience to a psychologically safe environment, where questions and ideas are appreciated, emotions are freely expressed, and wrong decisions and failures are discussed (Edmondson, 2023). This construct is particularly pertinent in educational contexts, where a psychologically safe classroom environment—facilitated by the educator—enables students to learn and experiment with failure aspects safely. It ultimately prepares them to establish psychological safety in their future ventures for progressive learning in this uncertain, changing world.

This chapter aims to propose a framework that addresses entrepreneurship failure management in EE using the Design Science Research approach (DSR). This framework can be used by EE educators to tackle an area that is seldom examined in EE and its course offerings.

From the several definitions of entrepreneurship failures, this study does not necessarily link entrepreneurship failure to mere bankruptcy but adopts a broader perspective by viewing it as non-attainment of an entrepreneurial goal (Cannon & Edmondson, 2005; Cope, 2011). Two research questions will guide the research. RQ1: Investigate the course offerings of entrepreneurship programs from selected universities around the world and whether these programs offer any courses related to preparing students to face entrepreneurship challenges and failures. RQ2: Based on the DSR approach, develop a learning protocol that can be used by entrepreneurship educators to address entrepreneurship failure and equip future entrepreneurs with the knowledge, skills, and traits to manage it, cope with it, and learn from it.

2 Literature Review

It is argued that EE has developed along with the development of entrepreneurial activities (González-López et al., 2019). Over the past decade, existing studies on EE have focused more on promoting youth entrepreneurial success (Boldureanu et al., 2020; Welsh et al., 2016) and improving youth entrepreneurial intention and willingness (Jena, 2020; Zhang et al., 2014) using different methods and applications such as qualitative comparative analysis (Luo et al., 2023) and meta-analysis (Martínez-Gregorio et al., 2021). Existing discussions on EE mostly guide and stimulate youth entrepreneurial behavior from the perspective of entrepreneurial success (Wang et al., 2023). Courses, teaching, and coaching have focused on delivering nuances associated with entrepreneurial desirability and feasibility. Reflections of success such as the smiling faces of young entrepreneurs are commonly seen in EE material. On the other hand, the nuances of entrepreneurship failure and its management are very little or even missing (Oser & Volery, 2012). Entrepreneurship educators expressed concerns that exposing students to the concept of failure may dampen their motivation toward pursuing entrepreneurial ventures (Cohen et al., 2023). The anti-failure bias that exists in today's EE curricula focuses on delivering the experiences of successful entrepreneurs yet avoids addressing common entrepreneurial failures (Liu et al., 2019).

Apart from failure itself, it is argued that the existing EE still lacks soft skills training that equips entrepreneurs with the ability to face business challenges and look forward (Ayala & Manzano, 2014; González-López et al., 2019). Competencies such as managing emotional difficulties, coping with uncertainty, and deriving lessons from setbacks are crucial elements of entrepreneurial training that warrant more highlighting (Bledow et al., 2017; Byrne et al., 2014; Loi et al., 2016).

In his review of the curricula of MBA programs that specialize in entrepreneurship and related fields at the world's top business schools, Widiawan (2017) found that only 0.79% of courses are focused on self-development content. This offering is mainly found in universities in the United States and Europe. Each school offers an average of 0.35 courses that are related to self-image, self-leadership, and the soft skills associated with psychological development. While some business schools teach risk analysis, very few courses cover subjects related to crisis management, and none of them address coping with failure. Entrepreneurship curricula do not include courses or modules on how to deal with the psychological effects of failure.

EE has also been criticized for its role and unintended consequence in producing failures and undesired outcomes due to its lack of addressing entrepreneurial risk awareness and the ability to recover from failure (Bandera et al., 2021).

2.1 The Failure-Averse Approach in EE

The disproportionate entrepreneurial failure rate in both boom and bad times has prompted entrepreneurship educators to reconsider the learning material and pedagogy. More EE for youth has begun to focus on entrepreneurial failure in teaching content and incorporating the perspective of failure learning in the educational pedagogy (Hameed & Irfan, 2019; Shepherd, 2004; Wang et al., 2023). The objective of such an approach stems from the willingness to facilitate success and prevent or avoid failure whenever possible. When addressed in EE, failure is often viewed as an important source of learning for implementing preventative measures to reduce risks and avoid future failure (Widiawan, 2017).

Resilience acquired particular attention in EE failure-related studies (González-López et al., 2019; Botha et al., 2015; Costa et al., 2016; Spagnoli et al., 2016) and is considered a fundamental component of personal development (Jing et al., 2016; Nabi et al., 2017). Despite its acknowledged importance, resilience remains underexplored in EE literature, particularly in practical application within educational curricula (Noble & McGrath, 2014). However, it has been incorporated in the classroom by means of increasing self-image and self-confidence (St-Jean & Audet, 2012) and by learning from the failing experiences of entrepreneurs to help develop preventative future mechanisms (Cope, 2011).

Studies that addressed entrepreneurial failures in EE emphasized the necessity for a nuanced understanding beyond the conventional traits of achievement, resilience, and risk-taking propensity commonly attributed to entrepreneurs (Oser & Volery, 2012) by considering the motivations, senses, and emotional aspects related to failure. A distinction between motivations associated with success and others associated with failure was recognized (Gonul & Litzky, 2018; Oser & Volery, 2012). It was also recommended to conduct a classification of entrepreneurship students based on their motivational tendencies of achievement versus anxiety as a way of preparing them for market challenges. The motivations included failure avoidance and achievement anxiety as subdimensions (Gonul & Litzky, 2018).

Based on regulatory-focused theory (Higgins, 1998; Sitkin & Weingart, 1995), Oser and Volery (2012) explored entrepreneurial self-regulation in time and context. With a "sense of success," entrepreneurs adopt promotion-focused behaviors aimed at achieving goals. Conversely, when motivated by a "sense of failure," their motivations shift toward prevention, emphasizing responsibility and alignment with their "ought" selves. A balanced approach to EE integrates both perspectives, equipping entrepreneurs with strategies for both promotion and prevention to enhance venture success. Oser and Volery (2012) further outline the elements of the "sense of failure" including awareness of inherent risks in start-ups, commitment to corrective action through responsibility and risk management, and a cultivated awareness of potential errors for enhanced failure prevention.

2.2 *Other Dimensions of Failure in EE*

Despite EE's objectives to deliver knowledge on failure avoidance, failure is inherent in entrepreneurship. Its economic and personal impacts can be devastating to the entrepreneur. Camuffo et al.'s (2024) experimental research, building on Camuffo et al. (2020), demonstrated that following a scientific approach can dynamically shape entrepreneurs' decision-making, particularly in areas of termination, pivoting, and performance. The scientific approach envisions entrepreneurs as "scientists" (Zellweger & Zenger, 2023) who are more likely to critically evaluate their business ideas and view the novelty of their business through reasoning, evidence, and strong argument (Kerr et al., 2014). The scientific approach relies on two mechanisms: efficient search and methodic doubt. Efficient search enables entrepreneurs to leverage theory for identifying and testing exploration opportunities, while methodic doubt encourages challenging entrepreneurial ideas. The interplay between efficient search and methodic doubt determines whether an entrepreneur pivots or terminates a business idea. When methodic doubt outweighs efficient search, entrepreneurs may decide to terminate; when the reverse holds, pivoting is preferred. Entrepreneurs trained in this approach are less likely attached to unsuccessful ideas and more decisive in either terminating projects or pivoting more focused way. Over time, this scientific method reduces overconfidence with the business idea (Åstebro et al., 2014) and unawareness (Karni & Vierø, 2017). It thus fosters superior performance and success in the long run, as entrepreneurs apply stricter decision rules. The relevance of Camuffo et al. (2024) to EE lies in its adoption of the framework of "entrepreneurs-as-scientists" (Zellweger & Zenger, 2023) and its theoretical-based training conduct. Camuffo et al.'s (2024) process—involving theory development, hypothesis formulation, testing, and adjusting initial beliefs based on evidence—aligns with the scientific approach, theoretical underpinning, and evidence-based results emphasized in EE.

Particular failure-associated feelings were discussed in EE as a learning pedagogy that addresses emotional intelligence. Managing "grief" to enhance learning from failure was proposed as a classroom learning activity that aims to guide students in dealing with their emotions in a sense that they can effectively leverage emotions to navigate between a loss-orientation process and a restoration-orientation process and attain a balance that prevents from succumbing to cognitive inefficiency (Shepherd, 2004). The feeling of "shame" after failure was discussed by Widiawan (2017) from the lens of the cognitive shame model by Poulson (2000). Similarly, anxiety, fear, and giving up on pursuing subsequent entrepreneurship career choices were also addressed in several EE studies (Widiawan, 2017; Al-Alawi et al., 2023; Wang et al., 2023; Cohen et al., 2023). A change in curricula to include modules and courses on psychological content in terms of starting a business, facing obstacles, and handling shame after failure was recommended (Widiawan, 2017).

A pedagogy that addresses emotional management and supports decision-making processes that contribute to superior performance and successful entrepreneurship in the long run is valuable for students preparing for future involvement in entrepreneurial endeavors as it expands from managing particular emotions of grief or shame to more general emotional intelligence (Shepherd, 2004).

However, the challenge in such a pedagogy is transferring the classroom theory into a management practice (Wren et al., 1994) when focusing on students' feelings rather than their thinking (Shepherd, 2004). Hence, the methods that can be applied in emotional learning need to have management relevance and the potential to produce a positive post-learning outlook on entrepreneurship.

Cohen et al. (2023) employed this experimental approach with entrepreneurship students to study the significance of having an optimistic mindset in entrepreneurship. They recognize that optimism serves as a moderating factor, mitigating the adverse effects of failure on the likelihood of pursuing future entrepreneurial efforts. Furthermore, the study differentiated failure not as a singular experience but as varying in magnitude, distinguishing between small and large failures. Accordingly, the entrepreneurial mindset toward failure will vary based on its magnitude.

Building on the concept of small failures, Seckler et al. (2017) studied the role of having an "error management mindset"—a perspective that acknowledges errors as inevitable aspects that cannot be completely prevented—on entrepreneurship after-failure consequences and negative emotions. Accordingly, a high error management mindset decreases the intensity of negative emotions and allows for viewing failures as a learning experience.

On a parallel line, Edmondson (2019) in her book *The Fearless Organization: Creating Psychological Safety in the Workplace for Learning, Innovation and Growth* identified failure archetypes and distinguished between preventable, complex, and intelligent failures. Preventable failures are "deviation from known process that produce unwanted outcomes" (p. 163) such as a behavioral deficiency. Complex failures are "unique and novel combinations of events and actions that give rise to unwanted outcomes" (p. 163) such as new factors imposed on a familiar situation. Intelligent failures, on the other hand, are "Novel forays into new territory that lead to unwanted outcomes" (p. 163). An example of this can be undertaking a new experiment. Intelligent failures represent a key learning opportunity given that the organization's leaders accept failures and promote psychological safety for sharing ideas and learning from failures (Edmondson, 2019).

3 Teaching Methods Proposed in EE Literature

Certain pedagogical approaches aimed at refining and assimilating knowledge derived from failures by engaging in comprehensive analyses and reflections on cases of entrepreneurial failure to enhance the entrepreneurial literacy of the youth when confronted with entrepreneurial challenges (Mohamed & Ali, 2021; Testa & Frascheri, 2015).

However, it is important to acknowledge that errors and failures cannot be prevented completely, and a learning strategy that is completely reliant on error prevention has its limitations (Frese & Keith, 2015). Pedagogical approaches that have acknowledged this incorporated preventive and productive dimensions in addressing failure in EE.

Wang et al. (2023) introduced an EE framework that prioritizes fault-tolerant environment as an abstract variable. This approach aims to assist entrepreneurs in attributing their failures, thereby mitigating the detrimental effects of self-doubt and external negation of their capabilities by external factors (willingness cognition). By incorporating fault tolerance, certain EE can work to counteract the pervasive entrepreneurial failure stigma. From another angle, failure-learning-based EE can empower young individuals to enhance their rational cognition (ability cognition) by fostering an improved preparedness for dynamic adaptation to entrepreneurial challenges through risk awareness, implementing preemptive measures, and systematically reducing entrepreneurial risks.

Recognizing that failure is not a singular experience but can take varying magnitudes and archetypes, entrepreneurship educators can develop pedagogical models to address failure accordingly. Edmondson (2019) encourages minimizing basic and complex failures for a higher focus while welcoming intelligent failures for enhanced development. Accordingly, failures can be destigmatized for psychological safety in the organization with productive responses to each failure archetype. Table 1 lists the suggested productive responses for each failure type.

This failure-based learning curve elevates to what is described as "failing well" characterized by praiseworthy attempts that carry new knowledge wherein the experience of failure fosters learning and growth (Edmondson, 2023).

In addition to fostering a fault-tolerant environment, Wang et al. (2023) proposed two pedagogical recommendations to prepare students to face and transcend failure in entrepreneurship. First, at the theoretical teaching level, the EE system should integrate courses on risk management, crisis management, and adversity

Table 1 Productive responses to different types of failure

	Preventable failure	Complex failure	Intelligent failure
Productive response	– Training – Retraining – Process improvement – System redesign – Sanctions, if repeated or otherwise blameworthy actions are found	– Failure analysis from diverse perspectives – Identification of risk factors to address – System improvement	– Failure parties – Failure awards – Thoughtful analysis of results to figure out implications – Brainstorming of new hypotheses – Design of next steps or additional experiments

Source: Edmondson (2019), p. 180

psychology, while also establishing a comprehensive case library of entrepreneurial failures. Second, active mentorship is proposed to help young entrepreneurs develop a mature and constructive perspective on the inevitable existence of failure in entrepreneurship. While the first level presents a preventative perspective to avoid future failures by learning about them, the second level presents a productive learning mechanism to experience and cope with failure. With these elements, a holistic strategy is proposed to dispel the fear associated with failure and shift the prevailing concept from "the victor becomes a king and the loser a bandit" to the more constructive notion that "failure is the mother of success." This multifaceted strategy seeks to instill resilience, encourage learning from setbacks, and foster a positive outlook on challenges within the entrepreneurial landscape.

Shepherd (2004) proposed a pedagogical approach that employs a combination of tailored lectures; indirect experiences including case studies and guest lecturers; and direct experiences including role-playing, reflections on the grief of business failure, and simulations. He also suggested a measurement implication to the learning-from-failure pedagogy. This measuring implication assesses students' competency to manage emotions associated with business failure in a pre-and post-intake of the new course content or change in the curriculum.

Other studies highlighted learning from stories about managerial failures (Bledow et al., 2017) through action-learning approaches and personalized mentoring (Cope, 2011), tutoring, counseling, and social networking support (Jing et al., 2016), as well as direct learning from experience (Crick & Crick, 2016).

4 Methodology

The study employed an analysis of universities that offered entrepreneurship courses worldwide, selected based on the region. Eight cases from eight different countries including the United Kingdom, Canada, Brazil, Australia, India, United States, and Morocco were chosen for the analysis. The universities were selected based on the convenience sampling method which is a technique used by researchers due to the ease of availability of the information. This method has been employed in this study due to the large availability of the course study plan through the universities' websites and databases online. The Design Science Research approach (DSR) was opted as a framework to analyze the findings. The relevance of DSR to EE lies in its focus on developing practical artifacts through iterative cycles that build on previous research findings for future problem-solving (Denyer et al., 2008). This characteristic allows for tackling various contexts in entrepreneurship while continuously refining solutions. It also considers stakeholders' collaboration and thus enhances the real-world impact of EE (Derre, 2023). The DSR approach enables researchers to recommend improvements on the way that failure management can be incorporated into the pedagogy as a strategic tool and a learning protocol (Derre, 2023). The DSR consists of six steps. They are (1) identification of the problem, (2) definition of objectives for a solution, (3) design and development of artifacts, (4) demonstration by using the artifact to solve the problem, (5) evaluation of the solution, and (6) communication of the problem, (Grenha et al., 2017) summarized in Fig. 1.

Furthermore, the research extended its scope to understand the perspectives of the program at an educator level. A total of 16 participants, consisting of 7 females and 9 males, were selected for interviews. These participants were drawn from universities offering entrepreneurship majors and were actively engaged in teaching entrepreneurship-related courses. The participants, whose professional roles are outlined in Table 3, were invited to participate in virtual interviews conducted via Microsoft Teams. A semi-structured interview format was employed to facilitate a comprehensive exploration of their insights and experiences. The questions asked are listed in Table 2.

Details of the participants are listed in Table 3.

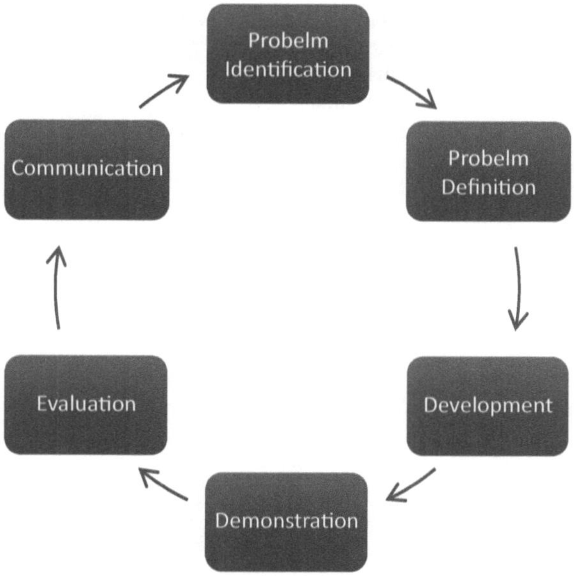

Fig. 1 Design science research approach model (based on Grenha et al. 2017)

Table 3 Participant profiles

Case	Country	Program	Participant ID	Title	Gender	Courses taught
1	United Kingdom (UK)	BSc business management	C1F1	Assistant professor	F	Entrepreneurship and Project Management; social science and modern business
			C1F2	Associate professor	F	Entrepreneurship and Project Management; business ethics and sustainability
2	Canada	Business management and innovation BCom (hons)	C2M1	Program coordinator	M	Entrepreneurship and innovation management; the global business environment; introduction to global management
			C2M2	Lecturer	M	Entrepreneurship and innovation management; Project Management
3	Brazil	Business administration and entrepreneurship	C3M1	Lecturer	M	Fundamentals of innovation and entrepreneurship; fundamentals of administration
			C3F3	Associate professor	F	Fundamentals of innovation and entrepreneurship; problem solving I
4	Australia	Bachelor of business management and innovation	C4F1	Assistant professor	F	Innovation and entrepreneurship; introduction to management
			C4M2	Assistant professor	M	Innovation and entrepreneurship; organizational behavior

(continued)

Table 3 (continued)

Case	Country	Program	Participant ID	Title	Gender	Courses taught
5	United Arab Emirates (UAE)	Bachelor of business administration entrepreneurship	C5F1	Program coordinator	F	Fundamentals of innovation and entrepreneurship; sustainability
			C5M2	Associate professor	M	Fundamentals of innovation and entrepreneurship; strategic management
6	India	Bachelor of business administration entrepreneurship	C6F1	Professor	F	Fundamentals of innovation and entrepreneurship; machine learning
			C6M2	Assistant professor	M	Fundamentals of innovation and entrepreneurship
7	United States of America (USA)	Management and innovation	C7M1	Program coordinator	M	Innovation and entrepreneurship; strategy
			C8F2	Lecturer	F	Innovation and entrepreneurship
8	Morocco	Bachelor of commerce and business management, double major in entrepreneurship	C8M1	Professor	M	Entrepreneurship and project management; commercial negotiation and business ethics
			C8M2	Lecturer	M	Entrepreneurship and project management; product innovation and commercialization

5 Findings

The interview with the program coordinators and the course instructors provided valuable insights into their institutional and personal perspectives on failure management in EE. Key topics discussed included their current pedagogical approaches, student capabilities and mindset, internal and external factors that contribute toward their mindset development, and broader dimensions toward failure management. All interviewees shared positive experiences teaching entrepreneurship, noting that while some institutions were highly focused on promoting entrepreneurial ventures, others prioritized intrapreneurial efforts. Notably, 12 out of 16 participants expressed concern that the curriculum primarily focused on preventative measures and strategies to avoid failure, rather than fostering a more balanced approach to learning from failure.

Table 2 Interview questions addressed to entrepreneurship educators in selected universities

Question number	Question wording
1	Tell us about your experience with teaching entrepreneurship to students.
2	Do you discuss risk-taking and failures entrepreneurs face with your students?
3	Do you believe it is important to talk about productive failures?
4	How do you engage in discussing the different dimensions of failure?
5	What pedagogical approaches do you use to discuss the view of failure in entrepreneurial journeys?
6	Do you believe that your current academic curriculum sheds light on failure management?
7	Do you believe that there is a scope to engage students to discuss and gain knowledge about failures as a separate course?
8	Would you say that several external and internal factors lead to the mindset development of students toward failure?
9	What recommendations would you suggest in incorporating productive failure and discussion in the classroom?
10	What trends do you see in academia regarding the incorporation of failure management into entrepreneurial education?

C6M2 commented:

> Entrepreneurship is all about pursuing opportunities, but at the same time has huge risks associated with it. And I think that's the whole beauty of it, so obviously, you are bound to fail. We teach students to always have that in the back of their mind and talk to them on the ways they can avoid certain situations.

C3F3 highlighted the curricula's inability to showcase failures:

> I mean we do talk to our students about failures as a part of developing their mindset, sort of like a terms and conditions (chuckles)… I think they already know what they are signing up for already. Essentially, we are not teaching them to fail but to figure out what could have been done to avoid them in the first place. We could never have a guidebook to navigate entrepreneurship since it's always experiential.

All participants highlighted the absence of formal frameworks for teaching failure management. Educators who addressed failure in their classrooms primarily relied on examples or case studies. Nevertheless, they noted that this method yielded mechanisms and strategies aimed at preventing failure.

Participant C1F1 said:

> I think most cases that we discuss lead to understanding the reason why a venture failed…like is it because of the CEO? Or is it the market?…. what possible reason could be there? I do this simple exercise in the class where I ask them, what would you have done? But that's quite a normal practice to engage in critical thinking, right?

Most participants agreed that it was important to discuss failures openly and that students should know when to call quits. They mentioned that some students always have high expectations of their business plan and lack the mindset to accept that things could not work as planned.

C5F1 stated:

> I believe that the fundamental reason why entrepreneurs end up failing has everything to do with their mindset. In most of the cases I have come across, a compelling reason why an entrepreneur never saw it coming was because they were so in love with their business plan.

All participants stated that they do not have a proper framework to refer to when identifying best practices for class discussions. Some participants also emphasized the numerous dimensions of failing and that pinning them down to a single framework could be challenging.

C7M1 added:

> I think it is obviously a good thing to talk to students about the possibilities of failure and what they should do to cope with it. But I think there are so many dimensions to it, and it could be from the emotional or psychological connection that carries the individual forward…I would say rather than just covering the business aspect of entrepreneurship, the practice of reflecting on actions and knowing when to tone things down can help.

C8M1 also commented:

> …there are always risks to the business and we always talk about ways to identify them. But sometimes, amidst these risks, other reasons also lead to the business failure, for example, lack of proper management, missing support, pressure to perform well and achieve their objectives, etc. I think many factors need to be discussed in the classroom to help students recognize and plan accordingly.

C4M2 provided an example:

> If I asked you to walk in broad daylight from point A to B, you would do it without a doubt since you can see where these points are. However, if the setting was pitch black, would you have gone in with the same confidence? Similarly, our students gather data and consume knowledge that prepares them for most of it. But if we do not discuss and be transparent about what all could go wrong and what they should or could do, they will always be afraid.

The participants identified internal and external factors they had observed as influencing the mindset of entrepreneurs. The internal factors include fear of failure, personal expectations, lack of knowledge/expertise, emotional and psychological factors, and personality and behavior. Meanwhile, the external factors include the mindset of family/friends/relatives/close social circle, lack of a support system, the societal stigma around failing, and the increasing percentage of unsuccessful entrepreneurs.

Finally, participants highlighted that teaching concepts such as productive failures, intelligent failing, and failing fast could enhance students' learning. They emphasized the importance of incorporating a pedagogy into the curriculum that addresses failure from an emotional perspective. This approach would help students develop soft skills, build resilience, improve decision-making when pivoting or discontinuing ventures, and foster continuous mindset development.

C1F1 said:

> Falling from a smaller height is much better than falling from a higher point because it can be tragic. I recommend the practice of productive failure where you may not be at the best performance now, but that leads you somewhere as a person…develops your long-term learning.

C3M2 remarked:

> Failures are meant to happen in an entrepreneurial journey, it is a normal thing to happen. But the way you react is what defines the failure. Some people are very quick to give up, some never give up (chuckles) and others just move on and never look back. But interestingly, some don't learn and end up repeating the same mistakes. I think we could agree that learning from mistakes and moving forward is good for the long run.

C3M1 recommended:

> I think it's best to engage optimistically and realistically by helping them identify when and what they should do if they are failing. I have seen so many of my friends who kept going till the end because they believed in a miracle. It doesn't quite work that way and we need to know that it's time to let go...... I think our approach should be concise and diplomatic where we talk to our students about realizing that their company is failing, pause and reflect on what happened, and then make a concise decision—should I continue or pivot or should I sell it? etc.

6 Discussion

In response to RQ1, the empirical investigation indicates that although some of the courses in entrepreneurship curricula address certain areas related to business and market challenges such as problem-solving, content that addresses entrepreneurship failure or the personal skills needed to navigate it is missing. Consequently, graduates from these programs are thrust into the realm of potential failure with minimal, if any, preparation. This outcome substantiates extant scholarly criticisms which have spotlighted the inherent inadequacy of EE in preparing future entrepreneurs to handle failure (Liu et al., 2019; Widiawan, 2017) or being adequately equipped with the required skills for that (Ayala & Manzano, 2014; González-López et al., 2019). This gap within EE underscores the urgent need for concerted attention to prevent successive cohorts of future entrepreneurs from being left in the dark when facing business failures.

The interviews with educators confirmed this critical gap in the current entrepreneurial curricula, particularly in their approach to the concept of failure. Many courses are primarily designed to prevent failures rather than engage with them, which may further contribute to establishing a pervasive fear of failure among aspiring entrepreneurs. Meanwhile, students often enter these programs with enthusiasm and optimism about starting their ventures, they also bring along unrealistic expectations and goals that may not align with the realities of a career in entrepreneurship. The findings underscore the necessity of integrating discussions and educational material on failure into the educational framework. By doing so, educators can help students develop a more nuanced understanding of entrepreneurship by encouraging them to view failure not as a setback, but as an essential part of the entrepreneurial learning process, equipping them with the mindset and skill necessary to navigate both success and failure effectively. This would require a revaluation of existing curricula to better prepare students for the challenges they will face in real-world scenarios.

The lack of established frameworks for teaching about failure in entrepreneurship suggests that educators may feel ill-equipped to address this topic effectively. Many discussions among educators focused solely on preventive measures, often neglecting to explore how to identify failures in the beginning and how to navigate their consequences after their occurrence. This oversight may leave the educator without a structured format for addressing failure in EE. It may also leave students unaware of and unprepared for the complexities of entrepreneurial life, where failures are not just common but can also serve as crucial learning opportunities. The findings highlight that failures are not merely obstacles to be avoided but significant events that shape an entrepreneur's journey. The way entrepreneurs respond to failure is influenced by a combination of internal factors, such as their mindset and resilience, as well as external factors like support systems and market conditions. These elements play a critical role in determining the way an entrepreneur would process setbacks and recover, or not, from them. Ultimately, the concept of "productive failure" emerges as vital in the context of EE. Embracing failures can lead to significant growth and development, fostering a more adaptive and innovative mindset among students. Productive failures are failure cases with high learning potential and provide important insight for future improvement. With the right mindset, which can be nurtured through an EE that embraces failures, productive failure can represent a learning curve on business and personal levels.

For that, it is critical to investigate the reasons and factors that lead to venture failure. This investigation comes as a priori for analyzing the failure, classifying it (Edmondson, 2023), and developing the relevant teaching method (Shepherd, 2004; Cope, 2011; Crick & Crick, 2016; Edmondson, 2023; Wang et al., 2023).

The outcome of the findings brings to attention the different dimensions of failures in businesses while emphasizing their relevancy in the learning process. In terms of entrepreneurial performance, personal factors and business factors possess a determining influence (Gomezelj & Kusce, 2013). Through the analysis of the literature and the data collected, it is evident that these two main constructs need to be jointly addressed in studying business failures. Research has investigated failure from a business and managerial lens (Lee et al., 2022) and from the lens of the entrepreneur's personality (Mayr et al., 2021; Othman et al., 2020). This study considers both components (1) Unwise Business Decisions, and (2) Personal Conflict and Status, as two main reasons for businesses ending up in very critical stages.

Investigating the components of the findings along with the literature review, it is evident that these two dimensions and the breakdown of each, as illustrated in Fig. 1, are important to be communicated and discussed in the classroom as this pedagogical approach will establish a robust foundation conducive to effective DSR framework development (Fig. 2).

Evaluating the first dimension of "Unwise Business Decisions," the findings of this study point out that most businesses fail due to the effects of their decisions and lack of management. For a thorough understanding of this factor, the study attributes it to elements related to "strategic management," and elements related to "risk

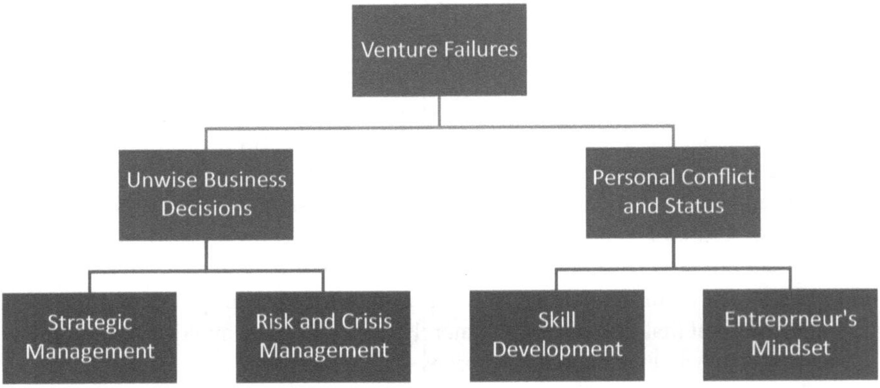

Fig. 2 Breakdown of factors leading to venture failure

and crisis management." The strategic management dimension represents a vital aspect of learning and managing businesses. It is considered a core course in six of the eight investigated study plans. The most common business failures point out that the lack of management and strategies is one of the critical reasons that lead to failures in many businesses. Similarly, "risk and crisis management" are important aspects of ensuring the continuity of the business and reducing the impact of adverse situations. Risk and crisis management have been highlighted as recommended study areas that equip students with the knowledge to navigate uncertainties and surmount failure in entrepreneurship (Wang et al., 2023; Widiawan, 2017).

Apart from the business decisions, the second dimension of "Personal Conflict and Status" reflects the personal and behavioral side of the entrepreneur. Several cases have provided indications that entrepreneurs face multiple internal conflicts and worry about their social status when things go wrong. The fear, shame, rumination, social stigma, and other negative emotions that result in negative effects on the entrepreneur's functions may precipitate catastrophic outcomes and deadly downfalls, potentially culminating in tragic endings for the entrepreneur (Council, 2019). Further investigating this deeper, the study attributes this factor to components such as lack of required skills, and the mindset of the entrepreneur (Seckler et al., 2017; Cohen et al., 2023). In the realm of research, there has been substantial attention devoted to the cultivation of personal skills within EE (Winarno et al., 2019). Pedagogically, courses focused on developing soft skills are predominantly integrated into American and European curricula (Widiawan, 2017). Similarly, a strong mindset is necessary for the ability to respond to varying situations that the entrepreneur stumbles upon. On an academic level, research in EE recommended stepping beyond the conventional traits of entrepreneurs such as resilience and risk-taking, and instead emphasizes the significance of emotional intelligence, which entails adept management of emotions such as grief and shame, alongside enhanced cognitive efficacy in periods of crisis (Shepherd, 2004).

RQ2 of the study revolves around providing a framework—as an artifact—for educators to address failures in entrepreneurship while interacting with students to come up with ways to apply decisions, this research uses the DSR approach to provide a learning protocol for this endeavor. Figure 3 provides an illustration of the DSR-based Artifact Failure Learning Protocol (AFLP) that educators can deploy in addressing entrepreneurship failure, particularly productive failure, in the

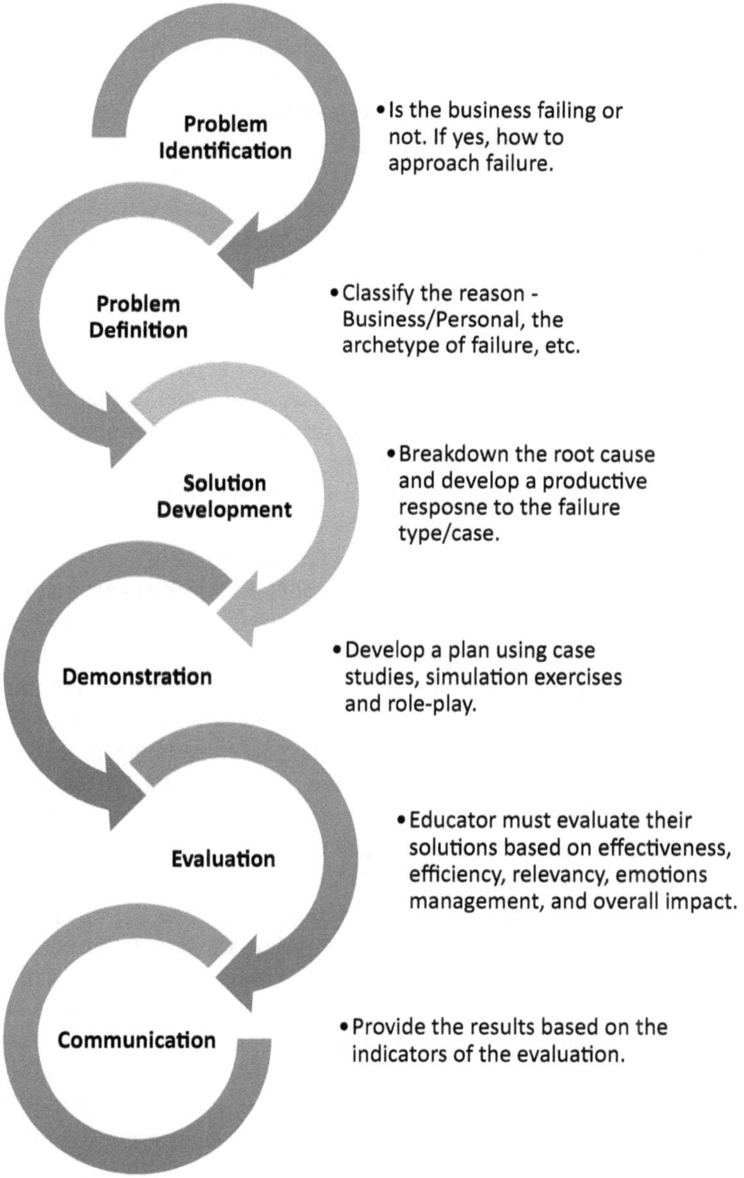

Fig. 3 Artifact failure learning protocol: educator's artifact in addressing entrepreneurship productive failure using the DSR approach

classroom. In this context, the learning protocol will comprise a set of consequential interventions to be followed in a given context (Van Aken & Andriessen, 2011) with causal dependency between interventions (Derre, 2023). This structure is not a rigid "cookie-cutter" uniform but rather a set of "master rules" guiding the sequence of interventions that educators can adapt (Weggeman & Cauffman, 2024). In this regard, a protocol represents an informed and creative framework refined through multiple iterations. Accordingly, a "learning protocol" encourages educators and students to continuously report their progress and application of DSR (Derre, 2023). While flowcharts often depict the protocols, they are not limited to the specific format; as DSR aims to produce prescriptive knowledge, protocols can take various forms, such as decision trees, manuals, or codes of conduct (Weggeman & Cauffman, 2024). Along this line, a protocol as an artifact can be described as—a step-by-step guide with sequential arrangement of interventions guiding educators through design steps and offering them a clear framework to support students (Derre, 2023).

The steps of the AFLP educate future entrepreneurs to identify the cause and take relevant actions to avoid further damage during times of crisis. The educator can follow this process to introduce the topics and follow exercises to stimulate an engaged and interactive learning experience. The first step is to help students identify whether the business is on the brink of failure. These can be identified through financial reports, management disruptions, or other business environmental reasons. In addition, educators can work on enhancing students' emotional intelligence. For example, educators can employ the dimensions of the sense of failure (Oser & Volery, 2012) such as awareness of weaknesses and intuition about mistakes to enhance students' emotional competencies. The next step is to explore and analyze the main reasons that resulted in this unfavorable and problematic status. In this regard, students may come to realize that a failure scenario often stems from complex, interacting, and escalating factors. Identifying a root cause that contributes to the problem in a higher weight and impact is critical. Such a factor can be either due to unwise business decisions vis-à-vis the internal and external environment that the business is passing through or personal conflicts. This can be approached by conducting background research and a hands-down investigation. The breakdown of factors leading to venture failures presented in Fig. 2 presents a relevant framework for this investigative step. Literature related to failure archetypes (Edmondson, 2019) can be employed at this step as well. The third step must further break down the identified problem and embark on a solution concerning the identified causes and their subdimensions. This step is crucial as it lays the foundation for their solution and further enables them to proceed to the next step. For example, at this stage, productive responses to the different types of failure presented in Table 1 (Edmondson, 2019) can be utilized. The fourth step involves interaction and demonstration of the thought solutions which can be conducted using different case studies, simulation exercises, and role plays, among other activities. Once the solution is demonstrated, the next step is to evaluate and analyze the solution. In this step, the educator must evaluate the solutions and decisions the students have made using indicators such as effectiveness, efficiency, relevancy, emotions management, and overall impact. The educator, at this step, can use the measurement implication to the learning-from-failure pedagogy (Shepherd, 2004) to assess students' competency to manage emotions associated with business failure in a pre-and post-intake of the learning cycle. They can also utilize the experiential scientific approach (Camuffo et al., 2024) to assess changes in students' decision-making processes. Finally, the educator integrates the steps of the process, revisions, feedback, and results. They are then communicated to the students, explaining the rationale for improvement. This final step will create a space for students to understand and make profound decisions and improvements to ensure that they are equipped with the necessary knowledge and skills to navigate through times of crisis.

7 Developing a DSR-Based Pedagogy to Help Students Handle and Learn from Entrepreneurship Failure

Entrepreneurship educators can increase and direct students' knowledge, skills, and mindset through methods that can be used at each step of the AFLP. These methods can minimize interference and maximize learning and preparedness to face potential failures. Furthermore, the DSR pedagogy development and implementation could also be integrated with experiential methods such as gamification principles to achieve higher student interaction and experiential learning (Al-Gindy et al., 2022; Yasin & Hafeez, 2018).

The first step of problem identification requires students and educators to delve into the reasons for failure. As with lectures, the content is based on theory, educators can introduce case studies of different businesses, their financial reports, and management disruptions. At this level, educators can utilize the experience of guest lecturers to solidify students' knowledge with indirect and real experiences. Along with the cognitive analysis of students, educators at this level can augment students' emotional intelligence by developing students' sense of failure, including its dimensions (Oser & Volery, 2012) to equip them with a proactive anticipation of potential crises in businesses.

Emotions experienced by past entrepreneurs through guest lectures and case studies in addition to psychological theories such as bereavement theory and psychological training on building an error management mindset (Seckler et al., 2017) and optimistic mindset (Cohen et al., 2023) can contribute to students' emotional intelligence and preparedness to adverse situations.

As for steps two and three, students can conduct the investigation and research through group work. For example, they can be guided by the factors and sub-factors illustrated in Fig. 2. Active participation in group work, which can also be conducted through simulations, aids students in attaining a more profound comprehension of various business facets, environmental factors, the entrepreneur's traits, and the implications of the entrepreneur's decisions on constraining firm growth and jeopardizing its viability.

In step four, students will process cognitive and emotional information and solutions through demonstrations. Educators can use simulations and role-playing at this stage. In simulations, students engage interactively as they think and feel that they are in a real failure scenario. They are prompted to contemplate the implications of a scenario, such as reflecting on their emotions and feelings devising strategies for potential failure recovery and post-failure subsequent entrepreneurship intent, using their critical thinking abilities. Meanwhile in role-playing, students can assume different situations that the entrepreneur goes through when experiencing failure. In this practice, students envision, analyze, and enact the various moments of business failure yet in a psychologically safe, low-risk environment. This practice helps build students' behaviors and personalities as they immerse themselves in the role of the entrepreneur (Shepherd, 2004).

The fifth step of evaluation offers a variety of methods for assessment including written evaluation and oral debriefing. At this level, educators can construct comprehensive pillars for evaluation. The ones that are suggested by this study are the evaluation of (1) effectiveness, (2) efficiency, (3) relevancy, (4) emotional management, and (5) overall impact. These evaluations entail in-depth feedback, critiques, and recommendations on the preceding four stages of the process. Oral debriefings foster dynamic class discussions, enabling students to reflect upon their roles, decisions, and emotions throughout the process. These discussions, guided by the educator, embrace a more open nature while remaining anchored in the established evaluation pillars of the exercise. Additionally, students may also take an active role in conducting evaluations themselves, fostering a collaborative and reflective learning environment exemplative of the DSR approach in considering stakeholders.

In the final phase of communication, the educator selects the communication platform(s) through which to convey the evaluation of the process to students. While the formal communication platform is determined by the university, the professor may choose additional channels of communication. Furthermore, the educator has the opportunity to disseminate insights and reflections on the DSR process, particularly failure learning protocols, within the EE community through avenues such as articles, conferences, and teaching notes.

8 Conclusion

Entrepreneurial education is currently under the microscope for larger research and findings to enhance the pedagogy. Throughout the research, it has been recognized that there is a lack of awareness and addressing of failure and its management in the curricula. While fostering the entrepreneurial mindset is crucial, it is equally important to equip students with the skills necessary to identify challenges, address them, and learn from their experiences. These skills are deemed to be essential to prepare students for future careers in entrepreneurship. The lessons that can be gleaned from failure enable educators to better prepare aspiring entrepreneurs, enhance their ability to navigate the challenges in their journeys, and enrich their capacity for long-term success.

The research provides a base for entrepreneurship educators to use the developed AFLP to introduce and engage students in experiencing and learning about failure management. From the study, it was evident that several reasons contribute to failure such as (1) Unwise Business Decisions and (2) Personal Conflict and Status. The learning protocol proposed in the model brings valuable contributions to the EE pedagogies with the objective of sustaining the entrepreneurial spirit and developing the learning from productive failures. Further curriculum development, particularly in embedding failure management, is critical for helping future entrepreneurs make informed decisions. This has been supported by multiple research examples that highlight the importance of addressing failure in the classroom and embracing it throughout the steps of the DSR approach. Furthermore, the research has been able to achieve the following (1) explore the course offering of the programs offered by the universities around the world; and (2) provide a DSR-based framework and pedagogy for entrepreneurship educators to address failure, its management, and skills. Future research could involve conducting DSR evaluation studies to test and refine the model's applicability.

References

Aftab, J., Veneziani, M., Sarwar, H., & Ishaq, M. I. (2022). Entrepreneurial orientation, entrepreneurial competencies, innovation, and performances in SMEs of Pakistan: The moderating role of social ties. *Business Ethics, the Environment & Responsibility, 31*(2), 419–437. https://doi.org/10.1111/beer.12415

Al-Alawi, A., Amjed, S., Elbaz, A. M., & Alkathiri, N. A. (2023). The anatomy of entrepreneurial failure: Antecedents of the performance failure appraisal inventory and the role of social support. *Sustainability, 15*(9), 7505. https://doi.org/10.3390/su15097505

Al-Gindy, A., Yasin, N., Aerabe, M., & Omar, A. A. C. (2022). Integrating digital Technology in Enterprise and Entrepreneurship Education. In D. Hyams-Ssekasi & N. Yasin (Eds.), *Technology and entrepreneurship education*. Palgrave Macmillan. https://doi.org/10.1007/978-3-030-84292-5_3

Åstebro, T., Herz, H., Nanda, R., & Weber, R. A. (2014). Seeking the roots of entrepreneurship: Insights from behavioral economics. *The Journal of Economic Perspectives, 28*(3), 49–69.

Ayala, J. C., & Manzano, G. (2014). The resilience of the entrepreneur. Influence on the success of the business. A longitudinal analysis. *Journal of Economic Psychology, 42*(3), 126–135.

Bandera, C., Santos, S. C., & Liguori, E. W. (2021). The dark side of entrepreneurship education: A Delphi study on dangers and unintended consequences. *Entrepreneurship Education and Pedagogy, 4*(4), 609–636. https://doi.org/10.1177/2515127420944592

Bledow, R., Carette, B., Kühnel, J., & Pittig, D. (2017). Learning from other's failures: The effectiveness of failure-stories for managerial learning. *Academy of Management Learning & Education, 16*(1), 39–53.

Boldureanu, G., Ionescu, A. M., Bercu, A. M., Bedrule-Grigoruţă, M. V., & Boldureanu, D. (2020). Entrepreneurship education through successful entrepreneurial models in higher education institutions. *Sustainability, 12*(3), 1267. https://doi.org/10.3390/su12031267

Botha, M., van Vuuren, J. J., & Kunene, T. (2015). An integrated entrepreneurial performance model focusing on the importance and proficiency of competencies for start-up and established SMEs. *South African Journal of Business Management, 46*(3), 55–65.

Bryant, S. (2024, June 24). *How many startups fail and why. investopedia.* https://www.investopedia.com/articles/personal-finance/040915/how-many-startups-fail-and-why.asp

Byrne, J., Fayolle, A., & Toutain, O. (2014). Entrepreneurship education: What we know and what we need to know. In E. Chell & M. Karatas-Özkan (Eds.), *Handbook of research on small business and entrepreneurship* (pp. 261–288). Edward Elgar.

Camuffo, A., Cordova, A., Gambardella, A., & Spina, C. (2020). A scientific approach to entrepreneurial decision making: Evidence from a randomized control trial. *Management Science, 66*(2), 564–586.

Camuffo, A., Gambardella, A., Messinese, D., Novelli, E., Paolucci, E., & Spina, C. (2024). A scientific approach to entrepreneurial decision-making: Large-scale replication and extension. *Strategic Management Journal, 45*(6), 1209–1237. https://doi.org/10.1002/smj.3580

Cannon, M. D., & Edmondson, A. C. (2005). Failing to learn and learning to fail (intelligently). How great organizations put failure to work to innovate and improve. *Long Range Planning, 38*(3), 299–319.

Cohen, D., Hsu, D. K., & Shinnar, R. S. (2023). Beyond educating students about business failure: The role of optimism training and hope. *Journal of Small Business Management, 62*(6), 2779–2805. https://doi.org/10.1080/00472778.2023.2275590

Cope, J. (2011). Entrepreneurial learning from failure: An interpretative phenomenological analysis. *Journal of Business Venturing, 26*(6), 604–623.

Costa, S. F., Caetano, A., & Santos, S. C. (2016). Entrepreneurship as career option: Do temporary workers have the competencies, intentions, and willingness to become entrepreneurs? *The Journal of Entrepreneurship, 25*(2), 1–26.

Council, Y. E. (2019, December 27). Is success scarier than failure? Confronting shame as an entrepreneur. *Forbes*. https://www.forbes.com/sites/theyec/2019/12/27/is-success-scarier-than-failure-confronting-shame-as-an-entrepreneur/?sh=2323bf6b6fc7

Crick, J. M., & Crick, D. (2016). Developing entrepreneurial resilience in the UK tourism sector. *Strategic Change, 25*(3), 315–325.

Denyer, D., Tranfield, D., & Van Aken, J. E. (2008). Developing design propositions through research synthesis. *Organization Studies, 29*(03), 393–413.

Derre, B. F. S. (2023). A design for effective entrepreneurial education in higher education. [Ph.D. Thesis (Research TU/e/Graduation TU/e). In *Industrial engineering and innovation sciences*. Eindhoven University of Technology.

Dobson, J. A., Jacobs, E., & Dobson, A. (2017). Toward an experiential approach to entrepreneurship education. *Journal of Higher Education Theory and Practice, 17*(3), 57–69.

Edmondson, A. C. (2019). *The fearless organization: Creating psychological safety in the workplace for learning, innovation, and growth.* Wiley.

Edmondson, A. C. (2023). *Right kind of wrong: The science of failing well.* Simon and Schuster.

Frese, M., & Keith, N. (2015). Action errors, error management, and learning in organizations. *Annual Review of Psychology, 66*(1), 661–687.

GEM (Global Entrepreneurship Monitor). (2023). *Global entrepreneurship monitor 2023/2024 global report: 25 years and growing*. GEM.

Gomezelj, D. O., & Kusce, I. (2013). The influence of personal and environmental factors on entrepreneurs' performance. *Kybernetes, 42*(6), 906–927. https://doi.org/10.1108/K-08-2012-0024

Gonul, O. O., & Litzky, B. E. (2018). Achieving success or avoiding failure? Motivational orientations of entrepreneurship students. *Journal of Higher Education Theory and Practice, 18*(4), 90–101. https://doi.org/10.33423/jhetp.v18i4.577

González-López, M. J., Pérez-López, M. C., & Rodríguez-Ariza, L. (2019). Clearing the hurdles in the entrepreneurial race: The role of resilience in entrepreneurship education. *Academy of Management Learning & Education, 18*(3), 457–483. https://doi.org/10.5465/amle.2016.0377

Grenha Teixeira, J., Patrício, L., Huang, K. H., Fisk, R. P., Nóbrega, L., & Constantine, L. (2017). The MINDS method: integrating management and interaction design perspectives for service design. *Journal of Service Research, 20*(3), 240–258. https://doi.org/10.1177/1094670516680033

Hameed, I., & Irfan, Z. (2019). Entrepreneurship education: A review of challenges, characteristics and opportunities. *Entrepreneurship Education, 2*(2), 135–148. https://doi.org/10.1007/s41959-019-00018-z

Higgins, E. T. (1998). Promotion and prevention: Regulatory focus as a motivational principle. *Advances in Experimental Social Psychology, 30*, 1–46.

Jena, R. K. (2020). Measuring the impact of business management student's attitude towards entrepreneurship education on entrepreneurial intention: A case study. *Computers in Human Behavior, 107*(2), 106275. https://doi.org/10.1016/j.chb.2020.106275

Jing, T., Dancheng, L., & Ye, Z. (2016). Study of impact on undergraduates' entrepreneurial failure based on the model of psychological resilience-knowledge acquisition. *English Language Teaching, 9*(8), 224–230.

Karni, E., & Vierø, M. (2017). Awareness of unawareness: A theory of decision making in the face of ignorance. *Journal of Economic Theory, 168*, 301–328.

Kerr, W. R., Nanda, R., & Rhodes-Kropf, M. (2014). Entrepreneurship as experimentation. *Journal of Economic Perspectives, 28*(3), 25–48.

Lee, C. K., Wiklund, J., Amezcua, A., Bae, T. J., & Palubinskas, A. (2022). Business failure and institutions in entrepreneurship: A systematic review and research agenda. *Small Business Economics, 58*, 1997–2023. https://doi.org/10.1007/s11187-021-00495-4

Liu, F., Ma, J., & Li, R. (2019). Which role model is more effective in entrepreneurship education? An investigation of storytelling on individual's entrepreneurial intention. *Frontiers in Psychology, 10*, 837. https://doi.org/10.3389/fpsyg.2019.00837

Loi, M., Castriotta, M., & Di Guardo, M. C. (2016). The theoretical foundations of entrepreneurship education: How co-citations are shaping the field. *International Small Business Journal, 34*(7), 948–971.

Luo, W., Ran, Q., & Cheng, S. (2023). What kind of support can promote academic entrepreneurial intention: An analysis of the qualitative comparative analysis configuration effect of multiple support. *Managerial and Decision Economics., 45*(3), 1414–1427. https://doi.org/10.1002/mde.4082

Martínez-Gregorio, S., Badenes-Ribera, L., & Oliver, A. (2021). Effect of entrepreneurship education on entrepreneurship intention and related outcomes in educational contexts: A meta-analysis. *The International Journal of Management Education, 19*(3), 100545. https://doi.org/10.1016/j.ijme.2021.100545

Mayr, S., Mitter, C., Kücher, A., & Duller, C. (2021). Entrepreneur characteristics and differences in reasons for business failure: Evidence from bankrupt Austrian SMEs. *Journal of Small Business & Entrepreneurship, 33*(5), 539–558. https://doi.org/10.1080/08276331.2020.1786647

Mohamed, N. A., & Ali, A. Y. S. (2021). Entrepreneurship education: Systematic literature review and future research directions. *World Journal of Entrepreneurship, Management and Sustainable Development, 17*(4), 644–661. https://doi.org/10.1108/wjemsd-07-2020-0084

Nabi, G., Liñán, F., Fayolle, A., Krueger, N., & Walmsley, A. (2017). The impact of entrepreneurship education in higher education: A systematic review and research agenda. *Academy of Management Learning & Education, 16*(2), 277–299.

Noble, T., & McGrath, H. (2014). Well-being and resilience in school settings. In G. A. Fava & C. Ruini (Eds.), *Increasing psychological Well-being in clinical and educational settings* (pp. 135–152). Springer.

Othman, A., Ng, W. K., & Mohamad, N. (2020). Factors of entrepreneurial personality characteristics on business failure of SMEs. *International Journal of Human and Technology Interaction, 4*(2), 23–29.

Oser, F., & Volery, T. (2012). «sense of failure» and «sense of success» among entrepreneurs: The identification of neglected twin entrepreneurial competencies. *Empirical Research in Vocational Education and Training, 4*(1), 27–44. https://doi.org/10.1007/BF03546505

Poulson, C. (2000). Shame and work. In N. Ashkanazy, C. Hartel, & W. Zerbe (Eds.), *Emotions in the workplace: Research, theory, and practice* (pp. 250–271). Quorum.

Seckler, C., Funken, R., & Gielnik, M. M. (2017). Learning from entrepreneurial failure: Integrating emotional, motivational, and cognitive factors. In J. Ellingson & R. A. Noe (Eds.), *In autonomous learning in the workplace* (pp. 54–77). Routledge.

Shepherd, D. A. (2003). Learning from business failure: Propositions of grief recovery for the self-employed. *Academy of Management Review, 28*(2), 318–328. https://doi.org/10.2307/30040715

Shepherd, D. A. (2004). Educating entrepreneurship students about emotion and learning from failure. *Academy of Management Learning and Education, 3*(3), 274–287.

Sitkin, S. B., & Weingart, L. R. (1995). Determinants of risky decision-making behavior: A test of the mediating role of risk perceptions and propensity. *Academy of Management Journal, 38*(6), 1573–1592.

Spagnoli, P., Santos, S. C., Caetano, A., & Lo Presti, A. (2016). A contribution towards the validation of the Italian version of the entrepreneurial potential assessment inventory. *Applied Psychology Bulletin, 64*(275), 37–49.

St-Jean, E., & Audet, J. (2012). The role of mentoring in the learning development of the novice entrepreneur. *The International Entrepreneurship and Management Journal, 8*(1), 119–140.

Testa, S., & Frascheri, S. (2015). Learning by failing: What we can learn from un-successful entrepreneurship education. *The International Journal of Management Education, 13*(1), 11–22. https://doi.org/10.1016/j.ijme.2014.11.001

Timmons, J. A. (1999). *New venture creation: Entrepreneurship for the 21st century*. Irwin McGraw-Hill.

Van Aken, J. E., & Andriessen, D. (2011). *Handboek ontwerpgericht wetenschappelijk onderzoek: wetenschap met effect [Handbook of design-oriented scientific research: science with effect]*. Boom Lemma Uitgevers.

Wang, P., Xiong, Z., & Zhao, Z. (2023). Exploring the relationship between failure-learning-based entrepreneurship education and youth entrepreneurial resilience: A mediated moderation model. *E&M Economics and Management, 26*(4), 51–65. https://doi.org/10.15240/tul/001/2023-5-001

Weggeman, M., & Cauffman, L. (2024). Using design science research to develop and validate the application of client-oriented psychological approaches illustrated by the design of a solution-focused approach. *Methods in Psychology, 100151*, 100151.

Welsh, D. H., Tullar, W. L., & Nemati, H. (2016). Entrepreneurship education: Process, method, or both? *Journal of Innovation & Knowledge, 1*(3), 125–132. https://doi.org/10.1016/j.jik.2016.01.005

Widiawan, K. (2017). A missing link on entrepreneurship education curricula. *International Journal of Industrial Research and Applied Engineering, 2*(1), 20–24. https://doi.org/10.9744/JIRAE.2.1.20-24

Winarno, A., Rahayu, W. P., Wijijayanti, T., & Agustina, Y. (2019). The failure of entrepreneurship education of vocational high school students and college students: Perspective of evaluation instrument of learning results. *Journal of Entrepreneurship Education, 22*(1).

Wren, D. A., Buckley, M. R., & Michaelsen, L. K. (1994). The theory/applications balance in management pedagogy: Where do we stand? *Journal of Management, 20*(1), 141–158.

Yasin, N., & Hafeez, K. (2018). Enterprise simulation gaming: Effective practices for assessing student learning with SimVenture classic and VentureBlocks. In D. Hyams-Ssekasi & E. Caldwell (Eds.), *Experiential learning for entrepreneurship*. Palgrave Macmillan. https://doi.org/10.1007/978-3-319-90005-6_3

Zellweger, T. M., & Zenger, T. R. (2023). Entrepreneurs as scientists: A pragmatist approach to producing value out of uncertainty. *The Academy of Management Review, 47*(4), 379–408.

Zhang, Y., Duysters, G., & Cloodt, M. (2014). The role of entrepreneurship education as a predictor of university students' entrepreneurial intention. *International Entrepreneurship and Management Journal, 10*(3), 623–641. https://doi.org/10.1007/s11365-012-0246-z

Samar Billi Noaman is an Assistant Professor at the Canadian University Dubai, United Arab Emirates. She received her Ph.D. in Management from Université Paris 1 Panthéon-Sorbonne, France, and her MBA from Les Roches School of Hotel Management, Switzerland. Her Ph.D. thesis was ranked second best thesis for 2018 by the Francophone Association of Tourism Management (AFMAT). She is a certified American Hotel and Lodging Educational Institute (AHLEI) educator. Noaman has over ten years of academic experience in hospitality and tourism, marketing, and management. From 2014 to 2016, Noaman chaired the Hospitality and Tourism Management Department at the Lebanese International University. Her research specialty and publications are in the fields of destination marketing, consumer behavior in tourism services, tourism entrepreneurship, and health tourism. On an industry level, Noaman conducted several soft skill-development training programs targeted at professionals and students.

Gayatri Nair is a Lecturer in the School of Management at Canadian University Dubai. She earned her Bachelor of Business Administration in Marketing from the university and a Master of Science in International Business from the University of Birmingham. Honoured with the 10-year UAE Golden Visa for her academic excellence, she has extensive experience in sales, marketing, and corporate training while actively engaging in startups and family businesses. As a passionate researcher, Mrs Nair has published in Scopus-indexed journals and contributed to prestigious conferences, highlighting her commitment to learning by practice.

From EntreComp to EntreAct: 16 Validated Design Principles for Making People More Entrepreneurial

Martin Lackéus

Abstract Sixteen action-reflection challenges around external stakeholder interaction were co-designed, developed and validated over a decade in close collaboration with around 350 entrepreneurship students at a venture creation-based entrepreneurship program at Chalmers University of Technology in Sweden. A novel research methodology termed Designed Action Sampling (DAS) was used alongside a digital reflection tool, resulting in capture of 754 qualitative student reflections and associated quantifications. This allowed for validating the effectiveness of these challenges in developing students' entrepreneurial competencies. Challenges were categorized into four groups: Ideas, Resources, Actions, and Emotions. Each challenge was described using a CIMO-logic (Context, Intervention, Mechanisms, Outcomes), providing insights on a micro level into implementation patterns and effects on student learning. Taken together, these challenges represent a framework that links actions to competencies, providing an answer to the question: "Learning-by-doing-what?". Such a framework is here termed an EntreAct framework, representing a further development of the well-known EntreComp framework of entrepreneurial competencies, previously developed by the European Commission. Findings demonstrate the importance of emotionally charged experiences in entrepreneurial learning and the value of external stakeholder interactions. A generic model for how to design EntreAct challenges is proposed, potentially serving as a starting point for a community of practice among entrepreneurship and enterprise educators using the DAS methodology to build context-dependent and empirically validated EntreAct frameworks for e.g. nursing, theology or pedagogy. This research contributes to bridging the gap between entrepreneurial competencies (EntreComp) and actionable teaching practices (EntreAct), offering educators empirically validated tools for fostering entrepreneurial competencies in diverse educational settings.

M. Lackéus (✉)
Technology Management and Economics, Chalmers University of Technology, Gothenburg, Sweden
e-mail: martin.lackeus@chalmers.se

© The Author(s), under exclusive license to Springer Nature Switzerland AG 2025
B. Derre, Y. Baggen (eds.), *Empowering the Next Generation of Entrepreneurial Change Agents*, Contributions to Management Science,
https://doi.org/10.1007/978-3-031-82251-3_8

1 Introduction

Design science has a strong inherent ability to bridge between theory and practice (Romme, 2003; Van Aken & Romme, 2009). For entrepreneurship educators, this ability can be used to invent, design, and try out new teaching practices to be used in real-world situations with students. The starting point could be more or less theoretical notions about how people might become more entrepreneurial. Design science then helps us reach the much-needed state of detailed articulations of practical teaching techniques, or design principles, for how to succeed with our educational mission in entrepreneurship education (EE).

I have for many years used design science in my own entrepreneurship teaching. In this chapter, I will report on a 10-year journey of crafting and testing various design principles together with my entrepreneurship students at the School of Entrepreneurship at Chalmers University of Technology in Sweden. I label the result EntreAct, since the 16 action-tasks presented here represent a link between entrepreneurial actions (here labeled EntreAct) and entrepreneurial competencies (often labeled EntreComp; a framework for entrepreneurial competencies designed by the European Commission). I have in my previous writing (e.g. Lackéus, 2020c) described rather general answers to a crucial question in EE: Learning-by-doing-*what*? Here I want to be more detailed. What can we invite our students to do, on a more practical level of taking action, in order for them to become more entrepreneurial? This represents a departure from philosophical and generic design principles such as ideation, business planning, venture creation, or value creation. General guidelines are still needed, but the practical nitty-gritty level of everyday techniques may be a more useful starting point for many teachers.

2 How It All Started a Decade Ago

I worked according to design science principles long before I learned about design science. Apprenticeship teachers in Uddevalla put me on this useful path. Back in 2014, they wanted to use my digital smartphone application for reflection data I had started to develop 2 years earlier. It is called Loopme, and I have used it for a decade to collect written reflections from my students (see Lackéus, 2014, 2020a). These apprenticeship teachers found my digital approach interesting but told me that it was not enough to merely collect emotionally charged free reflections from students, which was my approach at the time. An action-task function was also needed that specifies for students what they should first do and *then* reflect upon afterward. This helped complete the action-reflection cycle of experiential learning (Kolb, 1984).

We subsequently instructed our programmers to build such a function into Loopme. The technical development of it was the easy part. It was the non-tech part that really confused us. What now to ask students to *do* in order to *learn*? We spent a decade testing a broad array of action-tasks on around 350 students in entrepreneurship at Chalmers. It is the result of this decade-long trial-and-error process that I will be reporting from here. The student reflections we received on various attempts to prescribe entrepreneurial action made it clear to us that many action-tasks did not work out as we had hoped for. Some worked quite well, and a select few action-tasks made wonders to our students' learning journeys. These precious validated action-tasks represent novel and useful answers to the learning-by-doing-*what* question.

3 Methodology: Designed Action Sampling

The methodological process behind this work, and its relation to design science, has been described elsewhere under the label Designed Action Sampling (Lackéus & Sävetun, 2023). I will only very briefly describe the process here. From 2014 to 2024 we followed five steps each year: (1) First we (re)designed a set of around 5–30 mandatory action-tasks that our 35 students were to be given in the beginning of the second year of their Master's Programme in Entrepreneurship and Business Design. This is their final year when they are all expected to work in teams of 2–3 students to start a real-life tech venture based on someone else's idea. Two-thirds of each class start a new independent venture, and one-third start an internal venture in a large firm, i.e., intrapreneurship. (2) In August each year, the students were introduced to the action-tasks and subsequently took action. They were given from September to April to do up to ten action-tasks. (3) After each action-task was completed, they submitted digitally to us a short written reflection around what they did, how it went, and what they learned from it. They also quantified their emotional experience and their learnings according to the EntreComp model of entrepreneurial competencies (Bacigalupo et al., 2016). (4) We analyzed their reflections and quantifications continually and discussed a synthesis of them with the students twice per year. Students were invited to reflect upon how the action-tasks worked for them, per task and as a collective of tasks. (5) In the final step, insights were summarized and fed into a new design iteration, thus going back to step 1 again the following year. Each year the collection of action-tasks was thus redesigned, evolving organically based on reflections, quantifications, and collective analysis. Some years' modifications were more major than other years. The complete collection of discarded and currently active action-tasks can be seen at library.loopme.io. Here we will focus on the 16 most interesting and powerful action-tasks that we ended up with. These 16 action-tasks have been largely unchanged for the last 3 years, resulting in 754 reflections from 105 students on them, see Fig. 1.

The 16 action-tasks are presented in four groups of four, based on which quantified effects they resulted in according to the students who tried them out in practice. Three of these groups—Ideas, Resources, and Action—are aligned with the EntreComp definition of entrepreneurship competence as "the ability to transform *ideas* and opportunities into *action* by mobilising *resources*" (Bacigalupo et al.,

				Ideas					Resources							Action					Emotions				
		Number of reflections	Emotion average	Better at spotting opportunities	Better at valuing ideas	Improved sustainability thinking	Improved vision ability	Increased creativity	Better at finances	Better at mobilising others	Better att getting resources	Increased my perseverance	Increased self-awareness	Increased self-confidence	More motivated	Better at coping w uncertainty	Better at initiative-taking	Improved planning skills	Improved teamwork skills	Learned to learn more	Disappointed in myself	Disappointed in others	Expected a different outcome	Out of comfort zone	Team conflict
Ideas	Explore the value chain	58	1,24	26%	16%	10%	21%	19%	2%	9%	26%	5%	9%	16%	34%	-	16%	16%	3%	33%	-	-	12%	7%	2%
	Quantify and validate the value you can create	33	1,39	39%	42%	3%	9%	6%	15%	-	12%	6%	9%	24%	33%	21%	12%	9%	3%	18%	-	3%	9%	3%	-
	Build a prototype and get good feedback from an S-person	25	1,44	28%	28%	-	8%	52%	-	12%	8%	4%	12%	28%	44%	16%	8%	4%	4%	24%	4%	-	12%	8%	-
	Present your visionary dream to an S-person	21	1,33	38%	10%	10%	52%	19%	-	14%	14%	19%	14%	38%	52%	19%	19%	10%	14%	19%	-	-	10%	19%	-
Resources	Discuss value creation in your industry with a CSE alumni	73	1,48	32%	25%	4%	21%	15%	4%	10%	19%	3%	21%	22%	47%	22%	7%	11%	4%	30%	3%	1%	5%	12%	1%
	Discuss price issues with a potential customer	54	0,80	19%	22%	4%	4%	2%	30%	2%	15%	6%	9%	13%	15%	11%	9%	6%	-	11%	4%	9%	20%	19%	-
	Deliver real value to an S-person	33	1,64	33%	21%	3%	21%	15%	6%	30%	24%	15%	12%	48%	48%	6%	30%	12%	12%	12%	-	3%	3%	9%	-
	Sell a pilot project to a paying S-person	10	0,90	20%	10%	-	-	10%	-	30%	50%	20%	-	40%	30%	20%	10%	10%	-	10%	-	-	20%	20%	-
Actions	Talk to a potential and established competitor	63	1,21	37%	16%	2%	13%	21%	2%	6%	8%	10%	13%	24%	33%	27%	27%	8%	10%	29%	-	-	17%	29%	3%
	Immerse yourself in a deep tech lab	54	1,37	13%	9%	6%	9%	11%	2%	4%	11%	2%	7%	22%	28%	15%	24%	-	7%	57%	2%	-	7%	46%	-
	Talk to one hundred S-persons	38	1,47	37%	16%	5%	24%	26%	3%	8%	26%	24%	24%	42%	34%	29%	45%	11%	11%	32%	3%	3%	16%	37%	3%
	Pitch to a REAL investor asking for REAL money	23	1,39	22%	17%	4%	13%	17%	22%	13%	48%	4%	9%	61%	39%	17%	9%	17%	13%	22%	4%	-	9%	65%	4%
Emotions	Ignore feedback from an S-person based on personal conviction	84	0,69	15%	21%	5%	14%	8%	1%	6%	8%	30%	17%	46%	19%	17%	7%	4%	8%	17%	2%	19%	21%	20%	2%
	Ask an S-person for something and get rejected	67	-0,16	12%	4%	1%	6%	7%	-	4%	10%	27%	16%	10%	13%	13%	4%	6%	1%	18%	19%	33%	48%	22%	3%
	Get something for free from an S-person	65	1,58	34%	3%	8%	6%	12%	3%	8%	42%	3%	5%	26%	32%	3%	23%	2%	8%	8%	-	-	9%	6%	-
	Experience an emotional setback related to an S-person	53	-0,45	4%	8%	-	4%	6%	-	2%	2%	23%	32%	11%	9%	19%	6%	8%	15%	13%	13%	25%	58%	21%	9%
	Totals / averages / percentages	754	1,08	24%	16%	4%	13%	14%	5%	8%	18%	13%	14%	27%	30%	15%	15%	7%	7%	23%	4%	8%	19%	20%	2%

Fig. 1 The 16 action-tasks (left), the resulting emotional average per task and the resulting quantifications provided by 105 students during three academic years 2021–2024. Percentages represent the share of reflections upon an action-task that were tagged with the corresponding labels (top). Students could choose to associate one or many of the labels to each reflection

2016, p. 10, my added emphasis). A fourth group—Emotions—purports to capture some additional emotional effects. This was to make sure that the crucial role of emotions for entrepreneurial learning was not lost here (cf. Lackéus, 2013). Each student also had to quantify their emotional experience on a likert scale, see "Emotion average" in Fig. 1, which spans from −2 (very negative) to +2 (very positive) (cf. Lackéus & Sävetun, 2023). I used quantitative data from 2021 to 2024 to determine which of the action-tasks were the most powerful and interesting ones. I then picked 16 action-tasks that as a collective had been shown to result in a broad set of developed entrepreneurial competencies. I first aimed for 10 action-tasks, but to cover all competencies in EntreComp I needed to expand to 16 action-tasks.

Please keep in mind the limitation that stems from design principles being contextual (Romme & Dimov, 2021). The action-tasks were developed in a highly experiential and emotional full-venture creation program environment (Smith et al., 2022) where students get one full year to start a real-world high-technology independent or internal venture based on someone else's idea (see further in Lundqvist & Williams Middleton, 2024). Transferability of these action-tasks to other learning environments may thus vary. We also need to carefully take pragmatism into account, which stipulates that the question "What works?" should perhaps be replaced by "What works for whom, in what circumstances and why?" (Biesta & Burbules, 2003; Brentnall, 2023).

4 The 16 Action-Reflection Challenges

I will now describe the 16 most interesting and powerful action-tasks among all the ones that we have designed and tried out over a decade. For my students, I label them *action-reflection challenges*. They are all focused on external stakeholder interaction, or "s-person" interaction which I call it. To focus only on external stakeholder interaction was a decision made in 2021, after having observed that it was the student interaction with external stakeholders that triggered the most interesting reflections and the deepest learning each year. This is how I introduce these challenges to new students each year:

> You will be given a choice of 10 challenges among 30 possible interactions with so called S-persons—a Significant Stakeholder relevant to your venture but NOT part of your venture or emotional owner to your venture (i.e. NOT your idea partner, other close partner, funder, sponsor, internal coach, corporate coach, teammate, etc.). We meet once in the autumn and once in the spring to discuss your reflections, to see what you learned, in a collective analysis.

For each challenge comes first a verbatim description of it, the way it is presented to the students. Then follows a design science-inspired description, based on CIMO-logic (Denyer et al., 2008), where C stands for context, I stands for intervention, M stands for mechanisms, and O stands for outcome(s). Context is always the same here—a venture creation program in entrepreneurship. Therefore, only I, M, and O are described for each action-task below, based primarily on an analysis of the 754 qualitative student reflections, consisting of 141,000 words. For each group of challenges, I also introduce the group briefly. Each challenge description starts with "prove to me…", emphasizing that I always expect students to first give a comprehensive and convincing enough description of what they did. This is to lower the risk that students just pretend to have acted by writing a "zombie reflection" (De La Croix & Veen, 2018). Reflections are not graded but assessed through emotion-laden activity-based assessment in a pass-fail manner (Lackéus, 2022; Lackéus & Williams Middleton, 2018).

5 Developing "Ideas and Opportunities" Skills

Ideas skills can be developed by asking students to explore, dream, prototype, and quantify the future value they might one day be able to contribute with. Doing this together with external stakeholders seems to help them develop their ability to see in a more creative way a future where they become a novel part of an established value chain in society. The challenges in this group all illustrate how deeply relational the entrepreneurial job is, especially in the first stages of ideation.

Challenge 1: Explore the Value Chain

> Prove to me that you discussed and communicated value for others by discussing with an S-person who is NOT a potential customer but instead a representative of a value chain your project needs to become a part of in the future. Reflect here on how it felt, what you learned from it and how you will do next time around.

Intervention. Many students explored value chains through conversations with suppliers, experts, seniors, and customers' customers, discussing for example how an industry creates value, how it struggles in various structural ways, and how things actually work beneath the surface. Since discussions were held with noncustomers, it was often more open and less filtered than a typical customer discussion. It was a good way for students to start learning about a new industry.

Outcomes. This challenge often triggered a deeper overall understanding of the industry that students were attempting to enter. Many students reported that they learned how to scope their venture, who to create value for, who to initiate strategic collaborations with, how to structure a deal and which industry problems to try to solve. It also sometimes led to improved sustainability thinking (see Fig. 1), perhaps due to an emphasis on structural value creation and problems.

Mechanisms. Having a noncustomer value chain focus seems to help students zoom out and take a more overarching and strategic perspective than the more typical customer interview.

Challenge 2: Quantify and Validate the Value You Can Create

> Prove to me that you analyzed for value creation by quantifying the benefit your solution has to potential customers, and getting this validated in discussions with an S-person who

> is also a potential customer. Reflect here on how it felt, what you learned from it and how this impacts your project.

Intervention. Many students sat down with various potential customers to co-analyse, co-validate, co-quantify, and even co-create an interesting business case for them. Together they did the math and quantified the value that might be created, be it in terms of cost savings, time saved, increased quality, or some other value such as societal or enjoyment value. This was then often related to the customer's internal Key Performance Indicators (KPIs) or other industry-relevant quantitative benchmarks. Some customers then became interested in paying for a pilot test.

Outcomes. Many students got an early glimpse of real-world commercial negotiations and then learned how to develop customer empathy, insight, and understanding. This was a positive experience where they gained skills in spotting opportunities and valuing ideas, see Fig. 1.

Mechanisms. Quantification is a classic method of building trust (Porter, 1996). This could perhaps explain why asking students to quantify value together with potential customers may be an effective way to learn collaborative idea development skills in practice.

Challenge 3: Build a Prototype and Get Good Feedback from an S-Person

> Prove to me that you created value for others by building a prototype and getting good feedback on it from an S-person. Reflect here on how it felt, what you learned from it and how you will do next time around.

Intervention. Many students worked creatively to build a minimum viable product (MVP). The most tangible prototypes were built in the IT sector, e.g., mockups, wireframes, or fully working user interfaces. Also outside IT, many students created prototypes, such as physical devices, flow sheets, process diagrams, folders, models, videos, or other kinds of graphical visualizations. A prototype often triggered concrete and engaged discussions with external stakeholders. Sometimes it also helped students convey a powerful future vision for the industry.

Outcomes. Many students learned how to solicit really powerful and sometimes even painful customer feedback. Some students also learned about relationship-building through co-creative prototyping, thus creating buy-in and winning precious ambassadors for their vision. This challenge clearly developed many students' creativity, see Fig. 1.

Mechanisms. Concrete visualizations activate our brain's imagination more than abstract talk (Blakemore & Frith, 2005; Mulligan, 1993). Such activation through prototyping seems to foster both students' creative engagement and increase the quality of many customer dialogues.

Challenge 4: Present your Visionary Dream to an S-Person

> Prove to me that you envisioned something really new by presenting your visionary unreasonable artistic dream idea on how to do something really novel and unique in your area, and getting an S-person in your industry to still like it. Reflect here on how it felt, what you learned from it and how you will do next time around.

Intervention. Many students really pushed themselves here and dared to present a visionary and bold future dream that could potentially revolutionize an entire industry, to experts within that very industry. Some students remarked that such a fluffy, unrealistic, and perhaps even unreasonable dream needed to be backed up by data and facts. Others saw the need for a truly personal and genuine tone that conveys likeability. Many were surprised at how well a visionary dream was received by many experts.

Outcomes. These students got to practice and hone an important kind of visionary sales skill. They learned that visionary talk can help identify and attract like-minded innovators and early adopters amid larger crowds of people. They also learned the importance of having and nurturing a visionary dream, both for their own motivation as entrepreneurs and for early adopters and co-creators who become keen to share their enthusiasm.

Mechanisms. Playwright George Bernard Shaw once wrote that all progress depends upon unreasonable people who refuse to adapt to the world, but instead try to adapt the world to their visionary future dream (Elkington & Hartigan, 2008). This challenge uniquely shows how we can teach such a deviant skill. But we also need to keep context in mind. The 21 students who completed this challenge had been entrusted with someone else's quite mature high-tech idea to play around with. Can students who work with their own much less interesting ideas (cf. Jones & Penaluna, 2013, p. 807) even be given this challenge?

6 Developing "Mobilising Resources" Skills

There seem to be many different ways to work effectively with resource skills. An easy start is to let students discuss with alumni from the same entrepreneurship program. However, stronger development of resource skills instead comes from delivering real tangible value to someone else, in the form of a pilot project or in some other form. Finance skills are an outlier here, but can for example be developed by asking students to discuss price issues with potential customers.

Challenge 5: Discuss Value Creation in your Industry with an Alumni

> Prove to me that you analyzed for value creation by contacting an alumni from our program, asking for a meeting to discuss value creation in your industry. After the meeting, reflect here on how it felt, what you learned from it and implications for your project.

Intervention. Discussing one's entrepreneurial project with a friendly, helpful, and experienced alumni from the same program was emotionally comforting and boosting. Most students picked an alumni with work experience from the same industry or technology area. Topics varied greatly, e.g., early sales work, intellectual property, equity distribution, teamwork issues, networking, customer insights, etc. Many discussions centered around how to create value in their industry or with their type of technology.

Outcomes. Many students ended up more motivated and confident, less insecure, and more able to cope with the uncertainty of an early stage project. Many alumni gave the advice to avoid getting stuck in analysis and prioritize going out and talking to people (cf. Blank & Dorf, 2012; Brinckmann et al., 2010). The meeting often became the starting point of a very rewarding and trustful mentorship relation. Many students saw the meeting as a good example of effectuation, in terms of leveraging one's network to acquire a key resource for free (advice and mentoring).

Mechanisms. The fundamental mechanism here seems to be *alumni mentorship*. An alumni mentor can offer crucial emotional and motivational support based on high contextual understanding, but also practical tips that are specific to the industry or technology in question.

Challenge 6: Discuss Price Issues with a Potential Customer

> Prove to me that you explored pricing issues by discussing price issues with a potential customer. Reflect here on how it felt, what you learned from it and how you will do next time around.

Intervention. This challenge had a much wider variation in emotionality than the average challenge. Money talk can be both emotional and arbitrary in terms of customer reactions. Some customers are price sensitive, others may downplay the cost. Many students ended up in price discussions that at first felt uncomfortable but then ended up touching upon many key issues such as pricing strategy, production costs, competitor offerings, and potential pilot tests. Some even ended up in real negotiations and made real deals, and then reflected that a customer willing to talk money is a really interested customer.

Outcomes. Many students learned that it is more natural for people to talk about money than they had expected. A common conclusion was that one should not be afraid to have price discussions, even if it is still unclear what solution you offer or what problem you solve. It triggers a lot of important learning around the market and also highlights a need for financial and cost planning.

Mechanisms. Money is the most prominent resource in modern societies, so talking about it is a crucial skill to develop. This also allows for truly emotional and thus powerful learning (cf. Boekaerts, 2010). Students learn about their offering, their market, the alternatives, and also about themselves.

Challenge 7: Deliver Real Value to an S-Person

> Prove to me that you created value for others by delivering real value to an S-person at least once and in a non-scaleable way. Reflect here on how it felt, what you learned from it and how you will do next time around.

Intervention. Given the technical complexity of projects at this Master's program, most real value deliveries were in the form of epistemic value. Examples included collecting interesting data, analyzing new markets, conducting customer interviews, educating people around novel technology, and presenting their project in front of people who then gained new insights. A few prototypes were also mentioned, such as a team baking dog food for real "S-dogs" using food waste. Many teams also delivered real value outside their own project scope to gain goodwill, expand their network, or win ambassadors. This was a values trading that often ended well.

Outcomes. Many students reported about a strong boost in motivation and confidence, claiming that they learned to believe in their work and ability to create real value. Some saw it as a practical experience of open innovation where SMEs help each other to develop a novel field. Many learned how useful it is to help others, since they give back. This was especially the case for intrapreneurs who are embedded in a large hierarchy. The skill to mobilize others was clearly developed here.

Mechanisms. The many positive emotions and desirable effects of various others-focused activities seen here are good examples of prosocial motivation theory at work (Batson et al., 2008; Miller et al., 2012). We humans often find a deep sense of meaning in collective activity.

Challenge 8: Sell a Pilot Project to a Paying S-Person

> Prove to me that you created value for others by selling a pilot project to a paying S-person, before you even built a product/service, in a "Sell First Build Later" (SFBL) way. Reflect here on how it felt, what you learned from it and how you will do next time around.

Intervention. This challenge was very difficult, and was thus reflected upon only by one or two teams each year. Most of them got a paid pilot project up and running, and a few reported from their failed attempts. In all cases, students ended up in real negotiations involving real money in the range of 5–10.000 EUR. To succeed, the team needed to tick many boxes. Finding someone who had a problem important enough to be solved, who liked their vision around proposed value to be created, who could get a budget approved, and who was willing to spend it on an unproven student team. Most if not all pilots also came with significant technology or process uncertainty.

Outcomes. Trying to get a paid pilot project up and running entails many different aspects of being entrepreneurial. It could be one of the most complete challenges in this respect. Students thus reported having developed many different entrepreneurial competencies, such as flexibility, perseverance, courage, skills in sales, visioning, resourcing, negotiation, and planning.

Mechanisms. This could be one of the first formalized in-curricular examples of students learning through trying to sell a paid pilot project to a potential customer, in a sell-first-build-later manner. Given the broad set of learning outcomes observed, it represents a promising answer to the learning-by-doing-*what* question, striking an interesting middle ground between value creation and venture creation.

7 Developing "Into Action" Skills

All four action-tasks that develop action skills in a powerful way are associated to rather intense and deeply personal interactions that require courage, perseverance, and initiative. It can be intimidating to talk to a potential competitor, to one hundred people, to a real investor, or to laboratory staff who possess deep knowledge in an industry where oneself is a novice.

Challenge 9: Talk to a Potential and Established Competitor

> Prove to me that you discussed and communicated value to others by discussing your project with a potential and established competitor. Reflect here on how it felt, what you learned from it and how you will do next time around.

Intervention. Discussing with a potential market opponent is frightening for many reasons. Revealing your own tech secrets, annoying others through sneaky questions about their tech or market secrets, breaching the NDA of your corporate partner if you are an intrapreneur, and becoming demotivated by the superiority of your future rival. However, most students were pleasantly surprised by the friendliness they were greeted with. Many competitors openly shared their experiences and insights and were often truly interested in partnering to deliver on the same societal goal, sometimes in a co-opetition manner.

Outcomes. Many students learned to be more open-minded, curious, and relational when meeting people initially perceived as a threat. They often gained crucial insights about the industry, the market, trends, potential differentiators, and challenges. Learning about others' hard-earned facts gained through trying to solve similar problems can be helpful in a truly unique way. Many also reported being motivated by competition, seeing it as a sign of a genuine market need. Ethical skills were at times developed, since many students played the "student card" in an "undercover" way to make competitors reveal their secrets, which for many felt really awkward. They then advised others to be more open with their intentions. Honesty works fine too.

Mechanisms. This challenge exposed some key differences between competing and collaborating, thus representing a concrete way to refocus EE more on co-creation (cf. Watson & McGowan, 2020). Many students assume that entrepreneurship is all about competing, and here learn that novel solutions to vexing issues are often developed through effectuation-based collaboration.

Challenge 10: Immerse yourself in a Deep Tech Lab

> Prove to me that you had courage by immersing yourself in a deep tech lab and discussing your project with at least one S-person in the lab, even if you don't know the tech so well. Reflect here on how it felt, what you learned from it and how you will do next time around.

Intervention. Many students engaged in humbling and exciting conversations with researchers, specialists, and other experts at the forefront of a technological field. It could be in a deep tech academic lab, in a corporate technical development department, or in a factory. It became a concrete illustration of key principles such as effectuation (leveraging the resources present in a lab), learning-by-doing (a concrete and graspable experience triggering powerful reflective observation), and design thinking (becoming an insider feeling empathy with others). This was a scary experience for many students, feeling vulnerable but also empowered by the superior level of detailed knowledge provided. Many students prepared thoroughly through independent study.

Outcomes. Students learned to learn in many different ways. Not only by leaving their own building (cf. Blank & Dorf, 2012) but also by getting inside the *right* building. They learned to learn from experts by asking powerful questions, by being quiet, by building relationships, by forming interdisciplinary teams, and by embracing the uncertainty inherent in experts sharing deep knowledge. Many students saw it as an opportunity for them to become a crucial link between deep technology and commercial markets, between research and practice. This helped build emotional agency for the technical innovation students had been entrusted with. Many were also surprised by how fast they could learn in this way, how well they could cope with complex vocabulary, and how valuable it was for them to gain detailed technical knowledge.

Mechanisms. Visiting a deep tech lab helps students conduct a *techno-economic value analysis* (TEVA), an important step in technology-based intra- and entrepreneurship (Lundqvist & Williams Middleton, 2013). TEVA links detailed technical functionalities to valued customer utilities on the market, mediated by key performance indicators.

Challenge 11: Talk to One Hundred S-Persons

> Prove to me that you discussed and communicated value to others by talking to 100 S-persons, be it customers, experts, value chain people, network actors, etc. Reflect here on how it felt and what you learned from it.

Intervention. Many students first thought this was an impossible challenge. But every year, almost half the class proudly reported having reached the goal through phone calls, video meetings, and in-person meetings. Some used fairs and networking events, but most meetings were scheduled by painstakingly contacting people relevant to their project. Many used sales funnel and snowball sampling techniques. These conversations helped them understand the industry, emerging trends and customer needs, and pain points. They also identified innovators, early adopters, and co-creators. Many reported having built up a comprehensive industry network in just nine months. Some claimed having become experts in their niche thanks to these conversations.

Outcomes. Students learned practical techniques for how to make cold contacts and book meetings, how to overcome their fears, how to prepare meetings, how to ask good questions, how to make people excited, and how to make them open up to talk about their problems. Many reported going from nervous to confident in early stage entrepreneurial sales, even loving it. They learned how to decide which meetings to take and which ones to not waste time on. Perseverance was built when realizing that sales are a numbers game where more is always better.

Mechanisms. This was the most appreciated challenge among many students, thanking for this marathon forced upon them, and asking us to keep it in the curriculum forever. For many, it was really challenging, but also really rewarding for their project and impacting them for life. This challenge arguably captures much of what entrepreneurship is all about. To take action and throw yourself out there, even if your entire body screams NO at times, to then become an extreme learner who loves to see every single human interaction, especially the difficult ones, as a unique learning opportunity (cf. Smilor, 1997, p. 344).

Challenge 12: Pitch to a REAL Investor Asking for REAL Money

> Prove to me that you had courage by pitching to a REAL investor asking for REAL money. Reflect here on how it felt, what you learned from it and how you will do next time around.

Intervention. This challenge was the most uncomfortable of all, but also the most confidence-building, see Fig. 1. The students pitched for funding, either to an investor, to a large audience at a pitching event or to an internal corporate committee or management team. The money they asked for spanned from 5000 € to 500.000 €, with a typical amount being around 30.000 €. Some got what they asked for, many did not. Key components of their pitch were what value they intended to create, for whom, how this was unique, and which facts supported their claims. Intrapreneurs had the added complexity of aligning their pitch to corporate strategy. After their pitch, students got many different questions, some more challenging than others.

Outcomes. Students explained afterward that pitching is an experiential skill that requires real-world practice to be developed. They learned the importance of being genuine, showing enthusiasm, managing body language, preparing meticulously, practicing the actual pitch before, and managing a broad variety of tricky questions afterward. They became more confident in speaking to investors. They also learned about many different details to include in a pitch deck.

Mechanisms. Pitching is common in EE, often in front of a jury (Brentnall, 2023). But in this case, there is also an aspect of genuinely asking real investors or managers for their money. Each pitch had real-world consequences for their team. This addition could help explain why the effects were so strong in terms of student discomfort, confidence-building, and also ability to mobilize resources.

8 Developing "Emotions" Skills

While there is not a specific emotional skill in the EntreComp framework, many entrepreneurial skills such as self-awareness (a resource skill), uncertainty coping (an action skill), and opportunity spotting (an ideas skill) often require emotionally charged experiences to be more profoundly developed (Lackéus, 2020b). Some challenging activities that have been found to trigger deep learning are to ignore other people's advice, to get rejected, or to experience different kinds of emotional setbacks. However, also deeply positive experiences can play an important role here, such as managing to get something useful for free from an external stakeholder.

Challenge 13: Ignore Feedback from an S-Person Based on Personal Conviction

> Prove to me that you were dedicated on a personal level by getting feedback from an S-person in your industry, later to ignore that feedback to instead do what YOU believe is the right way forward. Reflect here on how it felt, what you learned from it and how you will do next time around.

Intervention. This was the most common challenge, see Fig. 1. Many students wrote that they ignored feedback all the time, such as if their entire project idea was blasted by an industry expert. Many were still nervous, fearing damaged relationships to key people. The ignored feedback was often deemed to be biased, diverging, out of context, guesswork, outdated, or simply at odds with the students' vision. Feedbackers could be innovation killers, overconfident know-it-alls, uninformed laggards, blatant promoters of their own niche, or representatives of old ways of doing things. Potential customers were often deemed to be wrong or asking for things they would not pay for. Some intrapreneurs also took the risk to ignore internal supervisors, managers, gatekeepers, or entire established corporate truths or cultures.

Outcomes. Ignoring bad advice often developed grit and perseverance. Many proudly reported gaining the courage and confidence to stick to their vision, to trust their instincts, and to listen to their gut feeling. But they also saw negative feedback as a learning opportunity and a way to practice a delicate balancing act between not giving up and knowing when to pivot. If negative feedback dominated, some saw the very few positive people as a sign that change is indeed needed. They then tried to turn these few likeminded early adopters into co-creators of radical innovation. Some students learned to manage their own inner negative thoughts, not losing their faith but instead going their own way to gather their own facts and proof. This filled them with a strong sense of ownership.

Mechanisms. Most people are not innovators or early adopters (Moore, 1999), so it is quite natural for students to meet many late adopters and laggards who are less able to give relevant feedback. Also, customers cannot be fully trusted to know what they actually want. This has been called the "faster horses" problem, after Henry Ford who was known for paying less attention to customers: "If I had asked them what they wanted, they would have said faster horses" (Gordon et al., 2019).

Challenge 14: Ask an S-Person for Something and Get Rejected

> Prove to me that you experimented by asking an S-person for something significant to your project (not just a meeting), and getting a clear no from this person, i.e. get rejected. Reflect here on how it felt, what you learned from it and how you will do next time around.

Intervention. The most common reason for rejection was when students tried to initiate collaboration with a potential customer. It could be to ask for a pilot project or a letter of intent. Other rejection examples were students asking for sensitive data, expert advice or help, a study visit at a factory, or free access to a database, industry report, or lab. Some rejections were about tangible resources such as funds, grants, or products. Rejections made students feel sad, frustrated, disappointed, and demotivated, see Fig. 1. But it also made them reflect on the importance of perseverance, trying harder next time, and eventually feeling the strong motivational power of overcoming challenges.

Outcomes. Many learning outcomes were related to sales strategy. Tactical sales insights around how to make new contacts, how to prepare and carry out effective sales meetings, and how to negotiate a deal. Strategic sales insights around how to build a sales pipeline, the importance of measuring progress, who to approach at what stage, and why an industry network is a crucial tool. Many key insights were also emotional and relational. Students learned how to master the art of coping with and even planning for failure, seeing it as a natural road to success instead of taking it personal. They also learned the importance of a positive growth mindset and building strong trustful relationships.

Mechanisms. This challenge lets students practice a crucial entrepreneurial skill—rejection management. Early stage entrepreneurial sales are often counter-intuitive in that the frequency of rejection is shockingly high. Most inexperienced people who get rejected by 90% or more would trust their gut feeling to give up. But when bringing novel and complex solutions to the world, initial rejection must be expected. This is described in sales and innovation literature (e.g. Rackham, 1989; Rogers, 1983) but needs to be learned viscerally.

Challenge 15: Get Something Tangible for Free from an S-Person

> Prove to me that you took emotional action by getting something tangible—an object, a resource, a gift of some kind—you needed for your project from an S-person in your industry, just because you showed this person that you care so much about your project. Reflect here on how it felt, what you learned from it and how you will do next time around.

Intervention. A broad range of tangible and useful gifts were given to those students who took emotional action by demonstrating their passion and personal dedication to key S-persons. Students received free entrance to expensive fairs, exclusive events, and influential committees. After trust and common interests had been established, they were sent confidential and useful documents and data of many different kinds, as well as valuable hard-to-find contacts. Also products and raw materials were given away to them, such as stoves, cameras, laptops, scooters, door locks, swimwear, whey, metals, and chemicals. Some students were even granted free office space and free exhibition space worth upwards of 2.000 €.

Outcomes. This challenge was the easiest and most common way to develop students' ability to acquire resources, see Fig. 1. Students learned to connect emotionally by showing engagement, passion, and vision, as well as by being nice, empathetic, and thankful. They learned that many people want to help when sympathy, relational trust, and reciprocity are present. Many students saw this as a way to practice effectuation principles such as *bird-in-hand* (leverage your resources such as your network), *crazy quilt* (co-create with those willing to commit), and *the ask* (dare to ask for commitments).

Mechanisms. This challenge lets students learn effectuation in a hands-on way. It also gives them insight into powerful mechanisms portrayed in Marcel Mauss' famous anthropological gift theory, stipulating that gifts are deeply relational (Graeber, 2001). Gifts carry a special power to nourish deep relationships by being personal, even spiritual, and by creating desire to reciprocate.

Challenge 16: Experience an Emotional Setback Related to an S-Person

> Prove to me that you revised by experiencing an emotionally charged setback involving an S-person. Reflect here on how it felt, what you learned from it and how you will do next time around.

Intervention. Most emotional setbacks occurred during meetings with potential customers who bluntly blasted the students as ignorant time-wasters, overly optimistic, or less unique than claimed. A few setbacks were about embarrassing demo failures, final rejections in pilot negotiations, being ghosted by customers amid positive talks, getting a very low response rate (<10%) on attempts to reach out to many, and late cancellations. Other setbacks were more personal, such as realizing one's lack of passion for the venture, realizing a bad choice of customer segment, or experiencing major collaboration issues in the team. Finally, a few really emotional setbacks were about project termination due to consistently negative feedback from customers or betrayals within the team.

Outcome. Many students were baffled by how deeply affected they were by an emotional roller-coaster, at times experiencing shock, shame, grief, hopelessness, and self-doubt. While they learned to see failures as creativity-sparking learning opportunities, they also learned the perils of being naïve. Don't trust everyone, prepare yourself meticulously, do your own checks, and try to spot early warning signs. A common theme was the crucial role of emotional intelligence and resilience, managing expectations better, not taking things too personal or becoming defensive, but instead staying flexible and open-minded, using new insights to revise and try again and again. Teamwork insights were triggered by seeing how important the team is when coping with difficulties, highlighting the need for transparent team communication, honesty, and trust.

Mechanisms. This challenge captured the naturally occurring crisis-triggered entrepreneurial learning events among these students (cf. Cope & Watts, 2000). Critical learning events are crucial to how entrepreneurs and intrapreneurs learn and should thus be monitored in experiential EE. Teachers can use these events for pedagogical purposes as they unfold, to show the entire class what can happen and what insights can be drawn from such crises.

9 Discussion

The Complex Beauty of Emotionally Charged Intra- and Entrepreneurship
Re-reading the 754 student reflections analyzed here has been a true joy. They illustrate the sheer beauty of the entrepreneurial lifestyle, where exhilarating moments of success and insight are mixed with life-impacting crises. Being entrepreneurial is a rollercoaster that truly makes life worth living for some people, but also makes other people search for a different and much calmer career. Analyzing the outcomes of these action-tasks has at times been surprising. Many unexpected links surfaced, such as between noncustomer talks and sustainability thinking, between alumni mentors and resource acquisition skills, and between deep tech lab visits and learning to learn.

What was not surprising to me, however, was to see how omnipresent and important emotions were in these student reflections. Entrepreneurship is deeply emotional labor (cf. Hochschild, 1983). If we want to understand EE better, we need to focus more on emotion-based impact indicators (Nabi et al., 2017). Figure 1 highlights a weak point of EntreComp as an outcome assessment framework in EE. If emotionality had been absent here, key entrepreneurial outcomes would have been invisible, such as ability to cope with rejections, setbacks, bad advice, disappointments, and missed expectations. What is also made visible is that external interaction is a very positive and motivation-triggering experience in most cases.

Figure 1 shows that two competencies stand out in relation to negative emotions; perseverance and self-awareness. Many student reflections illustrate how important negative experiences are for building these crucial competencies. However, deliberately triggering negative emotions in students has ethical and practical implications for teachers. Can we allow ourselves to inflict emotional pain on our students? How will it impact other kinds of learning? Can we cope with the anger and frustration it triggers? Many people deal with failure through *restoration orientation*; redirecting their negative emotions toward secondary sources of stress (Schut & Stroebe, 1999). At our program, we often see students distracting themselves from grief by engaging in conflicts with teachers and other university employees (Blomé & Simson, 2021).

From EntreComp to EntreAct: Tactics for Entrepreneurial Action

EntreComp is a framework for understanding what it means to *be* entrepreneurial, packaged as 15 different competencies of equal importance (McCallum et al., 2018, p. 13–14). But entrepreneurial competencies are evasive and fuzzy. Even if EntreComp helps many teachers by succinctly specifying what entrepreneurial competencies *are*, the framework gives scant support to teachers around what students can be asked to *do* in order to *develop* those competencies. There is a need to establish something we can call EntreAct—a corresponding framework for the doing required to *become* entrepreneurial (Lackéus & Sävetun, 2023, p. 22).

What would an EntreAct framework look like? Will we ever be able to specify 15 generic EntreAct action-tasks of equal importance, in a neat flower model like EntreComp? This is indeed a challenging proposal. The 16 action-tasks described here are only one example of how people can develop EntreComp competencies, taken from the specialized context of a venture creation program at a university of technology in Sweden.

EE is deeply contextual (Lindahl Thomassen et al., 2020), so one collection of EntreAct action-tasks might not work well in a different setting. Can we ask nursing students, theology students, or primary school kids to explore an industry's value chain or discuss price issues with a competitor? It could make them more confused instead of more entrepreneurial. We therefore need different action-task packages for different contexts. What the 16 action-tasks outlined here can hopefully achieve is inspiration to others when creating their own variation.

A Model for Designing EntreAct Challenges

In an effort to further help teachers design action-reflection challenges, Table 1 shows a generalization attempt based on commonalities across the 16 action-tasks. An EntreAct action-task includes taking action centered around a resource, or more generally around value. It specifies at least one of four different directions in an

Table 1 A generic inspirational model EE teachers may use when designing an action-reflection challenge of EntreAct type

Action	Resource	Direction	Interaction	Emotion	Reflection	Insight
Give Get Discuss Explore Propose Prototype Create Envision	..value ..help ..resources ..means ..an artifact ..a proposition ..a gadget ..some tech ..some future	..to ..for ..from ..with	…a previously unknown person that you establish a relation with… (could be a potential customer, partner, competitor, student, alumni, colleague, expert, or any other type of human being)	…in a way that triggers feedback from him/her which then causes emotions in you… (could be joy, surprise, engagement, pride, excitement, or, stress, anxiety, frustration, disappointment, etc.)	…and then reflect afterwards in preferably written form to your coach/teacher, individually, around what you…	..learned ..appreciated ..were surprised by ..felt strongly about ..found insightful ..found disturbing ..ignored/rejected ..relate to literature ..will revise/retry ..will not do again

Teachers pick one of eight action types, couple it with one of nine resource types and one of four direction types. This gives them a skeleton they can contextualize further for use with their students

emotion-laden personal interaction with a person previously unknown to the student. It also includes a request to reflect in writing afterward, both as a way to trigger deep insights and as a time-efficient way for the teacher to assess many students. The last part of the reflection is forward-looking, implying that it is an iterative process of up to hundreds of EntreAct interactions carried out by each student.

The Overarching Logic of EntreAct

Pedagogical advice to EE teachers can according to Mansoori (2018, p. 49) be offered on three different levels; (1) practical level of *tactics,* i.e., tools and techniques, (2) middle-level *models,* and (3) high-level overarching *logic.* If the 16 action-tasks in Fig. 1 represent a set of practical *tactics,* and Table 1 represents a middle-level *model*, what is then the overarching *logic* of EntreAct? This is a difficult question to which only provisional answers can be given here. One perspective is that EntreAct guides teachers in how to make their students experience all four aspects of the CAVE framework recently proposed by Sarasvathy (2024). CAVE stands for causal (e.g., hypothesis testing), adaptive (e.g., asking for advice), visionary (e.g., passionate pitching), and effectual (e.g., co-creation) tools and techniques used by entrepreneurs in their resource- and relationship-seeking activities. Together, the 16 action-tasks cover all four CAVE dimensions.

Sarasvathy often argues for the entrepreneurial *logic* to be taught to everyone, just like the scientific method is regularly being taught to all students (Sarasvathy, 2024, p. 24; Sarasvathy & Venkataraman, 2011, p. 115). What EntreAct-related efforts can contribute with, as well as a design science approach more in general, is to make such an endeavor actionable and reliable for teachers on a practical level of *models* and *tactics*. This is helpful in making entrepreneurial competencies broadly accessible to students of all ages and in all faculties, from primary school through high school to university and adult education—from ABC to PhD (Moberg, 2014).

An EntreAct Community Empowered by DAS Methodology
If many EE teachers would start to design EntreAct task packages similar to the one presented here, a strong community might emerge. These teachers could rely on DAS as a design science approach to design, test, validate, discuss, and diffuse a large number of EntreAct action-task packages in many different EE contexts. The DAS methodology could help such a community analyze in considerable detail how different EntreAct activities are causally linked to different EntreComp competencies. This could become an antidote to the prevailing McDonaldization of EE, where strikingly similar approaches such as competitions, inspirational lectures, business model canvas workshops, and money-making challenges dominate EE (Hytti, 2018).

The 16 challenges presented here do not at all rely on such McDonaldized approaches. Instead, they give students a broad variety of resource-seeking and relationship-seeking activities to choose from, where interactions with previously unknown people become the norm. Compared to isolated classroom-based approaches, this more accurately emulates the deeply intersubjective nature of entrepreneurship (Sarasvathy & Venkataraman, 2011, p. 126). More long-term, EntreAct could grow into a comprehensive framework consisting of many different context-sensitive logics, models, and tactics that give EE teachers access to empirically validated advice on how to make their students more entrepreneurial. This expands the pool of reliable answers to the "learning-by-doing-*what*?" question. Please contact the author if you want to join such a community.

Design Science as an Important Trend in EE
I hope this chapter has illustrated the usefulness of a design science approach. I personally believe that design science could be the next big thing in EE, and that we have exciting times ahead of us if design science gains traction. The editors of this volume are diligently leading the way here. I personally realized that it was design science I was doing when Bart Derre started to explain this to me some years ago. He introduced me to a new vocabulary, and a warm community, for which I am really thankful.

References

Bacigalupo, M., Kampylis, P., Punie, Y., & Van den Brande, G. (2016). *EntreComp: The entrepreneurship competence framework*. Publication Office of the European Union.

Batson, C. D., Ahmad, N., Powell, A. A., & Stocks, E. (2008). Prosocial motivation. In J. Shah & W. Gardner (Eds.), *Handbook of motivation science* (pp. 135–149). Guilford Publications.

Biesta, G., & Burbules, N. C. (2003). *Pragmatism and educational research*. Rowman & Littlefield Lanham, MD.

Blakemore, S. J., & Frith, U. (2005). *The learning brain: Lessons for education*. Blackwell Publishing.

Blank, S. G., & Dorf, B. (2012). The startup owner's manual: The step-by-step guide for building a great company. : .

Blomé, A., & Simson, W. (2021). *Entrepreneurial failure and learning – The role of affect in learning from failure and its impact on nascent entrepreneurs Master thesis*. Chalmers University of Technology Gothenburg.

Boekaerts, M. (2010). The crucial role of motivation and emotion in classroom learning. In H. Dumont, D. Istance, & F. Benavides (Eds.), *The nature of learning* (pp. 91–111). OECD Publishing.

Brentnall, C. (2023). *Theorising competitive enterprise education*. PhD thesis, Sheffield Hallam University Sheffield.

Brinckmann, J., Grichnik, D., & Kapsa, D. (2010). Should entrepreneurs plan or just storm the castle? A meta-analysis on contextual factors impacting the business planning–performance relationship in small firms. *Journal of Business Venturing, 25*(1), 24–40.

Cope, J., & Watts, G. (2000). Learning by doing – An exploration of experience, critical incidents and reflection in entrepreneurial learning. *International Journal of Entrepreneurial Behaviour & Research, 6*(3), 104–124.

De La Croix, A., & Veen, M. (2018). The reflective zombie: Problematizing the conceptual framework of reflection in medical education. *Perspectives on Medical Education, 7*(6), 394–400.

Denyer, D., Tranfield, D., & Van Aken, J. E. (2008). Developing design propositions through research synthesis. *Organization Studies, 29*(3), 393–413.

Elkington, J., & Hartigan, P. (2008). *The power of unreasonable people: How social entrepreneurs create markets that change the world*. Harvard Business Press.

Gordon, A. V., Rohrbeck, R., & Schwarz, J. O. (2019). Escaping the 'Faster Horses' trap: Bridging strategic foresight and design-based innovation. *Technology Innovation Management Review, 9*(8), 30–42.

Graeber, D. (2001). *Toward an anthropological theory of value: The false coin of our own dreams*. Springer.

Hochschild, A. (1983). *The managed heart: Communication of human feeling*. University of California Press.

Hytti, U. (2018). Critical entrepreneurship education: A form of resistance to McEducation? In K. Berglund & K. Verduijn (Eds.), *Revitalizing entrepreneurship education - Adopting a critical approach in the classroom* (pp. 228–234). Routledge.

Jones, C., & Penaluna, A. (2013). Moving beyond the business plan in enterprise education. *Education+ Training, 55*(8/9), 804–814.

Kolb, D. A. (1984). *Experiential learning: Experience as the source of learning and development*. Prentice Hall.

Lackéus, M. (2013). Developing entrepreneurial competencies – An action-based approach and classification in education. Licentiate Thesis, Chalmers University of Technology Gothenburg. (ISSN: 1654-9732).

Lackéus, M. (2014). An emotion based approach to assessing entrepreneurial education. *International Journal of Management Education, 12*(3), 374–396.

Lackéus, M. (2020a). Collecting digital research data through social media platforms: Can 'scientific social media' disrupt entrepreneurship research methods? In W. B. Gartner & B. Teague (Eds.), *Research handbook of entrepreneurial behavior, practice, and process*. Edward Elgar Publishing.

Lackéus, M. (2020b). Comparing the impact of three different experiential approaches to entrepreneurship in education. *International Journal of Entrepreneurial Behavior & Research, 26*(5), 937–971.

Lackéus, M. (2020c). Entrepreneurial education, its unique and novel contribution to education. In P. M. & H. R. (Eds.), *Encyclopedia of educational innovation*. Springer.

Lackéus, M. (2022). *Den värdeskapande eleven - en handbok för meningsfullt lärande i skolan* [The value-creating student - English translation available at vcplist.com/book]. Studentlitteratur.

Lackéus, M., & Sävetun, C. (2023). *Designed action sampling as a new research method to help build active communities in entrepreneurial education*. Entrepreneurship Education & Pedagogy.

Lackéus, M., & Williams Middleton, K. (2018). Assessing experiential entrepreneurship education: Key insights from five methods in use at a venture creation program. In D. Hyams-Ssekasi & E. Caldwell (Eds.), *Experiential learning for entrepreneurship - Theoretical and practical perspectives on enterprise education*. Palgrave Macmillan.

Lindahl Thomassen, M., Williams Middleton, K., Ramsgaard, M. B., Neergaard, H., & Warren, L. (2020). Conceptualizing context in entrepreneurship education: A literature review. *International Journal of Entrepreneurial Behavior & Research, 26*(5), 863–886.

Lundqvist, M., & Williams Middleton, K. (2013). *Transformative and transactional mechanisms in action-based entrepreneurship education* 22nd Nordic Academy of Management conference, Reykjavik.

Lundqvist, M., & Williams Middleton, K. (2024). Making the whole university entrepreneurial – Decades of legitimacy-building through Chalmers School of Entrepreneurship. *Technovation* (In press), 1–11.

Mansoori, Y. (2018). *Entrepreneurial methods as vehicles of entrepreneurial action*. Thesis for Doctoral Degree, Chalmers University of Technology Gothenburg, Sweden.

McCallum, E., Weicht, R., McMullan, L., & Price, A. (2018). *EntreComp into action: Get inspired, make it happen*. Publications Office of the European Union.

Miller, T. L., Grimes, M. G., McMullen, J. S., & Vogus, T. J. (2012). Venturing for others with heart and head: How compassion encourages social entrepreneurship. *Academy of Management Review, 37*(4), 616–640.

Moberg, K. (2014). *Assessing the impact of entrepreneurship education - From ABC to PhD*. Doctoral Thesis, Copenhagen Business School.

Moore, G. A. (1999). Crossing the chasm.

Mulligan, J. (1993). Activating internal processes in experiential learning. *Using experience for learning*, 46–58.

Nabi, G., Liñán, F., Fayolle, A., Krueger, N., & Walmsley, A. (2017). The impact of entrepreneurship education in higher education: A systematic review and research agenda. *Academy of Management Learning & Education, 16*(2), 277–299.

Porter, T. M. (1996). *Trust in numbers: The pursuit of objectivity in science and public life*. Princeton University Press.

Rackham, N. (1989). *Major account sales strategy*. McGraw-Hill.

Rogers, E. M. (1983). *Diffusion of innovations* (3rd ed.). The Free Press.

Romme, A. G. L. (2003). Making a difference: Organization as design. *Organization Science, 14*(5), 558–573.

Romme, A. G. L., & Dimov, D. (2021). Mixing oil with water: Framing and theorizing in management research informed by design science. *Designs, 5*(1), 13.

Sarasvathy, S. D. (2024). Lean hypotheses and effectual commitments: An integrative framework delineating the methods of science and entrepreneurship. *Journal of Management, 01492063241236445*, 3035.

Sarasvathy, S. D., & Venkataraman, S. (2011). Entrepreneurship as method: Open questions for an entrepreneurial future. *Entrepreneurship Theory and Practice, 35*(1), 113–135. https://doi.org/10.1111/j.1540-6520.2010.00425.x

Schut, M., & Stroebe, H. (1999). The dual process model of coping with bereavement: Rationale and description. *Death Studies, 23*(3), 197–224.

Smilor, R. W. (1997). Entrepreneurship: Reflections on a subversive activity. *Journal of Business Venturing, 12*(5), 341–346.

Smith, K., Rogers-Draycott, M. C., & Bozward, D. (2022). Full curriculum-based venture creation programmes: Current knowledge and research challenges. *International Journal of Entrepreneurial Behavior & Research, 28*(4), 1106–1127.

Van Aken, J. E., & Romme, G. (2009). Reinventing the future: Adding design science to the repertoire of organization and management studies. *Organization Management Journal, 6*(1), 5–12.

Watson, K., & McGowan, P. (2020). Rethinking competition-based entrepreneurship education in higher education institutions: Towards an effectuation-informed coopetition model. *Education+ Training, 62*(1), 31–46.

Martin Lackéus is a researcher in entrepreneurial education at the Division of Entrepreneurship and Strategy at Chalmers University of Technology in Sweden. He is also a teacher at Chalmers School of Entrepreneurship. Martin's research focuses on how individuals develop entrepreneurial competencies in education through value creation processes, and how such processes can be assessed. His research has been published in leading scholarly journals such as Small Business Economics, International Journal of Entrepreneurial Behaviour Research, and Journal of Small Business Management. In 2016, Martin defended his PhD thesis on value creation as educational practice. Martin also works part-time as a social entrepreneur with an IT company he co-founded; Loopme Group, building a digital research tool.

Design Science Approach to Building a Large University Entrepreneurship Education Ecosystem (EEE)

Steven A. Gedeon

Abstract In this chapter, I would like to present my practitioner insights by applying DSR to entrepreneurship education (EE) and sharing artifacts and empirical research results from one of the largest entrepreneurship education ecosystems in the world at Toronto Metropolitan University (TMU). In the current chapter, the entrepreneurship education ecosystem (EEE) refers to the ecosystem of TMU, including all incubators, programs, and other initiatives related to stimulating entrepreneurial skills and mindset development among students and staff.

1 Context: Toronto Metropolitan University (TMU)

TMU has more than 75 different entrepreneurship courses, 15 full-time entrepreneurship faculty, AACSB (i.e., accreditation for business schools) accredited undergraduate and graduate degree programs and specializations, an angel network, VC fund, and 10 on-campus incubators including the DMZ, ranked by UBC (2018) as the world's #1 university-based incubator, helping over 800 companies raise over $2 billion and creating more than 5000 new jobs. Zone Learning at TMU includes course credit for experiential learning in one of our incubators and has supported more than 5000 startups that have collectively raised over $2.5 billion. Over 7000 students take our entrepreneurship courses per year.

I characterize the current size and extent of the TMU EEE as being "large," but it wasn't always that way. When I first joined TMU, our entrepreneurship posters might have been torn down across campus because we were associated with the Business School. Building relationships, harmonizing language, and changing the university culture to embrace entrepreneurship did not happen overnight. The

S. A. Gedeon (✉)
TorontoMet Entrepreneur Institute and Entrepreneurship and Strategy Department, Ted Rogers School of Management, Toronto Metropolitan University (TMU), Toronto, ON, Canada
e-mail: sgedeon@torontomu.ca

© The Author(s), under exclusive license to Springer Nature Switzerland AG 2025

B. Derre, Y. Baggen (eds.), *Empowering the Next Generation of Entrepreneurial Change Agents*, Contributions to Management Science,
https://doi.org/10.1007/978-3-031-82251-3_9

creation of design artifacts through our journey helped us to grow beyond the reach of specialized degree programs in entrepreneurship to build the university ecosystem by creating specialized incubators (e.g., Social Venture Zone, Fashion Zone, Legal Innovation Zone), Zone Learning, an Office of Social Innovation and becoming Canada's first Ashoka Changemaker Campus.

In this chapter, I will highlight key methods, lessons, artifacts, and design rules created during our learning journey to build new courses, degree programs, and incubators and grow into and/or flourish as a large EEE. I have taught, shared, received feedback, and heard stories about implementing many of these methods with over 200 entrepreneurship professors through my involvement in the EntreTime Teach-The-Teacher program (Gedeon et al., 2022). I will summarize and provide updated and condensed artifacts, share previously unpublished longitudinal research results, and propose design rules based on my practitioner experiences and scholarly publications.

2 Context: Accreditation and How to Design EE

Policymakers, employers, parents, and university administrators increasingly demand evidence-based proof that education can deliver its promised benefits to students and society. While such calls for quality assurance, regulation, or oversight are criticized as neo-liberal managerialism by some within academia (Jarvis, 2014) other disciplines, particularly business, engineering, and other so-called professional degree programs have embraced the Total Quality Management principles associated with accreditation (e.g., EQUIS, AACSB) and various government support programs designed to improve university impact.

To assist universities in implementing the New Skills Agenda for Europe, the OECD and European Commission created HEInnovate (2024), a set of eight key priorities universities should adopt that empower students with an entrepreneurial mindset. These encourage universities to go beyond simply teaching EE in courses to provide a supportive culture, eco-system, resources, and leadership as well as reward entrepreneurial behavior within the university "EEE." EntreComp (2024) was created to articulate the key entrepreneurial competencies and educational learning outcomes desired and ConneeectU (Educating Entrepreneurship Educators) and EntreTime (2024) were founded to support educators and university administrators through Teach-The-Teacher programs, expert mentorship, and international collaboration. Through ConneeectU and EntreTime, best practices and case studies are shared with university professors on course and program design, pedagogical techniques, assignments, and assessment methods to implement quality assurance for the attainment of learning outcomes such as those described by EntreComp (Gedeon et al., 2022).

Design Science Research (DSR) provides a critical approach to learning from these efforts to advance knowledge and the application of knowledge through the creation of innovative artifacts (Vom Brocke et al., 2020). DSR applies the scientific method to improve design practice, create artifacts that capture long-lasting knowledge, integrate disciplines, and connect research and practice (Telenko et al., 2016). Unlike descriptive science which deals with historical facts to be organized and interpreted, design science is primarily about future possibilities to be enacted (Dimov, 2016, 2020) and is thus a vital approach to improving the design, delivery, and performance of EE within universities.

In the specific case of building TMU's EEE, I will point to the various design science artifacts and methods that have informed our practice to date and reference the descriptive science publications and research results that document the past. Where appropriate, I will also reference some of my experiences, artifacts, and observations from teaching in the ConneeectU and EntreTime programs. Finally, I will propose several design rules so that others might enact their own future possibilities in university EE and EEE.

DSR and the field of design in general have inspired new ways of dealing with the limitations of traditional planning-based management theories that suggest stable courses of action based on data from the past (Martin, 2004, 2009). Unlike causal-based reasoning methods, design embraces the complex, changing, unpredictable, and ambiguous "wicked problems" inherent in the real world (Dorst, 2011; Liedtka & Ogilvie, 2011). Designers use abductive logic to explore "What might be?" and envision new products, services, and systems without having proof of their success (Dorst, 2011; Liedtka, 2014; Martin, 2009, 2004).

Friedman (2003) defined design as a goal-oriented process that involves creating something new (or reshaping something that exists) to solve a problem or to improve upon a less-than-desirable situation even though we may not yet be able to specify the preferred situation.

The tools, methods, principles, and mindsets that designers use to empathize, understand, discover, experiment, and co-create their way to a solution integrate analytical methods with intuition and creativity and are referred to as "designerly ways of thinking" (Cross, 1982). From a theoretical perspective, design may be considered a problem-solving activity (Buchanan, 1992; Ho, 2001); a way of reasoning/making sense of things (Lawson, 2005; Cross, 1982); a reflexive practice (Rylander, 2009); and as creation of meaning (Krippendorff, 2006).

Designing a university course or degree program is normally a highly structured and regulated process with clearly defined agents, requirements, and constraints that are informed by the field of instructional development or instructional systems design and may be conceptualized as a topic within the broader field of education (Gustafson & Branch, 2004). Most instructional designers approach this as a problem-solving process that includes Analysis, Design, Development, Implementation, and Evaluation—referred to as ADDIE (Molenda, 2003).

There are many different instructional development models that course and degree program EE design teams may choose from, as compiled, for example, by Gustafson and Branch (2004). The Diamond (2008) model is among the most common methods where one starts the process by setting goals, objectives, and design criteria for the program (this is often referred to as an instrumental method). Accreditation methods also use this approach where you start by setting learning outcomes, measure your ability to meet these goals by auditing Assurances of Learning (AoL) assignments, and then use continuous process improvements to increase the number of students who meet these requirements.

3 EE Program Design Artifacts from TMU

Most entrepreneurship degree programs emerge out of entrenched academic bureaucracies, growing in fits and start from a single course or donor-led entrepreneurship center program (Kuratko, 2005; Solomon, 2007). In the case of TMU, the entrepreneurship program grew from within the Ted Rogers School of Management to include an undergraduate Major and Minor, graduate specializations, and a wide range of service courses available to other programs at the university. Coming from the largest business program in Canada, we collaborate, share resources, and compete for students and resources with all the other Majors and Minors such as accounting, finance, economics, HR, marketing, global management, IT, real estate, retail, hospitality, and tourism. The entrepreneurship program spread a culture of entrepreneurship across campus to support the creation of TMU's EEE through the TorontoMet Entrepreneur Institute, Entrepreneurship Research Institute, 10 incubators, TorontoMet Angel Network, VC fund, Zone Learning, Office of Social Innovation, and various entrepreneurship and innovation-related degree programs.

In 2011, the Ted Rogers School of Management became accredited by AACSB through a formal design process that had significant and ongoing positive effects on our program objectives, design decisions, and assessment methods. It offered us the opportunity to analyze and re-design our entrepreneurship degree program with fresh eyes and a beginner's mindset. The mission-driven Total Quality Management approach offered by AACSB forced us to confront important design questions like what our stakeholders want, what exactly we mean by entrepreneurship, what our mission is, how we measure quality, who we want our students to be and who we would like to help them become.

Table 1 shows some of the design artifacts that my colleagues and I have created during our EE and EEE journey so far. I reproduce some of the tables and figures that I believe will be most relevant to your own design challenges in this chapter.

We first reviewed EE best practices worldwide to build a Program Design Framework and evaluate different program goals and pedagogical techniques (Gedeon, 2014). Then we analyzed the quality expectations of different stakeholders including employers, governments, accreditation agencies, award and rating organizations, faculty, and students and adopted the student transformation model to prioritize and harmonize our program goals (Gedeon, 2017). Ultimately, we improved upon the PDF to create the Comprehensive Framework for Entrepreneurship Education (CFEE) which is reproduced in Fig. 1 (Valliere et al., 2014).

The CFEE is taught through the EntreTime Teach-The-Teacher program as a robust and theoretically validated model for embedding EE into a course, degree program, or university-wide eco-system (Gedeon et al., 2022). The major design

Table 1 Artifacts arising from the design of TMU's EE and EEE

Artifact reference	Description of artifacts	Artifact reproduced here
Gedeon (2014) "Application of Best Practices in University Entrepreneurship Education" *European Journal of Training and Development*	This article reviews the literature to identify and apply best practises in EE. Artifacts in this article include (i) the Program Design Framework used to design an MBA program, (ii) a list of primary, secondary, and tertiary goals of the program, (iii) course list and learning outcomes, and (iv) list of pedagogical techniques and where they are used in the program	Not included
Gedeon (2017) "Measuring Student Transformation in Entrepreneurship Education Programs" Special Issue on Entrepreneurship Education with Impact: Opening the Black Box (EEI) in Education, Research International	This article includes a (i) stakeholder analysis and quality expectations for each stakeholder, (ii) detailed description of the accreditation stakeholder requirements and (iii) goal setting framework using student transformation as the primary goal	Not included
Valliere, Gedeon and Wise (2014) "A Comprehensive Framework for Entrepreneurship Education" Special Issue on Entrepreneurial Education in the *Journal of Business and Entrepreneurship*	This article provides a theoretical foundation for the Comprehensive Framework for Entrepreneurship Education (CFEE) and a step-by-step method for using the CFEE. Two tables show how each element of the CFEE applies to case studies for an undergraduate and graduate program	Figure 1
TorontoMet Entrepreneur Institute Website (2024) https://entrepreneurinstitute.ca/for-educators/	Resources for Entrepreneurship Educators include what is entrepreneurship, how to design an entrepreneurship program, how to teach entrepreneurship, how to measure learning outcomes, how to design EEE and how to work with Angels. Open Education Resources (OER)	Not included
Gedeon (2010) "What is Entrepreneurship?" Entrepreneurial Practice Review	This article describes the four domains of entrepreneurship as taught by EntreTime and embedded in our school's Mission Statement	Table 2

(continued)

Table 1 (continued)

Artifact reference	Description of artifacts	Artifact reproduced here
Grant and Gedeon (2019) "Teaching and Learning in the 21st Century University" in "The University of the Future" book	This book chapter describes the integration of experiential learning (student-centric learning) to replace lectures and exams (teacher-centric teaching). It provides a guide to integrating different student-centric learning pedagogies throughout the entire curriculum and the use of technology and space	Table 3
Gedeon (2020) "Theory-Based Design of an Entrepreneurship Micro-Credentialing and Modularisation System within a Large University Eco-System" Entrepreneurship Education and Pedagogy (EE&P)	This article describes the design and implementation of the EEE at TMU using the CFEE including historical description, case study and lessons learned	Table 4
Gedeon and Valliere (2018) "Closing the Loop: Measuring Entrepreneurial Self-Efficacy to Assess Student Learning Outcomes" *Entrepreneurship Education and Pedagogy* (EE&P)	This article describes a new valid and reliable entrepreneurial self-efficacy (ESE) scale that measures students' self-perception of whether they have gained the program's learning outcomes	Appendix and Figs. 4, 5 and 6
Gedeon (2024) "Building an Entrepreneurial Mindset" textbook and learning platform	OER Textbook and Interactive learning platform (Articulate Storyline) for ENT 101: Building an Entrepreneurial Mindset. Required introductory course for over 2000 business students/year	Not included
Bygrave, Wise & Zacharakis (2014) "Entrepreneurship Canadian Edition" Wiley textbook	Textbook for ENT 526: Entrepreneurial Behaviour and Strategy. First required course for second and third year students in the entrepreneurship Major and Minor degree. Customized textbook with Canadian content	Not included
Wise and Feld (2017) "Startup Opportunities: Know when to quit your day job" textbook	Textbook for ENT 601: Identifying Opportunities. Second required course for third year students in the entrepreneurship Major and Minor degree	Not included
Valliere (2019) "Entrepreneurial Thinking: Think Different" textbook	Textbook for ENT 527: Theories in Entrepreneurship. Required course for third and fourth year students in the entrepreneurship Major degree. This is, to my knowledge, the only theory-based entrepreneurship course and textbook	Not included

(continued)

Table 1 (continued)

Artifact reference	Description of artifacts	Artifact reproduced here
Gedeon (2021) "Entrepreneurial Career and Life Design" textbook and 22-episode YouTube Series	OER Textbook and 22-episode YouTube Series for ENT 801: Entrepreneurial Career and Life Design. Elective course for third and fourth year students. Custom-created textbook during the pandemic to replace in-person design thinking pedagogies	Not included
Nicholls-Nixon, Valliere, Gedeon and Wise (2020) "Entrepreneurial Ecosystems and the Lifecycle of University Business Incubators: An Integrative Case Study" *International Entrepreneurship and Management Journal*	This article is a Case Study analysis of TMU's EEE	Tables 5 and 6

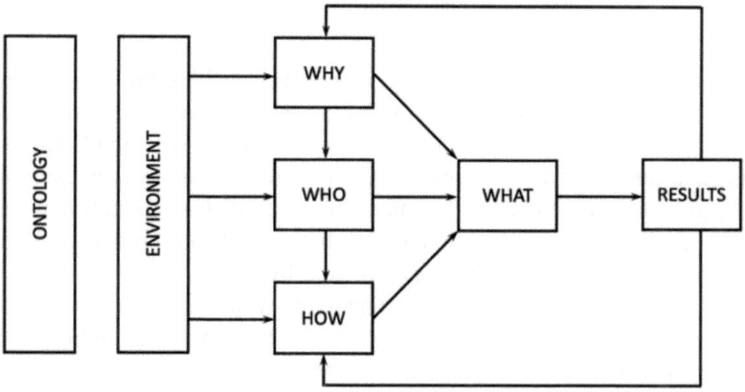

Fig. 1 Comprehensive Framework for Entrepreneurship Education (CFEE) recreated based on Valliere et al. (2014)

elements may be addressed at the institutional level, the degree program, or the individual course level, and the model has been applied to undergraduate, graduate, corporate, and youth empowerment programs in Europe and North America (Gedeon, 2022).

Some of the specific design choices we made at TMU for each element of the CFEE are described by Valliere et al. (2014) and on the Resources for Educators section of the TorontoMet Entrepreneur Institute (2024) website.

First of all, it is important that all stakeholders have a mutual understanding (or "ontology" or "philosophy") of what we mean by EE and what the purpose of education is. Here TMU embraced the broad definition of entrepreneurship as taught by EntreTime and produced in Table 2 (based on Gedeon, 2010, 2020, 2022). By ontologically separating an entrepreneurial mindset and behaviors from the specific

Table 2 Design artifact for ontology and "Why"—four primary domains of entrepreneurship (summarized from Gedeon, 2010, 2020, 2022)

Domain	Description
Starting Up a New Business or Venture	This is the form of entrepreneurship mostly portrayed by the media and popular press and also includes side hustles and self-employment. These new business entities stimulate the economy and account for virtually 100% of all new job growth in modern economies
Intrapreneurship	Being entrepreneurial within an existing venture or organization. Also termed innovation, employee entrepreneurship or corporate entrepreneurship
Social Entrepreneurship	Being entrepreneurial by creating primarily social or other forms of noneconomic values or organizations. Also termed social innovation, change making or active citizenship. This can involve starting a new program, entity (for profit or nonprofit) or creating change within a community or institution
Personal Empowerment	Being entrepreneurial toward your life and character through personal growth and transformation. The application of entrepreneurial principles toward your own career and life design. Often this form of entrepreneurship must take place prior to the other forms. "To change the world you first have to change yourself"

context in which they are performed, EE is seen as "teaching *through* entrepreneurship using the student transformation model to achieve entrepreneurial learning outcomes (e.g. entrepreneurial mindsets and behaviors such as described by EntreComp or in Figs. 2 and 3). This is a profoundly different ontology, for example, than "teaching *for* entrepreneurship" (i.e., teaching students how to start new ventures) or teaching *about* entrepreneurship (e.g., teaching about entrepreneurs and their role in the economy, society, innovation, and prosperity).

At TMU, all four domains of entrepreneurship were explicitly incorporated into the Mission Statements ("Why" in the CFEE) for the entrepreneurship degree program, Department of Entrepreneurship and Strategy, and the TorontoMet Entrepreneur Institute (Gedeon, 2020). We embedded both the startup and intrapreneurship domains into the 2-year, 4-semester set of experiential learning capstone courses for the entrepreneurship major. We also created domain-specific elective courses such as "Applied Social Entrepreneurship and Changemaking" and "Entrepreneurial Career and Life Design."

Defining entrepreneurship, the purpose of entrepreneurship education, and the student transformation model in peer-reviewed journal design artifacts enhance credibility and legitimacy when trying to build bridges and form a common vocabulary with colleagues in your own faculty as well as across campus. I experienced this when the TMU entrepreneurship degree program was accredited (Valliere et al., 2014) and when growing the EEE at TMU (Gedeon, 2020), but I've also experienced this at other universities around the world and through EntreTime.

The University of Applied Science Munich, for example, used this approach to get entrepreneurship embedded as one of the university's three key pillars (along with sustainability and internationalization) which enhanced the ability of their

Table 3 Design artifact for "How"—student-centric learning pedagogies (Grant & Gedeon, 2019)

Pedagogical technique	Sample references	Guide to use
Role Playing, Simulations, Game Playing	Stumpf et al. 1991; Low, et al. 1994; Hindel, 2002	In-class use or distance education, good for developing skills in a risk-free learning environment
Extra-Curricular Activities, Student Clubs, Startup Incubators	Haensly, 1985; Ollis, 2012	Used primarily to enhance the overall student experience. Can also be integrated into the curriculum for project-based courses
Case Studies, Living Cases	Learned, 1991; Katz, 1995	In-class use, good for theory integration and problem-based learning
Project-Based Learning, Experiential Learning, Service Learning	Bringle and Hatcher, 1996; Kolb, et al. 2001; Beard and Wilson, 2002; Gedeon, 2014	The deepest level of student-centric learning, good for skill and attitudinal learning outcomes
Field Experience, Internships, Co-Op Programs	Marchioro, et al. 2014	Good for tying student jobs to their education. Good for learning skills and gaining relevant experience
On-Line Videos, Flipped Classroom, Micro-Certification, MOOCs	Tucker, 2012; Gilboy, et al. 2015; Gedeon, 2019	Integrative capstone courses, good for tying extra-curricular activities into course credit
Interviews, Life Stories, Field Trips, Journals, Self-Reflection Assignments	Solomon et al. 1994; Rae and Carswell, 2000; Mitchell and Chesteen, 1995	Good for introductory courses and to provide students with role models and motivation. Good for learning values, expert scripts and principles

entrepreneurship center to co-teach 26 "wide entrepreneurship" courses per year in collaboration with 15 of the 16 faculties across the university (Turgut-Dao et al., 2015).

As presented at 3E (i.e., the ECSB Entrepreneurship Education Conference) in 2015, they say: "We have found that these more inclusive, holistic, four domains of entrepreneurship allowed us to form collaborative partnerships across campus including with engineering, social sciences, humanities, art, and design. In particular, broadening the preconceived notions of entrepreneurship beyond strictly a business discipline into a more holistic philosophy of personal growth, creativity, leadership, problem solving and teamwork has encouraged the collaboration of diverse perspectives" (Turgut-Dao et al., 2015).

At TMU, we also published design artifacts related to the "How" and "Results" elements of the CFEE model (see Fig. 1). In Grant and Gedeon (2019), we identified and documented best practices in student-centric teaching pedagogies and where these might best fit within the overall degree program as reproduced in Table 3.

4 Measuring and Auditing TMU's EE Program

In Gedeon and Valliere (2018), we defined our program's learning outcomes and, in addition to the Assurances of Learning (AoL) assignments designated for accreditation purposes, we also created a valid and reliable survey instrument, reproduced in the appendix, to measure "Results"—students' perceptions of whether they had attained the accredited learning outcomes of our program. We specifically identify and measure 12 independent sub-domains of Entrepreneurial Self-Efficacy (ESE), including Core Self Evaluation, Opportunity Identification, Alertness, Planning under Uncertainty, Resource Marshalling, Adaptability, Financial Management, Teamwork, Critical Thinking, Communication, Persuading and Selling, and Self-Management. (I should note that our design committee identified these program learning outcomes before EntreComp was established.)

We measured these longitudinal survey results for students in our degree program over a 5-year period and compared them to two control groups—students from the business school not enrolled in entrepreneurship and students from outside the business school taking introductory entrepreneurship courses.

Figures 2 and 3 show in which specific required core courses we introduced, reinforced, and measured each of these and other program goals (such as exposure to inspirational stories, entrepreneurial theories, and entrepreneurial processes and methods) during our degree program. This figure is a moving target as new textbooks are written for specific courses and as administrative pressures cause us to reduce courses and/or add new ones. Table 1 references five new textbooks written by our professors for five of our courses.

We audited AoL assignments in the courses shown in Fig. 3 to ensure that all passing students "Met Expectations" or "Exceeded Expectations" in accordance with AACSB accreditation guidelines. We've passed several 5-year accreditation reviews of the program since implementing these changes. According to AACSB,

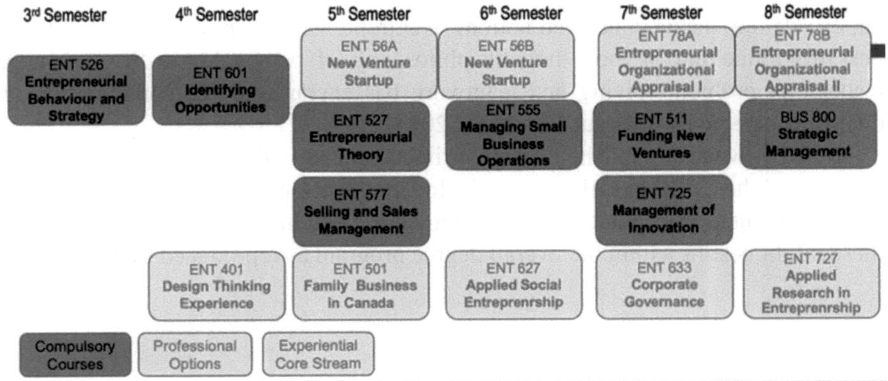

Fig. 2 Diagram showing the required course sequence in the Entrepreneurship and Innovation Degree Program at TMU

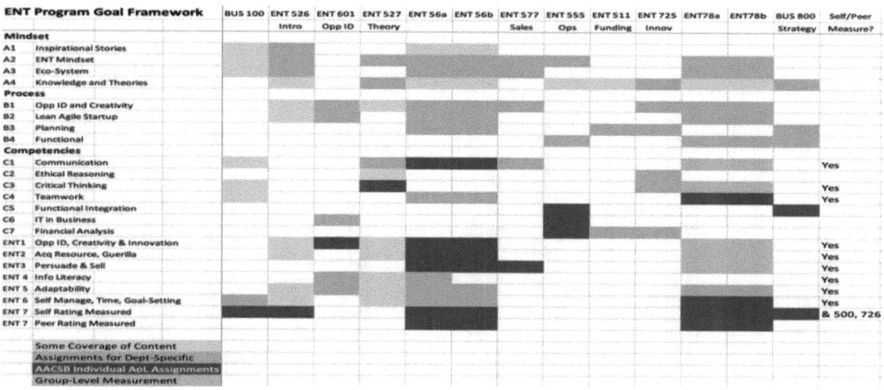

Fig. 3 Degree program goal framework that maps AACSB learning outcomes and AoL assignments to the 13 required courses in the Entrepreneurship & Innovation Degree Program at TMU

all students were achieving the designated learning outcomes as measured by AoL assignments using the embedded course method.

But did our students also believe they were achieving these learning outcomes as measured by the scale? Did they believe they possessed the competencies we were trying to instill?

Students progressing through our degree program took the Entrepreneurial Self-Efficacy (ESE) survey in the appendix when they first declared entrepreneurship as their major in 2nd year. They took the survey again at the start of their 3rd year and at the end of their 4th year. We conducted the surveys for 5 years, including over 300 students majoring in entrepreneurship and control samples with over 2700 non-entrepreneurship students following the experimental procedures described in Gedeon and Valliere (2018).

Figure 4 represents a longitudinal analysis comparing the individual student scores at the start of 3rd year (ENT 56A shown in blue) and the end of 4th year (ENT 78B shown in brown). As can be seen, overall average ESE (first column) and all learning outcome sub-domains of ESE increased during the 2-year 4-semester capstone sequence. Thus, students are not only passing the AACSB learning outcome assignment audits, but they also believe that they are improving at the learning outcome skills we were trying to instill.

How did this compare to control groups of students not majoring in entrepreneurship? Figure 5 shows a cohort analysis of the overall average ESE score sampled from six different courses that include non-entrepreneurship and nonbusiness students (note that these cohort-wide scores are not longitudinal changes in individual students—they are class averages). The results are perhaps not too surprising. Students in introductory-level classes had lower scores, and nonbusiness students had lower scores than business students. In all cases, the students exposed to our entrepreneurship courses appeared to increase their overall average ESE. I note that not all sub-domains of ESE were higher in the entrepreneurship majors. For example, in the ESE sub-domain of financial literacy, 4th year business students

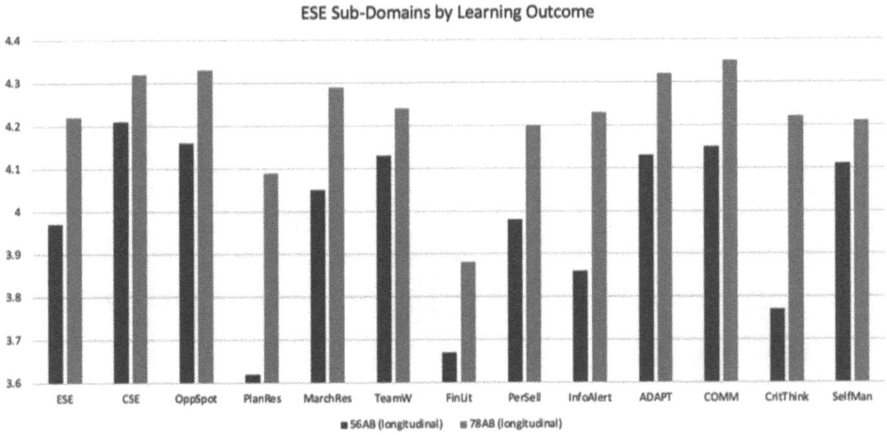

Fig. 4 Longitudinal Analysis of the Change in ESE Learning Outcomes for Students at the Start of 3rd year (ENT 56AB shown in blue) and End of 4th year (ENT 78AB shown in brown). Each pair of outcomes corresponds to the Survey Instrument shown in the appendix (Gedeon & Valliere, 2018). ESE = average ESE for the 11 sub-domains; CSE = Core Self Evaluation

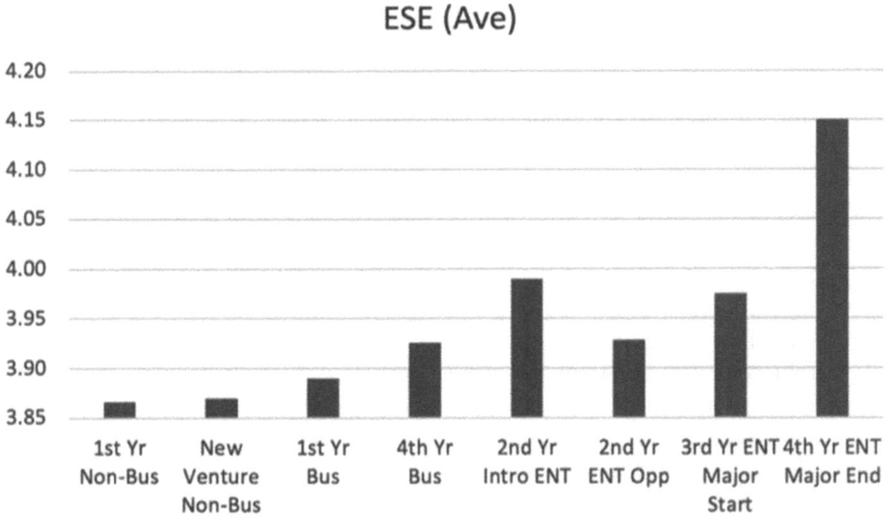

Fig. 5 Cohort-Wide Average ESE score in different courses at TMU

(some of whom were majoring in accounting or finance) scored higher than our 4th year entrepreneurship students, even though they had lower overall average ESE.

Figure 6 shows the level of entrepreneurial intent of the various control groups compared to students majoring in entrepreneurship. Business students had higher intent than nonbusiness students. However, for business students who were non-entrepreneurship majors, intent actually went down during the 4-year business program. Entrepreneurship majors have fairly high intent at the start of 3rd year, which

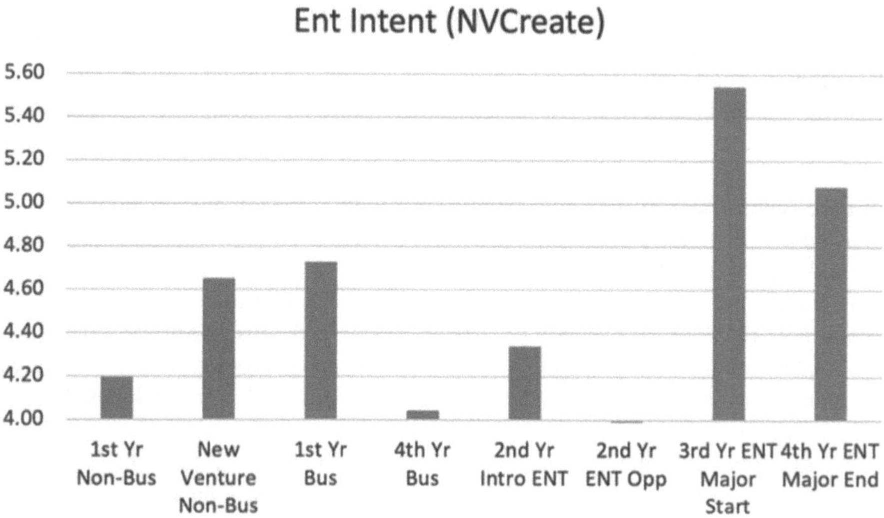

Fig. 6 Cohort-Wide Average Entrepreneurial Intent score in different courses at TMU

reduces somewhat by the end of 4th year, but is still higher than all other students measured across the university. Not surprisingly, students in the new venture startup elective course for nonbusiness students, had higher intent than other nonbusiness students, but not as high as entrepreneurship majors.

Even though we do not intend to teach intent—our mission is to teach *through* entrepreneurship not *for* entrepreneurship—entrepreneurship majors still increase their desire for, and intention to create, a new venture soon after graduation.

These design artifacts all seem to indicate that our EE is going well according to the design criteria we established. All passing entrepreneurship Majors are able to demonstrate their achievement of all learning outcomes (their AoL documents all passed every AACSB audit). We have continually tweaked our degree program by writing several of our own textbooks and we have expanded the number, popularity and variety of service courses to students outside our major to the point that over 7000 students take our courses per year. Students majoring in entrepreneurship indicate they also believe they have acquired our learning outcomes as measured by our valid and reliable ESE survey instrument (compared to all control groups).

5 EEE Design Artifacts from TMU

Throughout this entire ADDIE process of analyzing, designing, developing, implementing, and evaluating our EE program, we have simultaneously been helping design, implement, and grow our university's EEE (the "Environment" element in the CFEE in Fig. 1). Table 1 references the case studies and articles we've published on this and the related design artifacts reproduced here.

When we first wanted to expand the entrepreneurship program beyond the business school, we were generally met with either cold indifference or open hostility. We began to change this culture by hiring "entrepreneurial ambassadors" from outside the business school to run entrepreneurship-related events relevant to their majors (Gedeon, 2009). We offered free idea consultations, coaching sessions, and training programs, mostly organized by our Enactus student club (formerly Students In Free Enterprise—SIFE) under a program called StartMeUp. Eventually, having built up a critical mass of startup teams that wanted their own incubator space, we created the Digital Media Zone (later renamed the DMZ) on a shoestring budget as a by-students-for-students incubator. This marked the first major milestone in the creation of TMU's EEE. Gedeon (2020) describes the details and process by which we created and institutionalized a network of incubators, funding programs, degree programs, specializations, and administrative support. Table 4 reproduces the lessons we learned.

Being involved in the formation and growth of the DMZ from its original conception through to being awarded the world's #1 university-based incubator has enabled us to document some of the transitions and challenges associated with this. Nichols-Nixon et al. (2020) provide a detailed case study of the lifecycle of the DMZ which contributes to a deeper understanding of the lifecycle of other university incubators. Tables 5 and 6 reproduce two design artifacts from this publication that document how an incubator's stakeholders, logic, objective, focus, resources, audience, norms, and values change as the incubator goes from the conception stage to professionalization to growth. These artifacts help administrators, faculty, and staff understand what stage an incubator is in and how to meet the challenges of transitioning to the next stage without damaging relationships along the way.

6 Design Rules Based on Practitioner Experiences and Scholarly Publications

I would like to summarize and conclude this chapter by proposing five design rules for an entrepreneurship course, degree program, incubator, or EEE following the methods described by Plsek et al. (2007).

Design rules are used to bridge the theory-practice problem and capture how-to tacit knowledge by theorizing "forward-looking" real-time practice from the detached retrospective "backward-looking" viewpoint of the researcher (Selden & Fletcher, 2019). Design rules are heuristic statements frequently used in engineering, medicine, organizational planning, and computer science in the form: "If you want to achieve outcome Y in situation S, something like X might help" (Plsek et al., 2007).

Table 4 Lessons learned designing the TMU EEE (Gedeon, 2020)

1—Start all planning with a consistent and validated theoretical framework	Integrating scholarly research with any teaching proposals gives administrators and fellow professors confidence that they are making the right decisions. Being able to produce peer-reviewed papers based on established theoretical frameworks and pedagogical research provides significant credibility to any proposal. These design artifacts also become a record of why certain historical decisions were made when administrators change every few years
2—Use a holistic definition of entrepreneurship	Expanding entrepreneurship beyond merely starting a business, allows other disciplines to embrace this positive force for social innovation and personal transformation. This meant that the ENT Department had to relinquish control and trust others to make reasonable decisions, or no decisions at all
3—Encourage grassroots innovation, but then institutionalize	Most of the TMU programs began as student-run initiatives with no funding and lectures provided by volunteers. These activities were later funded, institutionalized, and rebranded once sufficient demand was proven. Many of the incubators were started by faculty members or run by students for some time before later becoming fully funded and institutionalized. Unleashing this ground-up innovation is important but so is the top-down institutionalization, funding, and professional management to make the initiative sustainable. The transition of ownership can result in hard feelings if not done properly—nobody wants their baby stolen from them
4—Take the long view—Administration and staff change frequently	If you don't get your way, be patient, be polite, be supportive, and bide your time. Focus on long-term, positive, supporting relationships with other professors. Continue to support and encourage students, continue to publish peer-reviewed research, continue to help write funding proposals, and eventually many of the stakeholders will change and new decisions will be made
5—Create cross-disciplinary integrating mechanisms	Programs such as the Ashoka Changemaker Campus (Ashoka, 2019) and HEInnovate (2019) provide an excellent opportunity for new ideas and actions to arise from collective action not initiated solely by the ENT Department or grassroots organizations like Enactus. Becoming an Ashoka Changemaker Campus also helps provide legitimacy, formalize sharing across faculties, and solidify key stakeholder groups across the university
6—Use microcredentials to transfer knowledge and augment experiential learning programs	Microcredentials should not be used as ends in themselves, but rather as part of a larger credential, like a course, that is administered by a professor or facilitator who ensures the relevancy and integration of the microcredential into a greater holistic understanding

Design Rule #1: If you want to design a stand-alone module/course that incorporates EE, and the course is not part of a larger entrepreneurship program, then:

1. Identify all relevant stakeholders, decision-makers, approval processes, and deadlines.

(a) If the designer is also the module/course instructor, they will probably be in charge of all major design considerations and course delivery. Often the instructor/designer will be adding entrepreneurial elements into their non-business degree program (e.g. over half the professors in the entreTime Teach-The-Teacher program were from outside business and entrepreneurship and primarily interested in improving their own courses (Gedeon et al., 2022)).

(b) If the designer is a department curriculum committee (or entrepreneurship center) creating this module/course as a service offering to students across campus ("wide entrepreneurship"), determine which other degree programs might add or promote your course. Be aware of the potential for the new course to be perceived as cannibalizing other programs rather than enhancing them.

2. Consider all elements of the CFEE Framework (Fig. 1).
3. Start with "Why." If the designer is the instructor, start with the instructor's Personal Statement of Teaching Philosophy. If the designer is a committee or center start with its mission statement.

   (a) Consider whether or not the purpose is teaching *about*, *for*, or *through* entrepreneurship. Is the course primarily about starting a new venture or about learning to become more entrepreneurial? Consider which sub-domain of entrepreneurship the module/course will emphasize (see reference Table 2).

4. Identify your course Learning Outcomes ("Results')

   (a) Does the module/course need to introduce or reinforce any overall program learning outcomes?
   (b) Consider adopting 2–4 EntreComp learning outcomes. Introductory courses should focus on Ideas and Into Action competencies.

5. Select your primary module/course pedagogies. The most widely accepted pedagogy is team-based experiential learning using project-based or challenge-based methods (combined with a self-reflection assignment). If this is not feasible, other pedagogies may be considered from the "How" (reference Table 3).
6. Identify available resources (textbooks, videos, course content).
7. Sketch out the primary assignment deliverables ("What").
8. Complete all documentation needed for the approval process and deadlines. This will likely include a calendar course description and draft course outline.
9. Once all approvals are in place, complete course development ("What").
10. Consider advertising and promoting the new module/course to your target audience to generate sufficient enrollment/registrations.

Design Rule #2: If you want to design a new entrepreneurship module/course and the new module/course is part of an accredited university entrepreneurship degree program, then:

1. The department-level curriculum committee will normally be given the mandate to create this new module/course by some higher authority such as an academic department, faculty council, periodic program review, accreditation review, and/or Dean. Often this mandate will include various design goals and constraints (e.g. plug a gap in the curriculum, add more experiential pedagogies, focus on specific learning outcomes). A member of the curriculum committee will normally be assigned primary responsibility for the course design and development, but other instructors may ultimately deliver the course(s).
2. Ideally, some or all elements of the CFEE Framework (Fig. 1) can be clearly identified in documents such as school, department, and program mission statements, accreditation and period program reviews, committee meeting minutes, and the academic plan.
3. The committee should review the relevant documents and go through the CFEE to identify how THIS SPECIFIC MODULE/COURSE might be in harmony with these often vague and aspirational statements.

   (a) Identify your course Learning Outcomes ("Results").
   (b) Select your primary course pedagogies ("How" reference Table 3).
   (c) Identify available resources (textbooks, videos, course content).
   (d) Sketch out the primary assignment deliverables ("What").

4. Identity any other courses that might be impacted by the new course.

   (a) Are there any prerequisites, anti-requisites or should the new course be a pre-requisite for any other courses? Will any other departments or programs be affected? How will students currently in the degree program be impacted? Coordinate with any impacted course instructors/departments/programs and identify any additional documentation or approvals required.

5. Complete documentation and coordination needed for the approval process and deadlines. This will likely include a calendar course description and draft course outline.
6. Once all approvals are in place, complete course development and delivery ("What").
7. Communicate with students, student services, and staff to ensure a smooth roll-out of the new course.

Design Rule #3: If you want to design (or re-design) an entrepreneurship degree program and the program will be accredited, then:

1. The Associate Dean or other designated individual (reporting to a school-level curriculum committee or faculty council) will normally be given the mandate to create this new degree program by the Dean in response to a perceived need. Often this mandate will be quite vague.

2. Most likely, few elements of the CFEE Framework (Fig. 1) can be identified other than the school's mission statement. All of these elements of the CFEE will need to be created from scratch. This presents a rare opportunity to "breathe life" into the degree program, so consider adopting a formal definition of entrepreneurship (e.g., Table 2) and formally adopting the student transformation model (teaching *through* entrepreneurship) in the program's mission statement (e.g., as in Gedeon, 2020).
3. The degree program design proposal will normally focus on "Who" to demonstrate market demand, societal need, and graduate employability. Often the name of the degree program will be modified to better suit market demand (e.g. changing the degree from "entrepreneurship" to "technology management and innovation" or "social changemaking").
4. Identify Degree Program Learning Outcomes ("Results").
    (a) Consider adopting EntreComp learning outcomes with potential tweaks to better suit the target market and institutional mission statements.
5. Map Modules/Courses to Learning Outcomes (reference Figs. 2 and 3) and identify specific Assurances of Learning (AoL) assignments that will be used for accreditation audit purposes.
6. Complete all documentation and coordination needed for the approval process and deadlines. This is normally a highly proscribed and regulated process.
7. Once all approvals are in place, complete course development and delivery ("What").
8. Communicate with students, student services, and staff to ensure a smooth rollout of the new degree program.

Design Rule #4: If you want to create a new university-based incubator and there is no obvious long-term sustainable funding, then:

1. As a startup, use design thinking and lean startup methods (e.g., user-centricity, prototyping, iterating, bootstrapping), effectuation principles (e.g., Bird-in-the-Hand, Affordable Loss, Pilot-in-the-Plane, see the work of Saras Sarasvathy) and entrepreneurial mindsets (e.g., proactivity, resilience, empathy, growth mindset).
    (a) Do more with less. All you really need to start is a name, logo, website, and engaged students. You don't necessarily need physical space, staff, funding or formal permission to put up posters, run events, book rooms, or coach startups.
    (b) Empower students and student clubs. Consider starting an Enactus club. Our university's Enactus team has won over 50 regional and national entrepreneurship competitions by empowering TMU student entrepreneurs with idea consultations, training tracks, new venture competitions, and starting the first three of our university's incubators. Put students in positions of leadership (Board of Directors of the incubator, VP marketing, VP of startup services, VP events, VP corporate development and fundraising).

2. Consider various incubator-university fit configurations.
   (a) Who "owns" the incubator? Is it managed and administered by the university's central administration, Office of Research and Innovation, or by a specific faculty, department, institute, or student club? Is the aspiration to become a separately incorporated entity with its own board of directors and external funding?
   (b) Will the incubator be managed by a student, professor, staff, or outside executive hired to fill the position? To whom will that person report?
   (c) Will the incubator primarily have an educational mission (e.g., expose students to entrepreneurial experiences to change their mindset (the student transformation model), an economic development mission (create lots of successful startups that create jobs), or a marketing mission (enhance the prestige of the university and generate lots of publicity)?
   (d) How will deal flow be created and "Who" will primarily be incubated? It's very difficult to build a critical mass in more than one of these three target customers per incubator: university spinoffs (professors and graduate students based on university IP), student teams, and existing startups from the community. How will you stimulate demand for your incubator?
   (e) What university courses can be used to create deal flow and/or give course credit for being incubated?
3. Consider research implications. If you want to get professors involved in promoting, coaching, speaking, creating content, granting course credit, or supporting your incubator, it always helps if these activities support their research obligations. Adding a research component, along with appropriate academic citations and rigour, is also an essential element of most large government grant applications.
4. Measure what supports your mission. If you have an educational mission (e.g., changing mindsets), then collect survey data, stories, and testimonials that showcase your accomplishments. If you have an economic mission, then reach out to involve existing startups in your community and help them raise funding and create more jobs. If you have a marketing mission, then do search engine optimization and collect media metrics.
5. When challenges and moments of transition arise, reference Tables 4, 5, and 6. Consider joining an incubator network like StartForFuture or the Global Consortium of Entrepreneurship Centers.

Design Rule #5: If you want to expand your university EEE and you already have 1–3 incubators, an entrepreneurship center, and 1–3 entrepreneurship-related degree programs, then:

1. It's difficult to articulate "design rules" for an ecosystem because, by definition, an ecosystem has no central designer or design team. A university's EEE may be considered a loose conglomeration of mostly autonomous academic units and administrative centers that compete for scarce resources with limited central authorities. What active involvement the central administration does have will

Table 5 DMZ Typology evolution (reproduced from Nichols-Nixon et al. (2020))

Typology dimension	Conception stage	Professionalization stage	Growth stage
Stakeholders	University President Entrepreneurship faculty members Students (*Enactus*) Entrepreneurship students	University TMT Professional managers All students Community entrepreneurs	University Deans Professional managers Students Community entrepreneurs Investors Corporate partners Governments
Dominant logic	Academic: experiential education, production of knowledge, open sharing	Political: promotional awareness, legitimacy, policymaker influence	Commercial: return on investment, risk management, sustainability
Objectives	Enhance student experience Leverage faculty expertise	Efficacy Increased scale Job creation Earned media coverage Consultation by policymakers	Efficiency Portfolio financial performance Success of graduated ventures
Strategic focus	Student startups Digital media No revenue model Student governance	Students and alumni Digital technologies Replication across campus as sister zones University governance	Community startups Sector agnostic Fee revenues International expansion (e.g., India, Jordan, Vietnam, Kenya) External governance
Incubation process	Ad hoc intake Ad hoc development processes No graduation criteria	Formalized continuous intake and graduation Ad hoc development processes	Formalized continuous intake and graduation Standardized development processes
Resources and services	Scrounged space Ad hoc programming by students Ad hoc mentoring by faculty members	Dedicated high-profile space Regular programming by partners Affiliated capital (*RFI*)	Multiple locations Regular programming by partners Referrals to external capital (ecosystem VCs)
Performance	Ad hoc performance monitoring Numbers of students involved Number of new ventures Beat other universities	Ongoing performance monitoring Media mentions Engagement by policymakers	Standardized external performance monitoring High-profile acquisitions of graduates Follow-on capital raised by graduates *UBI Global* ranking

often change when a new President, Rector, or Provost is hired. There are various ways, however, to influence and set up structures that support an expanded EEE.

(a) When possible, incorporate language related to entrepreneurship, enterprise, innovation, and other relevant concepts in the university's, schools', and programs' mission statements. Leverage this formal direction, but don't be upset when this language is diluted or replaced in the next 5-year cycle.

2. Consider adopting a formal framework for analysis and implementation, such as HEInnovate (2024), The Entrepreneurial Campus (Tuffee & Little, 2023), or the Kaufman Campus (Torrance, 2013).
3. Create university-wide institution-level collaboration mechanisms.

   (a) Create an office that reports directly to the central administration and is not associated with any specific faculty. In our university, we created an Office of Zone Learning (our 10 incubators are all called "Zones") and an Office of Social Innovation. At other universities, I've seen a Vice President of Entrepreneurship, Dean of Entrepreneurship and Enterprise, and various other appropriate titles.
   (b) Consider applying for relevant awards and recognitions. This will generate traction, enthusiasm, and administration interest. At TMU we applied for, and received recognition as an Ashoka Changemaker Campus and won awards from the Despande Foundation, UBI Global, and others.

4. Create incentives for ground-up entrepreneurial initiatives and unleash restraints on collaboration. A little bit of money goes a very long way to incentivize behaviors. Find ways to eliminate competition for scarce resources and instead reward collaboration.
5. Encourage students to get course credit for entrepreneurial behavior. While it is certainly important to encourage students to engage in extra-curricular entrepreneurial activities, the more closely you can tie entrepreneurial behavior to the core educational mission of the university, the more you will ensure long-term sustainable funding. You can see a few of the micro-credentialing approaches we used at TMU in Gedeon (2020).
6. Use government funding to enhance infrastructure, but don't become dependent on it. It is tempting to use temporary funding to increase headcount, but it is hard to create a sustainable ecosystem without sustainable funding. When possible, try to use the funds to build something sustainable that will remain long after the money is spent.

   (a) Consider using funds to build video libraries of useful educational content, educational resources, new modules/courses, endowments, chairs, centers, and high-quality marketing materials such as brochures, websites, testimonials, and impact numbers. Leverage government funding to find more sustainable sources.

Table 6 DMZ lifecycle and audience of resource providers (reproduced from Nichols-Nixon et al. (2020))

Audience concerns	Conception stage	Professionalization stage	Growth stage
Audience	Students Faculty advisors President's office	University administrators External funding agencies (*NRC*, *OCE*) Professional service firms	External funding agencies International corporate partners
Goals	Create startups Provide experiential education Focal point for campus entrepreneurship, university differentiation, shelter from skeptics	National reputation as entrepreneurial university, city-building Engage with local ecosystem	Extend reputation internationally End funding subsidy through sustainable business model Academically legitimate and fundable
Norms	Voluntary Action-oriented Academic norms and expectations	Strengthen *DMZ* brand, premier location for VIP tours and political announcements.	Commercial evaluation of graduated ventures Reconnect to academic university
Values	Student-centric, openness Education as a public good	Knowledge commercialization Risk aversion Engagement with external stakeholders	Generate return on investment, portfolio risk management. Role model for sister zones
Control	Faculty board, student management Milestone progress Informal organization, role fluidity	Directly accountable to university President Paid professional director Formalized processes for selection and reporting Metrics aligned to external norms	External advisory board Director and VP of Zone Learning roles created Formalized processes for service delivery
Attention	Recruiting startups Bootstrapped services (*StartMeUp*, *RAN*, idea consultations with faculty members)	External visibility Reducing financial subsidy by university	Expansion (cross-campus and internationally) Formalized and accredited educational elements (e.g., *StartupSchool*)
Summary orientation	Physical space with meaningful services Messaging to focus on student orientation, entrepreneurship is cool *Enactus* championship	Showpiece to earn awareness from ecosystem (esp. governments) Declare victory as the primary entrepreneurial university	Leverage success to raise international reputation of the university *UBI Global* awards

7. When things don't change, change too quickly, or change unpredictably, reference some of the lessons learned in Table 4 and check to see if you are going through any of the ecosystem lifecycle changes shown in Tables 5 and 6. Then please contribute your own lessons and design rules back to the entrepreneurship community and publish your own artifacts through conferences such as the annual 3E (ECSB Entrepreneurship Education) conference run by the European Council for Small Business and Entrepreneurship (ECSB). See you there!

Appendix Survey Instrument Developed to Measure ESE (Reproduced from Gedeon & Valliere, 2018)

	Strongly disagree ... Strongly agree				
Opportunity Identification and Creativity					
I have the ability to ...					
Think outside the box	1	2	3	4	5
Identify opportunities for new ways to conduct activities	1	2	3	4	5
Come up with new and different solutions	1	2	3	4	5
Information Alertness					
I have the ability to ...					
Be alert to proactively discovering new information of value	1	2	3	4	5
Identify, select, and process information from a variety of sources	1	2	3	4	5
Implement successful information seeking and research strategies	1	2	3	4	5
Document and communicate information clearly, logically, and accurately	1	2	3	4	5
Planning under Uncertainty					
I have the ability to ...					
Estimate customer demand for a new product or service	1	2	3	4	5
Determine a competitive price for a new product or service	1	2	3	4	5
Estimate the amount of start-up funding and working capital necessary to start my business	1	2	3	4	5
Design an effective marketing/advertising campaign for a new product or service	1	2	3	4	5
Create a project plan	1	2	3	4	5
Resource Marshaling					
I have the ability to ...					
Get others to identify with and believe in my vision and plans for a new venture	1	2	3	4	5
Network (i.e., make contact with and exchange information with others)	1	2	3	4	5
Establish new contacts	1	2	3	4	5
Bootstrap (i.e., get a lot done with few resources)	1	2	3	4	5
Adaptability					
I have the ability to ...					

	Strongly disagree … Strongly agree				
Deal with sudden changes and surprises	1	2	3	4	5
Work under stress and pressure	1	2	3	4	5
Continue work despite problems	1	2	3	4	5
Manage uncertainty in projects and processes	1	2	3	4	5
Financial Management					
I have the ability to …					
Organize and maintain the financial records of my venture	1	2	3	4	5
Manage the financial assets of my venture	1	2	3	4	5
Estimate a budget for a new project	1	2	3	4	5
Teamwork					
I have the ability to …					
Supervise employees and/or team members	1	2	3	4	5
Recruit and hire employees and/or team members	1	2	3	4	5
Delegate tasks and responsibilities to employees and/or team members	1	2	3	4	5
Train employees and/or team members	1	2	3	4	5
Critical Thinking					
I have the ability to …					
Make correct inferences from data	1	2	3	4	5
Deduce conclusions from information or data provided	1	2	3	4	5
Interpret whether conclusions are warranted on the basis of data given	1	2	3	4	5
Communication					
I have the ability to …					
Apply active listening skills to communicate with others	1	2	3	4	5
Read and understand complex issues	1	2	3	4	5
Write clear and effective reports	1	2	3	4	5
Communicate with others	1	2	3	4	5
Persuading and Entrepreneurial Selling					
I have the ability to …					
Come up with new ideas for satisfying customer needs	1	2	3	4	5
Generate and evaluate multiple alternatives for novel customer problems	1	2	3	4	5
Have fresh perspectives on old problems	1	2	3	4	5
Improvise methods for solving a problem when an answer is not apparent	1	2	3	4	5
Self-Management					
When I work toward something, it gets all my attention	1	2	3	4	5
I keep focused on tasks I need to do even if I do not like them	1	2	3	4	5
I become very aware of what I am doing when I am working toward a goal	1	2	3	4	5
I make sure to track my progress regularly when I am working on a goal	1	2	3	4	5
I pay close attention to my thoughts when I am working on something hard	1	2	3	4	5
I know I can track my behavior when working toward a goal	1	2	3	4	5

References

Buchanan, R. (1992). Wicked problems in design thinking. *Design Issues, 8*, 5–21.

Bygrave, W. D., Wise, S., & Zacharakis, A. (2014). *Entrepreneurship* (Canadian ed.). Wiley.

Cross, N. (1982). Designerly ways of knowing. *Design Studies, 3*(4), 221–227.

Diamond, R. M. (2008). *Designing and assessing courses and curricula. A practical guide* (3rd ed.). Jossey-Bass.

Dimov, D. (2016). Toward a design science of entrepreneurship. In *Models of start-up thinking and action: Theoretical, empirical and pedagogical approaches* (Vol. 18, pp. 1–31). Emerald Group Publishing Limited.

Dimov, D. (2020). *The entrepreneurial scholar*. Edward Elgar Publishing Limited.

Dorst, K. (2011). The core of 'design thinking' and its application. *Design Studies, 32*(6), 521–532.

EntreComp. (2024). Accessed on Oct 1, 2024 from https://www.entrecomp.nu/ and https://entre-comp.eu/

EntreTime. (2024). Accessed on Oct 1, 2024 from https://test-et.sce.de/ and from https://eismea.ec.europa.eu/document/download/ef1b9904-33cb-47d7-aa0e-98f52d53306d_en?filename=entreTime%20Learning%20Programme.pdf

Friedman, K. (2003). Theory construction in design research: Criteria: Approaches, and methods. *Design Studies, 24*(6), 507–522.

Gedeon, S. A. (2009). Instilling an entrepreneurial culture. In T. V. Menzies (Ed.), *University-based entrepreneurship Centres in Canada: Strategies and best practices* (pp. 119–128). Dobson Foundation. ISBN: 978-0-9683539-4-3.

Gedeon, S. A. (2010). What is entrepreneurship? *Entrepreneurial Practice Review, 1*(3), 16–35.

Gedeon, S. A. (2014). Application of best practices in university entrepreneurship education: Designing a new MBA program. *European Journal of Training and Development, 38*(3), 231–253.

Gedeon, S. A. (2017). *Measuring student transformation in entrepreneurship education programs*. Special issue on entrepreneurship education with impact: Opening the Black Box (EEI) in education research international, 1–12.

Gedeon, S. A. (2020). Theory-based design of an entrepreneurship micro-credentialing and modularisation system within a large university eco-system. *Entrepreneurship Education and Pedagogy Special Issue on Modularisation and Micro-Credentialing of Entrepreneurship Education, 3*(2), 107–128.

Gedeon, S. A. (2021). *Entrepreneurial career and life design*. Toronto Metropolitan University Retrieved from https://pressbooks.library.torontomu.ca/ecld/. Open educational resource. ISBN 978-1-77417-093-9.

Gedeon, S. A. (2022). Empowering students for future work and productive citizenry through entrepreneurial education. *Public Affairs Quarterly, 36*(3), 197–210.

Gedeon, S. A., & Valliere, D. (2018). Closing the loop: Measuring entrepreneurial self-efficacy to assess student learning outcomes. *Entrepreneurship Education and Pedagogy, 1*(4), 272–303.

Gedeon, S. A., Westerberg, M., Fee A., Gabriel, B., Huxtable-Thomas, L., Javorka, Z., Mancini, M. A., Redford D. T., Sailer, K., Singer, S., Stolze, A., & Stoycheva, M. (2022). *Case history of entreTime: European train-the-trainer programme for teaching through entrepreneurship*. Conference proceedings: 8th Innovation & Entrepreneurship Teaching Excellence Awards held at the 17th European conference on innovation and entrepreneurship in Cyprus on 15–16 September 2022.

Grant, K. A., & Gedeon, S. A. (2019). Teaching and learning in the 21st century university. In D. Remenyl, K. Grant, & S. Singh (Eds.), *The university of the future* (pp. 91–104) ACPIL, Reading, UK. ISBN: 978-1-912764-51-8.

Gedeon, S.A. (2024) "Building an Entrepreneurial Mindset" Toronto Metropolitan University Library, Open Educational Resource. ISBN 978-1-77417-101-1. (book)

Gustafson, K. L., & Branch, R. M. (2004). *Survey of instructional development models* (4th ed.). ERIC Clearinghouse.

HEInnovate. (2024). Accessed from https://www.heinnovate.eu/en on Oct 1, 2024.
Ho, C. (2001). Some phenomena of problem decomposition strategy for design thinking: Differences between novices and experts. *Design Studies, 22*, 27–45.
Jarvis, D. S. L. (2014). Regulating higher education: Quality assurance and neo-liberal managerialism in higher education—A critical introduction. *Policy and Society, 33*(3), 155–166.
Krippendorff, K. (2006). *The semantic turn: A new foundation for design*. Taylor and Francis.
Kuratko, D. F. (2005). The emergence of entrepreneurship education: Development, trends, and challenges. *Entrepreneurship Theory and Practice, 29*(5), 577–598.
Lawson, B. (2005). *How designers think: The design process demystified* (4th ed.). Architectural Press.
Liedtka, J. (2014). Perspective: Linking design thinking with innovation outcomes through cognitive bias reduction. *Journal of Product Innovation Management, 32*(6), 925–938.
Liedtka, J., & Ogilvie, T. (2011). *Designing for growth: A design thinking tool kit for managers* (1st ed.). Columbia University Press.
Martin, R. (2004). The design of business. *Rotman Management, Winter*, 7–10.
Martin, R. (2009). *The design of business: Why design thinking is the next competitive advantage*. Harvard Business Press.
Molenda, M. (2003). In search of the elusive ADDIE model. *Performance Improvement, 42*(5), 34–36.
Nicholls-Nixon, C., Valliere, D., Gedeon, S. A., & Wise, S. (2020). Entrepreneurial ecosystems and the lifecycle of university business incubators: An integrative case study. *International Entrepreneurship and Management Journal*, 1–29.
Plsek, P., Bibby, J., & Whitby, E. (2007). Practical methods for extracting explicit design rules grounded in the experience of organizational managers. *The Journal of Applied Behavioral Science, 43*(1), 153–170.
Rylander, A. (2009). Design thinking as knowledge work: Epistemological foundations and practical implications. *Design Management Journal, 5*, 7–19.
Selden, P. D., & Fletcher, D. E. (2019). The tacit knowledge of entrepreneurial design: Interrelating theory, practice and prescription in entrepreneurship research. *Journal of Business Venturing Insights, 11*, e00122.
Solomon, G. (2007). An examination of entrepreneurship education in the United States. *Journal of Small Business and Enterprise Development, 14*(2), 168–182.
Telenko, C., Sosa, R., & Wood, K. L. (2016). Changing conversations and perceptions: The research and practice of design science. *Impact of Design Research on Industrial Practice: Tools, Technology, and Training*, 281–309.
TorontoMet Entrepreneur Institute. (2024). Accessed from https://entrepreneurinstitute.ca/for-educators/ on Oct 1, 2024.
Torrance, W. E. (2013). *Entrepreneurial campuses: Action, impact, and lessons learned from the Kauffman campuses initiative*. Ewing Marion Kauffman Foundation Research Paper.
Tuffee, R., & Little, J. (2023). The entrepreneurial campus: The higher education sector as a driving force for the entrepreneurial ecosystem. *Scottish Government.*
Turgut-Dao, E., Gedeon, S.A., Sailer, K., Huber, F., & Franck, M. (2015) *Embedding experiential learning in Cross-faculty entrepreneurship education*. Conference proceedings, 3E conference – ECSB entrepreneurship education conference, Lüneburg, Germany 22–24 April 2015. ISSN 2411-3298.
Valliere, D. (2019). *Entrepreneurial thinking: Think different*. Edward Elgar Publishing.
Valliere, D., Gedeon, S. A., & Wise, S. (2014). A comprehensive framework for entrepreneurship education. *Special Issue on Entrepreneurial Education in the Journal of Business and Entrepreneurship, 26*(1), 89–120.
Vom Brocke, J., Hevner, A., & Maedche, A. (2020). "Introduction to design science research" Design science research. *Cases*, 1–13.
Wise, S., & Feld, B. (2017). *Startup opportunities: Know when to quit your day job*. Wiley.

Steven Gedeon is Chair of the TorontoMet Entrepreneur Institute and Associate Professor of Entrepreneurship and Strategy at Toronto Metropolitan University (TMU), one of the largest entrepreneurship programs in the world. Steven is an entrepreneurship educator, angel investor, and technology commercialization expert who has founded or led 15+ private, public, venture capital, and nonprofit organizations including the DMZ—named the World's #1 University-Based Incubator. He has published over 100 articles, reports, books, and patents, and delivered over 100 public speaking engagements and videos on entrepreneurship, happiness, life design, angel investing, and best practices in education. Over 2000 students take his ENT 101: Building an Entrepreneurial Mindset course per year. Steve's student teams have won over 50 regional and national entrepreneurship championships by empowering others in need and running some of the largest student-run social entrepreneurship programs in the world.

Part III
Future Outlook: Advancing the Design Science Approach in Entrepreneurial Education

Moving Design Science Research and Practice in Entrepreneurial Education Forward

Yvette Baggen and Bart Derre

Abstract The aim of our book was to introduce a design-science research approach as a promising way for teaching and investigating entrepreneurial education. The book focuses on supporting educators as designers of entrepreneurial education, so that they are able to educate students as change agents. Such change agents have the essential skills and mindset to create sustainable value with and for others in circumstances characterized by uncertainty. As such, we frame entrepreneurial education in the book beyond its more traditional, economic orientation—we argue that entrepreneurial education has transformative potential and we perceive entrepreneurial education as a way to empower a new generation of change agents with entrepreneurial mindsets, who are capable of addressing the complex, "wicked" challenges of our time.

In this final chapter, we as editors synthesize the contributions of the authors and provide an overview of emerging developments in design science research within the field of entrepreneurial education. We present a way forward for both practitioners and researchers and describe the design process behind the VLAIO EntreDesign Canvas. The collaboration with VLAIO, a Flemish government agency that supports entrepreneurship and entrepreneurial education in Flanders (Belgium), offered a unique opportunity to apply design science research and bricolage in a real-life context, further building upon the artifacts created by the authors in Part II of this book.

Y. Baggen (✉)
Education and Learning Sciences, Wageningen University and Research, Wageningen, The Netherlands
e-mail: Yvette.baggen@wur.nl

B. Derre
HOGENT University of Applied Sciences and Arts, Center for Entrepreneurship, Ghent, Belgium

Faculty of Psychology and Educational Sciences, VUB, Brussels, Belgium
e-mail: bart.derre@hogent.be

© The Author(s), under exclusive license to Springer Nature Switzerland AG 2025
B. Derre, Y. Baggen (eds.), *Empowering the Next Generation of Entrepreneurial Change Agents*, Contributions to Management Science,
https://doi.org/10.1007/978-3-031-82251-3_10

1 The Entrepreneurial Education Method as an Overarching Model

Shavelson et al. (2003) emphasize that, given the complex, messy nature of classrooms and schools, design studies are essential for developing and testing educational theories, as well as for creating instructional tools and learning environments that can withstand the demands of everyday practice. As described in chapter "Advancing the field of Entrepreneurial Education: Leveraging a Design Science Approach for Educating the Change Agents of the Future", descriptive and explanatory research alone cannot fully inform or guide practice in these contexts, as the social complexity of the environment, combined with the chosen intentionality, requires adaptations to hypothesis-driven knowledge. Therefore, Design Science Research (DSR) plays a crucial role in bridging science and practice (Van Aken, 2004; Dresch et al., 2015; Hevner et al., 2004), a theme further explored in the other chapters of the first part of the book. The insights presented in chapter "Designing Artifacts in Entrepreneurial Education Research" help to understand how DSR differs from a more linear approach to tackling problems—and why DSR is specifically targeted toward addressing wicked problems, which is how we can understand entrepreneurial education. In chapter "The Entrepreneurial Educator as an Architect of Effective Entrepreneurial Education: Design and Redesign of the CBL course "innovation Space Project: Innovation and Entrepreneurship Processes"", the course "innovation Space project: Innovation and Entrepreneurship processes" is presented, illustrating how DSR can be applied in designing and evaluating entrepreneurial education.

The contributing authors in Part II of the book present various tools (i.e., artifacts) that provide educators with concrete support. These tools were developed using DSR, which is itself evolving and offers researchers multiple avenues to further advance these tools as artifacts that help transform current education programs into desired outcomes—in the case of this book, entrepreneurial education that fits a certain intentionality and context.

More specifically, in chapter "The Entrepreneurial Education Canvas", Baggen et al. present cases from vocational education and a university of applied sciences. The "Entrepreneurship Education Canvas" specifically focuses on the "how" of entrepreneurial education and presents 11 design principles to support educators in developing and evaluating entrepreneurial education.

In the chapter "The Entrepreneurial Educational Method: A DSR Artifact to Support Educators in Designing Entrepreneurial Education", Derre et al. introduce the Entrepreneurial Educational Method (EEM), an artifact developed through DSR to support higher education educators in their instructional decision-making processes. The EEM consists of three nested layers: the first layer includes a set of ten design propositions, the second layer contains a sub-artifact called the ELED protocol, and the third layer comprises multiple CIMOs and tools, all structured like Russian dolls.

In the "Two Flows Framework" of Wetters et al. (chapter "A Two Flows Framework Leveraging Challenge-Based Learning for Entrepreneurial Education: A Design Science Approach"), "learning to learn" and "cracking the challenge" nicely come together in one framework, embedding the authentic nature of entrepreneurial education in challenge-based education for students. The Two Flows Framework supports educators in realizing education in which the narrow and wide approach to entrepreneurship (i.e., new venture creation and new value-creation) come together in challenge-based education.

In chapter "Embracing Failures: Advancing the Entrepreneurship Education Pedagogy Through Design Science Approach", Noaman and Nair discuss the role of emotions in entrepreneurship and entrepreneurial learning from the perspective of entrepreneurial failure. The "Failure Learning Protocol" of Noaman and Nair can help educators to include entrepreneurial failures as part of education—in which it is important that students first learn from small failures throughout the entrepreneurial journey, before having to deal with large failures, that cause more emotional struggles.

The "16-action tasks" of Lackéus (chapter "From EntreComp to EntreAct: 16 Validated Design Principles for Making People More Entrepreneurial") help to truly develop and implement entrepreneurial education in practice. Just like Noaman and Nair, Lackéus highlights the emotional nature of entrepreneurial learning, of which the impact on students should not be underestimated. Learning from emotions should be part of entrepreneurial learning journeys in a responsible way. What we learn from chapters "Embracing Failures: Advancing the Entrepreneurship Education Pedagogy Through Design Science Approach" and "From EntreComp to EntreAct: 16 Validated Design Principles for Making People More Entrepreneurial" is how important it is to perceive failure as a potential learning experience.

Lackéus also emphasizes the contextuality of entrepreneurship education. What might work in one situation, does not necessarily work in another context. This importance of context was also illustrated in chapter "The Entrepreneurial Education Canvas": The Entrepreneurial Education Canvas has the most value for educators in designing their entrepreneurial programs, when adjusted and translated toward a certain context.

In chapter "Design Science Approach to Building a Large University Entrepreneurship Education Ecosystem (EEE)", Gedeon shares his reflections on how entrepreneurial education and the entrepreneurship education ecosystem have been developed, built, and implemented at the Toronto Metropolitan University. He presents the different artifacts that supported the journey of creating an entrepreneurial ecosystem at such a large university. He concludes the chapter with design rules for creating entrepreneurship courses, degree programs, and incubators. Whereas, for instance, Lackéus presents action-tasks that can help to design entrepreneurial learning activities in class, the work of Gedeon helps in understanding how to create entrepreneurship support programs and facilities at an organizational level.

The framework of the Entrepreneurial Educational Method (EEM), introduced in chapter "The Entrepreneurial Educational Method: A DSR Artifact to Support

Educators in Designing Entrepreneurial Education", provides a structure for organizing and comparing the various artifacts presented in Part II. The EEM framework, inspired by Mansoori's Entrepreneurial Method and structured into three levels, can serve as a tool for organizing and comparing various artifacts. Level 1 encompasses the logic, or core design principles, that guide the design process in developing entrepreneurial education. Level 2, the model or protocol, refers to a set of minimal activities related to the design process that facilitate the implementation of these design principles. Finally, Level 3 involves the tactics or tools that support the implementation of the activities outlined in the model or protocol. Table 1 offers an overview of the different contributions, along with the specific levels to which each designed artifact contributes.

Baggen et al., Derre et al., Wetters et al., Noaman and Nair, and Lackéus offer a method or protocol that positions educators as designers, incorporating minimal activities to support them in decision-making. Derre et al. and Gedeon offer concrete tactics for implementing entrepreneurial education at the level of the classroom, course, curriculum and ecosystem. Existing tools, such as competency frameworks, are not overlooked in this design-oriented approach; rather, they are actively integrated, as clearly demonstrated by Lackéus in his EntreAct model. Regarding tools, it is worth noting that CIMO configurations represent an

Table 1 Overview of the specific levels of the designed artifacts

Authors and chapter	Design principles	Method (or protocol)	Tactics (tools/ CIMO's)
Baggen et al. (Chapter "The Entrepreneurial Education Canvas")	Design principles	Canvas	
Derre et al. (Chapter "The Entrepreneurial Educational Method: a DSR Artifact to Support Educators in Designing Entrepreneurial Education")	Design principles	ELED protocol	16 EL-CIMO's
Wetters et al. (Chapter "A Two Flows Framework Leveraging Challenge-Based Learning for Entrepreneurial Education: A Design Science Approach")	"Cracking the Challenge Flow" and "Learning to Learn Flow"	Two flows framework	
Noaman and Nair (Chapter "Embracing Failures: Advancing the Entrepreneurship Education Pedagogy Through Design Science Approach")		Failure learning Protocol	
Lackéus (Chapter "From EntreComp to EntreAct: 16 Validated Design Principles for Making People More Entrepreneurial")	Design principles	EntreAct	
Gedeon (Chapter "Design Science Approach to Building a Large University Entrepreneurship Education Ecosystem (EEE)")			Design rules

interesting path forward for design-oriented support, based on both emerging practices and theoretical insights from hypothesis-testing explanatory science.

In this final chapter, we aim to propose new pathways forward for both researchers and educators in DSR, empowering them to become trailblazers in designing and delivering entrepreneurial education that can help students become impactful change agents. There are numerous possibilities, and with each choice comes tradeoffs. As editors, after carefully reading and synthesizing all the contributions in this book, we have made a selective choice of recommendations. However, this does not preclude readers from identifying and designing their own new pathways after engaging with this book.

2 Bricolage as an Interesting Way Forward

Following Kincheloe's (2001) perspective on bricolage, we reach out to researchers working in DSR to embrace this methodology. For researchers in entrepreneurial education, bricolage means using what one has and building on each other's work while simultaneously expanding the boundaries of knowledge and methodologies. By embracing bricolage, researchers can design powerful new artifacts with great impact, facilitating the transformation from an "as-is" to a "to-be" state. We encourage researchers to engage in profound collaborations across disciplines, co-creating innovative artifacts for realizing entrepreneurial education by designing knowledge with critical insight and openness.

As editors of this book, we had the opportunity to engage directly with this call ourselves, applying a bricolage approach to bridge the epistemological differences present in our original design work—see the artifacts as we present in chapter "The Entrepreneurial Education Canvas" (Baggen et al.) and chapter "The Entrepreneurial Educational Method: A DSR Artifact to Support Educators in Designing Entrepreneurial Education" (Derre et al.) which we created and introduced in the field from different points of departure, but with the similar aim of supporting teachers in designing entrepreneurial education. Despite epistemological differences, a bricolage approach helped to merge the different models and enabled the creation of a new artifact, which we named EntreDesign, representing a step forward in supporting educators to design entrepreneurial education. The process of bricolage was perceived as a strengthening catalyst for creating a new artifact—which we present in the next section. We welcome researchers and educators to further shape this (and other) artifacts and would encourage them to translate the artifact to their own context.

By sharing this design-oriented bricolage process, we hope to encourage more researchers in the field of entrepreneurial education to transcend epistemological trenches and work together toward continuously improving entrepreneurial education for preparing future change agents for their demanding role in society.

2.1 *The EntreDesign Canvas: A New Artifact*

During the writing of this book, the editors were approached by VLAIO, a Flemish government agency that supports entrepreneurship and entrepreneurial education in Flanders (Belgium), to assist in developing a website aimed at promoting a design-oriented approach to entrepreneurial education. This presented a unique opportunity to apply bricolage in a real-life case. It became, in essence, a process of creating an overall artifact within the process of creating the artifacts as presented in Part II of this book.

2.1.1 The Field Challenge Presented by VLAIO

Flanders Innovation and Entrepreneurship—VLAIO for short—is the point of contact of the Flemish Government for all entrepreneurs in Flanders. VLAIO stimulates and supports innovation and entrepreneurship and contributes to a positive business climate that strengthens sustainable economic growth and job creation. This mission aims to create and enhance opportunities for every youngster to gain positive entrepreneurial experience throughout their formal education, develop an entrepreneurial mindset and competencies, and consider entrepreneurship as a feasible career path.

VLAIO aims to design and implement a website to support educational professionals in delivering high-quality entrepreneurial education. The website will provide clarity on what entrepreneurial education entails and its importance, serving as both a knowledge and learning platform. It will offer conceptual frameworks and theoretical insights to deepen understanding, along with a broad array of applications, ranging from fostering an entrepreneurial mindset in schools or universities to developing specific teaching and learning practices across formal and informal learning contexts.

In developing the website, VLAIO intends to emphasize a design-oriented approach to entrepreneurial education, grounded in the understanding that there is no single "best" method for practicing entrepreneurial education, as it depends significantly on context. However, some approaches have proven to be more effective than others. Building on research-based insights into the effectiveness of entrepreneurial education, VLAIO intends to include a section on the website that provides both a comprehensive design-focused (didactic) process and a toolbox of content-based resources that educational professionals, especially VLAIO's partners, can use. As such, the launch of the website offered a great opportunity to develop and share the overall artifact that we intended to develop based on the artifacts from Part II of this book.

Furthermore, VLAIO aims to facilitate the documentation and sharing of practices in a way that enhances data-driven insights into the actual effects of practices, as well as into the underlying processes, interventions, and mechanisms. To succeed in this task, VLAIO subsidizes and collaborates closely with UNIZO Education &

Entrepreneurship (UNIZO E&E[1]) and Flanders Young Enterprises, Vlajo as main operational partners in the domain of entrepreneurial education. VLAIO aims to actively involve these partners—next to the editors of the book—in developing a prototype that will serve as a foundation for building the website.

UNIZO E&E stimulates entrepreneurship, entrepreneurial skills, and an enterprising mindset within education in a sustainable way. Unizo E&E inspires, informs, and initiates entrepreneurial competencies and a spirit of entrepreneurship. They create opportunities for enterprising talent and build a bridge between the field of education and the entrepreneurial landscape.

Vlajo supports all levels of education, from kindergarten to university, in four ways: through growth projects, challenges, career exploration, and training programs. Vlajo aims to prepare young people for a turbulent future in which they are expected to address societal challenges. For this, Vlajo believes that young people should not only develop factual knowledge but also entrepreneurial skills such as collaboration, creativity, innovation, courage, and perseverance. With over 200,000 participating students and pupils, 9000 teachers and educators, 4000 projects, and 1500 experts from various business sectors each year, Vlajo positions itself as the reference point for entrepreneurial education in Flanders.

2.1.2 A Bricolage Design Science Research Approach to Co-create the Averarching Artifact: The EntreDesign Canvas

To design a prototype of the overarching artifact, a design-oriented, co-creative methodology based on Van Burg's (2010) work was applied. A working group[2] was formed, including representatives from VLAIO, the editors of this book, Unizo E&E, Vlajo, Sustainable education center,[3] and the VLAIO stakeholders group. These partners co-creatively engaged in the following design-oriented phases:

- *Ex ante empirical research*: This phase led to the development of design requirements and principles. The methodology described by Van Burg (2010) was used to extract design principles. This approach (van Burg & Romme, 2014; Sagath et al., 2019) combines "emergent" and "deliberate" design. Specifically, the design principles were created based on existing, scientific literature on entrepreneurial learning, the expertise of the working group, and the artifacts from Part II of the book. Written input and a focus group were organized with the working group to clarify and synthesize the practice and research-based design principles in a coherent set of design propositions.

[1] In Dutch: Unizo O&O.

[2] Participants working group: Johan Poisquet, PhD (VLAIO); Reineke Vandevenne (VLAIO); Nele Lintermans (VLAIO); Sylvie Cannoot (Unizo O&O); Peter Coenen (Vlajo); Julie Vanstraelen (Vlajo); Yolan Gielen (Duurzaam Educatiepunt); Filip Burgelman (Forum Entrepreneurial Higher Education and EntreComp Champion). Yvette Baggen and Bart Derre (editors of the book).

[3] In Dutch: Duurzaam Educatiepunt.

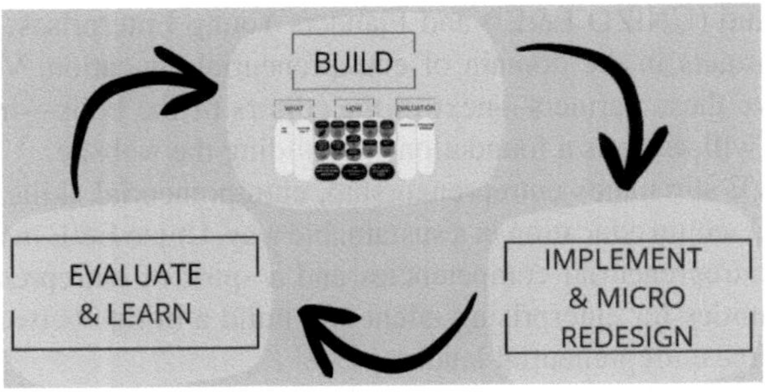

Fig. 1 Design process within which the EntreDesign Canvas is embedded

- *Designing the artifact*: During the design process, the *bricolage* technique was used, combining existing artifacts and the set of design propositions to create a new artifact, resulting in an early version of the EntreDesign Canvas.
- *Evaluating the artifact*: This phase involved an ex ante formative evaluation conducted during the VLAIO Summer Meeting in August 2024. Adjustments were made to the artifact, resulting in the next version of the EntreDesign Canvas. After the implementation of the website, an ex post-testing phase for evaluating the artifact is planned. This artifact is considered a minimum viable product that will be frequently updated based on user input over time, meaning that the evaluation will include on ongoing process of receiving and processing formative feedback.

Below, we present the current version of the resulting EntreDesign Canvas.

2.1.3 The EntreDesign Canvas

The EntreDesign Canvas (EDC) supports educators with a structured roadmap, along with various tools and resources, to facilitate the creation, implementation, and evaluation of entrepreneurial education aimed at educating change agents. It assists educators in their decision-making processes when designing learning interventions that foster an entrepreneurial mindset, skill set, and ultimately, wide entrepreneurial behavior among students. The EDC is embedded within a co-creative, iterative approach for designing educational artifacts in entrepreneurial education, structured around three main phases: Build, Implement and Micro-Redesign, and Evaluate and Learn (see Fig. 1).

The core principle of the EDC is the view of educators *as architects of entrepreneurial education*,[4] emphasizing the importance of contextualization and intentionality in designing learning artifacts. This approach helps educators in creating

[4]The concept of educators as architects of entrepreneurial education originates from a personal communication between Bart Derre and Filip Burgelman.

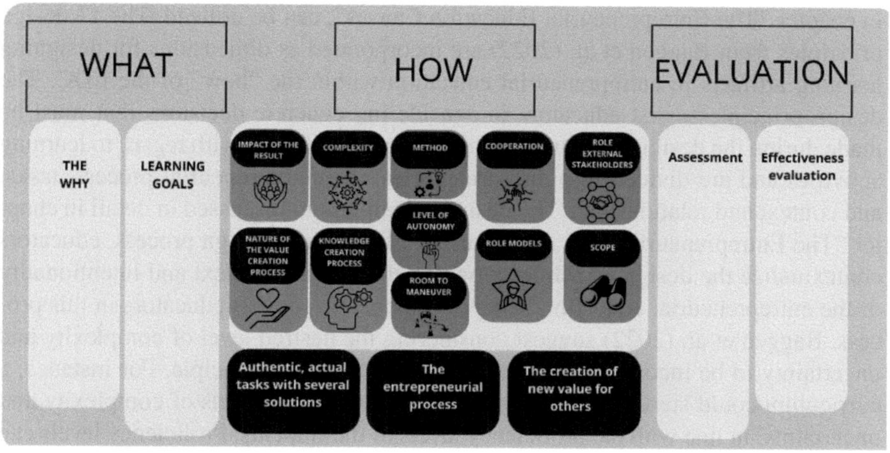

Fig. 2 The complete EntreDesign Canvas (EDC)

comprehensive learning interventions that are not only effective but also relevant and meaningful for students.

Contextualization involves adapting education to the specific context in which students learn and operate. This includes not only the learning environment and activities but also the characteristics of the students, educators, and the institution itself. By incorporating these factors, educators can provide a more holistic and impactful learning experience.

Intentionality refers to the idea that each learning activity and instructional method is driven by a clear educational purpose or "why", such as educating entrepreneurial change agents. This helps students engage in goal-oriented learning, fostering self-regulation and ultimately contributing to the intended learning outcomes. Importantly, intentionality does not exclude room for emergent learning effects.

Educators are specifically encouraged to pay close attention to aligning the constructs of "what—how—evaluation" when designing (i.e. building) entrepreneurial education learning interventions (see Fig. 2).

When considering the "what", educators are encouraged to reflect on the "why" of entrepreneurial education, which refers to the overarching aim of entrepreneurial education. In this book, the overarching aim is framed in the context of educating entrepreneurial change agents. Next to the overarching aim, educators formulate aligned learning objectives to realize the overarching aim in courses or other forms of entrepreneurial education, such as extra-curricular activities. Various tools are available to support educators in the process of formulating the why and learning objectives, which are presented by Derre et al. in chapter "The Entrepreneurial Educational Method: A DSR Artifact to Support Educators in Designing Entrepreneurial Education".

To support educators in designing the "how" of entrepreneurial education, the Entrepreneurial Education Canvas developed by Baggen et al. (2022), as introduced in chapter “The Entrepreneurial Education Canvas”, can be utilized. The 11 design principles from Baggen et al. (2022) are incorporated as dimensions for designing learning artifacts in entrepreneurial education within the “how” of the EDC. The design principles assist educators in considering concrete decisions that must be made during the design process of entrepreneurial education with regard to learning activities and are divided into three categories: the entrepreneurial process, tasks, and context and relationships. The design principles are discussed in detail in chapter “The Entrepreneurial Education Canvas”. During the design process, educators contextualize the design principles based on the specific context and intentionality of the entrepreneurial education being developed. To support educators in this process, Baggen et al. (2022) suggest considering the desired level of complexity and uncertainty to be incorporated in relation to each design principle. For instance, a curriculum could start with low levels and end with high levels of complexity and uncertainty, in line with the proficiency levels of the students. Proficiency levels can refer to both entrepreneurial mindset or competencies and the subject-specific knowledge related to the course. There is not necessarily a right or wrong choice here. The team can make conscious decisions about how much complexity and uncertainty should be introduced in the educational design, aligned with the learning objectives and target audience. It is the purpose of the design principles to engage in discussions about how these currently fit within your entrepreneurial education, and the variations or structure you have implemented across a larger program or within a specific course. We would encourage educators to reflect on how well the current design of entrepreneurial education matches with the “why” of education and to jointly identify areas for potential change.

In terms of "evaluation", it is recommended that educators consider both assessment and evaluation. Assessment refers to evaluating individual students concerning the learning gains achieved, often including grading in formal education settings. Evaluation typically incorporates assessment data but is supplemented with additional data and processed differently, providing educators insights into the impact of the learning artifact at the group level for which the artifact was designed.

Within the logic underpinning the EDC, it is important to note that data-driven DSR in entrepreneurial education diverges from traditional hypothesis-testing methodologies. In DSR, data plays a critical role not only in the synthesis-evaluation iterations during the design phase, but also in the post-design testing phase. These iterations involve the continuous evaluation of design artifacts against predefined design requirements, using various data sources to iteratively inform and refine the design.

Within the synthesis-evaluation process, assessment can take place, allowing for ongoing monitoring of individual learning gains and enabling educators to make adjustments to the design as needed. Data collected during these iterations reveals the strengths and weaknesses of each design decision, guiding further refinements and modifications.

Once the design phase concludes, post-design (ex post) evaluations become essential for testing the designed artifacts in real-world conditions. These evaluations may be summative, assessing the overall effectiveness of the design, or formative, aimed at understanding the underlying mechanisms and reasons behind the design's success or failure. In this phase, evaluation within the framework of educational effectiveness is classified, utilizing data from assessments and additional sources to provide educators with insights into the impact of the learning artifact at a group level.

When designing evaluations, educators can be guided by the following heuristics:

- *Reflect on the concept of "learning gains"*: As discussed in chapter "Embracing Failures: Advancing the Entrepreneurship Education Pedagogy Through Design Science Approach", it is important to consider both short-term and long-term learning gains in the context of productive failure. A failure experience can potentially lead to significant learning outcomes. Particularly when grading, it is crucial to distinguish between the entrepreneurial process the student has undergone - in which failure is an important opportunity for learning - and the final output they have achieved.
- *Consider capturing emerging learning gains*: A design-oriented approach can detect unexpected, unplanned learning outcomes (also referred to as "learning surprises," Baggen et al., 2022). As such, a design approach can help to identify and leverage a broader range of learning results.
- *Utilize quantitative and qualitative data*: In DSR, both quantitative and qualitative data can be used. Quantitative data can be collected through validated instruments that measure entrepreneurial competencies and mindset, while qualitative data provide deeper insights into students' learning experiences and perceptions. Students can easily share their experiences, and you can immediately use these insights to adapt the learning artifact.

2.1.4 The further development of the EntreDesign Canvas

In collaboration with the partners involved in the co-creation design process, we jointly agreed to perceive the EDC as a minimum viable product (MVP) and to approach its development through the same iterative process recommended for designing entrepreneurial learning artifacts. This design-oriented approach, characterized by rapid and overlapping iterations between the problem and solution spaces (Schön, 1987) rather than a linear design process, suits the complex process of building, implementing, learning and refining the MVP.

To enable such iterative process and allow the MVP to be evaluated and evolved, it is essential that a sufficiently large and, preferably, diverse group of educators adopt the EDC when designing their entrepreneurial education. This means we aim to disseminate the EDC widely and would like to ensure it is easily accessible to many different educators. In this regard, we appreciate the unique and long-term collaboration between VLAIO, their partners Unizo E&E and Vlajo, and the international EntreDesign research community. As part of this collaboration, VLAIO will adopt the EDC and further promote it under the name *VLAIO EntreDesign Canvas (VLAIO EDC)*. As explained, this initiative will include translating the

VLAIO EDC into an easily accessible website,[5] where tools, techniques, and scientific knowledge for creating entrepreneurial education can be readily consulted. Additionally, the collaboration will support educators in utilizing the VLAIO EDC through partnerships with Unizo E&E and Vlajo.

A distinctive feature of the VLAIO EDC will be the collaboration and interaction with educators, resulting in a joint process of value-creation, with educators, policymakers and other stakeholders as co-creators of entrepreneurial education. Educators are warmly invited and encouraged to communicate innovative, emerging practice-based CIMOs (for more information on CIMOs, see chapters "Designing Artifacts in Entrepreneurial Education Research" and "The Entrepreneurial Educational Method: A DSR Artifact to Support Educators in Designing Entrepreneurial Education"). Ideally, this input will also generate insights that can lead to substantive adjustments to the VLAIO EDC artifact. This means that the VLAIO EDC will become a living artifact, iteratively improved over the years based on practical experience.

Within the process of creating a living VLAIO EDC not only a collaboration will be established with educators, but also with the broader scientific community. This means that all research domains that are willing to contribute to the design of entrepreneurial education will have an easy and joint way to share their findings, translated into research-based CIMOs. In particular, the design-oriented research community will have the opportunity to create additional artifacts to further strengthen and complement the VLAIO EDC. The website will serve as a catalyst for realizing a scientifically informed approach to designing entrepreneurial education, as described in chapter "Advancing the Field of Entrepreneurial Education: Leveraging a Design Science Approach for Educating the Change Agents of the Future".

3 The Potential of Using Causal and Effectual Approaches in Educational Design

In 2001, Saras Sarasvathy, under the mentorship of Herbert Simon, introduced "effectual reasoning." Building on William Gartner's argument in a seminal 1987 publication—that to truly understand successful entrepreneurship, we should shift from asking "who is an entrepreneur?" to "what does an entrepreneur do?"—Sarasvathy documented the actions and decision-making processes of expert entrepreneurs. These individuals had over 15 years of experience, founded multiple ventures, and successfully taken at least one company public. Her findings revealed that expert entrepreneurs employ a distinct decision-making process, different from that of traditional managers.

[5] www.VLAIO.be/EntreHub

Sarasvathy (2001) observed that entrepreneurs use two forms of reasoning in their decision-making: causal and effectual, with effectual reasoning being typical among expert entrepreneurs. In causal reasoning, entrepreneurs begin by gathering facts, potentially developing a business plan, and then seeking resources to achieve predefined goals. In contrast, effectual reasoning starts with the resources at hand, leveraging them to create new opportunities and possible futures within uncertain environments. Sarasvathy (2001) found that expert entrepreneurs employ high levels of effectual thinking, particularly in the early stages of a startup.

Effectual thinking is increasingly recognized as essential for entrepreneurs, especially in volatile and uncertain environments (Peng et al., 2020). Sarasvathy (2001) and other researchers regard effectuation as an entrepreneurial method, akin to the scientific method, that can be learned and applied broadly.

Sarasvathy (2001) formulated five core principles to characterize effectual thinking, which can be useful in designing entrepreneurial education, especially as a design science approach requires something different from educators. Such an approach requires teachers that are flexible, able to improvise, and deal with uncertainty - if we would like students to deal with uncertainty, we should also embrace uncertainty ourselves and acknowledge unexpected challenges as part of learning and teaching. The five principles of effectuation can inspire educators and support the application of DSR in practice:

1. *Bird in Hand*: Maximize creativity using the resources you have as an educator. These include tangible resources, such as money and technology, but also intangible ones. Consider, for instance, the capacities and networks of colleagues.
2. *Affordable Loss*: Do not make decisions based on expected return, but on the maximum acceptable loss. In education, this might mean setting minimum learning goals as the baseline for acceptable outcomes of entrepreneurial learning. For instance by formulating learning goals on learning how to deal with uncertainty, or by challenging students to formulate personal learning goals and to come up with an actionable plan to develop such learning goals, and at the same time aiming for greater emerging learning gains throughout the learning process. Such greater aims could for instance relate to addressing societal issues in a joint process of value creation.
3. *Crazy Quilt*: Avoid a status quo bias rooted in established practices or literature; instead, co-create entrepreneurial education with committed stakeholders. Identify who these stakeholders might be, and consider how existing networks or social media can lower barriers for rapid testing and identifying meaningful collaborators. Think for instance of valuable collaborations between the industry, policy-makers, and educators in realizing authentic, entrepreneurial education in which students are challenged to address societal issues in education.
4. *Lemonade*: Rather than expending energy anticipating unforeseen circumstances, adapt to them as they arise, using a minimum viable product approach. View unforeseen challenges as opportunities to enrich your resources and turn them into learning experiences for students participating in entrepreneurial education. Especially in entrepreneurial education we argue that opportunities for

entrepreneurial learning can be captured in such unforeseen challenges, which we call learning surprises (Baggen et al., 2022). Think for instance of interaction with non-academic stakeholders such as potential customers - validation processes with potential customers could steer students in unforeseen directions in developing their idea. Try to train your capability to detect and respond to these unforeseen circumstances effectively.

5. *Pilot in the Plane*: Instead of trying to predict what will happen in entrepreneurial education, try to focus on creating it by focusing on the steps that are within your control. Under uncertain conditions, traditional planning becomes unreliable. As COVID-19 has taught us, the educator who adopts effectual thinking embraces the mindset that "if we create the future ourselves, there's no need to predict it."

Together, these five principles provide a framework for approaching educational design as an entrepreneurial process. However, it must be noted that the value of supporting educators in adapting a design approach in developing, implementing and evaluating education cannot be underestimated. Tailored training could, for instance, further support educators to develop the relevant skills and mindset to apply a DSR approach. Furthermore, although we emphasize the use of effectual thinking, both causal and effectual reasoning can be useful in designing entrepreneurial education. Causal thinking, and more specifically planning, is certainly useful in preparing education, especially when students participate in credited education programs. Key is to learn to recognize when causal or effectual reasoning can help most in designing entrepreneurial education - which is often determined by the amount of uncertainty in a given situation or context.

4 And Last but Not Least, Our Final Call to Researchers and Practitioners: Let's Work Together

We would like to close this book with a call to educators and researchers to join forces and collaborate in advancing the design science approach in entrepreneurial education. As the cases discussed in this book illustrate, entrepreneurial education is a highly complex endeavor—it can be perceived as a wicked problem itself—requiring collaborative processes of co-learning and co-creation between educators and researchers. Such collaborative efforts enable us to create entrepreneurial education that empowers the next generation of change agents who are capable of perceiving uncertainty as an opportunity (Walmsley & Wraae, 2022), as momentum to create something new that can help address societal challenges. Let us together create entrepreneurial education that embraces the way of thinking and acting that we also expect from our students as change agents, who flexibly and courageously deal with uncertainty while addressing pressing, societal challenges.

We would like to extend our sincere thanks to all the contributing authors and to VLAIO for initiating the EntreDesign website project, which has the potential to exponentially improve connections between practitioners and researchers in the coming years. We encourage other regions and countries to develop similar initiatives and collaborate to further embed a design science approach, thereby strengthening entrepreneurial education for all future change agents.

References

Baggen, Y., Lans, T., & Gulikers, J. (2022). Making entrepreneurship education available to all: Design principles for educational programs stimulating an entrepreneurial mindset. *Entrepreneurship Education and Pedagogy, 5*(3), 347–374. https://doi.org/10.1177/2515127420988517

Ball, L. J., & Christensen, B. T. (2019). Advancing an understanding of design cognition and design metacognition: Progress and prospects. *Design Studies, 65*, 35–59.

Denyer, D., Tranfield, D., & Van Aken, J. E. (2008). Developing design propositions through research synthesis. *Organization Studies, 29*(3), 393–413. https://doi.org/10.1177/0170840607088020

Dresch, A., Lacerda, D., & Antunes, J., Jr. (2015). *Design science research: A method for science and technology advancement*. Springer.

Hevner, A. R., March, S. T., Park, J., & Ram, S. (2004). Design science in information research. *Design Science in IS Research MIS Quarterly, 28*(1), 75.

Kincheloe, J. L. (2001). Describing the bricolage: Conceptualizing a new rigor in qualitative research. *Qualitative Inquiry, 7*(6), 679–692.

Peng, X. B., Liu, Y. L., Jiao, Q. Q., Feng, X. B., & Zheng, B. (2020). The nonlinear effect of effectuation and causation on new venture performance: The moderating effect of environmental uncertainty. *Journal of Business Research, 117*(May), 112–123. https://doi.org/10.1016/j.jbusres.2020.05.048

Sagath, D., Van Burg, E., Cornelissen, J. P., & Giannopapa, C. (2019). Identifying design principles for business incubation in the European space sector. *Journal of Business Venturing Insights, 11*(February), e00115. https://doi.org/10.1016/j.jbvi.2019.e00115

Sarasvathy, S. D. (2001). Causation and effectuation: Toward a theoretical shift from economic inevitability to entrepreneurial contingency. *Academy of Management Review, 26*(2), 243–263. https://doi.org/10.5465/AMR.2001.4378020

Schön, D. A. (1987). *Educating the reflective practitioner*. Jossey-Bass.

Shavelson, R. J., Phillips, D. C., Towne, L., & Feuer, M. J. (2003). On the science of education design studies. *Educational Researcher, 32*(1), 25–28. https://doi.org/10.3102/0013189X032001025

Sweller, J. (1988). Cognitive load during problem solving: Effects on learning. *Cognitive Science, 12*(2), 257–285. https://doi.org/10.1016/0364-0213(88)90023-7

Sweller, J. (2016). Working memory, long-term memory, and instructional design. *Journal of Applied Research in Memory and Cognition, 5*(4), 360–367. https://doi.org/10.1016/j.jarmac.2015.12.002

Van Aken, J. E. (2004). Management research based on the paradigm of the design sciences: The quest for field-tested and grounded technological rules. *Journal of Management Studies, 41*(2), 219–246. https://doi.org/10.1111/j.1467-6486.2004.00430.x

van Burg, E. (2010). *Creating spin-off designing entrepreneurship conducive universities Elco van Burg*. Eindhoven University Press.

van Burg, J., & Romme, A. (2014). Creating the future together: Toward a framework for research synthesis in entrepreneurship. *Entrepreneurship Theory and Practice, 38*(2), 369–397.

Walmsley, A., & Wraae, B. (2022). Entrepreneurship education but not as we know it: Reflections on the relationship between critical pedagogy and entrepreneurship education. *The International Journal of Management Education, 20*(3), 100726. https://doi.org/10.1016/j.ijme.2022.100726

Bart Derre is Director at HOGENT University of Applied Sciences and Arts in Ghent, Belgium, and holds the (HOGENT-Xerius) research chair on entrepreneurial learning at the Vrije Universiteit Brussel, Brussels, Belgium. As Director of the Center for Entrepreneurship, he has overseen numerous entrepreneurial education programs. His research, including a Ph.D. from TU Eindhoven (The Netherlands), focuses on the design and implementation of entrepreneurial education that drives meaningful impact.

Yvette Baggen is Assistant Professor at the Education and Learning Sciences group of Wageningen University & Research, specializing in entrepreneurial learning and ecosystems in higher education. Her work empowers students and professionals as change agents, equipping them to tackle real-world challenges. Yvette's research integrates education, entrepreneurship, and societal impact, promoting transformative learning experiences that prepare learners for impactful careers.

MIX
Papier aus verantwortungsvollen Quellen
Paper from responsible sources
FSC® C105338

If you have any concerns about our products,
you can contact us on
ProductSafety@springernature.com

In case Publisher is established outside the EU,
the EU authorized representative is:
Springer Nature Customer Service Center GmbH
Europaplatz 3, 69115 Heidelberg, Germany

Printed by Libri Plureos GmbH
in Hamburg, Germany